THE WITCH-HUNT IN EARLY MODERN EUROPE

Fourth Edition

The Witch-Hunt in Early Modern Europe, now in its fourth edition, is the perfect resource for both students and scholars of the witch-hunts written by one of the leading names in the field. For those starting out in their studies of witch-beliefs and witchcraft trials, Brian Levack provides a concise survey of this complex and fascinating topic, while for more seasoned scholars the scholarship is brought right up to date. This new edition includes the most recent research on children, gender, male witches and demonic possession, as well as broadening the exploration of the geographical distribution of witch prosecutions to include recent work on regions, cities and kingdoms, enabling students to identify comparisons between countries.

Now fully integrated with Brian Levack's *The Witchcraft Sourcebook*, there **SOURCE BOOK** are links to the sourcebook throughout the text, pointing students towards key primary sources to aid them in their studies. The two books are drawn **COMPANION WEBSITE @** together on a new companion website with supplementary materials for those wishing to advance their studies, including an extensive guide to further reading, a chronology of the history of witchcraft, a detailed glossary and an interactive map to show the geographical spread of witch-hunts and witch trials across Europe and North America.

A long-standing favourite with students and lecturers alike, this new edition of *The Witch-Hunt in Early Modern Europe* will be essential reading for those embarking on or looking to advance their studies of the history of witchcraft.

Brian P. Levack is the John E. Green Regents Professor in History at the University of Texas at Austin. His publications on witchcraft and demonology include *The Witchcraft Sourcebook* (2nd edition, 2015), *The Devil Within: Possession and Exorcism in the Christian West* (2013) and *Witch-hunting in Scotland: Law, Politics, and Religion* (2008). He has also edited *The Oxford Handbook of Witchcraft in Early Modern Europe and Colonial America* (2013).

Praise for this edition:

"*The Witch-Hunt in Early Modern Europe* has become widely regarded as the best introduction to the subject. This fourth edition, incorporating new material and new findings, ensures that the book will continue to be of fundamental importance to students and their tutors as they grapple with this complex historical phenomenon."

James Sharpe, *University of York, UK*

"As a single volume survey of the fascinating phenomena of witches, witchcraft and witch-hunting in early modern Europe, Levack's careful elaboration is without antecedent or peer. Intelligent, engaging, up-to-date, and highly recommended."

Thomas A. Fudge, *University of
New England, Australia*

"Witchcraft is one of the most, popular, fascinating, and difficult topics in early modern European history. Brian Levack's *The Witch Hunt in Early Modern Europe* has long been unrivalled as an introduction to the field. The new edition incorporates new scholarship, but maintains the clarity of earlier editions. Moreover, it has a companion website with a wealth of accompanying materials that will facilitate both teaching and studying."

John Ødemark, *University of Oslo, Norway*

"For anyone approaching the history of witch trials in Europe, Brian Levack has written the indispensable book – a thorough, accessible and extremely intelligent guide to a complex and often misunderstood phenomenon. Extensive notes and bibliographies in the revised edition provide a road map to further reading and research at all academic levels."

Mary R. O'Neil, *University of
Washington, USA*

"The fourth edition of this outstanding work ensures the continuing currency of what is by far the best single-volume introduction to the early modern European witch-hunt. For general readers and students alike, it offers a clear, crisp, strongly-informed thematic study of the rise and fall of the witch-hunt and a skilful assessment of the continuing debate about the causes, motors and nature of the early modern hunt. Levack provides a balanced and judicious guide not only to a fiendishly complex field of history but also to a generous selection of primary and contemporary source material."

Peter Gaunt, *University of Chester, UK*

Praise for previous editions:

"Fearlessly, Brian Levack tackles a vast, complex subject and reduces it to a concise and lucid synthesis with consummate skill, challenging old assumptions and casting light into the darkest corners . . . the essential starting point for the study of early modern witch-beliefs and witchcraft trials."

Malcolm Gaskill, *University of East Anglia, UK*

"Now, at last, with Brian Levack's careful scholarly and critical survey, a thoroughly reliable introduction to the whole literature is available."

History Today

"Levack's logical sorting of a prodigious amount of material has resulted in one of the most informative and comprehensive works of its genre."

American Historical Review

THE WITCH-HUNT
IN EARLY MODERN
EUROPE

Fourth edition

Brian P. Levack

Routledge
Taylor & Francis Group

LONDON AND NEW YORK

This edition published 2016
by Routledge
2 Park Square, Milton Park, Abingdon, Oxon OX14 4RN

and by Routledge
711 Third Avenue, New York, NY 10017

Routledge is an imprint of the Taylor & Francis Group, an informa business

© 2016 Brian P. Levack

First edition published 1987 by Pearson Education Limited

Third edition published 2005 by Routledge

British Library Cataloguing-in-Publication Data
A catalogue record for this book is available from the British Library

Library of Congress Cataloging-in-Publication Data
Levack, Brian P.
   The witch-hunt in early modern Europe / Brian P. Levack. –
   Fourth edition.
   pages cm
   Includes bibliographical references and index.
   1. Witchcraft – Europe – History. I. Title.
   BF1571.L48 2015
   133.4'309409031—dc23
   2015003554

ISBN: 978–1–138–80809–6 (hbk)
ISBN: 978–1–138–80810–2 (pbk)
ISBN: 978–1–315–68552–6 (ebk)

Typeset in Garamond Three
by Florence Production Ltd, Stoodleigh, Devon, UK
Printed and bound by CPI Group (UK) Ltd, Croydon, CR0 4YY

For Nancy

CONTENTS

ILLUSTRATIONS, TABLES AND MAP

Illustrations

Tables

Map

PREFACE TO THE
FOURTH EDITION

In preparing this edition of *The Witch-Hunt*, I have taken into account the needs of the two audiences I have kept in mind ever since I wrote the first edition nearly thirty years ago. For the scholars and postgraduate students who rely on the book as a synthesis of scholarship on the subject, I have incorporated the results of the substantial amount of research that has appeared in print since I prepared the third edition ten years ago. This has entailed rewriting many sections, updating the bibliography, and expanding some of the notes to deal with historiographical questions. These new additions to the text draw on some of my own scholarship on the subject and the essays in *The Oxford Handbook of Witchcraft in Early Modern Europe and Colonial America* (2013), which provides an overview of the state of the field in 2012. For under-graduates who use the book in courses on witchcraft or early modern Europe I have made two major changes. The first is to provide links, indicated by icons in the margins of the book, to the primary sources in *The Witchcraft Sourcebook*, which Routledge published in a new edition in 2015. The second change, related to the first, is the construction of a website linking both books. The website includes a timeline, a glossary, additional images, a list of films on the subject, supplementary bibliography, and an interactive map that provides information on prosecutions in locations where significant numbers of witches were tried and executed.

Let me take this opportunity to thank my colleagues in witchcraft studies in the United States, Britain, Europe and Australia for copies of their publications, responses to my queries and suggestions for improvement. They have saved me from making more mistakes than those that might still remain in the book, for which of course I am solely responsible. Their recommendations have made me value, even more than in the past, the scholarly co-operation and spirit of collegiality that prevails in the inter-disciplinary field in which we work.

B. P. L., Austin, Texas, February 2015

PREFACE TO THE
THIRD EDITION

The main reason I decided to prepare this third edition was to take into account the large volume of publications on the subject since I completed work on the second edition in 1993. Despite many predictions to the contrary, the profusion of witchcraft studies that began in the 1970s still shows no sign of abating. It would of course be impossible to keep up with all this literature, which is grounded in many different disciplines. I remain confident, however, that the breadth of my reading as well as my own archival work in Scottish and English records provides a sufficiently broad foundation for the arguments I advance here. Neither those arguments nor my approach to the topic has changed radically in the course of three editions. In particular, I have found no cause to reduce my emphasis on the legal context of witchcraft prosecutions, which is probably the most distinctive feature of the book. Nor have I seen fit to retreat from the position I have taken regarding the purported connection between state-building and witch-hunting, which I have discussed more fully in other publications.

The main structural change in this edition is the division of the final chapter of the first two editions, 'Decline and survival', into two separate chapters. I have devoted the first of these chapters entirely to the decline and end of witch-hunting. This chapter is informed by a long essay I published in 1999 in *Witchcraft and Magic in Europe: The Eighteenth and Nineteenth Centuries*. The new Chapter 9, 'Witch-hunting after the trials', also includes a considerable amount of new material, especially on witch-hunting in contemporary Africa, where witch-hunting has reached an intensity comparable to that recorded in some German territories in the early decades of the seventeenth century. I have also rewritten substantial portions of the other chapters, especially Chapter 5. In a few chapters I have added some material on demonic possession, about which I have written elsewhere and which is the subject of my current research. I have also made a downward estimate of the total number of witch-craft prosecutions and executions. When I published the first edition in 1987, my estimates were criticized in some quarters for being too conservative.

Recent research, however, has suggested figures even lower than the ones I first advanced. We will never be able to determine how many witches were tried or executed over the course of roughly three hundred years, but my new estimates, which are still fairly close to the figures I published in the first two editions, will hopefully put an end to the wildly inflated figures that some writers are still citing.

One of the few pleasures I have had while writing on this grim topic has been the opportunity to work with an international community of exceptionally talented scholars. Within that group I have benefited in particular from correspondence and discussions with Richard Kieckhefer, Erik Midelfort, Bill Monter, Stuart Clark, Julian Goodare, Jim Sharpe, Malcolm Gaskill, Richard Golden, Wolfgang Behringer, Johannes Dillinger, Willem de Blécourt, Owen Davies, Marijke Gijswijt-Hofstra, Valerie Kivelson, Gustav Henningsen, Marko Nenonen, Rune Hagen, Robin Briggs and Alfred Soman. My debt to their scholarship should be evident in the pages that follow, even in those places where our interpretations of witch-hunting differ.

B. P. L., Austin, Texas, February 2005

PREFACE TO THE
SECOND EDITION

In preparing a second edition of this book I have made an effort to take into account the large volume of scholarly literature on witchcraft that has appeared since I completed the first edition eight years ago. The process of revision has led to the inclusion of a significant amount of new information, a rewriting of some sections, and the expansion of both the Notes and the Bibliography.

The appearance of numerous regional studies, many of them dealing with witchcraft on the periphery of Europe, has only served to underline my argument regarding the complexity and diversity of the great witch-hunt and the difficulty of establishing a single explanation of its origins and development. The same can be said of those thematic studies which have emphasized different aspects of the subject, especially gender and popular beliefs. I have tried to take these works into account in presenting my own multi-causal approach to the problem. At the same time I have not seen fit to reduce my own emphasis, greatly neglected in other treatments of the subject, on the judicial aspects of the great witch-hunt, especially in explaining the geographical distribution of prosecutions. I am also more convinced now than I was eight years ago that the original impetus for prosecution came mainly from the localities rather than from the centre, and that the central authorities of the state had more to do with the restriction of witch-hunting than with its spread.

B. P. L., Austin, Texas, November 1993

PREFACE TO THE
FIRST EDITION

The idea for this book originated in the lecture courses and seminars I have given on the history of witchcraft during the past ten years. In teaching these courses I became aware of the need for a one-volume study of the entire European witch-hunt – the accusation, prosecution and execution of thousands of persons for the crime of witchcraft between 1450 and 1750. On this depressing but important subject much has been written, especially in recent years. The sheer volume of this work, however, has created problems of digestion, and the proliferation of theories regarding witch-hunting has created more confusion than enlightenment. My aim has been both to present a coherent introduction to the subject and to contribute to an ongoing debate.

This essay attempts to explain why the great European witch-hunt took place. It also attempts to explain why it reached its peak in the late sixteenth and early seventeenth centuries, why it was much more severe in some countries than in others, and why it came to an end. There are no simple answers to these questions. One reason for this is that the European witch-hunt was not a single historical event or episode but a composite of thousands of individual prosecutions that took place from Scotland to Transylvania and from Spain to Finland over a 300-year period. Although these prosecutions shared many common characteristics, they also arose in different historical circumstances and they often reflected witch beliefs that were peculiar to a certain locality. Another reason is that witch-hunting was an extremely complex enterprise. Since it involved both the educated classes and the common people, it reflected both elite and popular ideas about witchcraft. It had both religious and social dimensions, and it was conditioned by a number of political and legal factors. It is not surprising, therefore, that monocausal explanations of the witch-hunt have proved to be singularly unconvincing, if not demonstrably false.

In discussing the witch-hunt I have taken pains to emphasize both its complexity and diversity. Four chapters are devoted to the different causes of witch-hunting throughout Europe. Chapters 2 and 3 discuss the two main preconditions of the great hunt: the formation of the cumulative concept of witchcraft and the development of legal procedures that were capable of convicting witches in large numbers. Chapters 4 and 5 deal with the general religious and social developments which served as inducements to witch-hunting, especially in the late sixteenth and early seventeenth centuries, when the hunt entered its most intense phase. In Chapter 6 the focus of the book shifts from the general causes of the European hunt to the specific hunts that it comprised. My purpose there is both to explain why individual hunts began and to show the different ways they developed and eventually came to an end. Chapter 7 places even more emphasis on the diversity of witch-hunting, suggesting reasons for the uneven chronological and geographical distribution of prosecutions. In Chapter 8 the focus of the book shifts back to the entire European hunt in an effort to explain its decline. There too I have empha-sized the complexity of the process, showing that the reduction in the number of prosecutions was the result of legal, intellectual, religious and social developments.

Although this book covers a very large geographical area and many centuries of European history, it does not pretend to be a comprehensive history of European witchcraft. With the exception of some background material on the Middle Ages and a few observations on witchcraft in modern times, it is concerned exclusively with the early modern period. It also deals more with witch-hunting than with witchcraft, if by the latter term we mean the beliefs and activities of the witches themselves. There is certainly a need for a synthesis of popular witch beliefs and practices in the various parts of Europe, but this book does not attempt to provide one.

I should like to express my gratitude to the University Research Institute of the University of Texas at Austin for the financial assistance that enabled me to write a large portion of this book. I also wish to thank Myron Gutmann, Richard Kieckhefer and Guy Lytle for reading drafts of various chapters of the manuscript and for giving me much valuable criticism. I am likewise indebted to Travis Hanes for reading the entire manuscript and making a number of helpful suggestions. In developing my ideas regarding the legal aspects of witch-hunting I have benefited from the thoughtful comments of Edward Cohen, John Langbein, Bruce Mann and Edward Powell. My greatest personal debt is to my wife, Nancy, who gave me both criticism and support when I most needed them.

B. P. L., Austin, Texas, July 1985

1

INTRODUCTION

During the early modern period of European history, stretching from roughly 1450 to 1750, thousands of persons, most of them women, were tried for the crime of witchcraft. About half of these individuals were executed, usually by burning. Some witchcraft trials took place in the various ecclesiastical courts of Europe, institutions that played an important role in regulating the moral and religious life of Europeans during the Middle Ages and the early modern period. More commonly, especially after 1550, the trials were held in the secular courts – the courts of kingdoms, states, principalities, duchies, counties and towns. The geographical distribution of cases throughout Europe was extremely uneven. In some jurisdictions there were very few prosecutions, if any at all, whereas in others hundreds and sometimes thousands of persons were tried over the course of three centuries. There was also an uneven chronological distribution of witchcraft trials. A gradual increase in the number of prosecutions during the fifteenth century was followed by a slight reduction in the early sixteenth century, a dramatic increase in the late sixteenth and early seventeenth centuries, and finally a gradual decline in the late seventeenth and early eighteenth centuries. Within each jurisdiction there were even more pronounced fluctuations in the number of trials. Instead of a steady stream of prosecutions we often find some periods when large numbers of witches were prosecuted and others when the crime does not appear to have been a problem.

Although the number of witches who were tried varied from place to place and from time to time, all of these witchcraft prosecutions can be considered parts of one very large judicial operation that took place in Europe during the early modern period. This general but nevertheless clearly defined historical development is usually referred to as either the European witch-craze or the European witch-hunt. The former term, which is the one most commonly employed, should be used with great caution. It is appropriate only to the extent that European authorities and communities harboured such deep fears of witches during this period that they manifested frenzied, irrational or manic forms of behaviour in pursuing them. In some instances the number of suspected witches was so large, and the fear of them so profound, that entire communities became caught up in a panic. The problem with the word 'craze', however, is its implication that the set of beliefs that underlay the prosecution of witches was the product of some sort of mental disorder, which was certainly not the case.

The latter term, witch-hunt, is preferable to witch-craze because all witchcraft prosecutions, even those that gave no indication of collective psychoses, involved some sort of search for malefactors. Witch-hunts did not usually involve the physical pursuit of a named individual, as in the case of a hunt when a prisoner escapes from gaol or evades the law. Occasionally witches who escaped or went into hiding were hunted in that way, but the essential process in combating witchcraft was discovering who the witches were rather than where they were located. Witch-hunting involved the identification of individuals who were widely believed to be engaged in a secret or occult activity. Witches were hunted, therefore, in the same way that members of an underground movement or secret organization would be hunted today. This was a task undertaken by various individuals, usually judicial authorities but sometimes professional witch-finders. Acting on the basis of accusations, denunciations or sometimes mere rumour, these men arrested persons whose names came to their attention, interrogated them, and did everything in their power to extract confessions from them. Sometimes judicial authorities continued this investigation by forcing confessing witches to name their accomplices, the type of legal prosecution most commonly associated with the word 'witch-hunt' today.[1] The final stage of the witch-hunt was, in most cases, the formal conviction of the accused, followed by their execution, banishment or imprisonment.

The main purpose of this book is to explain why the great European witch-hunt took place. On this historical question there is no scholarly consensus. Indeed, it is difficult to think of any other historical problem over which there is more disagreement and confusion. During the past century the witch-hunt has been attributed, in whole or in large part, to the Reformation, the Counter-Reformation, the Inquisition, the use of judicial torture, the wars of religion, the religious zeal of the clergy, the rise of the modern state, the development of capitalism, a series of agricultural crises, the widespread use of narcotics, changes in medical thought, social and cultural conflict, an attempt to wipe out paganism, the need of ruling elites to distract the masses, opposition to birth control, the spread of syphilis, and the hatred of women. This book does not endorse any one of these all-encompassing explanations of the hunt. Rather, it adopts a multi-causal approach which sees the emergence of new ideas about witches and a series of fundamental changes in the criminal law as the necessary preconditions of the witch-hunt, and both religious change and social tension as its more immediate causes. Only by studying all of these factors, which will be the subject of Chapters 2–5, and by seeing how they reinforced each other, can we begin to understand why the hunt occurred. Even then, however, it is necessary to go beyond these general causes of the hunt and explore the specific circumstances and events that triggered individual witch-hunts, for the European witch-hunt was little more than a series of trials and separate hunts, each of which had its own precipitants. Each of these hunts also had its own dynamic, and therefore in Chapter 6 I try to explain why witch-hunts, once they had begun, followed many different patterns of development.

The complexity of the great European witch-hunt is evident not only in an analysis of its causes but also in a study of its chronological and geographical development. Since witch-hunting was more intense in some areas than in others and at certain times than at others, it is imperative that we explain why these variations occurred. Only in this way can we appreciate the relative importance of some of the more general causes of the entire European witch-hunt. Throughout the book, therefore, I make an effort to explain this diversity, and in Chapter 7 I adopt a more systematic approach to the entire question.

Chapter 8 deals with the decline and end of witchcraft prosecutions in the late seventeenth and eighteenth centuries. Although many different societies from ancient to modern times have identified certain individuals as witches, the extensive criminal prosecution of Europeans for practising witchcraft occurred only during the early modern period. It is important, therefore, that we understand how this massive judicial operation came to an end and why witchcraft was considered no longer to be a crime. Even after the trials ended, however, communities occasionally lynched people whom they suspected of being witches, and in the twentieth century members of various groups have been relentlessly pursued by authorities much in the same way as witches. Chapter 9 explores these different forms of witch-hunting after the trials had ended. The last section of that chapter deals with witch-hunting in Africa in the late twentieth century, after decolonization. These African witch-hunts, which have been in large part conducted without official governmental sanction, have revealed deep conflicts between groups of people determined to take action against witches and the post-colonial courts that refuse to recognize the reality of the crime.

The meaning of witchcraft

In dealing with such a complex issue as witchcraft, it is important to establish what the word means. Since contemporaries themselves assigned different meanings to the word, and since they also used many other terms as the equivalents of 'witch' and 'witchcraft', this is no simple task. When early modern Europeans used the word witchcraft, however, they were almost always referring to either or both of two types of activity. The first was the practice of harmful, black or maleficent magic: the performance of harmful deeds by means of some sort of extraordinary, mysterious, occult, preternatural or supernatural power. This type of magic would include the killing of a person by piercing a doll made in his or her image, inflicting sickness on a child by reciting a spell, bringing down hail on crops by burning enchanted substances, starting a fire by leaving a hexed sword in a room, and causing impotence in a bridegroom by tying knots in a piece of leather and leaving it in his proximity. Such harmful magic was usually referred to in Latin as *maleficium*, while the plural form identifying such magical acts was *maleficia*. In English *maleficia* were sometimes called 'witchcrafts'.[2] The agents of these deeds were often referred to as *malefici* or *maleficae*, the Latin words that were commonly used to identify male and female witches during the late medieval and early modern periods.

It was in the performance of *maleficium* that European witchcraft most closely resembled the practice of witchcraft in some African and Native American societies today. In all witch-believing societies witches are regarded as individuals who possess some sort of extraordinary or mysterious power to perform evil deeds. The essential characteristics of these deeds are that they are magical rather than religious, and harmful rather than beneficial. These distinctions, however, are not always clear and call for some sort of explanation.

In its purest sense magic is a power that is activated and controlled by human beings themselves. The power is very much the magicians' power, which they use to produce readily observable, empirical results in the world. They almost always use this power in critical situations and they usually act secretly and individually. The assumption of magicians is that if they practise their art correctly, it will automatically bring about the desired result. If they fail, they conclude that they have not performed their spell or ritual properly. In practising religion, however, people, whether they be priests or laity, do not exercise the same type of control over the power they are employing. They merely supplicate spirits or gods, who they hope or trust will achieve the desired result. If they fail, it is because the gods did not deign to satisfy their request. The ends that they pursue, moreover, are generally non-empirical, 'supernatural' goals, such as the achievement of life after death. Religion is also a more communal, organized form of activity than magic, and its practice is not confined to critical situations. Unlike magic, religion uses the art of persuasion in attempting to realize its goals, and since it deals with superior beings, it is more capable of filling the people who practise it with a sense of awe.[3]

Although it is possible to draw clear distinctions between magic and religion in their purest or most ideal senses, in practice these distinctions are often blurred.[4] This should not surprise us, for many religions have slowly developed out of magic, while others have often deteriorated into magic.[5] One example of the way in which religion can resemble magic is the fact that priests sometimes recite prayers or perform rituals with the magician's certainty that if they act according to form, the desired outcome will automatically ensue.

The results of religious activity, moreover, are very often empirical, worldly benefits, just like those of magic, and they may have been sought in order to solve an immediate crisis. Magic, on the other hand, can easily become conflated with religion whenever it uses the powers of gods or other spirits to achieve its intended effects. In ancient Greece and Rome, for example, the very same gods who were the object of supplication and who inspired awe in their worship played an important part in the practice of magic. And, as we shall see, the early Christian Church insisted that all magical activity involved the power of the pagan gods, who were considered to be demons.

Because of the frequent blurring of the distinctions between religion and magic, it is worthwhile to imagine a continuum of activities that involve the use of some sort of preternatural, supernatural or non-empirical power. At one end of the continuum would be magic in the purest or ideal sense, in which the gods would not be involved and in which the objective would be immediate, worldly and empirical. At the other end would be religion in its most organized, public, supplicatory and theological sense, its objectives being essentially non-empirical and other-worldly. Between the two would be various forms of magic that are public and involve the intervention of gods or other spirits and various forms of religion that exhibit 'magical' characteristics.[6] Within this continuum, however, it would still be possible to distinguish between magic and religion on the basis of the criterion of compulsion.[7] Those forms of activity in which human beings command or manipulate mysterious forces, supernatural or otherwise, would be essentially magical; those in which they supplicate and leave the power to the spirit or god would be essentially religious.

The second essential characteristic of *maleficia* is that they are by definition harmful, not beneficial. They are intended to bring about bodily injury, disease, death, poverty or some other misfortune (see Figure 1.1). They are to be contrasted, therefore, with acts of so-called white magic, the purpose of which is to bring about some benefit to oneself or another. White magic can be productive, in the sense of helping crops to grow or women to bear children; it can be therapeutic, in the sense of healing a person who is ill; or it can be protective, in the sense of preventing some misfortune from occurring or warding off some evil spirit or witch. The distinction between black and white magic can easily become blurred, especially when magicians harm someone in order to protect themselves, or when they cure someone by transferring the disease to another person. Acts of love magic very often fall into this grey area, since one person's gain in love might easily be another's loss. Amatory magic could also be considered harmful, at least by communal standards, when it resulted in an adulterous liaison but beneficent when it reunited an estranged husband to his spouse.

The concept of *maleficium* comes very close to, but nevertheless cannot be equated with, that of sorcery. There is no universally accepted definition of sorcery, but in all contexts the word denotes the practice of magic by some

Figure 1.1 Man afflicted with a disease of the eyes, which the optometrist Georg Bartisch attributed to sorcery. Bartisch, who has been called the founder of modern ophthalmology, offered both natural and supernatural explanations of ocular diseases. The illustration appeared in Bartisch's treatise, *Ophthalmodouleia* (Dresden, 1583).

sort of mechanical, manipulative process. Sorcery is an acquired skill. It might involve the destruction of an image of a person in order to bring him harm, the pronunciation of a spell, or the use of a potion. Sorcery can be distinguished from *maleficium* on two possible grounds. The first is that in the view of some scholars, sorcery can be beneficial as well as harmful.[8] In that sense it is a broader category. The second is that some malefecent acts do not involve the use of any particular technique, substance or paraphernalia. In that sense it is a more limited category. *Maleficium* can be the result of a witch's general power to inflict harm rather than her practice of any particular art. One example of this type of *maleficium* in Europe was the harm allegedly caused to individuals by the witch's evil eye. Another was the harm done to a person by some completely internal act of the witch, such as wishing that a person were dead. These actions were certainly *maleficia* in every sense of the word, but they were not acts of sorcery.[9]

One further distinction should be made regarding the magic performed by witches. All magic, whether beneficial or harmful, can be classified as either high or low. Once again the distinction is not always clear, but high magic is a sophisticated and speculative art that requires a certain amount of education. The most common forms of high magic are alchemy, which is the changing of base metals into precious ones, and divination, which is the use of various means to acquire secret or otherwise unknown knowledge. Astrology, the use of the position of the stars to obtain such knowledge, and necromancy, the use of the spirits of the dead for similar purposes, are the most commonly known methods of divination, but more than one hundred different methods, including scapulomancy (divination by inspecting animals' shoulders), dactyliomancy (by means of a finger-ring) and oneiroscopy (by the interpretation of dreams), have been employed by various societies. Low magic requires little or no formal education, and can be learned by oral transmission, apprenticeship or even individual experimentation. It usually takes the form of simple charms and spells. Most of the *maleficia* ascribed to witches in the early modern period fall into this category of low magic, both because the overwhelming majority of witches came from the lower levels of society and because most high magic was white. It is important to note, however, that practitioners of high magic did occasionally incur accusations of witchcraft and that the practice of divination was specifically prohibited by many witchcraft laws. Moreover, a particular type of learned or semi-learned magic, the ceremonial art of summoning up demons, often referred to as necromancy, played an important role in the development of witch beliefs in medieval Europe, as shall be discussed in Chapter 2.

The performance of *maleficium* is only one of the two types of activity contained in the early modern European definition of witchcraft. The second concerned the relationship that existed between the witch and the Devil, the supernatural foe of the Christian God and the personification of evil. A witch in the fullest sense of the word was a person who not only performed harmful magic but who also made a pact with the Devil and paid some sort of homage to him. Witchcraft was therefore diabolism, the worship of the Devil. The two types of activity that witches were accused of – magic and diabolism – were closely related, for at this time it was widely believed that a witch acquired her powers to harm people magically by making a pact with the Devil. The alleged connection between magic and diabolism derived from the writings of theologians, who ever since the fourth century had argued that magic could only be performed by demonic power.

During the Middle Ages this idea that magicians had some sort of commerce with demons underwent a significant development. As an increasing number of men began to practise ceremonial magic, theologians argued that magicians made face-to-face pacts with the Devil and were therefore heretics and apostates. In the early fifteenth century they began to argue that people who performed simple *maleficia* – including women from the lower ranks of society – worshipped the Devil as their god in large nocturnal assemblies, to which they often flew. At some of these gatherings, witches not only paid homage to the Devil but also engaged in a variety of gluttonous, lewd, infanticidal and cannibalistic practices, all of which represented an inversion of the moral standards of society.

The emergence of the belief that witches were not merely practitioners of *maleficia* but also Devil-worshippers changed the nature of the crime of witchcraft. It made witches not simply felons, similar to murderers and thieves, but heretics and apostates, intrinsically evil individuals who had rejected their Christian faith and had decided instead to serve God's enemy, the Devil. Now, it is true that throughout the history of Christianity magic had been viewed as the work of the Devil, a form of heresy, and a lapse in one's faith. But by the late fifteenth century the heresy and apostasy of the witch had become much more deliberate, organized and threatening, and theologians identified it as a new and especially virulent form of heresy. As that change took place, the diabolical practices of the witch – the pact with the Devil and the collective worship of him – assumed much greater significance than her practice of harmful magic. Indeed, many lawyers came to regard the pact as the essence of witchcraft, while many theologians, especially those in the Protestant camp, claimed that witchcraft was a purely spiritual crime. Consequently many individuals tried for witchcraft were not accused of performing any *maleficia* at all; their crime was only worshipping the Devil.[10] Whenever large witch-hunts took place, those persons who were implicated by confessing witches were almost always accused simply of participating in such nocturnal assemblies, not of practising specific acts of magic.

It is the diabolical component of early modern European witchcraft that distinguishes it most clearly from the witchcraft of many African and non-Western societies in the world today. The belief in magic, even harmful magic, exists in almost all cultures, but the belief in the Christian Devil, defined as he was by generations of medieval theologians, is unique to Western civilization and its derivative cultures. Many African societies do, of course, believe in evil spirits and gods, and some believe that these spirits can assist magicians in their work. Some of these societies also believe that witches engage in activities that reverse or invert the established norms of society. But none of them has developed a set of beliefs that duplicates or even approximates those of late medieval demonologists, and none of them has nurtured the belief that a large sect of flying magicians worships demons secretly in orgies characterized by cannibalistic infanticide. In this regard late medieval and early modern European culture is unique.

There were, therefore, two quite different but related types of activity denoted by the word witchcraft as it was used in early modern Europe, one being the practice of *maleficium*, the other being diabolism. Both notions were contained in the prevailing stereotype of the witch, so much so that the presence of one usually implied the other.[11] In artistic representations of witchcraft, *maleficium* and diabolism were often combined. A seventeenth-century engraving of the witches' sabbath, as the nocturnal gathering of witches was often called, shows witches not only dancing naked and sacrificing children to the Devil but also standing over a cauldron preparing unguents to be used in harming other human beings (see Figure 1.2). Despite this fusion of the two components of witchcraft, the word witchcraft and its equivalent in European languages sometimes connoted only one of these two alleged practices. On the one hand, some people were accused of witchcraft simply on the basis of having attended the sabbath (*sabbat* in French) without any evidence that they had performed *maleficia* or 'practised witchcraft'.[12] On the other hand, some individuals were accused of performing *maleficia* but avoided the additional charge of diabolism.

This latter situation usually occurred when witchcraft accusations originated in accusations of *maleficia* by the witches' neighbours rather than judicial officials and were not embellished by judges and prosecutors who were preoccupied with diabolical fantasies. Neighbours of witches were generally much more concerned about the misfortunes that they believed they had suffered as a result of a witch's magical power than the witch's alleged dealings with the Devil. They were not completely ignorant of such things as the witch's pact with the Devil and her alleged worship of him, and during large witchcraft panics they often received instruction from clerics regarding such matters.[13] But ideas of diabolism were shared mainly by scholars, lawyers, judges and magistrates – the literate and ruling members of society – and witches were generally accused of such activities when the members of these educated elites either brought charges against witches on their own initiative or used judicial torture to force people accused of *maleficia* to confess to diabolical activity. In England, where judges had none of these legal powers and where almost all witchcraft prosecutions came from below, the crime of witchcraft remained essentially one of performing harmful magic, not one of worshipping the Devil. In other regions, such as Russia, Denmark and Norway, the crime was viewed in the same way, either for legal reasons or because the ideas of diabolism that were current in France, Germany and Italy never fully penetrated these peripheral regions. The witches' relationship with demons was present in some witchcraft trials in these countries, but the large majority of these prosecutions were based on charges of malefic rather than diabolical witchcraft.

The word witchcraft, therefore, will be used in this book to denote the practice of either harmful magic or diabolism, and when it is used in the fullest sense of the word it will designate both. The word can, moreover, be extended to cover two other types of activity that are very closely related to this definition of witchcraft. The first is invocation, in which a person calls upon the Devil or more commonly one of the lesser demons to obtain instruction or assistance. This invocation was usually performed as part of a ritual or ceremony, the purpose of which was to practise some sort of magic, usually

Figure 1.2 Jan Ziarnko's depiction of the witches' sabbath. In the top right corner witches sacrifice an infant to the Devil, seated on his throne, flanked by the queen and princess of the sabbath. At the bottom right witches and demons feast on the dismembered and sacrificed children. To the left and the right witches dance naked. In the centre, witches fly to this assembly on broomsticks and the backs of animals. Below them, witches stand over a cauldron, preparing potions that will be used to cause harm, showing that *maleficium* remained a central feature of the witches' crime, even at the sabbath. From Pierre de Lancre, *Tableau de l'inconstance des mauvais anges et démons* (1613).

divination. Ritual magicians were not generally classified as witches in the sixteenth and seventeenth centuries, but in certain instances they were prosecuted as such. These trials usually occurred when the magic that was being performed was maleficent and when the relationship between magician and demon appeared to be that of servant and master. In fact that was rarely the case. Ritual magicians almost always sought to establish a contractual relationship with the demons they conjured. Nevertheless, as part of this contract, they often made offerings to these demons that appeared to be signs of reverence, and this made them vulnerable to prosecution.

The second activity that can be included within a broad definition of witchcraft is that of 'white witchcraft', which in early modern Europe denoted either the practice of magical healing or the use of rather crude forms of divination in order to foretell the future, locate lost objects or identify enemies. By definition white witchcraft did not involve the practice of *maleficium*, but because all magic was believed to involve the agency of the Devil, white witches could easily be regarded as having made pacts with him. In those witchcraft treatises that viewed the pact as the essence of witchcraft, very little distinction was made between white and black witches.[14] In actual practice, however, white witches were usually treated more leniently than their maleficent counterparts. In England they were usually prosecuted in the ecclesiastical rather than the secular courts and given only spiritual penalties. In some areas they were not even prosecuted. Nevertheless, many white witches, being known to cure the sick, were also suspected of harming them and thus became assimilated to malefic witches.[15]

A final terminological distinction must be made between witchcraft and demonic possession. The belief that evil spirits can actually inhabit the body of human beings and control their physical movements and behaviour is present in all societies. In Christianity the belief has a long history, having a scriptural foundation in the exorcism performed by Christ.[16] Victims of possession were reported to have manifested a wide variety of symptoms, including severe convulsions and fits, bodily contortions, stiffness of the limbs, temporary blindness and deafness, vomiting nails or other alien objects, displaying abnormal strength, speaking in foreign languages previously unknown to them, and levitating. Sometimes demonic possession afflicted groups of people, such as nuns in convents, children in orphanages and young girls in small towns and villages. A further distinction can be made between possession, in which demonic spirits reputedly enter the body, and obsession, in which the demons assail the body from outside and produce some of the symptoms of possession.[17]

The victims of possession, known as demoniacs, can be distinguished from witches on the grounds that, being the involuntary victims of demonic power, they were not morally responsible for their actions. They could, and sometimes did, claim that 'The Devil made me do it'. In some situations the symptoms of possession were viewed as 'good' or 'divine', being the product of the spiritual regimen followed by Catholic women, especially nuns, to achieve sainthood or possibly mystical union with the deity. Nevertheless, possessions could lead to the claim that the demoniac was morally suspect. The belief that some demoniacs suffered their afflictions because of their own sins or the sins of their parents often led to the suspicion, especially in Protestant communities, that they might actually be witches themselves.[18]

The main connection between possession and witchcraft, however, is that witches could cause the possession of others. During the early modern period theologians claimed that there were two methods of possession. The first and most common was that the Devil could inhabit the person's body by his own power, presuming of course that he did so with God's permission. The second was that the Devil possessed a person at the command of a witch. In those latter cases the symptoms of possession were considered among the various maleficent deeds performed by witches. Many of the witchcraft prosecutions of the early modern period, especially those between 1590 and 1700, were directed against witches for causing the possession or obsession of other people. The demonologist Henri Boguet began his influential treatise on witchcraft with an extended discussion of the prosecution of a witch for causing the possession of an eight-year-old girl, Loyse Maillat.[19] One of the most famous witchcraft prosecutions of the entire period was based on the charge that Urbain Grandier, a parish priest in Loudun, caused the demonic possession of an entire convent of Ursuline nuns. A majority of the prosecutions for witchcraft in the Calvinist republic of Geneva in the early seventeenth century began as cases of alleged possession, as did many of the witch trials in New England and Scotland in the last decade of the seventeenth century.[20] In seventeenth-century England the connection between witchcraft and possession was so common that the words 'possessed' and 'bewitched' became almost synonymous.[21] The distinction between witchcraft and possession, therefore, does not in any way deny the important connection between them.

SOURCE BOOK

The reality of witchcraft

Witchcraft is often referred to, at least by sceptics, as an imagined crime, an elaborate fantasy that has no foundation in reality. Those who were tried as witches, therefore, are viewed as innocent victims of a deluded judiciary and an oppressive legal system. Are these assumptions valid? Did the European witch-hunt produce thousands of criminals who had not committed any crimes, or did witches actually perform some of the deeds for which they were prosecuted? In addressing these questions we need not determine whether magic works or whether the Devil actually exists, for such problems lie outside the realm of historical investigation. But historians can and must ask whether those persons accused of witchcraft did in fact engage in any of the *activities* for which they were prosecuted. The answer to this historical question inevitably affects the answer to the related question of the witches' legal guilt, since guilt is determined at least to some extent by the reality of the alleged crime. If witches did not in fact perform the various deeds of which they were accused, and if they did not actually attempt to perform them, then they could not have been guilty as charged.

In discussing the reality of witchcraft it is necessary first to distinguish between the two main components of the crime: *maleficium* and diabolism. The first has a solid basis in reality, in that certain individuals in virtually all societies do in fact practise harmful or evil magic. Concerning the reality of such deeds in the past, there is an abundance of physical, legal and literary evidence. In the ancient Roman Empire, for example, individuals were known to inscribe curses on lead tablets, dedicate the tablets to demons, and then drive nails through the tablets. We know that this form of sorcery, which is

called *defixio*, was actually practised, since the tablets themselves have
survived.[22] In similar fashion the dolls and other paraphernalia used in image
magic have survived from many societies in the past. When necromancers were
prosecuted in the Middle Ages, the tools of their trade were usually produced
as evidence of their guilt. And the literature of magic – the hundreds of
manuals and guides to the practice of both white and black magic that have
survived from many different historical periods – all provide ample proof that
people have in fact practised sorcery and continue to do so today.

Whether any of the European witches of the early modern period actually
attempted to harm people by using magical power is more difficult to
determine. The tools of their alleged art were rarely produced in court, and
since they were for the most part illiterate, they could not be expected to have
books of magic in their possession.[23] The legal evidence for their sorcery
consisted of their confessions and the depositions of neighbours who accused
them of causing harm or misfortune. Both types of evidence are suspect: the
confessions because they were very often adduced under torture, the depositions
because they were made by hostile parties. Nevertheless, the depositions do
often contain records of spoken curses, spells and even the use of the tools of
image magic, all of which suggest that at least some of the people accused of
witchcraft did in fact try to harm their enemies by magical means. Indeed,
sorcery was one of few means by which women, especially older, unmarried
women, could protect themselves in early modern European communities. In
a study of the well-known witch-hunt that took place at Salem, Massachusetts,
in 1692, Chadwick Hansen has argued that at least three of the women
prosecuted for witchcraft were in fact practitioners of sorcery.[24]

Even if some of the witches of the early modern period did actually engage
in the practice of maleficent magic, we must not assume that all of them, or
even a majority of them, did likewise. We shall never know how many of the
thousands of executed witches did in fact perform maleficent magic, but the
number was certainly very low. A somewhat larger number, but still a distinct
minority, were probably guilty of practising some form of white magic,
which their neighbours and superiors misinterpreted or perhaps deliberately
misrepresented as being maleficent. The majority of accused witches did not
practise any sort of magic at all but were accused either of causing harm by
magical means when unexplained misfortune struck one of their neighbours
or when they were named as the accomplices of other witches in the course
of a large witch-hunt.

When we turn to the subject of diabolism, the problem of establishing the
reality of the witches' actions becomes more difficult, for the only evidence
we have regarding such deeds are the confessions of the witches themselves
and the accusations made by their alleged accomplices. These pieces of
evidence are suspect for a number of reasons.[25] First, they frequently contain
references to the performance of manifestly impossible deeds, such as flying
through the air. Such statements do not by themselves invalidate the entire

testimony, but they do call its veracity into question and require supporting evidence. This evidence has never been produced in any recorded case of diabolism. Never once, for example, did the neighbours who accused witches of *maleficia* testify that they had witnessed the collective worship of the Devil or even the conclusion of a formal pact between a witch and the Devil. Even more importantly, no impartial or detached observer ever testified or claimed in writing that he had witnessed such an act. Even the rather credulous Italian inquisitor, Paulus Grillandus, writing in the early sixteenth century, admitted that he had never seen or heard of any witch caught *in flagrante crimine*.[26] Never once did authorities conduct a raid on a witches' coven, even though the same authorities showed that they were quite capable of breaking into the meetings of other subversive groups. In fact, whenever independent, impartial investigations were conducted into the alleged practice of diabolism, they produced negative results. When, for example, the Spanish inquisitor Alonso de Salazar Frías interrogated hundreds of witches from the Basque country who had confessed to attending witches' sabbaths, known in the Basque language as *aquelarres*, in 1610, he concluded on the basis of numerous retractions and contradictions that the entire affair was 'nothing but a chimera'.[27]

A second reason for calling into question the confessions of witches to acts of diabolism is that they were often extracted under torture or the threat of torture. Confessions obtained in this way contained evidence that was contaminated, since it was more likely that the confession would indicate what the torturer wished to hear rather than what the accused had actually done. Most clerical judges and secular magistrates in Europe during the sixteenth and seventeenth centuries had a fairly clear, preconceived idea of the diabolical activities that witches engaged in. When accused sorcerers were brought before them, they assumed that these people, in addition to practising magic, were also members of a secret, heretical, Devil-worshipping sect. Using highly effective methods of torture, they often forced them to confess to having made face-to-face pacts with the Devil and having worshipped him collectively. In an effort to wipe out the entire sect of witches, moreover, they then used torture once again to elicit the names of their alleged accomplices.

The best evidence we have regarding the close connection between torture and confessions to diabolical activity is that accusations of Devil-worship usually did not arise in witchcraft trials until that stage of the proceedings when torture was applied.[28] Sometimes this was in the early, preliminary stages, shortly after the arrest of the witch, but at other times it did not take place until after witnesses had made their depositions. These depositions were almost always concerned exclusively with *maleficium*, not diabolism. Once torture was employed, then charges of diabolism arose. For this reason it is valid to claim that torture in a certain sense 'created' witchcraft, or at least created diabolical witchcraft.

The crucial role that torture played in securing confessions to diabolism is most clearly illustrated in a trial of three witches in the Channel Island of

Guernsey in 1617. In this trial torture was not administered until very late in the proceedings, after the defendants had been convicted and sentenced. Up to that point the trial had dealt only with charges of *maleficia*. Numerous witnesses had testified that the three women had cast spells on inanimate objects, inflicted strange diseases upon many persons and beasts, cruelly hurt a great number of men, women and children, and caused the death of many animals. On the basis of this testimony, which made no reference to the worship of the Devil, the three were convicted and sentenced to death.[29] As soon as the sentence was pronounced one of the witches, a widow by the name of Collette Du Mont, confessed that she was a witch, but since she refused to specify which crimes she had committed, she was taken to the torture chamber.

It was at this point that diabolism entered the trial. Once Collette was put to the question, she admitted that the Devil had appeared to her in the form of a cat on numerous occasions and that he had incited her to take revenge on her neighbours. In this way a connection was established between her relationship with the Devil and the maleficent deeds with which she had been charged. Her confession, however, did not stop there but went on to describe diabolical practices that were very often associated with witchcraft:

> That the Devil having come to fetch her that she might go to the SOURCE BOOK
> Sabbath called for her without anyone perceiving it: and gave her a
> certain black ointment with which (after having stripped herself), she
> rubbed her back, belly and stomach: and then having again put on
> her clothes, she went out of her door, when she was immediately
> carried through the air at a great speed: and she found herself in an
> instant at the place of the Sabbath, which was sometimes near the
> parochial burial ground: at other times near the seashore in the
> neighbourhood of Rocquaine Castle: where, upon arrival, she met
> often fifteen or sixteen wizards and witches with the devils who were
> there in the form of dogs, cats and hares; which wizards and witches
> she was unable to recognise, because they were all blackened and
> disfigured: it was true, however, that she had heard the Devil summon
> them by their names, and she remembered among others those of
> *Fallaise* and *Hardie* . . . Admitted that her daughter Marie, wife of
> Massy, now condemned for a similar crime, was a Witch: and that
> she took her twice to the Sabbath: at the Sabbath, after having
> worshipped the Devil, who used to stand up on his hind legs, they
> had connection with him under the form of a dog; then they danced
> back to back. And having danced, they drank wine (she did not know
> what colour it was), which the Devil poured out of a jug into the
> silver or pewter goblet; which wine did not seem to her so good as
> that which was usually drunk; they also ate white bread which he
> presented to them – she had never seen any salt at the Sabbath.

The confession concludes with a report of the way in which the Devil, on leaving the sabbath, gave Collette certain black powders that she could throw on human beings and cattle to cause harm.[30]

Collette Du Mont's account of the sabbath can readily be dismissed as the product of judicial coercion. What are we to do, however, with those confessions to diabolism that are reported to have been free or unforced? Some of these voluntary confessions were not free at all, having been made shortly after the conclusion of one stage of torture and before the next. Nor can we consider as free the confessions of those who decided on rational grounds that it was preferable to confess and be executed than to endure the excruciating tortures that awaited them if they remained silent. These people might very well have recognized that the situation was hopeless anyway and elected therefore to avoid some of their agony by confessing. The confessions of Johannes Junius at Bamberg in 1628 fall into this category. Even when accused witches thought they might survive the torture and be acquitted, the intolerable prospect of social isolation and communal hatred after they returned to their villages occasionally induced 'voluntary' confessions.[31] In all of these cases, confession led to what we might call judicial suicide, an alternative to the completely self-inflicted suicide that many witches resorted to while in prison. Whenever a witch committed this type of suicide, the evidence contained in her confession lacked credibility, for in making her statement she was at least to some extent willing to tell her interrogators what they wanted to hear. The same problem arises in dealing with those confessions that witches made in the hope of obtaining judicial leniency. In some cases that hope was based on false promises of the authorities or the unwarranted expectations of the accused; in others it rested on the established judicial policy of giving reprieves to those who confessed. Whatever the rationale, however, these confessions could easily be fabricated in order to win acceptance and therefore cannot be relied upon for their factual accuracy.

Not all 'free' witchcraft confessions represented conscious efforts to avoid some form of pain or suffering. Some, for example, might very well have been the product of psychological disorder. We need not accept the argument of Johann Weyer, the sixteenth-century critic of witch-hunting, that witches were afflicted with melancholy to appreciate the fact that some of the old women who were prosecuted for witchcraft were of unsound mind. Such women were capable of developing a variety of fantasies and providing their interrogators with material that could easily be shaped into accounts of diabolical activity. We also know enough about people today who confess to crimes they did not commit – and even to crimes that no one *could* commit – to dismiss the possibility that some of the individuals who made free confessions to diabolism were mythomaniacs.

Even if witches who made free confessions were not psychologically disturbed, they might very well have confessed to having performed activities that they dreamed they had done. Such dreams were probably conditioned by cultural traditions, such as when children dreamed or imagined that they had been taken to places where they had been told witches usually gathered. It is also possible, although highly unlikely, that salves made from widely available hallucinogenic plants, such as such as belladonna, henbane and mandrake, resulted in ecstatic experiences that influenced the content of the witchcraft confessions.[32] The problem with this theory is that there is no reliable evidence that accused witches actually anointed themselves in this manner, even if demonologists claimed that they did.[33] In any case, neither dreams of having attended the sabbath nor ecstatic experiences induced by unguents made from psychotropic plants go very far to establish the 'reality' of witchcraft.

Even when all the confessions that were the product of judicial coercion, psychological disorders or dreams are accounted for, we are still left with a number of apparently free confessions to diabolism, especially in jurisdictions where torture was prohibited or strictly limited.[34] These confessions do not conform to the learned stereotype of the witches' sabbath, but they do provide evidence of the witches' belief that they made pacts with the Devil. One example of such a confession was made by an English witch, Elizabeth Sawyer, in 1621. Sawyer's confession might not be viewed as completely voluntary, **SOURCE BOOK** since she made it only after the local minister Henry Goodcole visited her in gaol. But since she made the confession after a jury had convicted her, and since Sawyer was not tortured, her confession does provide some indication of her beliefs regarding the Devil and her relationship to him. In response to Goodcole's questioning, Sawyer admitted that the Devil appeared to her on several occasions and that after threatening her, she 'granted for fear unto the Devil his request of my soul and body'.[35]

Like Elizabeth Sawyer, some of the individuals who were accused of witchcraft probably did genuinely believe that they had make pacts with the Devil. We need not believe that the Devil actually exists or that he actually appeared to witches and conversed with them to admit this possibility. All we must do is recognize that in the early modern period many poor, often old women, realizing that their plight was desperate, and believing that the Devil offered people material pleasures in exchange for adoration, pledged their service and sold their souls to him.[36] Other witches may have invoked his aid in critical situations. If such people did in fact believe that they had made pacts with the Devil, inquisitors would have had a relatively easy time convincing them that they had engaged in other, less credible forms of Devil-worship. The same people, it should be added, would probably have appeared in the trial records as feeling a deep sense of guilt and remorse for their actions, which is exactly how many witches have been described.[37]

Although individual witches may have actually tried to make pacts with the Devil, there is no foundation to the widespread belief that they worshipped him collectively. Unless independent, non-contaminated evidence can be produced to support the existence of a witch cult, we must take the sceptical position that all such activities existed in the minds of the accused or their prosecutors, or both.[38] Nor can we argue with any degree of certainty that people accused of witchcraft organized themselves for some other, non-diabolical purposes that were interpreted by judicial authorities as the collective worship of the Devil. There is no shortage of historical theories that interpret witchcraft in this way. The most famous is that of Dame Margaret Murray, an anthropologist who in three different studies argued that the witches of the early modern period were really members of an ancient, pre-Christian fertility cult whose beneficent rituals were misrepresented by alarmed clerics and judges as harmful and diabolical.[39] Other scholars, sharing a romantic interpretation of witchcraft, have interpreted the witches' assemblies as organized protests either against the established economic and social order or against patriarchy. One historian has seen the witches' sabbath as the work of goliards parodying the current ecclesiastical order.[40] The problem with all these interpretations is that there is no proof that witches ever gathered in large numbers for any purpose, diabolical or otherwise. The fear of collective Devil-worship may have been based on the reality of the secret assemblies of other groups. We know, for example, that heretics did gather in fairly large numbers for purposes of religious worship. But witches, if they ever practised any of their craft at all, did so individually or in small groups.

Murray's theory appears to have received some reinforcement from the work of Carlo Ginzburg, who discovered that a number of witches from the Italian province of Friuli in the late sixteenth and early seventeenth centuries were in fact members of a fertility cult. The *benandanti*, as these persons called them-selves, wore their cauls around their necks as amulets and claimed that they went out at night to battle the witches, the enemies of fertility. Under the pressure of the Inquisition these men came to believe that they themselves were witches and confessed. Ginzburg claims that his discovery confirmed a 'kernel of truth' in Murray's thesis, for the *benandanti* prove that 'witchcraft had its roots in an ancient fertility cult'.[41] That may very well be true, if 'witchcraft' is taken to mean the witch beliefs or myths held by the common people. But Ginzburg's book does not support the position that witches were pagans or that they actually practised their religion. Not only did the *benandanti* frequently profess their loyalty to the Catholic Church, but even more importantly, they never actually travelled at night to fight the witches. Instead they went out in spirit, while their bodies entered a cataleptic state. Ginzburg entertains the possibility that the *benandanti* may have actually gathered under some circumstances, but there is no evidence that they ever did so.

The possibility that witches dreamed or imagined that they were engaging in certain activities is the only legitimate basis for a romantic interpretation of witchcraft. The peasants who were accused of witchcraft had their own fantasies, just as their inquisitors did, and these fantasies could easily reinforce those of their prosecutors. We know, for example, that many women believed that they flew at night and copulated with demons, beliefs that reinforced the conviction of inquisitors that the same women engaged in these activities at the sabbath. We also know from the work of Emmanuel Le Roy Ladurie that many of the peasants of Languedoc imagined an inverted social order as a form of symbolic protest and that the revelation of their fantasies could easily have been interpreted as accounts of the sabbath, at which everything was believed to be upside down.[42] But we must keep in mind that the reality of this inversion was mental, not physical. We still do not have any evidence that either a witch cult or a group of persons performing some ritual that was interpreted as witchcraft actually existed.

The fact that the great European witch-hunt involved so much fantasy – the fantasies of the witches themselves as well as those of their accusers – has led many historians, mainly those of the liberal or rationalist school, to regard witchcraft as a massive delusion or illusion, which was dispelled by the growth of scientific knowledge and by the general enlightenment that occurred in Europe in the late seventeenth and eighteenth centuries. This characterization of witchcraft as a delusion is inappropriate, both because it impedes an open-minded investigation into the functions that witch beliefs served in early modern European society and because it suggests that witchcraft, as it was viewed at this time, had no foundation in reality. As argued above, that was not the case. There were clearly individuals who practised magic, even harmful magic, and others who claimed to have made pacts with the Devil. One might contend that the magician and the diabolist were deluding themselves; such a contention would depend upon one's beliefs regarding the effectiveness of magic and the existence of a Devil who could converse with humans. But when writers and judicial authorities tried to wipe out witchcraft, they were not dealing with an entirely fabricated threat.

The size of the hunt

There are two sets of figures that can be used to estimate the size of the great European witch-hunt. The first is the number of witches who were prosecuted (i.e. those who were arrested and formally charged before a court). The second set of figures is the number who were executed. Because so many judicial records have been destroyed or otherwise lost, and because the trials of many witches were never even officially recorded, neither figure can be determined with any degree of accuracy. Some estimates, ranging as high as nine million executions, have been grossly exaggerated.[43] These estimates have been inflated both by the claims of witch-hunters themselves, who often boasted about how many witches they had burned, and by subsequent writers, who for different reasons wished to emphasize the gravity of the process they were discussing.[44] Detailed scholarly studies have generally led to a downward estimate of the total numbers of victims. It has long been believed, for example, that an early seventeenth-century witch-hunt in the Basque-speaking Pays de Labourd in France resulted in 600 executions, but it now appears that the actual figure was closer to 80.[45] In the German ecclesiastical territory of Bamberg, where another 600 witches were allegedly burned between 1625 and 1630, the total was probably closer to 425.[46] In Scotland, where Henry C. Lea claimed that 7,500 persons were executed for witchcraft, the actual tally was probably about 1,500.[47]

Even if we make allowances for trial records that have been lost or destroyed, the total number of Europeans who were prosecuted for witchcraft probably did not exceed 90,000. About half of these persons lived in German lands within the Holy Roman Empire.[48] The other heavy concentrations of European prosecutions were in the lands bordering on Germany. To the south, Switzerland, long recognized as a centre of the witch-hunt, tried at least 10,000 witches,[49] while to the west a string of French and Spanish territories within the Empire (including Lorraine, Franche-Comté and the Spanish Netherlands) held another 5,000 trials. By comparison, the areas under the control of the king of France – known as royal France – were far more restrained, mainly because the provincial parlements superintended the process. Between 1565 and 1640 the Parlement of Paris, which had jurisdiction over about one-half of the country, reviewed 1,123 cases from the lower courts, but since appeals were not automatic until 1624, one can assume that the total number of original trials was slightly higher.[50] More intense witch-hunting took place in the Pays de Labourd in the southwest, but all in all the number of French subjects tried for witchcraft probably did not exceed 3,000, a figure that takes into account witches tried by the lower courts whose cases did not reach the parlements.

In addition to these areas of relatively intense witch-hunting, there were no more than 5,000 prosecutions in the British Isles (more than half of them in Scotland) and another 3,000 in the Nordic countries. There were even fewer trials – probably not more than 5,000 in all – in Bohemia, Hungary, Transylvania and Russia. In Poland, once considered a centre of witch-hunting, there were probably no more than 3,000 prosecutions.[51] Finally, in the Mediterranean countries of Europe – the Spanish kingdoms and the Italian states – there were about 10,000 prosecutions.[52] Some of these trials, however, were for various forms of magic and 'superstition' rather than for diabolical or malefic witchcraft.[53]

The true horror of witch-hunting lies not in the number of prosecutions but in the number of people who were executed. Determining this figure is just as imprecise an exercise as estimating the number of prosecutions. Table 1.1 establishes the execution-rate of witches in a number of European kingdoms or territories.[54] The number of trials upon which these rates are calculated are very small, since they include only those cases whose outcomes are known. In most of these locations the execution-rate was less than 70 per cent, and in some areas, such as Essex county, Ostrobothnia and Geneva, it was less than 25 per cent. Only in the Pays de Vaud, in Switzerland did the execution-rate reach the severe level of 90 per cent.[55]

On the basis of the statistics in Table 1.1, the average execution-rate for Europe was 46 per cent, but the table does not include data for any German

Table 1.1 Regional execution-rates in witchcraft trials

Region	Years	Persons tried (fates known)	Executions	% Executed
Fribourg	1607–1683	162	53	33
Geneva	1537–1662	318	68	21
Neuchâtel	1568–1677	341	214	63
Pays de Vaud	1537–1630	102	90	90
Luxembourg	1509–1687	547	358	69
County of Namur	1509–1646	270	144	54
Isle of Guernsey	1563–1634	78	33	46
Dept. of the Nord, France	1542–1679	187	90	48
Finland	1520–1699	710	115	16
Iceland	1625–1683	120	22	18
Norway	1551–1760	730	280	38
County of Essex, England	1560–1672	291	74	24
Scotland	1563–1727	307	206	67
Hungary	1520–1777	932	449	48
Poland	1511–1775	455	246	54

territories, which accounted for about half of all European prosecutions and which appear to have had relatively high execution-rates. In the city of Kiel, for example, at least 67 per cent of the witches tried between 1530 and 1676 were executed, and the figure may have been as high as 81 per cent.[56] These relatively high figures, however, are balanced to some extent by those from German territories like Rothenburg ob der Tauber, which executed only three out of 65 accused witches between 1549 and 1709.[57] In southeast Germany there were about 3,000 trials but only 1,000 to 1,500 executions.[58] It is impossible to calculate a precise number of executions for all German territories, but one fairly conservative estimate puts it at about 22,500, a figure that would be consistent with an execution-rate of about 50 per cent.[59] Using the same average execution-rate for all of Europe, we might reasonably conclude that European courts executed about 45,000 witches during the early modern period.[60]

A total of approximately 90,000 witchcraft prosecutions and 45,000 executions may be significantly lower than many estimates, but these figures still represent a grim reality, especially if we keep in mind that most witches were tried either for crimes they did not commit or for crimes that were greatly exaggerated. The total figures, moreover, do not convey the full dimensions of the European witch-hunt. The number of people arrested and brought to trial does not, for example, reveal how many others lived under suspicion of witchcraft or became the object of informal accusations. We know from church court records, where individuals who were called witches brought charges of slander against their accusers, that there were many more witchcraft accusations than actual prosecutions.[61] Even in places where there were relatively few trials, like the Dutch Republic, women lived in constant fear of being named as witches.[62] Witchcraft accusations, therefore, were a much more common feature of early modern European village life than the number of trials would suggest.

There were also many individuals who were formally accused of witchcraft but were never brought to trial. Many of these people were named as witches by their alleged confederates, usually under torture, but for one reason or another they were not themselves prosecuted. In some cases the failure to prosecute can be explained by the decision of judicial authorities to bring the hunt to an end before all suspects had been tried. In other cases the time and cost of imprisoning and prosecuting hundreds of suspects may have tested the resolve of even the most zealous witch-hunter or taxed the financial resources of the local community. In any event, a comprehensive study of witch-hunting cannot ignore these accused but untried persons, who shared much of the terror of those who were actually prosecuted, and who often endured social ostracism and continued suspicion after the hunt ended.

The figures regarding total prosecutions and executions also fail to provide any indication of the effect that witch-hunts had on individual towns and villages. Only when we break down the composite figures year by year and village by village can we appreciate how intense witch-hunts could be. When we learn, for example, that 121 witches were executed in the city of Osnabrück during the summer months of 1583 and that some 300 persons were executed for witchcraft in the prince-bishopric of Würzburg in 1617 alone, we gain a much better sense of the toll that witch-hunting could take than when we calculate figures for an entire country during a 300-year period.

For people living in the sixteenth and seventeenth centuries the main statistical question as far as witchcraft was concerned was not how many witches had been executed but how many were still loose. Some of these estimates were astonishingly high. At the height of a particularly intense witch-hunt in 1587, the judge of the French village of Brieulles claimed that he had evidence of 7,760 witches in the single duchy of Rethelois.[63] In 1571 a French witch by the name of Trois-Eschelles told King Charles IX that there were 300,000 witches in his realm, and in 1602 the demon-ologist Henri Boguet used this figure to project a total of 1,800,000 for all of Europe. According to Boguet, there were 'witches by the thousands every-where, multiplying upon the earth even as worms in a garden'.[64] The number of participants at the witches' assemblies was estimated to be at least 500 by one demonologist and as high as 100,000 by another.[65] These estimates help to explain why educated elites in Europe were so frightened of witchcraft. They also help to explain why they prosecuted witches with such ferocity. A threat of this size could not be ignored; it had to be met head-on with all the judicial power that European states could muster.

Notes

1. The word 'witch-hunt' was coined only in the twentieth century. It connotes the relentless judicial pursuit of groups of people, often because of their political views or undesirable social characteristics, on the basis of contrived or artificial charges. See C. Larner, *Witchcraft and Religion: The Politics of Popular Belief* (Oxford, 1984): 88–91.

2. On the distinction between 'ordinary witchcrafts' and bewitchments in England and New England see R. Weisman, *Witchcraft, Magic and Religion in Seventeenth-Century Massachusetts* (Amherst, MA, 1984): 47–9. In Scotland acts of harmful magic were often referred to as malefices.

3. See H. Sebald, *Witchcraft: The Heritage of a Heresy* (New York, 1978): 147–57; E. Nottingham, *Religion: A Sociological View* (New York, 1971): 88–91.

4. See K. Thomas, *Religion and the Decline of Magic* (London, 1971): chapter 2; M. Tausiet, *Urban Magic in Early Modern Spain: Abracadabra Omnipotens* (Basingstoke, 2014): 4–8.

5. See D. L. O'Keefe, *Stolen Lightning: The Social Theory of Magic* (New York, 1982) for the argument that magic derives from religion and not vice versa; A. A. Barb, 'The Survival of Magic Arts', in *The Conflict between Paganism and Christianity*, ed. A. Momigliano (Oxford, 1963): 100–25.

6. Nottingham, *Religion*, 91; Sebald, *Witchcraft*, 150–2; W. Goode, *Religion Among the Primitives* (Glencoe, IL, 1951): 52–5.

7. E. Peters, *The Magician, the Witch and the Law* (Philadelphia, 1978): xv; Barb, 'Survival', 101.

8. See, for example, C. Larner, *Enemies of God: The Witch-Hunt in Scotland* (Baltimore and London, 1981): 9; R. A. Horsley, 'Who Were the Witches? The Social Roles of the Accused in the European Witch Trials', *Journal of Interdisciplinary History* 9 (1979): 696. For an opposite view see F. E. Lorint and J. Bernabe, *La Sorcellerie paysanne* (Brussels, 1977): 25; A. Macfarlane, *Witchcraft in Tudor and Stuart England* (New York and London, 1970): 4, 310.

9. Horsley, 'Who Were the Witches?', 701, emphasizes this distinction. See also Macfarlane, *Witchcraft in Tudor and Stuart England*, 4.

10. H. C. E. Midelfort, *Witch Hunting in Southwestern Germany, 1562–1684: The Social and Intellectual Foundations* (Stanford, 1972): 52–3.

11. See, for example, N. Remy, *Demonolatry*, tr. E. A. Ashwin, ed. M. Summers (London, 1930): vii.

12. Henri Boguet, *An Examen of Witches*, tr. E. A. Ashwin, ed. M. Summers (London, 1929): 203–4.

13. D. Hall (ed.), *Witch-Hunting in Seventeenth-Century New England: A Documentary Collection, 1638–1692* (Boston, 1991): 9; G. Henningsen, 'The Papers of Alonso de Salazar Frias', *Temenos* 5 (1969): 105.

14. W. Perkins, *A Discourse of the Damned Art of Witchcraft* (Cambridge, 1608): 173–6, considers white witches the most dangerous of all. The definition of witchcraft given by Joseph Glanvill in *Saducismus Triumphatus* (London, 1681), II: 4, would accommodate either white or black magic.

15. On white witches see G. Henningsen, *The Witches' Advocate: Basque Witchcraft and the Spanish Inquisition, 1609–1614* (Reno, 1980): 303; Thomas, *Religion and the Decline of Magic*, 212–53; Weisman, *Witchcraft, Magic and Religion*, 61; E. W. Monter, *Witchcraft in France and Switzerland: The Borderlands during the Reformation* (Ithaca, 1976): 167–90.

16. G. H. Twelftree, *Jesus the Exorcist* (Tübingen, 1994).

17. On demonic possession see B. P. Levack, *The Devil Within: Possession and Exorcism in the Christian West* (New Haven and London, 2013).

18. C. Karlsen, *The Devil in the Shape of a Woman: Witchcraft in Colonial New England* (New York, 1987): 242–4; H. C. E. Midelfort, 'Catholic and Lutheran Reactions to Demon Possession in the Late Seventeenth Century: Two Case Histories', *Daphnis* 15 (1986): 625–8; S. Olli, 'The Devil's Pact: A Male Strategy', in *Beyond the Witch Trials: Witchcraft and Magic in Enlightenment Europe*, ed. O. Davies and W. de Blécourt (Manchester, 2004): 111–12.
19. Boguet, *An Examen of Witches*, 1–14.
20. Monter, *Witchcraft in France and Switzerland*, 59–60.
21. Thomas, *Religion and the Decline of Magic*, 478.
22. For examples of these curses see H. A. Harris, *Sport in Greece and Rome* (Ithaca, NY, 1972): 235–6; B. P. Levack (ed.), *The Witchcraft Sourcebook*, 2nd edn (London, 2015): 14–15.
23. For a few rare cases in which accused witches used books see Sebald, *Witchcraft*, 44; C. Garrett, 'Witches and Cunning Folk in the Old Regime', in *The Wolf and the Lamb: Popular Culture in France from the Old Regime to the Twentieth Century*, ed. J. Beauroy, M. Bertrand and E. T. Gargan (Stanford, 1976): 59. For the case of Jean Michel of Moulins see Humanities Research Center, University of Texas at Austin, Pre-1700 MS 142.
24. C. Hansen, *Witchcraft at Salem* (New York, 1969): 94–104, 284–6; E. Bever, *The Realities of Witchcraft and Popular Magic in Early Modern Europe: Culture, Cognition, and Everyday Life* (Basingstoke, 2008): 154–85.
25. For the strongest denial of the reality of diabolism see N. Cohn, *Europe's Inner Demons: The Demonization of Christians in Medieval Christendom*, rev. edn (Chicago, 1993): chapters 7 and 8.
26. R. H. Robbins, *The Encyclopedia of Witchcraft and Demonology* (New York, 1959): 236.
27. Henningsen, *The Witches' Advocate*, 247.
28. See R. Kieckhefer, *European Witch Trials: Their Foundations in Popular and Learned Culture, 1300–1500* (London, 1976): chapters 3 and 5; M. Madar, 'Estonia I: Werewolves and Poisoners', in *Early Modern European Witchcraft: Centres and Peripheries*, ed. B. Ankarloo and G. Henningsen (Oxford, 1990): 272.
29. J. L. Pitts, *Witchcraft and Devil Lore in the Channel Islands* (Guernsey, 1886): 9–10.
30. Ibid., 12–14.
31. Sir George Mackenzie, *The Laws and Customes of Scotland in Matters Criminal* (Edinburgh, 1678): 87.
32. See for example M. Harner, 'The Role of Hallucinogenic Plants in European Witchcraft', in *Hallucinogens and Shamanism*, ed. M. Harner (New York, 1973): 125–50; and more recently, Bever, *The Realities of Witchcraft and Popular Magic*, 129–50.
33. Cohn, *Europe's Inner Demons*, 175–80; M. Ostling, 'Babyfat and Belladonna: Witches' Ointment and the Contestation of Reality', *Magic, Ritual, and Witchcraft*, forthcoming.
34. On reading such confessions in England see D. Purkiss, *The Witch in History: Early Modern and Twentieth-Century Representations* (London, 1996), especially part II; M. Gibson, *Reading Witchcraft: Stories of Early English Witches* (London, 1999).
35. H. Goodcole, *The Wonderful Discovery of Elizabeth Sawyer, a Witch, late of Edmonton* (London, 1621).
36. See Thomas, *Religion and the Decline of Magic*, 516–26.
37. Monter, *Witchcraft in France and Switzerland*, 137.
38. See Henningsen, *Witches' Advocate*, 93–4.
39. M. Murray, *The Witch-Cult in Western Europe* (Oxford, 1921); idem, *The God of the Witches* (London, 1933); idem, *The Divine King in England* (London, 1954).
40. E. Rose, *A Razor for a Goat* (Toronto, 1962).

41. See C. Ginzburg, *The Night Battles: Witchcraft and Agrarian Cults in the Sixteenth and Seventeenth Centuries*, tr. J. Tedeschi and A. Tedeschi (Baltimore, 1983).

42. E. Le Roy Ladurie, *Les Paysans de Languedoc* (Paris, 1966): 407–13.

43. See, for example, A. Dworkin, *Woman Hating* (New York, 1974): 130. W. von Baeyer-Katte, 'Die Historischen Hexenprozesse: Der Verbürokratisierte Massenwahn', in *Massenwahn in Geschichte und Gegenwart*, ed. W. Bitter (Stuttgart, 1965): 222, estimates close to one million cases on the basis of lost records and unrecorded trials. For a late eighteenth-century estimate see H. C. Lea, *Materials toward a History of Witchcraft*, arr. and ed. Arthur C. Howland, 3 vols (New York, 1957), III: 1075. For a summary of a wide variety of estimates see R. M. Golden, 'Satan in Europe: The Geography of Witch Hunts', in *Changing Identities in Early Modern France*, ed. M. Wolfe (Durham, NC, 1997): 220–1.

44. Luis de Páramo boasted that inquisitors alone had executed 30,000 persons for witchcraft by the middle of the sixteenth century. H. C. Lea, *A History of the Inquisition of the Middle Ages*, 3 vols (New York, 1955), III: 549.

45. Henningsen, *Witches' Advocate*, 23–5, 480–1. R. Briggs, *Communities of Belief: Cultural and Social Tension in Early Modern France* (Oxford, 1989), suggests that the figure may be as low as thirty.

46. B. Gehm, *Die Hexenverfolgung im Hochstift Bamberg und das Eingrefen des Reichshofrates zu ihrer Beendigung* (Hildsheim, 2000): 109–11. All told, 642 persons were arrested and at least 415 were executed.

47. H. C. Lea, *History of the Inquisition in Spain*, 4 vols (New York, 1906–7), IV: 246–7; J. Goodare, J. Miller and L. Yeoman, *The Survey of Scottish Witchcraft*, www.shca.ed.ac.uk/Research/witches/.

48. G. Schormann, *Hexenprozesse in Deutschland* (Göttingen, 1981): 8–15, 71. Schormann is confident that the number was less than 100,000. Wolfgang Behringer has calculated that there were certainly more than 15,000 and perhaps more than 20,000 *executions* in Germany. W. Behringer, '"Erhob sich das ganze Land zu ihrer Ausrottung . . .": Hexenprozesse und Hexenverfolgungen in Europa', in *Hexenwelten: Magie und Imagination vom 16.–20. Jahrhundert*, ed. Richard van Dülmen (Frankfurt, 1987): 165. Some historians have speculated that the number of executions in Germany may be as high as 40,000. R. Briggs, 'Number of Witches', in *Encyclopedia of Witchcraft: The Western Tradition* (Santa Barbara, 2006), III: 839–41, estimates roughly the same numbers as presented here, with perhaps 100,000 prosecutions and at most 50,000 executions.

49. G. Bader, *Die Hexenprozesse in der Schweiz* (Affoltern, 1945): 211–20, gives a total of 8,888 persons tried and 5,417 executed, but subsequent research has shown that these totals are too low. Behringer, 'Erhob sich das ganze Land', 161–2, estimates that the number of executions may be as high as 10,000.

50. A. Soman, 'The Parlement of Paris and the Great Witch Hunt (1565–1640)', *Sixteenth Century Journal* 9 (1978): 35.

51. B. Baranowski, *Procesy czarownic w Polsce w XVII i XVIII wieku* (Lodz, 1952): 178. Baranowski's estimates of 10,000 legal executions and 5,000 illegal ones is greatly exaggerated. See W. Wyporska, 'Poland', in *Encyclopedia of Witchcraft: The Western Tradition*, ed. R. M. Golden (Santa Barbara, 2006), III: 907–10. In Russia there were probably not more than 900 prosecutions. V. Kivelson, *Desperate Magic: The Moral Economy of Witchcraft in Seventeenth-Century Russia* (Ithaca, NY, 2013): 36.

52. G. Parker, 'Some Recent Work on the Inquisition in Spain and Italy', *Journal of Modern History* 54 (1982): 529, gives a figure of 3,687 persons tried for witchcraft in Spain between 1560 and 1700. That figure does not include prosecutions in the secular courts.

53. Trials for witchcraft in the Spanish and Roman Inquisitions comprised only a portion of those for various offences categorized as 'superstition'. Trials for witchcraft in these tribunals could be for *maleficium* or diabolism. Trials for other types of magic were usually not classified as witchcraft, but these distinctions were not always maintained.

54. Sources for Table 1.1: Monter, *Witchcraft in France and Switzerland*, 49; M.-S. Dupont-Bouchat, 'La Répression de la sorcellerie dans le duché de Luxembourg aux XVIᵉ et XVIIᵉ siècles', in M. Dupont-Bouchat, W. Frijhoff and R. Muchembled, *Prophètes et sorciers dans les Pays-Bas XVIᵉ–XVIIIᵉ siècles* (Paris, 1978): 127; Pitts, *Witchcraft and Devil Lore*, 28–32; J. Goodare *et al.*, *Survey of Scottish Witchcraft*; A. Heikkinen and T. Kervinen, 'Finland: The Male Domination', in *Early Modern European Witchcraft: Centres and Peripheries*, ed. B. Ankarloo and G. Henningsen (Oxford, 1990): 321; H. E. Naess, 'Norway: The Criminological Context', in *Early Modern European Witchcraft: Centres and Peripheries*, ed. B. Ankarloo and G. Henningsen (Oxford, 1990): 371; M. Rafnsson, *Angurgapi: The Witch-Hunt in Iceland* (Hólmavik, 2003): 25–6; Macfarlane, *Witchcraft in Tudor and Stuart England*, 57; G. Klaniczay, 'Hungary: The Accusations and the Universe of Popular Magic', in *Early Modern European Witchcraft: Centres and Peripheries*, ed. B. Ankarloo and G. Henningsen (Oxford, 1990): 222; M. Ostling, *Between the Devil and the Host: Imagining Witchcraft in Early Modern Poland* (Oxford, 2011): 89.

55. The execution rate in Lorraine was also about 90 per cent. See R. Briggs, 'Witchcraft and Popular Mentality in Lorraine, 1580–1630', in *Occult and Scientific Mentalities in the Renaissance*, ed. B. Vickers (Cambridge, 1984): 338. In Russia, however, the execution rate was less than 15 per cent during the period 1600–1760, a percentage comparable to that of Finland. Kivelson, *Desperate Magic*, 36.

56. D. Unverhau, 'Kieler Hexen und Zauberer zur Zeit der grossen Verfolgungen (1530–1676)', *Mitteilungen der Gesellschaft für Kieler Stadtgeschichte* 68 (1981): 45–6.

57. A. Rowlands, *Witchcraft Narratives in Germany: Rothenburg, 1561–1652* (Manchester, 2003), 12. Similar restraint was evident in the palatinate. See J. M. Schmidt, *Glaube und Skepsis. Die Kurpfalz und die abendländliche Hexenverfolgung 1446–1685* (Bielefeld, 2000).

58. W. Behringer, *Witchcraft Persecutions in Bavaria: Popular Magic, Religious Zealotry and Reason of State in Early Modern Europe* (Cambridge, 1997): 64.

59. See W. Behringer (ed.), *Hexen und Hexenprozesse* (Munich, 1988): 193. Behringer, *Witches and Witch Hunts: A Global History* (London, 2004): 150, rounds this figure up to 25,000 executions.

60. This figure corresponds roughly with the more detailed calculations of Richard Golden, who offers a figure somewhere between 40,638 and 52,738 executions. Golden, 'Satan in Europe', 234. For the more conservative estimate of 30,000–35,000 for all Europe, with only 5,000 outside Germany, see W. Monter, 'Witch Trials in Continental Europe, 1560–1660', in *Witchcraft and Magic in Europe: The Period of the Witch Trials*, ed. B. Ankarloo and S. Clark (London, 2002): 12–16.

61. Macfarlane, *Witchcraft in Tudor and Stuart England*, 60, 66–75; J. A. Sharpe, *Witchcraft in Seventeenth-Century Yorkshire: Accusations and Counter Measures*, Borthwick Paper no. 81 (York, 1992).

62. W. de Blécourt, 'The Making of the Female Witch: Reflections on Witchcraft and Gender in the Early Modern Period', *Gender and History* 12 (2000): 309.

63. A. Soman, 'Witch Lynching at Juniville', *Natural History* 95 (1986): 10.

64. J. Bodin, *De la Démonomanie des sorciers* (Anvers, 1586): 365; Boguet, *An Examen of Witches*, xxxii, xxiv.

65. Remy, *Demonolatry*, 56; Lea, *Materials*, III: 1297.

2

THE INTELLECTUAL
FOUNDATIONS

By the end of the sixteenth century many educated Europeans believed that witches, in addition to practising harmful magic, engaged in a variety of diabolical activities. First and foremost, they believed that witches made an explicit, face-to-face pact with the Devil. This pact not only gave witches the power to perform *maleficia* but also initiated them into the Devil's service. The conclusion of the pact was a formal ceremony that took place after the Devil had appeared to the witches and enticed them with the promise of material reward or sexual pleasure. The witches agreed to reject their Christian faith, often symbolized by their trampling on the cross, and to be re-baptized by the Devil. They then paid homage to the Devil, either by bowing down (often backwards) before him or by kissing his buttocks. As a sign of their allegiance the Devil imprinted a distinctive mark on the witches' bodies, usually in a concealed spot. He then gave them careful instructions for the performance of their maleficent work, equipping them if necessary with the potions, unguents and images they would need to ply their trade.

A second witch belief that many educated Europeans subscribed to in the late sixteenth century was that the witches, having made a pact with the Devil, gathered periodically with other witches – sometimes numbering in the hundreds or even thousands – to perform a series of blasphemous, obscene and heinous rites. At these meetings the Devil would appear in various forms, together with subordinate demons. The witches would very often sacrifice children to the Devil, feast on the bodies of these infants and on other unsavoury dishes, dance naked, and engage in sexual intercourse with the Devil, his subordinate demons or other witches. At some time during these assemblies a parody of the Christian communion service might very well take place, and throughout the entire affair witches would make preparations for continuing their maleficent work. Closely associated with all these activities was a belief that witches could use the power of the Devil to fly through the air and thus gain quick access to assemblies that often took place a considerable distance from their homes.

27

Now it is important to note at the outset that these witch beliefs, all of which concern the relationship between witches and the Devil, were mainly the property of the literate and ruling elites, and not the common people. Although popular beliefs in witches, demonic spirits, sexual commerce with demons, witches' flight, orgies and cannibalism had provided some of the raw material out of which such ideas had been fashioned, the synthesis of those ideas had been the work of theologians, philosophers and lawyers, and the men who subscribed to them were judges, clerics, magistrates and educated landlords. Peasants could gain a limited amount of information about the diabolical activities of witches from the public reading of the charges against them at the time of their execution and from the deliberate efforts of authorities to instruct the populace regarding witchcraft during a witch panic or hunt. Once these ideas were presented to them, they had little difficulty accepting them; the idea of a miserable peasant making a pact with the Devil in order to improve his lot and of attending a shocking orgy in order to gain culinary and sexual pleasure was hardly alien to a peasant mentality.[1] But illiterate peasants could not fully understand the sophisticated theories of the demonologists, nor were they likely to become as frightened of diabolical activity as were monks and theologians. Their concern with, and fear of, witchcraft centred on the witch's ability to cause harm by occult means, not her relationship with the Devil. Identification of the Devil as the source of the witch's magic probably aggravated the fears of common folk, especially after the Reformation heightened their consciousness of the Devil's powers, but their primary concern remained the maleficent magic rather than the diabolism of the witches.[2]

The great European witch-hunt could not have taken place until the members of the ruling elites of European countries, especially those men who controlled the operation of the judicial machinery, subscribed to the various beliefs regarding the diabolical activities of witches that we have briefly described above. The mere belief in the reality of the magic that witches practised was not capable of sustaining the systematic prosecution and execution of large numbers of witches. The crime of *maleficium*, as allegedly committed by witches in early modern Europe, while clearly felonious, was not serious enough or practised widely enough to elicit the type of judicial campaign that was in fact mustered against them. In order for the intensive hunting of witches to take place, it was necessary for ruling elites to believe that the crime was of the greatest magnitude and that it was being committed on a large scale and in a conspiratorial manner. They had to believe not only that individual witches were harming their neighbours by magical means but that large numbers of them were rejecting their Christian faith and undermining Christian civilization. They had to believe that magicians belonged to an organized, conspiratorial sect of Devil-worshippers.

The subscription of many influential and politically powerful Europeans to this set of beliefs regarding witches raises a number of important questions.

First, where did all these ideas regarding the pact with the Devil, the sabbath and the ability of witches to fly come from and how were they integrated into the early modern concept of witchcraft? Second, how were these ideas developed and then disseminated throughout Europe, especially among educated people? Third, why did these ideas have such great appeal at this time and why were they not successfully challenged until the late seventeenth century?

The cumulative concept of witchcraft

The stereotype of the witch as both a harmful magician and a Devil-worshipper that emerged in the early years of the fifteenth century has been described as a composite or cumulative notion: composite because it consisted of ideas that formerly were not connected, and cumulative because the synthesis of these ideas occurred gradually, each new addition building upon or supplementing others. Once fully formed, the new concept of witchcraft was not evident in all witchcraft trials, but many of its elements were, and the stereotype of the witch as maleficent magician who made a pact with the Devil and worshipped him with other witches at the sabbath found expression in many witchcraft trials and in many of the witchcraft treatises that appeared in the next 250 years.

The Devil

The central figure in the cumulative concept of witchcraft was the Devil, the source of the witches' magic, the partner with whom they concluded the pact, and the object of their adoration. Before exploring the witch's relationship with the Devil, we need to establish who this spiritual power was and what attributes European writers ascribed to him. As with so many witch beliefs that involved demonic power, the very concept of him had changed noticeably by the time witch-hunts began.

Throughout the history of Christianity the Devil has often been identified as Satan, a Hebrew name meaning 'adversary' that appears in the Hebrew Bible, known to Christians as the Old Testament. In the early books of the Hebrew Bible Satan appeared as an angelic spirit who was not evil. In the later books he acquired a distinct personality but still was not considered an evil spirit or demon. In the Book of Job Satan was a member of God's court who accused human beings before God, and in the First Book of Chronicles he was the instrument of an angry God. Only in the New Testament where his Hebrew name was translated into Greek as *diabolos* (i.e. the Devil) did Satan become the chief of demons who not only tempted Christ in the desert but also became the powerful opponent of Christianity itself, enticing people to withdraw from Christ and reject his teaching.[3] A titanic struggle thus arose between the Kingdom of Christ on the one hand and the Kingdom of Satan on the other, a conflict that most believed would continue until the Second Coming.

As Christianity, the kingdom of Christ, spread throughout the East and the West, it was only natural that the Church fathers would consign the religions with which they were competing, both Jewish and pagan, to the kingdom of Satan. This process actually contributed to the visual depiction of the Devil in Christian art. One of the most effective tactics of the Christian Church in dealing with converts or potential converts who continued to worship their pagan gods was to demonize those gods – to claim that those deities were actually demons or the Devil himself. Because this equation was made so frequently, Christians began depicting the Devil in the ways that pagans viewed their gods. There was no standard image of the Devil in medieval art, and some of the features that he acquired in these depictions owe more to Christian theology than to pagan imitation. His depiction as black, for example, comes from the traditional association of black with sin rather than from the blackness of any particular pagan god. Likewise, the wings derive from the Devil's status as a fallen angel, not from the fact that many pagan gods were themselves winged creatures. Nevertheless, many of the features commonly given to the Devil were originally those of pagan gods. The goatee, the cloven feet, the horns, the wrinkled skin, the nakedness and the semi-animal form bear direct reference to both the Greek and Roman male god Pan and to the male Celtic god Cernunnos, while the female breasts, which appear often in seventeenth-century depictions of the Devil, came almost certainly from the goddess Diana.[4]

The resemblance between the medieval Christian Devil and the ancient pagan gods which Christianity replaced and demonized is one of the main pieces of evidence that scholars have used to support the thesis that the witches of the early modern period were in fact practising an ancient fertility religion. In many witch confessions there were references to the worship of a horned beast as a god. These confessions cannot, however, be taken at face value. Suggested almost certainly by the witches' inquisitor or judge, these descriptions reflect a Christian view of the Devil, whom the inquisitor believed the witches were worshipping as their god. It is only natural that in describing the appearance of this 'god' he would allude to the features most commonly assigned to the Devil, which in turn derived in large part from earlier images of pagan fertility gods.

Although Satan was the most commonly used name to refer to the Devil, it did have some competition. Occasionally the name of Lucifer, which the patristic writers assigned to the great archangel who rebelled against God and was cast down from Heaven into Hell, was used to describe the Devil. The name, a Roman word for the morning star, does not appear in the Bible, but some of the Church fathers identified it with the star in the book of Isaiah that tried to be like God and that God cast out of the heavens. Lucifer, therefore, became a name that could be used to describe Satan before the fall.

In addition to the Devil, referred to as Satan, Lucifer, or some other title like the Prince of Darkness or the Prince of this World, medieval and early modern Christians believed that there were large numbers of demons who assisted the Devil in his work of evil, temptation and destruction. One of the demons that Christ exorcized identified himself as 'legion', suggesting that there were 6,000 such evil spirits – the number of soldiers in an imperial Roman legion – but their exact numerical strength became a topic of speculation among demonologists. The fifteenth-century Spanish theologian Alfonso de Spina came up with a tally of 133,306,668, which was exceeded only by the much less precise calculation of 26 billion in one of the 'devil books' compiled by Sigmund Feyerabend in 1569.[5] Other estimates were usually much more conservative, in the range of six or seven million. Since these demons were believed to be fallen angels, they were often ranked, like the angels, hierarchically.

Some demons, especially those of the higher orders, were referred to by name, possessed distinct personalities and presided over certain sins. On such matters there was nothing even approaching a consensus, and the entire matter could become hopelessly confused when demonologists referred to the Devil (i.e. Satan) by the names of one of the chief demons, such as Beelzebub, Leviathan, Asmodeus, Belial or Behemoth, or demoted either Satan or Lucifer (or both) to a status of mere parity with his subordinates. This confusion is not surprising, since the source of these names was either the Bible or the apocryphal books of the pre-Christian period, in which the various names were used interchangeably. The confusion appears not only in the work of demonologists but in the reports of the witches' sabbath, where it frequently cannot be determined whether the lord of the ceremony, who was often depicted as a horned animal, was supposed to be the Devil or one of his chief demons.

The frequent references throughout the Middle Ages to the physical appearance of the Devil and the equally frequent references to his inhabitation of the bodies of human beings raises the important question of his metaphysical nature and his powers. These subjects remained the source of controversy during the entire medieval period, but in the twelfth and thirteenth centuries a group of scholastic theologians established a view that remained orthodox throughout the period of witch-hunting. According to the scholastics, demons, like angels, were pure spirits, possessing no flesh or blood. They could, however, take on the appearance of a human or an animal body by mixing the air with various vapours from the earth so as to create a non-corporeal or aerial body. This body, being composed of natural elements, did have a physical reality and it could perform certain bodily functions, such as dancing or the sexual act. According to some demonologists, the Devil could even procreate by using semen borrowed from another man, but this view was highly controversial.[6] The peculiar properties of demonic bodies also explain why the Devil and his numerous *incubi* or *succubi* demons are described as being cold during sexual intercourse. We need not postulate that witches were using stone phalluses as part of some sort of fertility rite to explain the frigidity of the Devil's sexual organs; the theological opinion that he had no blood suffices.[7] **SOURCE BOOK**

In addition to taking on the appearance of a human being or an animal, the Devil or his subordinate demons could enter and inhabit the body of a human being. Reports of such possessions appear in the Bible and continue throughout the early Christian and medieval periods. Very often the demoniacs were clerics, who complained about the control that the Devil thereby acquired over their organs or bodily functions. When the Devil possessed a person he did not have to compress or condense air to create an aerial body; he simply occupied the body of the afflicted person, using his power over matter to direct the functions of the human body. Contemporary belief that the skin was porous made such penetration of the body even more plausible. Demonic possession of individuals could, and eventually did, play a part in witchcraft, since the possession could take place as a result of a witch's actions. The witch could, in other words, supposedly command the Devil to possess a victim as part of the pact that the witch had concluded with the Devil. Nevertheless, possession could take place without any involvement of a witch and merely at the whim of the Devil himself, so long as God permitted him to do so.

One of the most important powers of the Devil was to create illusions. Like his power to take on the form of a human being, this derived from his power to move various substances, images and humours. Just as he was able to condense air, he could also take the images that were stored in people's minds and impress them upon their mental faculties so that they appeared to see something that was not in fact there. Scholastic theologians emphasized that many of the marvelous effects produced by the Devil were only illusions that he created. This is what they claimed was happening when, for example, he turned men into beasts or deprived a man of his 'virile member'. He did not actually change the substance of a man or alter his physical structure. He merely deluded the man into thinking that the change had been made.[8] Either he impressed the image of a beast or a memberless man on a person's imaginative faculty or he confused that person's perceptive faculties by a similar exercise of his powers of controlling local motion. Much of the magic that the Devil performed was accomplished in this way, although he could also perform magic by moving physical bodies together or apart, in defiance of the normal course of nature.

It should be clear from this discussion of the Devil's powers that he did not, according to the scholastic point of view, possess anything that came close to unlimited power over the physical world. He could not change the substance of things or perform miracles. Nor could he create new life in any form; he had to work with the natural world as God had created it. Whatever the Devil did was by the explicit permission of that immanent God, who retained many powers for His exclusive use. To declare that the Devil was in any way equal to God, that he had created matter or controlled its operation, was dualist heresy, the doctrine of such sects as the Manichaeans and Cathars. At times orthodox Christians came very close to subscribing to such ideas. Whenever they spoke of the Kingdom of Satan, whenever they expressed doubt that the struggle of Christ against Satan might not result in the victory of the former, whenever they felt that they might not be able to avoid the apparent control that the Devil had over them, they came dangerously close to assigning powers to him that the official doctrine of the Church condemned. Not surprisingly, these expressions of belief in overwhelming demonic power were most common during the period of witch-hunting.[9]

During the fifteenth century, as the power of the Devil in the world appeared to be increasing and as the first witchcraft trials were taking place, the figure of the Devil began to undergo a significant transformation. Throughout the Middle Ages the Devil had been described as the enemy and antitype of Christ, teaching hatred rather than love. Now, however, he was increasingly depicted as the anti-type of God the Father, the source and object of idolatry and false religion. One of the sources of this transformation was the insistence by late scholastic theologians on the Ten Commandments, rather than the Seven Deadly Sins, as the basis of Christian ethics. The first of the Ten Commandments prohibits the worship of false gods, an offence not readily subsumed under the Seven Deadly Sins. John Bossy has argued that the promotion of this new moral system, which all Catholics and Protestants would eventually adopt at the time of the Reformation, contributed to the transformation of the crime of witchcraft from that of *maleficium* to that of Devil-worship.[10] It is no coincidence that the late medieval theologian who was the main advocate of the new scriptural ethics, Jean Gerson, was the person SOURCE BOOK primarily responsible for the decision of the theology faculty of the University of Paris in 1398 to declare that all magicians, whether maleficent or beneficent, were guilty of idolatry.[11] It is also not surprising that Johannes Nider, the Dominican theologian and inquisitor who wrote one of the first witchcraft treatises, *Formicarius* [The Ant Hill], between 1436 and 1437, was one of Gerson's German disciples.[12] In that work, Nider described witches as men and women who not only cast spells but also paid homage to the Devil, renounced their Christian faith and trampled on the cross[13] (see Figures SOURCE BOOK 2.4–2.6).

The pact with the Devil

The central idea in the cumulative concept of witchcraft is the belief that witches made pacts with the Devil. Not only did the pact provide the basis of the legal definition of the crime of witchcraft in many jurisdictions, but it also served as the main link between the practice of harmful magic and the alleged worship of the Devil. In the fullest sense of the word a witch was both a harmful magician and a worshipper of the Devil, and the pact was the means by which the two forms of activity were most clearly related.

The belief that a human being could make a pact with the Devil can be found in the writings of St Augustine, but it did not become widespread in western Europe until the ninth century, when various legends regarding such pacts were translated into Latin. In these pacts the human party made an agreement resembling a legal contract, according to which the Devil provided wealth or some other form of earthly power in exchange for service and, of course, the custody of the human party's soul after death. In some of these accounts the pact involved the practice of magic. In one of the most famous accounts, a Jewish magician enticed St Theophilus into signing such an agreement, and as a result of this bargain Theophilus acquired, among other things, magical powers. In another legend, adopted from St Jerome by Archbishop Hincmar of Reims in the ninth century, a boy made a pact with the Devil at the urging of a magician in order to win the affection of a young girl. The boy himself did not acquire magical powers as a result of the pact, nor did the magician make a pact with the Devil, but the boy did obtain the desired object of the love magic, and one can assume that the magician had in fact previously concluded a similar pact. In other stories regarding pacts, such as that told of a ninth-century Italian bishop who wished to achieve great wealth, there was no allusion to the communication of magical power to the human from the Devil.[14] Nevertheless, the belief that magicians made pacts with the Devil was well enough established by the ninth century that Hrabanus Maurus, the archbishop of Mainz, could refer to the conclusion of the pact as one reason for condemning the practice of learned magic.[15]

The connection between magic and the demonic pact became much closer in the twelfth and thirteenth centuries, when the translation of many Islamic and Greek books of magic led to a dramatic increase in the actual practice of the art and when ecclesiastical writers became more explicit in their condemnation of it. The magic that began to be performed at this time involved the invocation and command of demons, and was frequently referred to as necromancy, a term that technically means the summoning up of the spirits of the dead. This ceremonial or ritual magic was practised mainly at the courts of European monarchs and even at the papal court. Its practitioners may have appeared to later Renaissance *magi* as 'ignorant necromancers' but they were by no means illiterate and in fact had more in common with both ancient and Renaissance learned magicians than with the witches who later were prosecuted in great numbers (see Figure 2.1). Summoning up demons in order to acquire secret or forbidden knowledge may not have required sophisticated scholarly learning, but it did require more expertise than the mere recitation of formulas. The methods of this conjuration varied greatly, but they usually involved adherence to a written formula, the purpose being to entrap the demon in a bottle, ring or mirror and then to command him to provide the desired assistance.

The condemnation of this new type of magic was mainly the work of scholastic theologians, but they gained considerable support from the papacy and from papal inquisitors like Nicholas Eymeric. In condemning such practices these writers needed to do more than simply reiterate the traditional theological attack upon magic; rather they had to answer the objection that

Figure 2.1 Ritual magician, standing in a protective circle, summoning up a demon. Unlike the early modern witch, the ritual magician was usually male and literate. From the title page of Christopher Marlowe, *Dr. Faustus* (1636).

the practitioners of this type of demonic magic were pursuing good objectives and were commanding, not serving, the demons that they conjured. The key to the scholastic response to this challenge was the plausible argument that demons did not provide services without demanding something in return. The very practices of the magicians suggested that this was so, since they often offered these evil spirits either reverence or some sort of physical object, such as a chicken or their own blood, in order to lure them into their service. The conclusion that the scholastics were able to draw from all this was that virtually all magicians made pacts with the Devil. When the magician actually summoned up the demons and offered them something it was explicit; at other times it was implicit or tacit, in the sense that although no direct negotiations took place, the actual practice of magic implied that some reciprocal relationship between the Devil and the magician had to have been established.[16] In either case the magician was to be condemned, because by entering into the pact he had given to the Devil something that was due to God alone. The magician was therefore a heretic, in that he was, at least by inference, denying God the exclusive position in the universe that Catholic doctrine claimed He had.[17] Even worse, he was an apostate, for the magician was abdicating his Christian faith by agreeing to worship or otherwise serve the demon.[18]

The designation of magicians as heretics and apostates was not new, and in making this claim the scholastics drew upon earlier patristic condemnations of magic. In a sense the theologians of the fourteenth century were confirming an earlier attitude of the Church towards magic in the face of protestations by ritual magicians that they were not heretics. The novelty of the scholastic position was the emphasis upon the pact as the reason for the heresy and the blanket condemnation of all ritual magic on such grounds. The significance of this thought concerning the pact in the development of learned witch beliefs is two-fold. First, the condemnation of all ritual magic as heresy could easily be extended to types of magic that did not concern the scholastics, in particular the practice of simple *maleficium* by illiterate villagers. By the logic of scholastic argument they too must have made pacts with the Devil, since only the Devil had the power to work magical effects, and in order to avail themselves of his magical powers they had to give him something in return. Second, the designation of magicians as heretics and apostates made witches susceptible to all of the charges that were made against heretics in the later Middle Ages, especially charges of secret, collective worship and totally perverse, amoral and anti-human behaviour. And since magicians were now also heretics, they could be prosecuted by papal inquisitors.

As the belief that magicians made pacts with the Devil was extended to the perpetrators of simple sorcery or, as one might say, the magician became a witch, the idea of the pact itself underwent a significant change. The pacts that ritual magicians made with the Devil always involved some sort of worship of the Devil and, at least according to scholastic commentators, the loss of the magician's spiritual integrity and faith, but they also gave the magician certain powers over the Devil. They placed the Devil at the magician's service and compelled the demon to provide him with the assistance he needed. The negotiation of the pact was generally an operation conducted by two equals, each of whom tried to outwit the other and entice him into giving more than he received. As the charges of practising magic and making a pact with the Devil were levelled against uneducated villagers, however, the official and learned characterization of the pact changed. The magician who was gradually being transformed into the witch became much more the servant than the master of the Devil. As King James VI of Scotland later put it, 'Witches are servants only, and slaves to the devil; but the necromancers are his masters and commanders'.[19]

It is true that a bargain was still struck between the two, but the control that the witch exercised over the Devil was restricted to her ability to compel him to perform *maleficium*, while the reverence that the witch paid to the Devil became much more voluntary, obsequious and unconditional. The Devil in many ways gained the upper hand in the process, a position he never had in dealing with the ritual magician. One clear sign of the change is that in the later cases the witch usually agrees to serve the Devil in exchange for meagre financial or material rewards. Very often he wins the allegiance of the witch with the offer of a small coin, which promptly turned to stone after the irrevocable pact was made. The Devil, it should be remembered, was viewed then as the great deceiver, and once the witch was no longer the equal of the Devil she could easily become his dupe. It is also interesting to note that as the master-magician was transformed into the servile witch, the sex of the malefactor changed from male to female.

The sabbath

The belief that witches made pacts with the Devil was a central witch belief among the clergy and the secular elite of early modern Europe. Many of those who held this belief also subscribed to another idea that was of equal and in some respects even greater importance. This was the belief that those witches who made pacts with the Devil also worshipped him collectively at night in remote locations. This belief was not as widely held as that of the pact, and it was less uniform in its various expressions. Nevertheless, like the belief in the pact, it served as an essential precondition of the great witch-hunt. Just as the belief in the pact made it imperative that witches be prosecuted, so the belief in the witches' nocturnal gatherings led European authorities to search for their confederates. Without the belief in the sabbath European witch-hunting would have been much more limited in its scope and intensity.

Although the two beliefs that witches made pacts with the Devil and attended nocturnal assemblies were closely linked in the minds of many members of the learned elite, and although homage and sometimes even sacrifice to the Devil were elements in both of them, the two ideas had somewhat different sources. Their merger in the cumulative concept of witchcraft did not take place fully until the fifteenth century. Even then, however, the two beliefs were not necessarily associated, even in the literary tradition. For example, the most famous witchcraft treatise ever written, the *Malleus maleficarum*, has a great deal to say about the pact but makes only passing references to the collective worship of the Devil.[20]

The belief in the sabbath has both general psychological and specific historical sources. The psychological roots, which are, to say the least, inadequately understood, are those that produce nightmares and fantasies about anti-human and amoral activities in many different societies. Every culture has been known to generate myths about persons, sometimes possessing peculiar powers or physical characteristics, who invert the moral and religious norms of society and who therefore present a threat to the very fabric of that society. It can be argued that a belief in the existence of such individuals is necessary in order to establish what those norms are, or at least to reinforce those that are generally accepted. The particular values that these people allegedly invert will vary in accordance with the norms of each society, but since all societies share some similar moral values, the nightmares that they produce possess some common features. Thus the practice of cannibalistic infanticide, which most societies consider to be the most egregious moral offence, has been a part of virtually all such nightmares. The same can be said of naked dancing, an activity which many societies, until very recent times, have considered to be socially and morally outrageous.[21]

To some extent the belief in the witches' sabbath, which included both naked dancing and cannibalistic infanticide, represents the late medieval and early modern European version of this standard or even universal nightmare. At the same time, however, the European sabbath had many distinctive characteristics that reflect the influence of medieval Christianity. Certainly the heavy emphasis that was placed on the erotic aspects of the sabbath – ritual intercourse with the Devil and the prevalence of promiscuous heterosexual and homosexual activity among the witches – derives from the negative attitude of the medieval and early modern Church towards sex. The parody of the Catholic Mass, which was by no means common to all descriptions of the sabbath but which appears in the accounts of many French, Spanish and Italian assemblies, also reflects the specifically Christian horror at the mockery of its most sacred ceremony. The parody never involved the saying of a Black Mass, an elaborate ceremony that some modern witches actually perform over the body of a naked woman and whose origins can be traced only to the eighteenth century. But some of the sabbaths that allegedly took place in the sixteenth and seventeenth centuries included the saying of the Nicene Creed backwards while the celebrant stood on his head, the use of such commands as 'Go in the name of the Devil', the blessing of the congregation with a black aspergillum, the consecration of a host made of offal, turnip or some black substance, and the singing of the choir in 'hoarse, gruff, and tuneless voices'.[22]

The specifically Christian, European depiction of an anti-society that appears in the confessions of witches has its origins mainly in the rhetorical invective that monks developed with respect to heretics in the twelfth and thirteenth centuries. Threatened with the frightening spread of heresies like Catharism and Waldensianism, these monks deliberately constructed a picture of an anti-human heretical society in order to prevent the growth of such movements and to encourage their suppression. In constructing this picture the monks, such as Ralph of Coggeshall, drew not only on the universal image of an anti-society but on a number of specific sources.[23] One was the image that Romans had developed of early Christians who practised cannibalistic infanticide – an image that had gained currency because the central rite of Christianity, the Eucharist, in which Christians consumed the bread and wine that had been miraculously transformed into the body and blood of Christ during the Mass, could easily be misinterpreted as cannibalism. Another source of the sabbath was the image that the theologians had developed of the heretic (as well as of the magician and the Jew) as idolaters and children of Satan. A third source, partially based on reality but ascribed to all heretics indiscriminately, was the conviction that they, like the early Christians in Roman times, met secretly, a charge that the failure of contemporary authorities to discover heretics only served to encourage.[24] A fourth source was the doctrinal content of heresy itself, or more accurately, the way in which heresy was being

38

interpreted. Cathars, for example, were dualists, which meant that they exaggerated the powers of the Devil and especially his control over the material world. The purpose of Christianity according to Catharist doctrine was to teach people how to free their souls, which were spiritual, from the evil matter in which they were entrapped. Christ, who was pure spirit, had provided people with the means by which this could be accomplished. Catharism was therefore emphatically anti-demonic, but it is easy to see how the exaggeration of the Devil's power in the universe and his elevation to a position of near parity with God could lead the defenders of orthodoxy to depict the Cathars, and by extension other heretics, as Devil-worshippers. In the same way, the Cathars' contempt for procreation, which to them was the work of the Devil, could lead to the charge that they practised abortion, and this in turn nourished fantasies, which had arisen from other sources, regarding the practice of cannibalistic infanticide.

Monastic writers of the late twelfth and early thirteenth centuries, drawing on all of these sources, constructed a stereotype of the heretic as a secret, nocturnal, sexually promiscuous Devil-worshipper. This image, which in many respects acquired a life of its own, could be applied indiscriminately to any heretic or deviant from orthodox Christianity. In the late Middle Ages it was in fact applied to heretics and ritual magicians. For our purposes the main question is how and when it came to be applied to *malefici*, the alleged practitioners of harmful low magic. For some time it was believed that the application first occurred in the trials of a number of Cathars in the dioceses of Toulouse and Carcassone in the fourteenth century.[25] These heretics were allegedly performing *maleficia*, and therefore the beliefs of their prosecutors, who were papal inquisitors, regarding the conduct of Cathars were easily transferred to them as *malefici*. The Cathars were, therefore, being turned into witches. This description of their trials and the confessions made in them have been shown, however, to be forgeries,[26] and so we must look elsewhere for the fusion of ideas of magic on the one hand and ideas about the secret and collective practice of heresy on the other.

The most important and celebrated case in which the connection was made was the trial of Dame Alice Kyteler and her associates in Kilkenny, Ireland, in 1324–5. Kyteler was accused of practising numerous *maleficia*, some of which involved murder, in order to increase her wealth. During the course of her trial, which took place in the court of the bishop of Ossory, she and her associates were accused not simply of *maleficia* but also of belonging to a sect of heretics that met secretly at night, renounced the Christian faith and made sacrifices to demons. Dame Alice, moreover, was accused of copulating with her own personal demon. The members of the sect were not accused of cannibalistic infanticide, but they were charged with having concocted potions out of the clothes of deceased unbaptized babies and the fat extracted from human corpses. The trial shows not only how charges of *maleficium*, which in this case were almost certainly politically motivated, suggested charges of ritual demonic magic but also how the charges of magic, which had become clearly identified with heresy, in turn suggested charges of secret Devil-worship and copulation with demons.

In the case of Dame Alice Kyteler the cumulative concept of witchcraft had not yet been fully formed. For reasons that will be explained below, neither she nor her associates were reported to have flown to their nocturnal gatherings. The sect that they belonged to was smaller than later witches' covens, consisting of only ten persons. The description of their assemblies, moreover, was not as lurid as the later accounts of the witches' sabbath, and, as mentioned above, the charge of infanticide was only implicit and that of cannibalism absent. Even the pact, which one would expect in a trial involving the alleged practice of ritual magic, does not appear explicitly.[27] Nevertheless, the case is a landmark in the formation of learned notions about witchcraft because it reflects for the first time the belief that practitioners of harmful magic were organized in a Devil-worshipping heretical sect. It places us, as Norman Cohn has argued, on the threshold of the European witch-hunt.[28]

A second case, in many ways similar to that of Kyteler, which took place in Boltigen, Switzerland, between 1397 and 1406, in some respects brings us closer. The trial, that of a man named Stedelen, resembled the Kyteler case in that it arose out of charges of *maleficia*. Stedelen was accused of destroying crops, causing sterility among cattle, and so forth. Like one of Kyteler's accomplices, Stedelen confessed under torture not only to the *maleficia* but to summoning up demons and to membership in a heretical sect of Devil-worshippers. The members of this sect renounced their faith in Christ and also killed babies by magical means, using the potions to make unguents (see Figure 2.2). Aside from the explicit charge of infanticide, the case differed from Kyteler's in two respects. First, all appearances suggest that Stedelen and his associates were not, like Kyteler, members of the aristocracy but were common folk, similar to most of the witches of the sixteenth and seventeenth centuries. Second, the trial took place, like many subsequent witchcraft prosecutions, in a secular court. In this case the court was that of the city of Bern, the judge being Peter of Greyerz, a lay magistrate. This shows that by the beginning of the fifteenth century not only clerics like the bishop of Ossory but secular magistrates like Greyerz could take originally clerical notions about heretical practices and impose them on individuals accused of *maleficia*. The application is especially noteworthy, since the original crime of which Stedelen was accused was not, like Kyteler's crime, heresy, but the secular crime of magic.[29]

The image of collective apostasy and Devil-worship that was applied to maleficent magicians in the trials of Kyteler and Stedelen was originally formulated by monks as a description of heretical practices. By the time of these trials, however, the image had lost its connection with heresy and had become associated exclusively with magic and witchcraft. Neither literary accounts of nor prosecutions for heresy in the fourteenth century or after

Figure 2.2 Witches burning and boiling infants. From Guazzo, *Compendium Maleficarum* (1610 edition).

depicted heretics in the extreme way that late twelfth- and early thirteenth-century monks had. The charges of secrecy and collective worship persisted, especially when they had a foundation in reality. But heretics no longer appeared, either in treatises written about them or in court records of their trials, as perpetrators of the same behavioural excesses that the monks had described. In particular, the charge of cannibalistic infanticide against heretics disappeared in the early twelfth century and did not reappear until the 1450s.[30] As more and more became known about the actual activities of heretics, those sensational charges devolved on to ritual magicians and witches. Then, in the sixteenth century, as the stereotype of the witch shed most of the remnants of its association with ritual magic – especially the conjuring up of demons – the charges became attached solely to witches. The fantastic stereotype of the heretic-magician became the stereotype of no one but the witch.[31]

Flight

The final major component of the cumulative concept of witchcraft was the belief that witches could fly. In many respects this was a corollary of the belief in the sabbath, in that it provided an explanation for the ability of witches to attend secret nocturnal gatherings in remote areas without their absence from home being detected. When the sabbath was held in very distant lands (such as the assemblies that French peasants from the Pays de Labourd allegedly attended in Newfoundland), and when it was believed that the number of participants was exceptionally large (the top figure was 100,000), the belief in the ability of witches to fly served as a necessary corollary.[32] Nevertheless, the belief in the sabbath could and did exist independently of the belief in flight, as it did in the description of nocturnal gatherings of witches in Scotland. The belief in flying witches, moreover, had sources that contributed only indirectly to the theory of the sabbath itself, and it did not gain acceptance among the educated elite of Europe until they had already come to believe that witches made pacts with the Devil and gathered collectively to worship him.

The belief that witches could fly had much more distinctly popular origins than the belief that they made pacts with the Devil or participated in nocturnal assemblies. There were in fact two originally distinct popular beliefs that lay at the basis of this notion. The first of these was the belief, traceable to classical times, that women could transform themselves at night into flying screech owls or *striges* who would devour infants. This belief in 'night witches' has been shared by many cultures, including many African cultures in modern times, and it was prevalent among the Germanic people even before the period of Roman influence. The *striges*, which became one of the many Latin words for witches, were also called *lamiae*, a reference to the mythical Queen of Libya, loved by Zeus, who sucked the blood of babies in revenge for Hera's killing of her children. The second belief was that women went out at night on a ride, sometimes referred to as a 'wild hunt', with Diana, the Roman goddess, who had close associations with the moon and the night and who was often identified with Hecate, the goddess of the underworld and magic. In medieval Germany Diana was often depicted as Holda or Perchta, a goddess who, like Diana, could be terrifying as well as nurturing. Just as Diana, a virgin, could slay would-be lovers and turn them into animals, so Holda could lead a 'furious horde' of those who had died prematurely through the sky. When Holda went on her earthly nocturnal journeys, however, she always served beneficent functions. In France and Italy this belief usually took the form of a belief in 'the ladies of the night', mysterious women under the direction of a queen who visited homes for beneficent purposes.[33]

The beliefs in both the *striges* and the ladies of the night were so strong among the common people of Europe that some women actually believed that they flew out at night as *striges*, while others believed that they joined the supernatural queen in her nocturnal meanderings. When the literate elite eventually accepted the reality of such activities, these credulous women were readily suspected and accused of witchcraft. Until the fourteenth century, however, educated men viewed all such beliefs as illusions caused by the Devil. Since the Church had always claimed that Diana and the other pagan gods, especially the chthonic or fertility gods, were in fact demons, it was only natural that the whole spectacle of ladies riding out with Diana should have been viewed as the work of the Devil. Those who imagined that they rode out at night, just like those who believed they were *striges*, were engaging in pagan superstition, as were those who simply believed that other humans performed these actions. Such beliefs, even if they had no foundation in reality, were not to be taken lightly, since those who held them were heretics.

The best example of the medieval Church's attitude towards such beliefs was the Canon *Episcopi*, a set of instructions written in the tenth century by Regino of Prüm that became part of the canon law of the Church in the twelfth century. The Canon *Episcopi* is usually referred to as an illustration of the scepticism of the medieval Church towards witchcraft. This is somewhat misleading, for the document deals with a number of practices and beliefs that only later became part of the cumulative concept of witchcraft, not with witchcraft as such. In addition to condemning the magical arts as a form of heresy, in the manner of the Church fathers, the Canon specifically singles out

> some wicked women, perverted by the Devil, seduced by illusions and phantasms of demons [who] believe and profess themselves in the hours of the night to ride upon certain beasts with Diana, the goddess of the pagans, and an innumerable multitude of women, and in the silence of the dead of night to traverse great spaces of earth and to obey her commands as of their mistress and to be summoned to her service on certain nights.

These women were accused of infidelity and of leading others into the same error.

SOURCE BOOK

During the course of the late Middle Ages the learned attitude towards belief in the *striges* and the women who rode out with Diana underwent a number of significant changes. First, the two ideas, which in popular culture were quite distinct, were often fused. The ladies of the night became perpetrators of cannibalistic infanticide while their procession or ride on beasts became airborne. The fusion of these ideas can be seen as early as the twelfth century in the work of John of Salisbury,[34] but it was not complete until the fifteenth century. Second, the literate elite, which before had argued that the activities described by common folk took place merely in their dreams, began to argue that they had a physical reality. The supernatural visitors were now, in their view, demons that actually took on the appearance of human beings, while the people who had previously only dreamt or imagined that they were following such demons did in fact do so in a fully awakened state. The women who before had dreamt that they flew at night on cannibalistic missions were now actually flying, the power of transportation being provided by the Devil. The reasons for this change in learned attitudes, which one can begin to detect in the fourteenth century, are unclear. The most likely explanation is that it was the product of scholastic demonology. Once the Devil was defined as having extraordinary powers over local motion, then his ability to move people through the air (which was his domain) naturally followed. At the same time the scholastic emphasis on the ability of the Devil to take on human forms and for individuals to make pacts with him encouraged the view that humans could and did attend him in the manner described in stories of the Dianic procession. The third change, partially a product of the other two, was the fusion of the two ideas of the *striges* and the Dianic procession with the belief in a secret, amoral, Devil-worshipping sect of magicians. That synthesis also took place in the early fifteenth century.

It should be noted that although many members of the European elite subscribed to the belief that the Devil could physically transport human bodies through the air, the older, more sceptical attitude that this happened as a result of diabolical imagination was never completely rejected, even in scholastic circles. The long discussion in the *Malleus maleficarum* of the ability of devils to transport witches from place to place bears this out. Faced with the unimpeachable authority of canon law, Heinrich Kramer, the primary author, could not deny the fact that some witches were transported only 'in imagination'. They merely stated, therefore, that one could not deduce from the canon that *all* witches were transported in this way. 'But who is so foolish as to conclude that they cannot *also* be bodily transported?' asked the *Malleus*. Kramer then went on to prove, on the basis of scholastic demonology, that the Devil could in fact transport himself from place to place. At the same time, however, he could not deny that transportation by phantasm was just as consistent with scholastic demonology. Much of what the Devil did, according to scholastics, was by deliberate delusion. Some, but not all, of the witches' magic was performed in this way, and the alleged metamorphosis of witches into beasts, an idea present in the popular notion of the *striges*, was clearly the result of the Devil's confusion of the imaginative faculty, not the actual transmutation of substances. It was not at all implausible, therefore, that some individuals would imagine that they were at the sabbath, while others would in fact be transported there bodily. Instead of claiming that the belief in reality of the witches' flight replaced the belief that the witch imagined such a venture, we should realize that after the fourteenth century both beliefs coexisted. As the *Malleus* concluded, 'they are transported both bodily and phantastically'.[35] The important change, however, was the admission by a long succession of writers in the late fifteenth and sixteenth centuries that 'sometimes witches are really transported from place to place by the Devil who, in the shape of a goat or some other fantastic animal, both carries them bodily to the sabbath and is present at its obscenities'.[36] Those who continued to maintain the older attitude of the Canon *Episcopi* in all cases were the humanist sceptics of the mid-sixteenth century.

The belief that witches could fly was one that admitted numerous differences in detail. Sometimes witches were described and depicted artistically as riding beasts in the manner of Diana's followers. At other times they rode on sticks, which could be forked in the manner of a divining rod. Male witches occasionally appear riding pitchforks or tridents, a symbol frequently associated with the Devil and derived ultimately from the trident of the classical god Poseidon (Neptune). Of all the witches' means of aerial transport, however, the most frequently cited and clearly the most enduring in popular culture was the broomstick. The broom is primarily a symbol of the female sex, since women were assigned the role of cleaning the house, and its use in the fantasy of the witches' sabbath might therefore reflect nothing more than the preponderance of female witches. In this sense the broom serves the same symbolic function as the distaff, which was used in the female activity of spinning cloth and which also appears occasionally in descriptions of witchcraft. The broom might have had added significance, however, in that it was often used in fertility rites, thus suggesting associations with ancient pagan goddesses. Last but not least, the broom served as a phallic symbol and therefore was appropriate in a scene that was suffused with sexuality.

Sometimes witches were depicted as having flown without any means of support, either in a gust of wind or simply by their own power. Since in some of these instances it was claimed that they anointed themselves with flying unguents, the question has arisen whether these ointments contained hallucinogens that made the witches feel as if they were covering vast distances and perhaps even imagine that they were attending the sabbath. Twentieth-century experiments with the ingredients listed in early modern recipes for such flying unguents have shown that they contained atropines and other poisons which, when rubbed into the skin, can produce high excitement, delusion and lifelike dreams.[37] We also know that the secretions from toads, which Basque witches allegedly kept as familiars, can have a hallucinogenic effect.[38] It is possible, therefore, that some individuals who used these ointments actually imagined that they were flying and attending sabbaths, an argument first advanced by sixteenth-century sceptics like Johann Weyer. But we must not leap to conclusions. Many of the earliest recipes for flying unguents, which come from the fifteenth century, contain nothing but inert elements like bat's blood and soot, and all early accounts of the use of flying unguents claim that the ointment was applied to the witch's stick or broom, not directly to her body.[39] Witches' unguents, therefore, should probably be viewed as products of either harmless folklore or demonological theory, and not as effective mind-altering substances.

Metamorphosis

One popular witch belief closely related to flight that was never fully integrated into the cumulative concept of witchcraft was that of metamorphosis. The belief that humans could change their shape was present in popular culture from earliest recorded times and still exists today. Since the

Figure 2.3 Witches, having changed themselves into animals, cast their spells at the door of a neighbour. One of the woodcuts in Francesco Maria Guazzo's *Compendium Maleficarum* (1610 edition).

process of metamorphosis involves the operation of some magical or super-natural power, it readily became associated with witchcraft, and the claim that witches transformed themselves (or others) into animals, especially wolves, appears in many witchcraft confessions (see Figure 2.3). Like the belief that witches could fly, belief in metamorphosis was considered heretical and illusory by the Canon *Episcopi* and by many other late medieval authorities. Unlike the belief in flight, however, the belief in the physical reality of shape-shifting was generally not accepted by early modern demonologists.[40] Even the highly credulous *Malleus maleficarum*, which insisted on the reality of witchcraft, concluded that metamorphosis was the product of demonic illusion. The equally credulous demonologist Henri Boguet, after citing the Bible and classical authority to prove that 'the metamorphosis of a man into a beast is possible', admitted that in his opinion the change was always illusory.[41] Scepticism regarding metamorphosis did not in any way prevent the prosecution of persons who claimed that they could transform them-selves into beasts. In certain areas of Europe, especially in heavily forested regions, a number of werewolves were tried and convicted as witches.[42] The charge of metamorphosis, however, did not appear frequently enough in witchcraft trials to become an essential component of the cumulative concept of witchcraft.

The dissemination of belief

By the middle of the fifteenth century the cumulative concept of witchcraft had acquired all of its basic elements. Indeed, in the 1420s and 1430s a number of trials took place in the Alpine regions of France, western Switzerland and northern Italy in which men and women were accused not only of practising harmful magic but also of worshipping the Devil in nocturnal rites, killing and devouring infants, and flying to these ceremonies.[43] Some of these witches were caught up in a massive hunt for Waldensian heretics in the duchy of Savoy and western Switzerland in the 1430s. Since both Waldensians and witches were accused of meeting secretly, inquisitors sometimes confused them and even used the same word, *vaudois*, to identify both groups of heretics.[44] The confusion between Waldensians and witches became more widespread in France and Switzerland during the 1440s and 1450s. Some inquisitors and demonologists, however, viewed the two groups of heretics as distinct, since charges of magic and flying out at night found no place in the accusations of Waldensians, an anti-clerical sect that denied the miracles of the saints, the power of relics and the efficacy of pilgrimages.[45] Heinrich Kramer explained that witchcraft differed from all other heresies, especially Waldensianism, in that the witches' heresy inhered in their maleficent deeds, not their theological beliefs or ecclesiastical practices.[46] By the turn of the sixteenth century, inquisitors generally agreed that witches were members of a new and very different heretical sect.

The stereotype of diabolical witchcraft that first appeared in the trials of the 1420s and 1430s endured for more than two centuries, but it was not yet complete. The belief, for example, that witches received a mark on their bodies from the Devil when they concluded a pact with him did not emerge with any clarity until the early sixteenth century. The mark was thought to be insensitive to pain and incapable of bleeding. Judicial authorities therefore developed the practice of pricking the witch with a needle to find the incriminating sign, usually shortly after arrest. Calvinist communities in Geneva and Scotland were among the most vigilant in searching for the mark, possibly because Calvinists emphasized the diabolical dimension of witchcraft.[47] Protestants might also have accepted the mark because it had a scriptural basis in Revelation 13:16, where the Antichrist marked the right hand or forehead of his followers. Some Catholic judges and demonologists, however, also accepted the theory of the Devil's mark and searched the bodies of suspected witches for the incriminating signs.[48]

SOURCE
BOOK

Descriptions of the sabbath were embellished in various ways during the period of intense witch-hunting. In some countries, such as Norway and Sweden, this belief was assimilated to a body of folklore regarding flights to distant locations. In the Italian region of Friuli learned belief in the sabbath was grafted on to a body of peasant belief regarding nocturnal struggles between the members of a fertility cult, the *benandanti*, and the witches.[49]

Testimony from witches, moreover, led to the introduction of details that varied from place to place and time to time. The Devil, for example, appears in a wide variety of guises, most commonly as a human being or a he-goat but also as a bull, cat, dog, horse or sheep. The feast or banquet also reflected local cuisine and could be described in either attractive or unpleasant, tasteless terms.

As witchcraft prosecutions intensified in the sixteenth century, the descriptions of sexual activity at the sabbath became more lurid. One new element was the claim that demons had homosexual relations with male witches. In the Middle Ages demons were thought to be repulsed by the prospect of sodomy, in keeping with the belief that they, no less than angels, obeyed the laws of nature. In an effort to magnify the evil of both demons and witches, the Italian demonologist Gianfrancesco Pico della Mirandola introduced a discussion of demonic sodomy in his treatise *Strix* (1524).[50] A group of Italian demonologists followed suit. This indiscriminate homosexuality became standard in subsequent descriptions of the sabbath, including that written by Pierre de Lancre in 1612, which devoted more space to the sexual activities of witches than any other demonological treatise. After discussing the indecent dances of the witches, which he claimed came from Spain rather than France, de Lancre described the 'demonic coupling' of the Devil with both male and female witches. In discussing the latter he added that the Devil had sexual relations with 'the beautiful witches from the front, and the ugly ones from behind'.[51]

SOURCE BOOK

Although reports of the witches' sabbath varied from place to place and from one period to the next, they still shared a number of common features. These similarities suggest strongly that learned notions about witchcraft were transmitted from one area to another and from one generation to the next. It is true, as discussed above, that certain elements of the cumulative concept of witchcraft, such as the belief in a collective, antichristian, amoral society, are capable of arising *sui generis* at any place and time, but this is not true of the entire set of learned European witch beliefs. These ideas were fused into a quite distinct amalgam by the fifteenth century, a composite product that could not have arisen by itself in the mind of one magistrate or inquisitor. This body of knowledge had to be learned, and hence it had to be transmitted from one time and place to another. The only way we can deny the fact of that transmission is to claim that organized witchcraft, or some activity closely resembling it, was in fact practised throughout all of Europe. This was the position taken by the French philosopher and judge Jean Bodin, who based his belief in the reality of a European witch cult on the uniformity of witches' confessions. It was also the position of Margaret Murray, who on the basis of the same confessions concluded that all accused witches were in fact practitioners of the same fertility religion. Neither Bodin's nor Murray's theory can be substantiated, however, and therefore we must explain how learned notions regarding activities that never occurred were actually transmitted.[52]

Both the development and the transmission of learned notions of witchcraft occurred as the result of the interaction between the judicial process on the one hand and a literary tradition on the other. Most learned witch beliefs were developed and fused with other notions in the actual trials of either magicians or witches. The development or fusion was invariably the work of the judge or inquisitor, who blended the charge against the accused with his own fantasies or obsessions, which were themselves often nourished by either theological and demonological knowledge or the reports of other cases that he or a colleague had adjudicated. By extracting confessions, usually under torture, to the activities that he believed the witch had engaged in, the inquisitor received confirmation of his suspicions, and thus the beliefs acquired validity. The results of these trials became known to other judges, first by word of mouth and then by written manuals for inquisitors, which used the testimony given at the trials to illustrate the various activities of the witches. In this way the set of learned beliefs could become cumulative, since a new inquisitor, in trying a case, would use the information contained in the manual to formulate the questions he would direct to witnesses and the accused. At the same time, however, he might use some of the specific charges against the accused or his own imagination to give a new twist to the standard charges. The confession that he would extract to these somewhat different charges, perhaps embellished by the witch's imagination and folk beliefs, might then be included in another manual or treatise on witchcraft and thus be transmitted to other inquisitors. The entire process of transmission was abetted by the universities, which exposed future judges to the growing body of demonological and inquisitorial literature and also advised local jurisdictions how to conduct witchcraft prosecutions.[53]

It is difficult if not impossible to determine whether the trials themselves or the large body of literature on witchcraft was more important in the development and transmission of learned witch beliefs. On the one hand, judges and inquisitors had often acquired extensive knowledge of witchcraft through their education and reading before actually prosecuting witches. On the other hand, the manuals and treatises they read tended to reflect rather than to anticipate juridical developments. Without oversimplifying a complex issue, one can argue that as the various notions included in the cumulative concept of witchcraft were being developed and fused, the trials themselves were of primary importance, the literature playing a secondary role in shaping the course of those trials and communicating their results to a wider audience.[54] As the stereotype of the witch became fairly well established, however, the literature became the main vehicle for transmitting knowledge about the crime. The importance of this literature also increased significantly with the introduction of printing in the second half of the fifteenth century. This innovation made it possible for learned beliefs to spread more broadly and more rapidly than in the manuscript age. As this witchcraft literature grew in size and popularity, the trials themselves began to serve only the ancillary functions of validating the beliefs contained in the literature, providing additional examples for new treatises, and making some of these ideas available to the illiterate population in the form of sentences that were read publicly at the time of execution.

The first witchcraft treatise that assumed a major role in making the cumulative concept of witchcraft available to a large audience was the *Malleus maleficarum* [The Hammer of Witches]. First published in 1486, and reprinted thirteen times before 1520, it appeared under the name of two Dominican inquisitors, Heinrich Kramer or Institoris (his Latin name) and Jacob Sprenger. Kramer, an elderly theologian who had been appointed inquisitor for Upper Germany in 1479, was the principal and probably the sole author. Kramer, an inveterate enemy of Jews and heretics, was zealous in his defence of papal authority and the Catholic faith, and in 1484 he turned his attention to the new heresy of witchcraft, conducting prosecutions in the town of Ravensburg in southern Germany.[55] When he encountered resistance from local ecclesiastical and secular authorities who resented his exercise of papal authority, Kramer succeeded in obtaining a bull, *Summis Desiderantes*, from Pope Innocent VIII authorizing him to proceed without obstruction. The bull also named Sprenger, a professor of theology at the University of Cologne, who had been serving as inquisitor in the archbishoprics of Mainz, Trier and Cologne since 1481, as his colleague.[56] On the basis of this papal authorization, Kramer conducted a brutal witch-hunt in the diocese of Brixen, which included the town of Innsbruck, in 1485. One year later, citing as examples many of the cases he had adjudicated, Kramer published the *Malleus*, to which he attached the papal bull as a preface. He also included an endorsement, which may have been forged from the theological faculty of the University of Cologne.

The *Malleus* was essentially a manual for inquisitors, similar to the *Directorium inquisitorum* [Guide for Inquisitors] produced by the Spanish inquisitor Nicholas Eymeric in 1376. Kramer's manual took the form of a scholastic disputation, in which a series of questions were asked and answered, and in so doing it relied heavily on scholastic thought, especially that of the Dominican theologian Thomas Aquinas. In addition to Aquinas, the book drew upon a broad range of theological and legal writers in a rather eclectic fashion, and it incorporated many of the popular beliefs regarding witchcraft that were current in southern Germany at the time.[57] In this way the *Malleus* became a statement of the cumulative concept of witchcraft, although it said very little about some of its components, especially the various ceremonies conducted at the sabbath. The only novel contribution that the book made to learned witch beliefs was Kramer's emphasis on the sexual nature and foundation of the crime. He claimed that the most powerful class of witches (those who inflicted every kind of harm and who devoured their children) all 'practise carnal copulation with devils' and that the root of all witchcraft was carnal lust.[58] The book has acquired the reputation for being misogynistic, and Kramer was deeply contemptuous of the intellectual and moral weakness of women, but misogyny of that nature was conventional in the fifteenth century, especially within the clergy.

Concentration on the sexual and misogynistic elements of Kramer's treatise can distract the reader from his larger mission of proving that witchcraft does in fact exist, claiming that those who deny its reality were themselves heretics, and persuading his large audience of the seriousness of the threat.[59] The effect that the book had on witch-hunting is difficult to determine. It did not open the door 'to almost indiscriminate prosecutions'[60] or even bring about an immediate increase in the number of trials. In fact its publication in Italy was followed by a noticeable reduction in witchcraft cases.[61] But even if it did not prompt hundreds of inquisitors and magistrates to inaugurate massive witch-hunts in their jurisdictions, it did make them more conscious of the crime of witchcraft and probably more credulous of its reality. We must recognize that the cumulative concept of witchcraft did not command instinctive and immediate belief, either among the educated or the illiterate. People had to be *told* that witches *could* and *did* perform the various acts of which they were accused. The *Malleus* was an appropriate tool in this educative process, since it contained enough information drawn from judicial experience and enough theological citation and argumentation to make it appear to be authoritative. The apparent papal approval that it gained from the inclusion of the bull of 1484 may have given it even greater authority, although obviously not among those Protestants who used the book in the sixteenth century.[62]

The *Malleus*, therefore, while not directly inspiring a frenzy of witchcraft prosecutions, nevertheless did make an important contribution to the development of the entire European witch-hunt. Like the cumulative concept of witchcraft that it helped to transmit, it served as a precondition of intensive witch-hunting. It is important to note, however, that the *Malleus* was only one of many important witchcraft treatises that were published during the period of witch-hunting.[63] Many of those that followed it into print were much more complete in their description of the cumulative concept of witchcraft, especially in dealing with the sabbath, and a few of these works achieved even greater popularity than the *Malleus*. In 1524 Paulus Grillandus, a papal judge who presided at a number of witchcraft trials in the vicinity of Rome, published *Tractatus de hereticis et sortilegiis* [A Treatise on Heretics and Witches]. This widely read work became one of the main sources of information regarding the sabbath, in which Grillandus fully believed.

After the appearance of Grillandus's book there was a forty-year lull in the production of witchcraft literature. Very few treatises were written during that period, nor were new editions of the older works forthcoming. For this surprising gap there are a number of possible explanations, including both a European-wide decline in prosecutions and a preoccupation of the educated elite with the Protestant Reformation. As Protestantism spread, moreover, and as papal inquisitions became less frequent in Catholic countries, interest in works written mainly by inquisitors naturally waned. After 1560, however, there was a marked upsurge in witchcraft prosecutions, and this development stimulated the printing of the old treatises and the authorship of new ones. Like the *Malleus*, the new treatises of the late sixteenth and seventeenth centuries were the product of judicial action, in that they used evidence from the trials themselves to embellish the stereotype of the witch and to provide officials, especially secular magistrates, with guidance.

In 1595 Nicolas Remy, a judge from the duchy of Lorraine who claimed to have executed more than 800 witches in sixteen years, published a treatise, *Demonolatreiae* [Demonolatry], which in many ways replaced the *Malleus* as the main source of information regarding the work of Satan on Earth. The readers of *Demonolatreiae* were treated to detailed discussions of the activities that allegedly took place at the sabbath: the obscene kiss, the feasting on **SOURCE BOOK** horrid foods and human flesh, and the dancing to unpleasant music. A few years later a Spanish Jesuit from Antwerp, Martín Del Rio, published his *Disquisitionum magicarum libri sex*, which served as an encyclopedia of magic and also gave specific instruction to judges. Printed twenty times and translated into French in 1611, Del Rio's work became the most popular **SOURCE BOOK** and authoritative witchcraft treatise in the seventeenth century.

Other late sixteenth- and seventeenth-century works supplemented that of **SOURCE BOOK** Del Rio and also achieved widespread popularity. In 1602 a Burgundian judge, Henri Boguet, wrote a treatise on the basis of his judicial experience, *Discours des sorciers* [A Discourse on Witches], which went into eight editions. A few years later Pierre de Lancre, a French judge who had conducted a large witch- **SOURCE BOOK** hunt in the Pays de Labourd, wrote a treatise, *Tableau de l'inconstance des mauvais anges et démons* (1612), which not only described the sabbath in unprecedented detail but also included a now famous engraving by the Polish artist Jan Ziarnko depicting the horrid affair (see Figure 1.2). In 1635 a Lutheran judge from Saxony, Benedict Carpzov, published his *Practica rerum criminalium*, a commentary on the laws of Saxony regarding witchcraft and a compendium of decisions by the Leipzig Supreme Court. Carpzov's book, which was reprinted nine times, gained a reputation as the *Malleus maleficarum* of Protestantism, especially since it provided specific instructions regarding the **SOURCE BOOK** prosecution of witches. In Italy the most comprehensive guide to witchcraft, the *Compendium maleficarum*, was written by a Milanese friar, Francesco Maria Guazzo, in 1608. Guazzo drew heavily on the works of Kramer, Remy and Del Rio, as well as hundreds of other authorities, thus showing that the work of demonologists was, like the concept of witchcraft that they were elaborating, cumulative. Guazzo included in his book a series of illustrations of witches concluding a pact with the Devil, thereby providing his audience with an important visual supplement to the fantasies he was describing (see Figures 2.4–2.6).

Taken together, the witchcraft treatises of the early modern period succeeded in making the literate members of European society aware of witchcraft and convinced of its reality. The readership of these works, however, was limited to a small portion of the population, consisting mainly of members of educated and ruling elites. This segment of society, which included the lawyers, judges and magistrates, was perfectly capable, on the basis of the knowledge it had acquired regarding witchcraft and the legal power it possessed, of conducting a witch-hunt. In order for intensive witch-hunting to have succeeded, however, it was necessary for illiterate villagers to have some understanding of the diabolical nature of the crime. Even when witchcraft prosecutions came from 'above' (i.e. initiated by officials and judges), the detection and prosecution of witches required the support of the entire community.

It was the witches' neighbours who were relied upon to identify suspects, facilitate their apprehension and testify against them. If a witch-hunt, especially a large hunt, were to be successful, it was necessary for the entire community to believe in witchcraft and to assist in the process. The problem was that most people in early modern villages did not share the learned notions

Figure 2.4 Witches showing subjection to their master, the Devil, by kissing him on the buttocks, a sign of their complete debasement. The witches, who are depicted as both male and female, are holding candles. From Guazzo, *Compendium maleficarum* (1610 edition).

Figure 2.5 The Devil re-baptizing a witch after the conclusion of the pact. This parody of the Christian sacrament of baptism signified the witches' initiation into the worship of the Devil as their god. From Guazzo, *Compendium Maleficarum* (1610 edition).

Figure 2.6 Witches trampling on the cross at the Devil's command, an act symbolizing their apostasy. From Guazzo, *Compendium Maleficarum* (1610 edition).

of witchcraft that made the crime so frightening. They believed in magic and its use for maleficent purposes and recognized the danger that such magic posed to them, but they did not necessarily identify the Devil as the source of that magical power. Many of them believed in *striges*, the ladies of the night, and metamorphosis, and some of them even believed in *incubi* and *succubi*, but they had not fused these disparate ideas in the way that theologians and inquisitors had, with all the frightening implications. Nevertheless, there is evidence that some of the learned notions of witchcraft and certainly the attendant fear of a widespread satanic conspiracy did penetrate the lower levels of European society, at least for brief periods of time. There are enough unforced confessions, for example, to show that many of the fantasies developed by the theologians and inquisitors had percolated down to simple villagers. When we discover that nearly 2,000 illiterate peasants in the Basque country freely confessed to having attended large sabbaths and described the activities that went on at those assemblies, we can be fairly certain that the ideas of the educated elite had reached them by one route or another.

One method of educating the populace in learned notions of witchcraft was the public reading of the charges against witches at their executions. Another was the deliberate instruction of the people in matters of witchcraft at the time of a large panic. During the Basque witch-hunt of 1609–11 the King of Spain sent letters to all the bishops in the afflicted areas and also to the heads of the preaching orders to have their subordinates preach against witchcraft, just as they had during an earlier hunt in 1526. The purpose of this programme was to prevent people in their ignorance from joining the witches' sect, to secure confessions from those who had already succumbed to the temptation, and to win the support of the people in wiping out the pernicious crime.[64] In the Low Countries ecclesiastical authorities included the activities of witches in the lists of errors that they periodically read to their congregations. Throughout Europe witchcraft sermons were preached during witch-hunts and especially before executions. Perhaps the best example of the role that sermons played in spreading witch beliefs among an entire congregation occurred at Salem, Massachusetts, where the minister of the church in Salem village, Samuel Parris, not only unconsciously prepared his congregation for witch-hunting by depicting a satanic menace both outside and within the village for years before the hunt, but also developed this theme once the actual hunt began.[65]

Although the learned elite did achieve a certain measure of success in educating the uneducated in their demonologically oriented theories of witchcraft, the process of imposing a higher culture on a popular one was not without its difficulties and could result in bitter social conflict. There is perhaps no better example of the gap that existed between learned and popular culture than the prosecution of the *benandanti* in the Italian province of Friuli in the late sixteenth and early seventeenth centuries. The *benandanti*, as we have seen, believed that they went out 'in spirit' at night during the Ember Days (quarterly fasting periods) to fight the witches. The officials of the Inquisition, incapable of comprehending this body of peasant folk belief and suspicious that the *benandanti* were in fact witches going to the sabbath, gradually convinced these members of an old fertility cult that they were maleficent witches. In one sense the entire episode serves as an example of the way in which learned beliefs were able to penetrate social barriers, for the final result was the imposition of a learned notion of the sabbath on a very different set of popular witch beliefs. But the difficulties that the inquisitors encountered in achieving this result are of perhaps greater significance than their ultimate success. Over and over again they interrogated suspects who insisted that they were 'fighting for Christ' against the witches, ensuring the fertility of the crops, and it took the courts more than fifty years to convince them otherwise.[66] When examined in this light, witch trials can be seen as a form of cultural and social conflict, in which literate ruling elites tried to bring an illiterate peasantry into conformity with its world-view and in the process suppressed or at least fundamentally transformed an entire set of popular beliefs.[67]

The sceptical tradition

Once the cumulative concept of witchcraft had been formulated and disseminated, it proved to be astonishingly durable for the next two centuries. It did not, however, ever win universal acceptance. In fact elements of the concept were contested throughout the period of witch-hunting. The authors of many witchcraft treatises were openly sceptical of at least some witch beliefs, especially metamorphosis and flight. A number of more credulous works, moreover, were written as responses to statements by sceptical judges or as rejoinders to sceptical treatises. It is useful, therefore, to think of the history of demonology as an extended discourse in which the reality of witchcraft was continually being debated. Even the authors of the more credulous treatises themselves, such as Kramer and Del Rio, apparently entertained doubts regarding certain elements of witchcraft and wrote the treatises to convince themselves as well as others that witches and evil spirits really did exist.[68] In those cases the discourse took place within the minds of the credulous demonologists themselves.

SOURCE
BOOK
There were four main sources of the sceptical tradition. The first was classical texts, such as *The Golden Ass* of Apuleius, who wrote in the first century CE, and the odes of the Roman poet Horace, who wrote in the early years of that same century.[69] These works helped to create a stereotype of the witch, but at the same time they never treated the witch as a real threat. Second, there was the Canon *Episcopi* itself, which certainly raised doubts about

the reality of nocturnal flight and forced authors like Kramer to explain away this component of church law. A third source was the writings of Renaissance humanists, who were openly contemptuous of the scholastic mentality that supported many witch beliefs. Renaissance humanists also revived many of the classical philosophical texts that denied the possibility of human beings attaining any certain knowledge at all.[70] Finally there was a theological tradition that became especially strong among Protestant clergymen which insisted that God Himself, rather than a witch operating with demonic assistance, was the source of all misfortune.

Scepticism about witchcraft was just as old as the belief in witchcraft itself. Works expressing disbelief in at least some aspects of witchcraft appeared throughout the period of the trials. Indeed, in 1489, shortly after the appearance of the *Malleus*, Ulrich Molitor, a doctor of canon law and a judge at the imperial court of the Holy Roman Emperor, published a dialogue entitled *De lamiis et pythonicis mulieribus* [On Witches and Female Fortune-tellers] that took a sceptical position regarding the ability of witches to perform *maleficia*, fly to the sabbath, or procreate with demons. Like most sceptics, Molitor did not deny the possibility that a person could make a pact with the Devil, but his book included six images of activities that he argued in the text were only illusions caused by the Devil.

Scepticism regarding witchcraft entered a new phase with the spread of Renaissance humanism throughout Europe in the early sixteenth century. Humanists like Desiderius Erasmus, Pietro Pomponazzi and Andrea Alciati attacked certain witch beliefs, while Cornelius Agrippa of Nettesheim, the great practitioner of learned magic, criticized both the *Malleus maleficarum* and the prosecution of witches.[71] The force of this humanist scepticism was blunted, however, by the fact that most humanists, especially those who were influenced by Neoplatonic thought, accepted both the reality of demonic power and the reality of magic. The demons of Neoplatonism bore little resemblance to the Devil of medieval scholasticism, but Renaissance intellectuals, once they conceded the existence and power of demonic forces, were hardly in the best position to assault the basic principles of medieval demonology.

The same is true for Renaissance magic. The learned *magi* of the Renaissance did everything in their power to distinguish the magic they practised and wrote about from the magic of the ignorant necromancers of the Middle Ages and the poor, illiterate witches of their own day. But the distinctions were not always clear, especially when learned *magi* employed demonic magic, and the belief in one type of magic could lead to belief in the other.[72] The connections between the two types of magic became even closer in the work of writers like Jean Bodin, who combined his attack on witches with an assault on the magic of Agrippa and Giovanni Pico della Mirandola.[73] In Italy the clerical confusion between magic and witchcraft may actually have contributed to the rise of witch-hunting.[74] Perhaps it is no coincidence that the introduction of humanism in Florence in the late fourteenth century was accompanied by a series of sorcery trials.[75]

Both the strengths and the limits of Renaissance scepticism regarding witchcraft are evident in the work of the most famous of all sixteenth-century critics of witch-hunting, Johann Weyer, a disciple of Agrippa and a physician in the service of Duke William V of Cleves. Weyer's work reflects the negative attitude of Agrippa towards necromancy as well as the tolerant attitude of Erasmus towards those accused of witchcraft. It also draws upon a tradition that was very strong in Lutheran theological circles which, on the basis of the Canon *Episcopi*, argued that witches were deceived by the Devil. The main purpose of Weyer's books, *De praestigiis daemonum* [On the Delusions of Demons] (1563) and *De lamiis* [On Witches] (1582), was to show that the ignorant women who confessed to witchcraft were suffering from delusion and should not be prosecuted. These books, therefore, constituted a frontal assault upon the views expressed in the *Malleus maleficarum*. In making his case Weyer used his medical knowledge, claiming both that the alleged *maleficia* of witches could be explained by natural, medical causes and that confessions of witches to diabolical activities were to a large extent the result of the female disease of melancholy. Weyer also used his knowledge of Roman law to prove that a witch's alleged pact with the Devil was not a valid contract and that the crime of having made such a pact was therefore impossible.[76] To Weyer, therefore, witchcraft was an attempt by a mentally disordered person to do something that was both physically and legally impossible.

Weyer's scepticism, nonetheless, was not as thoroughgoing as it might have appeared, since he still accepted the reality of demonic power in the world. In dealing with the alleged *maleficia* of witches, their pacts with the Devil, and the ceremonies of ritual magicians he admitted that the Devil could influence the human imagination and insinuate himself in human affairs. *Maleficia* might be attributable to natural causes, but the Devil was responsible for making the witches think that they had caused these harmful deeds. In similar manner the Devil played upon the imagination of the poor, ignorant, melancholic women who claimed that they made pacts with him, and he also deceived evil necromancers into performing the various acts of conjuration for which they were notorious. Weyer also accepted the possibility that the Devil could possess the bodies of human beings directly, by their own power; his scepticism on this issue consisted entirely of denying that witches were the cause of the possession.[77]

A second limitation of Weyer's scepticism was that he failed to free the melancholic old women who were accused of witchcraft from moral responsibility for their actions. Even if these persons were imagining that they made pacts with the Devil, they were still guilty of heresy in the same way that the women referred to in the Canon *Episcopi* were. Melancholy had only made these women more vulnerable to the Devil's power of delusion. In fact,

Weyer did not rule out the prosecution of these women by ecclesiastical authorities, although he did insist that none of them should be put to death.[78] He opposed their prosecution by the secular courts, since witches did not actually cause the harm attributed to them, which in any case had nothing to do with their spiritual crime. But by admitting that witches were guilty of a spiritual crime, Weyer gave Protestant authorities adequate justification for prosecuting witches on the grounds that witches had abandoned their Christian faith.

Because of the inconsistencies of Weyer's arguments, his views were almost entirely discredited by more credulous demonologists, who argued that if the Devil was capable of direct intervention in the natural world, why could he not also perform *maleficia* and involve human agents in his work? Without a philosophically and theologically sound refutation of the belief in demonic power, Weyer's treatise was vulnerable to the verbal assaults that were to be made upon it by a cluster of demonologists, which included the Swiss physician and political theorist Thomas Erastus, the German bishop Peter Binsfeld, the French lawyer Jean Bodin, and King James VI of Scotland.[79]

The emphatic restatement of the cumulative concept of witchcraft in the 1580s and 1590s did not put an end to the sceptical tradition. Quite to the contrary, a new group of sceptics continued the assault upon prevailing witch beliefs. The main voices of scepticism during these two decades were the English radical Protestant writer Reginald Scot, the German jurist Johann Georg Goedelman, the Calvinist minister Anton Praetorius, and the Dutch Catholic priest Cornelius Loos.[80] None of these writers categorically denied the reality of witchcraft, although Scot, the most radical of the group, came very close to claiming witchcraft was an impossible crime.[81] What all four of these sceptics shared was an insistence on the limits of demonic power. Like Weyer, Scot was influenced both by Renaissance humanism and by the theological ideas of the radical anti-Trinitarian Protestant sect known as the Family of Love. Scot treated biblical texts metaphorically rather than historically or literally, and he suggested that the Devil was nothing but the spirit of evil in ourselves.[82] He openly ridiculed the idea contained in the *Malleus maleficarum*, and he advanced a social explanation for accusations of witchcraft, claiming that witches were old women who went from house to house begging for assistance.[83]

SOURCE BOOK

Despite the vigour and persistence of the sceptical tradition, it did not prevail. Most theologians, jurists and local magistrates subscribed to the conventional belief in the reality and the danger of the crime. As long as the educated elite believed that the Devil could exercise power in the world, the arguments of the sceptics could be answered. Only in the late seventeenth century did a new breed of sceptics, reflecting new intellectual currents that found no place for the Devil in the natural world, begin to win the day. These new traditions will be discussed in Chapter 8.

Witchcraft and the fear of rebellion

The set of learned beliefs that we refer to as the cumulative concept of witchcraft proved, therefore, to be highly durable in the sixteenth and early seventeenth centuries. The acceptance of these ideas was sustained by many factors, the most significant being a firm conviction that the Devil had gained extraordinary powers over the course of human affairs. It was in fact this same conviction that originally inspired the construction of the cumulative concept of witchcraft; without this belief witches would never have been regarded as anything more than superstitious peasants. But why did the men who formulated and then disseminated learned witch-beliefs come to the conclusion that Satan's power was so pervasive and so frightening? What developments in the late medieval and early modern periods led them to believe that the Devil was loose and that he was recruiting large numbers of human accomplices?

There is no simple answer to this question. The apparent manifestations of demonic power during these centuries were many and varied. The numerous calamities of the late fourteenth century, especially the Black Death, may have encouraged intellectuals to assume greater demonic intervention in the world, whereas the profound economic crises of the early modern period, the trauma of the Reformation, and the frequency of war and plague might easily have reinforced the conviction of men like Remy, Boguet, Carpzov and Guazzo that the Devil was especially active. So too did the growing apocalyptic belief that the world was in its last days before the Second Coming of Christ, when the Antichrist had appeared. As we shall see, these very same developments created anxieties in early modern communities that encouraged magistrates to prosecute witches.[84] But if we wish to identify one factor that underlay both the construction and the transmission of the cumulative concept of witchcraft, one that most solidly buttressed the belief that the Devil was active in human affairs, then we should focus on the fear of rebellion, sedition and disorder that beset ruling elites throughout Europe during these years. It is no coincidence that the earliest descriptions of the witches' sabbath appeared when Europe had recently experienced a wave of social rebellions in the late fourteenth century.[85] Nor is it a coincidence that the learned belief in organized witchcraft spread through Europe during a period of profound instability and chronic rebellion. The intense witch-hunting that occurred in the late sixteenth and early seventeenth coincided with numerous peasant *jacqueries*, religious civil wars, and ultimately the first national revolutions of the modern world.[86] These disturbances terrified members of the ruling elite throughout Europe, and these fears were reflected in the imagery of the sabbath.

Like the Devil himself, who began his malevolent career with an act of rebellion against God, the witch was the quintessential rebel. Whether the individuals who were accused of witchcraft were in fact rebels is a separate question that we shall address in Chapter 5; the important consideration here is that theologians, magistrates and authors of witchcraft treatises viewed them in this way. As heretics and apostates witches were considered guilty of *lèse majesté* or treason against God; by gathering with other witches they were part of an enormous political conspiracy; by threatening entire communities with arson, poison, disease, and crop destruction they resembled modern-day political terrorists;[87] and by engaging in the amoral activities at the sabbath they were inverting the divinely established hierarchical order of society.[88] Sometimes the connection between rebellion and witchcraft was made explicit, as when witch-hunters, quoting the Bible, proclaimed that 'Rebellion is as the sin of witchcraft', or when Scottish royalists, convinced that witches and Covenanters were of the same ilk, proclaimed in 1661 that 'Rebellion is the mother of witchcraft'.[89] Churchmen at the Council of Basel in the early fifteenth century thought that rural rebellion was part of a satanic conspiracy to destroy clerical celibacy and therefore took steps to facilitate the prosecution of witches.[90] Many witches were in fact accused specifically of treason as well as witchcraft, especially during the early phase of the witch-hunt, when accusations of political sorcery arose frequently. It was not uncommon for Bohemian rebels to be accused of satanism, and during the English Civil War a radical clergyman, Thomas Larkham, was accused of 'faction, heresy, witchcraft, rebellion and treason'.[91]

If witchcraft and rebellion were as closely related as these examples suggest, then the fear of rebellion probably did play an important part in the construction and dissemination of the cumulative concept of witchcraft. Lionel Rothkrug has argued that the concern of the authors of the *Malleus maleficarum* with sorcerers who are archers reflects a widespread fear in German lands of Swiss infantry who had defeated the army of Charles the Bold in 1477 and of south German peasants who were hoping to enlist Swiss support in a rebellion against the Empire.[92] In similar fashion Pierre de Lancre's account of a massive diabolical conspiracy in the Pays de Labourd was conditioned by the fact that the area was a centre of Basque resistance against the French monarchy. Henri Boguet feared that if there were as many male witches as female ones and if they had a 'great Lord' as their leader, 'they would be strong enough to make war upon a king', which some witches had boasted they could do.[93] James VI of Scotland developed the credulous ideas that appear in his *Daemonologie* only after he became convinced that a coven of witches, headed by the earl of Bothwell, was engaged in a political conspiracy against him.[94] Perhaps Jean Bodin, whose absolutistic political views James fully endorsed, was thinking in similar terms when he wrote the *Démonomanie*.[95] Certainly William Perkins, the English theologian who wrote *A Discourse of the Damned Art of Witchcraft* in the closing years of the sixteenth century, had the image of the rebel witch in his mind. 'The most notorious traitor and rebel that can be', wrote Perkins, 'is the witch. For she renounceth God himself, the king of kings, she leaves the society of his Church and people, she bindeth herself in league with the devil'.[96]

SOURCE
BOOK

The construction, transmission and credulous reception of the cumulative concept of witchcraft by members of the learned and ruling elite served as one of the main preconditions of the great European witch-hunt. Without such beliefs there would have been no reason to pursue witches with the determination that judicial authorities manifested during the early modern period. Individual prosecutions for *maleficium*, ritual magic and the pact would certainly have taken place, just as they had in the past, but intensive campaigns against witchcraft and the search for the witches' alleged confederates would have been difficult to sustain. The construction of the cumulative concept of witchcraft was, however, only one of the two main preconditions of the hunt. The second was the development of legal procedures that facilitated prosecution and conviction of those who were suspected of this crime. To these equally important judicial developments we now turn.

Notes

1. See Ginzburg, *The Night Battles*, 135. C. Holmes, 'Popular Culture? Witches, Magistrates and Divines in Early Modern England', in *Understanding Popular Culture: Europe from the Middle Ages to the Nineteenth Century*, ed. S. Kaplan (Berlin, New York and Amsterdam, 1984): 100–1, argues that in England the propaganda of the clergy eventually resulted in the limited acceptance of the satanic pact in popular culture.
2. On the gap between popular and learned beliefs see Kieckhefer, *European Witch Trials*, 27–46; R. Muchembled, 'The Witches of Cambrésis: The Acculturation of the Rural World in the Sixteenth and Seventeenth Centuries', in *Religion and the People, 800–1700*, ed. J. Obelkevich (Chapel Hill, 1979): 232, 240; Weisman, *Witchcraft, Magic and Religion*, 53–72.
3. See E. Pagels, *The Origin of Satan* (New York, 1995).
4. See for example *The Devils Triumph Over Rome's Idol* (London, 1680).
5. Robbins, *Encyclopedia*, 130; Lea, *Materials*, III, 1084.
6. See Remy, *Demonolatry*, 92; H. Kramer and J. Sprenger, *The Malleus Maleficarum*, tr. and ed. M. Summers (London, 1928): 111–12; Lea, *Materials*, II: 993.
7. The coldness could also be attributed to the formation of the Devil's body from coagulated water or his use of a cadaver. See R. Masters, *Eros and Evil* (New York, 1966): 20–2.
8. Kramer and Sprenger, *Malleus Maleficarum*, 118–24.
9. On the loss of confidence that the Devil was totally subservient to God during the period of the great witch-hunt see F. Cervantes, *The Idea of the Devil and the Problem of the Indian: The Case of Mexico in the Sixteenth Century* (London, 1991): 11–19.
10. J. Bossy, 'Moral Arithmetic: Seven Sins into Ten Commandments', in *Conscience and Casuistry in Early Modern Europe*, ed. E. Leites (Cambridge, 1988): 229–31.
11. For the text of the condemnation see B. P. Levack (ed.), *The Witchcraft Sourcebook*, 2nd edn (London, 2015): 49–52.
12. Bossy, 'Moral Arithmetic'. On Nider's role as a reformer see M. D. Bailey, *Battling Demons: Witchcraft, Heresy, and Reform in the Late Middle Ages* (University Park, PA, 2003); A. Blauert, *Frühe Hexenverfolgungen* (Hamburg, 1989): 32–3.
13. See C. Ginzburg, *Ecstasies: Deciphering the Witches' Sabbath* (New York, 1991): 69–71. For an analysis of the different elements in Nider's treatise and the recognition of its novelty see Blauert, *Frühe Hexenverfolgungen*, 56–9.

14. J. B. Russell, *Witchcraft in the Middle Ages* (Ithaca, 1972): 84–5.
15. Peters, *The Magician, the Witch and the Law*, 16–17.
16. Russell, *Witchcraft*, 144; Cohn, *Europe's Inner Demons*, 113.
17. On the development of this definition of heresy, which does not necessarily involve intellectual error, see Russell, *Witchcraft*, 174.
18. Many writers insisted that some witches, while clearly apostates, were not heretics. See S. Leutenbauer, *Hexerei- und Zaubereidelikt in der Literatur von 1450 bis 1550* (Berlin, 1972): 48–70; Kramer and Sprenger, *Malleus Maleficarum*, 194–205.
19. (King) James VI, *Daemonologie* (1597), ed. G. B. Harrison (London, 1924): 9.
20. The authors simply state that some pacts with the Devil were made 'in a solemn ceremony . . . when witches meet together in conclave on a set day'. Kramer and Sprenger, *Malleus Maleficarum*, 99. They also refer to 'a congress of women in the night-time' at which a man 'saw them kill his child and drink its blood and devour it'. Ibid., 66.
21. See L. Mair, *Witchcraft* (New York, 1969): 40.
22. Russell, *Witchcraft*, 253; J. Caro Baroja, *The World of the Witches*, tr. O. N. V. Glendinnung (Chicago, 1965): 119, 149–50; M. Summers, *The History of Witchcraft and Demonology* (Secaucus, 1956): 147–57; Le Roy Ladurie, *Les Paysans de Languedoc*, 413.
23. W. L. Wakefield and A. P. Evans (eds), *Heresies of the High Middle Ages* (New York, 1969): 251–4.
24. Cohn, *Europe's Inner Demons*, 1–15.
25. J. Hansen (ed.), *Quellen und Untersuchungen zur Geschicte des Hexenwahns und der Hexenverfolgung im Mittelalter* (Bonn, 1901): 449–54.
26. Ibid., 132–8; Kieckhefer, *European Witch Trials*, 16–18.
27. L. S. Davidson and J. O. Ward (eds), *The Sorcery Trial of Alice Kyteler* (Binghamton, 1993).
28. Cohn, *Europe's Inner Demons*, 143.
29. Ibid., 204–5. The cases heard by Greyerz form the basis of Nider's description of a sect of *malefici* in the region of Bern and Lausanne.
30. Ginzburg, *Ecstasies*, 76–7.
31. Peters, *Magician*, 33–45.
32. Lea, *Materials*, III: 1296.
33. See Ginzburg, *The Night Battles*, 42–50; Cohn, *Europe's Inner Demons*, 167–75.
34. A. Kors and E. Peters (eds), *Witchcraft in Europe, 400–1700: A Documentary History*, 2nd edn (Philadelphia, 2001): 77–8.
35. Kramer and Sprenger, *Malleus Maleficarum*, 108. See also Ginzburg, *The Night Battles*, 20.
36. F. M. Guazzo, *Compendium Maleficarum*, tr. E. A. Ashwin, ed. M. Summers (London, 1929): 34.
37. Harner, 'The Role of Hallucinogenic Plants', 127–50; L. Gentz, 'Vad förorsakade de stora häxprocesserna?', *ARV* 10 (1954): 37.
38. Henningsen, *Witches' Advocate*, 94, 471–2.
39. Ostling, 'Babyfat and Belladonna'; Kieckhefer, *European Witch Trials*, 41. Harner, 'The Role of Hallucinogenic Plants', 131, argues that the stick served as an applicator to the sensitive vaginal membranes but the practical reasons for choosing this method are not made clear.
40. Jean Bodin was one of the few who did. His views, however, were rejected by Pierre Le Loyer, Martín Del Rio and J. de Nynauld. See J. Pearl, 'Humanism and Satanism: Jean Bodin's Contribution to the Witchcraft Crisis', *Canadian Review of Sociology and Anthropology* 19 (1984): 542–4.

41. Boguet, *An Examen of Witches*, 143.

42. Monter, *Witchcraft in France and Switzerland*, 144–51; C. Oates, 'The Trial of a Teenage Werewolf, Bordeaux, 1613', *Criminal Justice History* 9 (1988): 1–29.

43. R. Kieckhefer, 'The First Wave of Trials for Diabolical Witchcraft', in *The Oxford Handbook of Witchcraft in Early Modern Europe and Colonial America*, ed. Brian P. Levack (Oxford, 2013): 159–78; Cohn, *Europe's Inner Demons*, 202–6. Descriptions of metamorphosis also surfaced for the first time in some of these trials. Ginzburg, *Ecstasies*, 72–3. For trials at Rome in 1426 and at Todi in 1428 that had many of the same characteristics as those in France and Switzerland see F. Mormando, *The Preacher's Demons: Bernardino of Siena and the Social Underworld of Early Renaissance Italy* (Chicago, 1999): 54–77; D. Mammoli (ed.), *The Record of the Trial and Condemnation of a Witch, Matteuccia di Francesco, at Todi, 20 March 1428* (Rome, 1972); Kieckhefer, *European Witch Trials*, 73. The only element missing in these fifteenth-century Italian trials that is prominent in the French and Swiss cases is the claim that the witches could fly. The claim is implicit, however, in the charge that the witch of Todi assumed the form of a horsefly.

44. W. Behringer, 'How Waldensians Became Witches: Heretics and their Journey to the Other World', in *Communicating with the Spirits*, ed. Gábor Klaniczay and Éva Pócs (Budapest, 2005): 155–92. In the Jura region, many of the early vernacular words for 'witch' were derived from words for 'heretics'. Monter, *Witchcraft in France and Switzerland*, 22–3.

45. Inquisitors during these years often made distinctions between the Waldensians and the 'other pernicious sect'. Johannes Nider, who described the witches' sabbath in *Formicarius*, made a clear distinction between heretics and witches. See Bailey, *Battling Demons*, chapter 2.

46. On the distinction in the *Malleus*, see T. Herzig, *Christ Transformed into a Virgin Woman: Lucia Brocadelli, Heinrich Institoris and the Defense of the Faith* (Rome, 2013): 72–3.

47. Monter, *Witchcraft in France and Switzerland*, 159–66. In some cases more than one mark was found. Four marks were located on Janet Bruce of Tranent, Scotland, in 1657. National Archives of Scotland, JC 26/27.

48. Guazzo, *Compendium Maleficarum*, 14; Remy, *Demonolatry*, 9; C. Carena, *Tractatus de officio sanctissimae Inquisitionis* (Cremona, 1641).

49. Ginzburg, *The Night Battles*, 99–145. In *Ecstasies*, 76–8 *et passim*, Ginzburg argues that a similar body of folkloric culture was one of the main sources of the origin of the idea of the witches' sabbath in the western Alpine region in the late fourteenth and early fifteenth centuries.

50. T. Herzig, 'The Demons' Reaction to Sodomy: Witchcraft and Sexuality in Gianfrancesco Pico della Mirandola's *Strix*', *Sixteenth Century Journal* 34 (2003): 53–72.

51. P. de Lancre, *Tableau de l'inconstance des mauvais anges et démons*, ed. N. Jacques-Chaquin (Paris, 1982): 189–90, 197–9.

52. Bodin, *De la Démonomanie des sorciers*, 135–53; Murray, *Witch-Cult*, 13 *et passim*.

53. On the role of the universities in Germany see G. Schormann, *Hexenprozesse in Nordwestdeutschland* (Hildesheim, 1977): 9–44.

54. This was especially true in the fifteenth century. See Russell, *Witchcraft*, 243.

55. On these prosecutions, as well as the context, interpretation and dating of the *Malleus*, see W. Behringer, 'Heinrich Kramers *Hexenhammer*: Text und Context', in *Frühe Hexenverfolgung in Ravensburg und am Bodensee*, ed. A. Schmauder (Ravensburg, 2001): 83–124.

56. On the political nature of the papal Bull and the prosecutions in Brixen see E. Wilson, 'Institoris at Innsbruck: Heinrich Institoris, the *Summis Desiderantes* and the Brixen Witch-Trial of 1485,' in *Popular Religion in Germany and Central Europe*, ed. B. Scribner

and T. Johnson (New York, 1996): 87–100. On the career of Kramer as papal protégé and inquisitor and his relationship with Sprenger, see Herzig, *Christ Transformed into a Virgin Woman*, chapter 1.

57. See S. Anglo, 'Evident Authority and Authoritative Evidence: The *Malleus Maleficarum*', in *The Damned Art: Essays in the Literature of Witchcraft*, ed. S. Anglo (London, 1977): 1–31; H. P. Broedel, *The* Malleus Maleficarum *and the Construction of Witchcraft: Theology and Popular Belief* (Manchester, 2003).

58. Kramer and Sprenger, *Malleus Maleficarum*, 41–8, 99.

59. W. Stephens, *Demon Lovers: Witchcraft, Sex and the Crisis of Belief* (Chicago, 2002): chapter 2, claims that Kramer was most eager to respond to sceptical arguments that witches do not exist.

60. Sebald, *Witchcraft*, 36.

61. On the impact of the book on witch-hunting see G. Jerouschek, '500 Years of the Malleus maleficarum', in *Malleus maleficarum 1487 von Heinrich Kramer (Institoris)*, (Hildesheim, 1992): xlvi–xlviii; and Herzig, *Christ Transformed into a Virgin Woman*, 59–62.

62. Hansen, *Witchcraft at Salem*, 27, claims that the Puritan minister Increase Mather used the book in late seventeenth-century Massachusetts.

63. For lists of some of these see Russell, *Witchcraft*, 246–50; Leutenbauer, *Hexerei- und Zaubereidelikt*, xiv–xxi.

64. See Henningsen, *Witches' Advocate*, 206–7; 'The Papers of Alonso de Salazar Frías', 105.

65. P. Boyer and S. Nissenbaum, *Salem Possessed: The Social Origins of Witchcraft* (Cambridge, MA, 1974): 168–78.

66. Ginzburg, *The Night Battles*.

67. The role played by such popular ideas in the actual formation of the learned stereotype remains a matter of dispute. See Ginzburg, *Ecstasies*, 11 *et passim* for the argument that the stereotype was 'a hybrid result of a conflict between folk culture and learned culture'. For a different view see R. Muchembled, 'Satanic Myths and Cultural Reality', in *Early Modern European Witchcraft: Centres and Peripheries*, ed. B. Ankarloo and G. Henningsen (Oxford, 1990): 140–1.

68. Stephens, *Demon Lovers*, 27–31.

69. Levack, *Witchcraft Sourcebook*, 16–26.

70. On Renaissance scepticism see C. G. Nauert, *Agrippa and the Crisis of Renaissance Thought* (Urbana, 1965): 200, 240–1, 292–301.

71. E. W. Monter (ed.), *European Witchcraft* (New York, 1969): 56–7; H. A. Oberman, *Masters of the Reformation* (Cambridge, 1981): 174; H. R. Trevor-Roper, 'The European Witch-Craze', in H. R. Trevor-Roper, *The European Witch-Craze of the Sixteenth and Seventeenth Centuries and Other Essays* (New York, 1969): 132–3.

72. A. Williamson, *Scottish National Consciousness in the Age of James VI* (Edinburgh, 1979), 168; R. H. West, *Reginald Scot and Renaissance Writings on Witchcraft* (Boston, 1984): 4.

73. F. Yates, *The Occult Philosophy in the Elizabethan Age* (London, 1979): 67–71.

74. P. Burke, 'Witchcraft and Magic in Renaissance Italy: Gianfresco Pico and his *Strix*', in *The Damned Art: Essays in the Literature of Witchcraft*, ed. S. Anglo (London, 1977): 49.

75. G. Brucker, 'Sorcery in Early Renaissance Florence', *Studies in the Renaissance* 10 (1963): 8.

76. H. C. E. Midelfort, 'Johann Weyer and the Transformation of the Insanity Defense', in *The German People and the German Reformation*, ed. R. P. Hsia (Ithaca, NY, 1988): 234–61.

77. J. Weyer, *Witches, Devils and Doctors in the Renaissance: Johann Weyer's* De Praestigiis Daemonum, ed. George Mora (Binghamton, 1991): 304–7.

78. Ibid., 541.

79. T. Erastus, *Deux Dialogues. Histoires disputes et discours des illusions et impostures des diables, des magiciens infames, sorcieres et empoisonneurs, des ensorcel* (Paris, 1885); Bodin, *De la Démonomanie des sorciers*; James VI, *Daemonologie*; P. Binsfeld, *Tractatus de confessionibus maleficorum et sagarum* (Treves, 1596).

80. R. Scot, *The Discoverie of Witchcraft*, ed. M. Summers (London, 1930); J. G. Goedelmann, *De magis, veneficis et lamiis* (Frankfurt, 1592); J. Scultetus [A. Praetorius], *Gründlich Bericht von Zauberey und Zauberern* (Cologne, 1598); Loos, 'De vera et falsa magica', in Burr, *Witch Persecutions*.

81. On the limits of Goedelmann's scepticism see Sönke Lorenz, 'Johann Georg Goedelmann – Ein Gegner des Hexenwahns?' in *Beiträge zur pommerschen und mecklenberischen Geschichte*, ed. R. Schmidt (Marburg, 1981): 61–105. On Praetorius see G. S. Williams, *Defining Dominion: The Discourses of Magic and Witchcraft in Early Modern France and Germany* (Ann Arbor, 1995): 137–40. Scot did not include the 'working of wonders by supernatural means' in his summary of the 'absurd and impossible crimes' attributed to witches. Scot, *Discoverie of Witchcraft*, 18–20.

82. D. Wootton, 'Reginald Scot/Abraham Fleming/The Family of Love', in *Languages of Witchcraft: Narrative, Ideology and Meaning in Early Modern Culture*, ed. S. Clark (Basingstoke, 2001): 119–38.

83. Scot, *Discoverie of Witchcraft*, 4, 23, 46, 177.

84. See below, Chapter 5.

85. See Monter, *Witchcraft in France and Switzerland*, 18; G. Holmes, *Europe: Hierarchy and Revolt, 1320–1450* (New York, 1975): 125–33. Nider, who offers one of the earliest descriptions of the sabbath, claims that the sect had been active since about 1375. Ginzburg, *Ecstasies*, 71.

86. H. Kamen, *European Society 1500–1700* (London, 1984); P. Zagorin, *Rebels and Rulers: 1500–1660*, 2 vols (Cambridge, 1981).

87. J. Dillinger, 'Terrorists and Witches: Popular Ideas of Evil in the Early Modern Period', *History of European Ideas* 30 (2004): 167–302.

88. On the political nature of such inversion see S. Clark, 'Inversion, Misrule and the Meaning of Witchcraft', *Past and Present* 87 (1980): 110–27.

89. I Samuel 15:23; J. Kirkton, *The Secret and True History of the Church of Scotland*, ed. C. K. Sharpe (Edinburgh, 1817), 126. See also W. Kennett, *The Witchcraft of the Present Rebellion* (London, 1715).

90. L. Rothkrug, 'Religious Practices and Collective Perceptions: Hidden Homologies in the Renaissance and Reformation', *Historical Reflections* 7 (1980): 110–11. On the importance of the Council of Basel as the setting for the development of learned notions of witchcraft see Blauert, *Frühe Hexenverfolgungen*, 32–3.

91. R. J. W. Evans, *The Making of the Habsburg Monarchy, 1550–1700* (Oxford, 1979): 413; G. H. Radford, 'Thomas Larkham', *Reports and Transactions of the Devonshire Association* 24 (1892): 97. For the argument that belief in demonic intervention in the world was heightened at times of political strife in which the religious and political order was threatened, see P. Elmer, 'Towards a Politics of Witchcraft in Early Modern England', in *Languages of Witchcraft: Narrative, Ideology and Meaning in Early Modern Culture*, ed. Stuart Clark (Basingstoke, 2001): 101–18, esp. 104.

92. Rothkrug, 'Religious Practices', 108.

93. Boguet, *An Examen of Witches*, xxxi, xxxvi.

94. C. Larner, 'James VI and I and Witchcraft', in *The Reign of James VI and I*, ed. A. G. R. Smith (London, 1973): 74–90; S. Clark, 'King James's *Daemonologie*: Witchcraft and

Kingship', in *The Damned Art: Essays in the Literature of Witchcraft*, ed. S. Anglo (London, 1977): 156–81.

95. He certainly considered the witch to be a threat to the good order of the republic. See Bodin, *Démonomanie*, 334.

96. Perkins, *A Discourse of the Damned Art of Witchcraft*, 248–9.

3

THE LEGAL
FOUNDATIONS

The great European witch-hunt was essentially a judicial operation. The entire process of discovering and eliminating witches, from denunciation to punishment, usually occurred under judicial auspices. Even when witches took their own lives, they usually did so in order to avoid the often gruesome and apparently inevitable processes of the law.[1] Occasionally, agitated villagers took justice into their own hands and executed witches in vigilante style. In 1543, when Danish peasants were reported to have hunted witches 'like wolves', fifty-two suspected female witches were lynched in Jutland. During the 1580s some fifty witches in the northeastern French province of Champagne were lynched before the archbishop of Reims intervened to restore order.[2] During the Basque witch-hunt of 1609–11, large crowds broke into the houses of those who had been named as witches and attacked them, killing at least one woman, while in 1704 local residents of the Scottish burgh of Pittenweem, furious that a suspected witch, Janet Cornfoot, had been released by order of the Privy Council, pressed her to death.[3] There is no way to determine how many suspected witches died in this illegal manner. In the Polish countryside the numbers may have been fairly high.[4] Central governments, however, were very much opposed to this type of rough country justice, since it constituted a challenge to their authority, and they took steps to prevent its recurrence.[5] We can be fairly certain, therefore, that a large majority of those persons who were executed for witchcraft during the great hunt were formally and legally tried and sentenced.

Since witch-hunting usually took a judicial form, it is only reasonable to assume that the legal procedures used in criminal prosecutions and the ways in which European judicial systems operated had a good deal to do with the origins of widespread witch-hunting. Indeed, the intensive prosecution of witches in early modern Europe was facilitated by a number of legal developments that occurred between the thirteenth and the sixteenth centuries. First, the secular and ecclesiastical courts of continental Europe adopted a new, inquisitorial system of criminal procedure that made it far easier for witchcraft cases to be initiated and prosecuted. Second, these courts acquired the right to torture individuals accused of witchcraft, thus making it relatively easy to obtain confessions and the names of the witches' alleged accomplices. Third, the secular courts of Europe acquired jurisdiction over witchcraft, thereby supplementing and in many cases replacing the ecclesiastical courts as the judicial engines of witch-hunting.

None of these legal developments, or even all of them taken together, amounted to a sufficient cause of the great witch-hunt, but each of them served as a necessary precondition of that hunt. Just like the intellectual developments discussed in the previous chapter, they helped to make the witch-hunt possible. In fact, the legal and the intellectual foundations of the hunt were closely related, since the adoption of new criminal procedures facilitated the synthesis of the various ideas about the activities that witches allegedly engaged in. Legal developments also help to explain why the great witch-hunt took place when it did. Intensive witch-hunting did not begin until many European courts had adopted inquisitorial procedure and had begun to use torture. Equally important, intensive witch-hunting did not come to an end until magistrates and judges realized that they were sending innocent people to the stake and consequently instituted a number of significant legal reforms.

Changes in criminal procedure

Before the thirteenth century European courts used a system of criminal procedure that made all crimes, and especially concealed crimes, difficult to prosecute. This procedural system, which is generally referred to as accusatorial, existed in its purest form in the secular courts of northwestern Europe, but it was also followed, with some significant modifications, in the secular courts of Mediterranean lands and in the various tribunals of the Church.[6] In the accusatorial system, a criminal action was both initiated and prosecuted by a private person, who was usually the injured party or his kin. The accusation was a formal, public, sworn statement that resulted in the trial of the accused before a judge. If the accused admitted his guilt, or if the private accuser could provide certain proof, then the judge would decide against the defendant. If there was any doubt, however, the court would appeal to God to provide some sign of the accused person's guilt or innocence. The most common way of doing this was the ordeal, a test that the accused party would have to take to gain acquittal. He would have to carry a hot iron a certain distance and then show, after his hand was bandaged for a few days, that God had miraculously healed the seared flesh; or he would have to put his arm into hot water and in similar fashion reveal a healed limb after bandaging; or he would be thrown into a body of cold water and would be considered innocent only if he sank to the bottom; or he would be asked to swallow a morsel in one gulp without choking.

As an alternative to the ordeal the accused or his champion might engage in a duel with the champion of the wronged party, his victory in this 'bilateral ordeal' or trial by combat being construed as a sign of his innocence. He also might be allowed, as an alternative to the ordeal, a trial by compurgation. In this case the accused would swear to his innocence and then obtain a certain number of 'oath-helpers' who would solemnly swear to the honesty (and indirectly, therefore, to the innocence) of the accused. During the trial, in whatever form it took, the judge would remain an impartial arbiter who regulated the procedure of the court but who did not in any way prosecute the accused. The prosecutor was the accuser himself, and if the defendant proved his innocence of the charge, then the accuser became liable to criminal prosecution according to the old Roman tradition of the *lex talionis*.[7]

Regarding this early medieval system of criminal prosecution two observations are in order. First, it was a fundamentally non-rational process. The determination of guilt or innocence was usually not made by a rational inquiry into the facts of the case but by an appeal to divine intervention into human affairs. The court in effect abdicated its own responsibility to investigate crimes and left the matter in the hands of God. Second, the system did not prove to be particularly successful in prosecuting crime. Not only did every prosecution require an accuser who was willing to risk the possibility of a counter-suit on the basis of the talion, but the trial itself could also be manipulated in favour of the accused. Calloused hands and proper breathing techniques could, for example, help one to pass the ordeal, while men of high reputation (which admittedly many men accused of serious crimes were not) could usually secure acquittal by their mere oath or by compurgation. The system stands as a testament to men's faith in God's immanence but not to their efforts to use the law as an effective instrument of social control.

Beginning in the thirteenth century, however, the ecclesiastical and secular courts of western Europe abandoned this early medieval system of criminal procedure and adopted new techniques that assigned a much greater role to human judgement in the criminal process. The change from the old system to the new was stimulated to some extent by the revival of the formal study of Roman law in the eleventh and twelfth centuries,[8] but the main impetus came from the growing realization that crime – both ecclesiastical and secular – was increasing and had to be reduced. In bringing about this change the Church, which was faced with the spread of heresy, took the lead. The Church also encouraged the new procedures in the secular courts by formally prohibiting clerics from participating in ordeals at the Fourth Lateran Council of 1215.[9] Since the ordeals, being appeals to divine guidance in judicial matters, required clerics to bless the entire operation, the action taken by the Council signalled their end.[10]

The new system of criminal procedure that gradually took form during the thirteenth, fourteenth and fifteenth centuries and was employed throughout continental Europe by the sixteenth century is generally referred to as inquisitorial. Its adoption changed both the procedures by which criminal cases could be initiated and the procedures of the trials themselves. Regarding initiation, it is important to note that the adoption of inquisitorial procedure did not preclude the commencement of a legal action by individual accusation.[11] Many crimes tried according to inquisitorial procedure, including a large number of witchcraft cases, were initiated in this way.[12] The only difference between the new system and the old when suits were begun by accusation was that the accuser was no longer responsible for the actual prosecution of the case, as shall be discussed below. In addition to the initiation of cases by accusation, however, the new procedure allowed the inhabitants of a community to denounce a suspected criminal before the judicial authorities, a procedure that the church courts had used in certain circumstances during episcopal visitations as early as the ninth century.[13] Even more important, the new system allowed an officer of the court – either the public prosecutor, who was sometimes known as the fiscal, or the judge himself – to cite a criminal on the basis of information he had obtained himself, often by rumour.[14] Once again, the Church had employed this procedure in certain cases as early as the ninth century, claiming that the *infamia* or ill-repute of the criminal was the legal equivalent of the private accusation.[15] During the late Middle Ages this practice became widespread both in the ecclesiastical and secular courts. The initiation of cases in this way led to a significant increase in the number of criminal prosecutions, but it also made individuals vulnerable to frivolous, malicious, politically motivated or otherwise arbitrary prosecutions.

Even more important than the adoption of new modes of initiating criminal actions was the officialization of all stages of the judicial process once the charge had been made.[16] Instead of presiding over a contest between two private parties in which the outcome was at least theoretically left to God, the officers of the court – the judge and his subordinates – took it upon themselves to investigate the crime and to determine whether or not the defendant was guilty. This they did mainly by conducting secret interrogations of both the accused and all available witnesses, recording their testimony in written depositions. In this way they established the facts of the case, which they then evaluated, on the basis of carefully formulated rules of evidence, to determine whether or not the accused was guilty and to sentence him accordingly. The procedure, therefore, was not only completely officialized but also rationalized. Judicial officials were using their own judgement, which was informed by the rational rules of the law, to prosecute crime. It should not surprise us, therefore, to learn that the growth of the new system was closely related, as both cause and effect, to the emergence of a body of scientific legal literature, commonly known as jurisprudence. It also was related to the growth of a large legal profession.

Inquisitorial procedure can be contrasted not only to the accusatorial procedure that it replaced but also to the system of criminal procedure that developed at approximately the same time in England. English courts, like their continental counterparts, abandoned the ordeal and other 'supernatural probations' by the early thirteenth century, and they also entrusted the determination of guilt to human judgement, but they did not allow the criminal process to become as officialized as it did on the Continent. Whereas on the Continent officers of the court acquired the right both to initiate legal proceedings and to determine their outcome, in England lay jurymen – men not trained in the law – performed those functions. A presenting jury, acting in the name of the king, initiated or at least exercised prior review over all 'public' prosecutions, while the determination of guilt was left to a trial jury, whose duty it was to establish the facts of the case. Originally the jurymen were actual witnesses to the crime, but by the beginning of the sixteenth century they were no longer self-informed and sat in court as lay judges of evidence brought before them by local judicial officials. By the middle of the sixteenth century these officials regularly conducted a pre-trial examination of the prisoner and the witnesses, but the system nevertheless did not become inquisitorial because the lay jurors, and not the officials of the court, reached the verdict. In many respects, moreover, the English trial revealed the persistence of the older accusatory process. Technically, a private person, the individual who swore out the original complaint, not a legal official, prosecuted the crime. The trial remained public and oral and still resembled a contest between two adversaries, not a secret judicial investigation to establish the truth.[17] And the judge remained at least in theory (though hardly in practice) an impartial arbitrator who presided over the judicial process, rather than an official who was entrusted with the detection, investigation, prosecution and conviction of the crime.[18]

England was not the only country in Europe that resisted or otherwise avoided the introduction of inquisitorial procedure. Scotland maintained a jury system similar to that of England, while in Sweden and Poland many prosecutions continued to be initiated by private complaints. Hungary actually continued to use ordeals as late as the seventeenth century. These other countries, however, eventually adopted some features of inquisitorial justice. In Scotland judicial officials compiled large dossiers of written depositions that were used as evidence in criminal trials.[19] In the early seventeenth century Swedish courts and Polish town courts introduced the main features of inquisitorial procedure.[20] Similar criminal procedures were adopted in Hungary in the late seventeenth century, when a new judicial code prescribed the use of procedures advocated by the Saxon jurist Benedikt Carpzov in his treatise on criminal law. Even then, however, the new procedures encountered strong resistance and did not win full acceptance until well into the eighteenth century.[21]

The adoption of inquisitorial procedure facilitated the prosecution of all crime, but it proved to be most useful in the investigation and trial of heresy and witchcraft. Since most heretics were known only by general reputation, and since there were no victims of their crimes demanding retribution, the only effective way of bringing them to justice was through either denunciation or official promotion. It was, in fact, mainly to combat heresy that the Church adopted the new modes of initiation. Witches, who were often arrested on the basis of ill-repute, could likewise be proceeded against *ex officio*, but those whom they had harmed could also initiate judicial action against them. In those cases the main effect of the new system was the elimination of the liability of the accuser.[22] It stands to reason that under the old accusatory system a victim of sorcery would be reluctant to accuse his magical assailant with *maleficium* if there was a chance that he himself might be penalized for making the accusation.[23] Now, however, he could do so without taking that risk. Once heretics and witches were charged under the new procedures, the likelihood of conviction also increased, since the judge was able to use his powers of investigation to build up a dossier regarding the alleged crime. The direct interrogation of the accused was especially instrumental in this regard, since by this means the judge could elicit the information necessary for conviction.

The adoption of inquisitorial procedure led to the introduction of a very demanding standard of proof for establishing guilt in a capital crime. Since the adoption of inquisitorial procedure represented a shift from reliance upon divine intervention in human affairs to reliance upon personal rational judgement, jurists agreed that it was absolutely necessary for judges to have conclusive proof of guilt before passing sentence. The standard they adopted, which derived from the Roman law of treason and which we generally refer to as the Roman-canonical law of proof, was the testimony of two eyewitnesses or the confession of the accused. No other form of proof, no matter how convincing, would be considered sufficient. Unless two witnesses could testify that they actually saw the crime being committed, or unless the prisoner himself confessed to the deed, the accused could not be convicted. The rigidity of this law of proof can best be appreciated if we compare it with the standards of proof that English juries often used to convict criminals. English juries could and did deliver guilty verdicts on the basis of hearsay, circumstantial evidence or the testimony of only one eyewitness. Now, it is true that these same juries did require unanimity in their verdicts after 1367, and they often revealed a great reluctance to find the accused guilty. But when they did decide to convict, they often did so on the basis of rather flimsy evidence, even in the eighteenth century, by which time the English law of evidence had begun to take form.

Adherence to the Roman-canonical law of proof presented serious problems for judges in situations where eyewitnesses could not be produced. This was especially true in trials for concealed crimes, among which heresy and witchcraft were prominent. Heresy was essentially a mental crime, although witnesses could testify regarding a heretic's promulgation of his ideas. Witchcraft, which involved heresy, presented similar problems. The number of people who could testify that a witch performed *maleficia* before their very eyes was small indeed, while the only persons who could give eyewitness accounts of diabolism and the sabbath were the alleged accomplices of the witches, who could not be detected until at least one witch confessed and yielded their names. In such circumstances judges had to rely exclusively on confessions in order to obtain convictions. Confessions, however, were not always forthcoming, and consequently judicial authorities began to allow the use of torture in order to obtain them. The use of torture in heresy, witchcraft and other cases was therefore the direct result of the adoption of inquisitorial procedure. The logic of one led to the application of the other.

Torture

When we speak of judicial torture we do not mean the use of torture as a punishment for crime. Very often courts would sentence criminals to be tortured before their execution, and the methods used would be the same as those that had been employed during their trial. Some scholars distinguish between this type of *retributive* or *punitive* torture and *interrogatory* torture, but judicial torture, properly defined, refers only to the latter procedure. Judicial torture was a means employed to obtain either a confession or concealed information from an accused person or a recalcitrant witness.

The use of judicial torture in the late medieval and early modern periods had ancient and early medieval precedents. In ancient Greece and Rome, slaves who did not possess the same legal rights as free men were frequently tortured during their trials, while during the Roman Empire even free men were tortured in the prosecution of treason and other heinous crimes. In many Germanic kingdoms torture continued to be used on slaves, but not on free men, and its application was irregular and extra-judicial. Because of these precedents, it is proper to consider the introduction of torture in thirteenth-century Europe as a revival rather than an innovation. Like inquisitorial procedure, with which it is closely associated, its adoption was inspired to some extent by revival of the study of Roman law.[24] But the main reason for its reintroduction in the West was the need to prosecute crime more effectively.

The first documentary evidence we have of the use of torture in the late Middle Ages comes from the laws of the city of Verona in 1228. Within a few years many other city-states in Italy, the Holy Roman Empire and the kingdom of Castile followed suit. In these secular jurisdictions the main purpose of torture was to obtain evidence from notorious criminals who were suspected of concealed crimes. In 1252 the Church, which had taken the lead in the adoption of inquisitorial procedure, followed the example of the secular courts in allowing the use of torture. At that time Pope Innocent IV authorized papal inquisitors to use torture in the prosecution of heresy, which was in many ways the ultimate concealed crime. It was especially appropriate that suspected heretics should be tortured, since their crime was the ecclesiastical equivalent of treason, and the first free Romans to be subjected to torture had been traitors. The use of torture in heresy trials provided the foundation for its employment against witches in the church courts, while both the example of the ecclesiastical courts and the general practice of using torture in the prosecution of capital crimes led to its employment in secular witchcraft trials.

The use of judicial torture is predicated upon the assumption that when a person is subjected to physical pain during interrogation he will confess the truth. The assumption is not always valid. In many cases, it is true, the application of torture has elicited honest confessions or factual truth from the guilty or otherwise knowledgeable parties. In wartime the torture of military prisoners has often had the same effect. At other times, however, torture has proved to be a highly unreliable means of discovering the truth, for it has produced fabricated or at least partially misleading confessions. The likelihood of such falsification is greatest when (1) the person tortured is innocent of the alleged crime or ignorant of the desired information; (2) the details of the confession are suggested to him by means of leading questions; and (3) the amount of torture is excessive. There is an abundance of evidence from contemporary as well as historical sources to show that if torture is sufficiently painful, even the most tight-lipped, innocent person will perjure himself and confess to virtually anything his torturers wish him to say. The clearest historical evidence we have of this process is the great European witch-hunt SOURCE BOOK itself, in which thousands of individuals, when subjected to torture, confessed to crimes they did not commit and which in fact they could not have committed.

The architects of the system of judicial torture were not unaware of the unreliability of torture as a means of establishing the truth. They knew that although torture could elicit a great deal of otherwise unavailable, accurate, incriminating evidence, it could also seriously prejudice the rights of a defendant and lead to his or her unwarranted conviction. Before the middle of the thirteenth century the Church had prohibited torture for precisely this reason. When torture was revived in the thirteenth century, therefore, legal writers and judicial authorities devised a set of rules governing its application. The main objectives of the rules were to minimize the chances that an innocent person would be tortured, to prevent the fabrication of confessions, and to place some limits on the severity and duration of the torture. These rules did not serve as a justification of the use of torture: that lay in the necessity of obtaining confessions to crimes that threatened the state. But the rules did make the entire system more palatable to those who had a genuine interest in the protection of the rights of the accused and who wished to prevent the conviction of innocent persons.

The rules governing the use of torture varied from place to place and they also changed over time. In their original and strictest form they contained, first of all, a prohibition against the use of torture unless the judge could prove that a crime had in fact been committed.[25] Once that was ascertained, the judge still could not sentence a suspect to be tortured unless there was a solid presumption of guilt, which was usually provided by the testimony of one eyewitness (half the proof needed for conviction) or circumstantial evidence (*indicia*) that was the legal equivalent of the testimony of one eyewitness.[26] Even when this requirement was satisfied, the judge was forbidden to use torture unless it was the only way to establish the facts of the case, and before he ordered it he was required first to threaten the suspect with its use.

For both humanitarian and legal reasons, rules were also established to restrict the severity and the duration of the torture. The most widely recognized of these was that the torture should not result in the death of the victim, and it was for this reason that most courts used methods of torture that either distended or compressed the extremities. The most common instrument of torture that achieved such an effect was the *strappado*, a pulley that raised the person off the floor by his arms, which were tied behind his back (see Figure 3.1). Other instruments of distension, the rack and the ladder, were also used frequently. Of the instruments of compression the most common were the thumb screws, leg screws, head clamps, and tourniquets. All these had the advantage that they could be relaxed as soon as the tortured person agreed to confess or to provide the desired information. They also allowed the torture to be increased gradually. Most jurisdictions had rules governing the intensity of the torture. These depended on both the gravity of the crime and the strength of the presumption of guilt. When the *strappado* was used, these rules would determine how long the accused would hang from the ceiling and whether or not he or she would be jerked abruptly. When Niclas Fiedler, the former mayor of Trier, denied that he was a witch, the hangman took him to the torture room, bound him, 'pulled him up high, secured the cord to the wall, and beat on the rope with a stick, thereby inflicting great pain on the bound prisoner, as indicated by his screams'. In its most severe form, referred to as squassation, weights of anywhere from 40 to 660 pounds would be attached to the person's ankles and then the ropes would be jerked, a procedure that could dislodge a person's arms from their sockets. All of the grades of torture, however severe, were supposed to be performed on the same day; repetition of torture was forbidden. There were also rules that exempted certain classes of people, such as pregnant women and children, from torture.

Yet another set of rules was designed specifically to prevent the fabrication of confessions. The use of leading questions by the judge, which would of course alert the prisoner to what his interrogator wished to hear, was forbidden. Testimony taken in the torture chamber was not admissible, the prisoner being required to repeat his confession 'freely' outside the chamber within a period

SOURCE
BOOK

Vorstellung des bereits in der Luft aufgezogenen Inquisiten

Figure 3.1 The torture of a prisoner by means of the *strappado*. This procedure was usually not employed until other instruments of torture, such as the thumbscrews, had not resulted in a confession. The pain could be increased by jerking the ropes or adding weights, depicted here in the foreground, to the ankles. From *Constitutio Criminalis Theresiana* (1769).

of twenty-four hours. The judge was, moreover, required to verify the details of confessions extracted under torture.

If the courts of Europe had adhered strictly to these rules regarding the use of torture, then the adoption of this method of criminal investigation would not have led to the innumerable miscarriages of justice with which it is almost always associated. In particular, the European witch-hunt would have been much smaller than it was. As it turned out, however, these rules were greatly relaxed and the system was grossly abused. In some jurisdictions the rules were officially changed in order to facilitate the prosecution of all crime. In others the rules were routinely suspended in the prosecution of crimes that were considered to be especially grave and difficult to prosecute. It should be noted that witchcraft was regarded by some jurists as a *crimen exceptum*, an

exceptional crime, and in the prosecution of such an offence certain procedural rules, such as those regarding the qualification of witnesses, did not apply.[27] In still other jurisdictions judges flagrantly ignored or violated the rules, especially in witchcraft cases.

The most significant modification of the rules dealt with the requirement that the judge should first establish that a crime had in fact been committed. As John Langbein has argued, if this rule had been strictly enforced, 'the European witch-craze would never have claimed its countless victims'.[28] Unfortunately, however, an exception was often made for those occult crimes for which the evidence had vanished at the time of commission. This meant that judges could torture suspects for crimes that were believed to have been committed but for which there was no tangible evidence.[29]

Another official relaxation of the rules regarding torture concerned its repetition. In drafting his manual for inquisitors in 1376, Nicholas Eymeric circumvented the prohibition of repetition by allowing its *continuation* at a later time. Eventually European courts dispensed with this casuistry and permitted judges to repeat the torture at least once and sometimes two or more times if the prisoner proved to be recalcitrant.[30] In some witchcraft cases torture was applied indefinitely. There is at least one recorded instance of its repetition fifty-six times,[31] and in 1631 the hangman in the town of Dreissigacker in Germany revealed in a chilling statement to an accused witch how completely the safeguard against repeating torture had been abandoned. 'I do not take you for one, two, three, not for eight days, nor for a few weeks', said the hangman, 'but for half a year or a year, for your whole life, until you confess: and if you will not confess, I shall torture you to death, and you shall be burned after all.'[32] It should be noted that the prisoner was pregnant at the time and therefore should not have been tortured at all.

As the duration of the torture was indefinitely extended, so too was its severity. It appears that in many jurisdictions the most brutal tortures were reserved for witches. Certainly one gets that impression from reading the account of the prosecution of Anna Spülerin of Ringingen, who was tortured so gruesomely that her limbs were mutilated and her sight and hearing lost.[33] In Scotland Dr Fian, one of the many witches suspected of treason against the king, 'was put to the most severe and cruel pain in the world, called the boots', with the result that 'his legs were crushed and beaten together as small as might be, and the bones and flesh so bruised, that the blood and marrow spouted forth in great abundance'.[34] Some of these procedures were sanctioned by the criminal law of particular states, but others were employed illegally, at the mere command of an overzealous and perhaps sadistic judge. In Germany some courts, most notably that of the imperial city of Offenburg, used the witches' chair, which was heated by fire from below, while in Scotland a witch's fingernails were reportedly pulled out by pincers. In Spanish, French and German lands it was not uncommon for courts to force-feed their prisoners with large amounts of water – a procedure similar in some respects to the modern torture of waterboarding. Among the clearly illegal tortures were filling the nostrils with lime and water, tying the victim to a table covered with hawthorn twigs, rolling a pin with dagger-like points up and down the spine, gouging out the eyes, chopping off the ears, squeezing the male's genital organs, and burning brandy or sulphur over the victim's body.

Many of these especially brutal tortures were used originally or exclusively in witchcraft cases. This was not simply because witchcraft was considered the most heinous of all crimes and the most necessary, therefore, to prosecute successfully, but also because many judges feared that witches might employ sorcery to help them withstand pain. In such circumstances the judges may have believed that an especially cruel form of torture would succeed where others had failed. The method that was specifically designed for use in such cases, however, was one that caused no direct physical harm. The torture of forced sleeplessness, the *tormentum insomniae*, was considered to be the most effective antidote to the sorcery of the victim. Since this method, which kept the victim awake for forty hours or longer, did not actually hurt the body, it had great appeal to humane judges. It also was extremely effective, probably because it resulted in a form of brainwashing. One judge claimed that fewer than 2 per cent of all victims of this torture could endure it without confessing.

Just as the limits on the duration and severity of torture were raised or completely ignored, the rules guarding against false confessions were gradually modified or abandoned. Suggestive questioning became routine in witchcraft cases, a practice which the publication of sets of questions to be asked of witches only encouraged. Few attempts were made to verify the details of the confessions, and when an accused witch retracted a confession made under torture, judges allowed a second or even a third or fourth use of torture, thereby violating the rule against repetition.[35] It was not unusual for judges to give non-capital sentences to prisoners who retracted their confessions, but when the crime was that of witchcraft the judges showed great reluctance to follow that course of action. Some witches were not even given the opportunity for retraction, while others who retracted were executed anyway in the manner prescribed for unrepentant heretics.

The question remains, however, whether judges who applied torture with great severity and with apparent disregard of at least the original rules were worried that they might be forcing innocent parties to incriminate themselves. The answer is almost certainly 'No'. Either they believed that God would protect the innocent and allow them to endure the torture, just as the deity had allowed them to survive the ordeal, or they did not seriously consider the possibility that the accused might be innocent. Even when the evidence of a person's guilt was insufficient according to the law, judges proceeded with torture on the assumption that the accused was guilty and would therefore speak the truth when pain was threatened or applied. Whatever compunctions the judge might have about subjecting a human being to excruciating torture would be offset by his recognition of the enormity of the crime and the necessity of its effective prosecution. And, of course, once the torture had begun, judges had an additional motive for completing their task successfully, since the confession itself served as a justification of their use of torture in the first place.

The reintroduction of torture into the legal systems of western Europe and the relaxation of, or disregard for, the rules regulating its use had a profound effect on the origin and development of the great European witch-hunt. First, torture facilitated the formulation and the dissemination of the cumulative concept of witchcraft. Although the various ideas regarding witchcraft were synthesized and spread mainly by the authors of learned treatises, their fusion first occurred in the courtroom, where inquisitors used torture to confirm their suspicions and realize their fantasies. In most cases the treatises drew upon and developed ideas that had first emerged in the torture chamber. Once these ideas were put into writing, moreover, the production of confessions under torture confirmed their reality and facilitated their transmission. The importance of obtaining confessions to ratify beliefs that are otherwise available only in print can best be appreciated by studying the fate of certain witch beliefs in England. Ideas about witches attending the sabbath and worshipping the Devil were by no means absent from England, at least in literary form, during the sixteenth and seventeenth centuries, but these ideas never gained widespread acceptance among the elite. This was mainly because torture could not be used in witchcraft cases and confessions to diabolical activities could not, therefore, be readily obtained.

The second effect of the adoption of torture on witch-hunting was that it greatly increased the chances of witches being convicted. The introduction of inquisitorial procedure by itself should have had that effect, but the acceptance of the Roman-canonical law of proof threatened to negate its effectiveness in the case of concealed crimes. The use of torture, especially unrestricted torture, not only resolved the problem of insufficient proof but also made possible the conviction of almost anyone who incurred the suspicion of witchcraft. Although we do not have complete statistics, it appears that when torture was used on a regular basis in witchcraft prosecutions, the rate of convictions could be as high as 95 per cent.[36] When it was not used, as in England, the conviction rate was well below 50 per cent. Between the two extremes there were of course many intermediate positions, which could reflect the use of torture in only some cases, a greater or lesser adherence to the rules governing the use of torture, or different degrees of humaneness on the part of the judges.[37] In some jurisdictions torture was ineffective because some prisoners employed certain techniques to help them withstand the pain.[38] There is no question, however, that without torture the conviction of witches would have been less common and the pattern of witchcraft prosecutions and convictions would have probably resembled that of England more closely than that of Germany.

The third and most important effect of the adoption of torture on European witch-hunting concerns its use in acquiring the names of witches' alleged accomplices. Roman law had declared emphatically that a person who confessed to a crime could not be tortured regarding that of another person, but most European jurisdictions – with the notable exception of the Spanish and papal territories – abandoned this rule during the late medieval or early modern period. Only when this critical change was made, and when authorities began to believe that witchcraft was a conspiracy, did the conduct of large, chain-reaction hunts become possible. The torture of individual witches for their confessions could produce a high percentage of convictions, but only the torture of those witches for the names of their confederates could produce witch-hunts in which scores, if not hundreds, of individuals were tried for a collective crime.

Witchcraft and the secular courts

The third main legal development that made the great European witch-hunt possible was the deployment of the full judicial power of the state in the prosecution of a crime that was primarily spiritual in nature. To the extent that witchcraft involved the worship of the Devil it was a spiritual crime – the crime of apostasy and heresy – and as such it merited punishment by ecclesiastical authorities. Many witches were in fact prosecuted in episcopal courts and in those of papal inquisitors, whose main assignment ever since the early thirteenth century had been to combat the spread of heresy. From the earliest years of witch-hunting, however, the secular courts of western European states also took part in witch-hunting, either by cooperating with ecclesiastical courts or by trying witches on their own authority. As the hunt developed, the secular courts assumed an even greater role in the process, while that of the ecclesiastical courts declined. Governments defined witchcraft as a secular crime, and in some countries the temporal courts secured a monopoly over its prosecution. As this change took place, the Church continued to have an active interest in the matter of witchcraft. It often inspired or directed secular authorities to pursue witches aggressively,[39] but the driving judicial force of the witch-hunt became secular rather than ecclesiastical authority. Without the mobilization of this secular power, the great witch-hunt would have been a mere shadow of itself.

The extraordinarily durable notion that the European witch-hunt was essentially a clerical operation, inspired by clerical zeal and conducted under ecclesiastical auspices, derives both from the size of the contribution that churchmen made to the construction of the cumulative concept of witchcraft and from the role that church courts played in the prosecution of the crimes of heresy and magic during the late Middle Ages. That churchmen took the lead in the early formulation of witch beliefs cannot be denied, although lay theologians like Arnald of Villanova and lay magistrates who adjudicated cases of sorcery played a significant part in the process.[40] The important consideration in this regard, however, is that these ideas, whatever their source, became the property of the lay magistracy as well as of the clerical elite by the time witch-hunting began.[41] Once that happened, it was just as likely that the ideas would surface in secular as in ecclesiastical courtrooms.

Regarding the clerical role in the late medieval prosecution of magic, heresy and witchcraft, we must make a number of qualifications. First, the prosecution of magic was undertaken by both secular and ecclesiastical authorities, since it was clearly a crime of 'mixed jurisdiction'.[42] The Church condemned the practice because it involved some sort of commerce with demons, and it prosecuted it as a form of heresy, but secular authorities had a legitimate interest in the crime when it resulted in physical injury, and especially when it was used for political purposes. It was in fact the traditional jurisdiction that secular authorities had over *maleficium*, which can be traced back to Roman times, that provided the major foundation for later statutory prohibitions of witchcraft. Second, secular authorities also played a role, although admittedly a more limited one, in the prosecution of heresy. Almost all heresy trials in the late Middle Ages took place in the courts of episcopal or papal inquisitors, but these officials required and obtained a great deal of assistance in their work from secular authorities. Lay officials helped to locate and arrest suspects, and once they were convicted, executed them on the basis of secular laws. The cooperation of the secular authorities in punishing heretics was essential, since church courts could not inflict bodily harm and were therefore obliged to surrender condemned heretics to the secular arm for punishment. Of course there was very little concern that lay officials would not cooperate, since heresy was widely regarded as a source of civil disorder.[43]

Since secular courts had jurisdiction over magic and *maleficium*, and since they willingly provided indispensable services to the ecclesiastical courts in the prosecution of heretics, they naturally assumed a significant role in the prosecution of witches. When witch-hunting began in the fifteenth century, the trials took place not only in the courts of papal inquisitors and in the episcopal courts but also in various municipal courts. The notorious witch-hunting campaigns of Heinrich Kramer in Germany during the 1480s, which Pope Innocent VIII directly sanctioned in his bull of 1484, and the publication of the *Malleus maleficarum* by Kramer two years later, have led to a general assumption that most fifteenth-century witch-hunting activities occurred under the auspices of papal inquisitors. This is clearly not the case. It is true that inquisitors were primarily responsible for the numerous witch-hunts that took place in southern France in the early fifteenth century. These trials were to some extent a by-product of the pursuit of Waldensian heretics in that region. In other parts of Europe, however, episcopal and secular courts prosecuted witches, sometimes in cooperation with inquisitors or with each other and sometimes independently. In one of the very first witch-hunts, which took place in the Swiss Alps at the turn of the fifteenth century, the governor of Bern conducted the trials in an effort to establish the jurisdiction of the city over the region.[44]

As the witch-hunt gathered strength in the sixteenth and early seventeenth centuries, a number of developments resulted in the reduction of clerical jurisdiction over witchcraft and a corresponding increase in the amount of secular judicial concern with it. The first was the definition of witchcraft as a secular crime. Both the *Malleus maleficarum* and a treatise titled *Layenspiegel*, which was written in 1510 by Ulrich Tengler, the governor of Höchstädt, had established the theoretical foundation of such a definition, but only later in the sixteenth century did secular rulers take official action. Frightened that witchcraft was spreading and that its practitioners were evading prosecution, the legislative bodies of many European states either passed specific laws against witchcraft, promulgated edicts to the same effect, or included specific prohibitions of witchcraft in their criminal codes.[45] The *Reichstag* of the Holy Roman Empire included an article concerning witchcraft in the authoritative *Constitutio Criminalis Carolina* of 1532, while many German states within the Empire enacted their own particular laws against the crime. The English Parliament passed witchcraft statutes in 1542, 1563 and 1604; the Scottish Parliament did the same in 1563; and the rulers of Franche-Comté, Sweden, Denmark, Norway and Russia all issued edicts against witchcraft in the late sixteenth and early seventeenth centuries.[46] Most of these witchcraft laws were based upon the traditional jurisdiction that the state claimed over *maleficium*, but in some cases the law allowed prosecution for the exclusively spiritual crime of making a pact with the Devil or, more vaguely, covenanting with an evil spirit.[47] These laws not only gave secular courts an indisputable right to hear witchcraft cases, but also contributed directly to the growth of witch-hunting by publicizing the crime and facilitating its prosecution.

A second development that caused a significant shift of witchcraft cases from ecclesiastical to secular tribunals was the decline of both the papal Inquisition and other ecclesiastical courts. The general weakening of papal authority in the late fifteenth and early sixteenth centuries, and the later Protestant rejection of that authority at the time of the Reformation, left the Inquisition, which had never been an organized institution to begin with, in a permanently enfeebled state.[48] Only in Spain, where an Inquisition had been established as a national institution under the authority of the king in the late fifteenth century; in Portugal, which in similar fashion had three inquisitorial tribunals that remained independent of Rome; and in Italy, where a new Roman Inquisition was established on the Spanish model in 1542, did the Inquisition continue to show any signs of vitality.[49] The papal Inquisition was not, however, the only instrument of ecclesiastical justice that declined at this time. Throughout Europe, especially in Protestant countries but also in those that remained Catholic, church courts lost much of their authority and found themselves clearly subordinated to the secular power of the state.[50] Their coercive and jurisdictional powers were restricted in many countries, and by the middle of the sixteenth century they appear to have become much weaker instruments than the secular courts in the increasingly important task of extirpating witchcraft. In many countries the role of church courts in prosecuting 'witchcraft' was restricted to those who practised various forms of magic.[51]

A third reason for the reduction of clerical involvement in witch-hunting was the growth of a considerable reluctance among church lawyers and judges to tolerate the procedural abuses upon which successful witch-hunting depended. There is no little irony in the fact that papal inquisitors, who earlier had taken the lead in violating many of the procedural rules governing the use of torture, were among the first to recognize that these violations had resulted in numerous miscarriages of justice and to recommend caution in further proceedings. Ecclesiastical officials, moreover, manifested a greater reluctance to mete out harsh sentences in the sixteenth and seventeenth centuries, indicating a return to the traditional penitential and admonitory functions that ecclesiastical justice had originally served. Secular courts, by contrast, being concerned for the maintenance of a public order that was being seriously challenged, generally manifested fewer compunctions in this regard.

The assumption of secular control over the crime of witchcraft had a profound impact on the process of witch-hunting in many European countries. In Scotland, for example, large-scale witch-hunts did not begin until after the Scottish Parliament defined witchcraft as a secular crime in 1563 and until after the secular courts established a virtual monopoly over witchcraft prosecutions. In Transylvania, where few witches had been executed when the ecclesiastical courts had jurisdiction over the crime in the fifteenth and sixteenth centuries, the assumption of secular control in the seventeenth century was accompanied by a striking increase in executions.[52] In Poland the process of secularization was very slow to develop, and it was only after the fairly tolerant ecclesiastical courts reluctantly allowed municipal courts to prosecute witches that witch-hunting claimed many victims in that country.[53]

At the same time that the assumption of secular control over witchcraft led to an increase in prosecutions in some countries, the retention of ecclesiastical jurisdiction over the crime helped to keep prosecutions at a minimum in others. The two countries in Europe where ecclesiastical tribunals, and in particular the courts of the Inquisition, maintained primary jurisdiction over witchcraft in the late sixteenth and seventeenth centuries were Spain and Italy. In both areas the number of witchcraft prosecutions and executions during this period remained relatively low by European standards. In Italy this judicial mildness is especially interesting, for during the fifteenth and early sixteenth centuries, when papal inquisitors had exercised less restraint in witch-hunting, northern Italy had been one of the main centres of prosecution.[54] In Spain the authority of the ecclesiastical courts was so great that they were able, even in the seventeenth century, to mitigate the severity of sentences that secular courts imposed in witchcraft cases.[55]

It is important to note that the decline of ecclesiastical jurisdiction over witchcraft did not involve the clergy's abandonment of their interest in witch-hunting. The clergy remained just as concerned with the worship of the Devil and the practice of maleficent magic as they had been in the past. The clergy did, however, change their tactics, becoming auxiliaries to judicial authorities in roughly the same way that lay officials had earlier provided assistance to the ecclesiastical judges. In the sixteenth and seventeenth centuries the clergy often put pressure on secular authorities to take stronger action against witches, assisted in the apprehension of suspects, and used the power of the pulpit to maintain witch-hunts. In Salem, Massachusetts, the clergy actively encouraged the prosecution of witches, even though the trials took place in the secular courts.[56] In Scotland the clergy not only interrogated witches after their apprehension but collectively urged the government on several occasions to step up its witch-hunting operations.[57] In the Cambrésis region in the southern Netherlands parish priests were closely involved in the process of identifying and prosecuting witches.[58] The most direct clerical influence on secular witchcraft prosecutions occurred in those German and Burgundian territories where bishops or monks exercised temporal power.[59] In these quasi-ecclesiastical states the ruling clerics used secular officials and secular authority to prosecute witches, a tactic that gave them more procedural latitude than if they had used the church courts and also freed them from any misgivings they might have had about inflicting corporal punishment through an ecclesiastical tribunal.[60] The witch-hunts that took place in the Catholic ecclesiastical territories of Ellwangen, Mergentheim, Trier, Würzburg and Bamberg were as large as those occurring in any other parts of Germany.[61]

Although witchcraft became a secular crime, triable in the secular courts, and although most secular authorities claimed jurisdiction over it on the grounds that it involved *maleficium* rather than heresy, the form of punishment that the secular courts adopted for this crime reflected its heretical rather than its felonious nature. Except in England and New England, where witches who had been sentenced to death were hanged like other felons (see Figure 3.2), witches were usually burned at the stake. This was the punishment that was traditionally inflicted on relapsed heretics, and its use in witchcraft cases served the purpose of identifying the witch with the heretic, both of whom were believed to be servants of the Devil.[62] The practice of burning heretics had a scriptural foundation in the statement that 'if a man not abide in me, he is cast forth as a branch that is withered; and men gather them and cast them into the fire, and they are burned'.[63] Burning witches also was a ritual of purification, which in all mythologies is associated with fire, and it also may have served as an implicit substitute for the ordeal by fire, which the Church abolished just about the time that it started prosecuting and executing people for heresy. Much more practically, death by fire may have provided guarantees for nervous judges that witches would not return from the dead by means of sorcery. But the main reason why secular courts usually decided upon this sentence was that witches were guilty of a crime that was similar to, if not identical with, heresy.[64]

Figure 3.2 The hanging of the Chelmsford witches, 1589. In England witches were hanged, not burned. The small animals in the foreground are familiar spirits or imps who were believed to receive nourishment from witches and aided them in performing their magic. From *The Apprehension and Confession of Three Notorious Witches* (1589).

Most witches were not burned alive. Although this was the usual practice in Spanish and Italian territories (where relatively few witches were executed), witches in France, Germany, Switzerland and Scotland were usually strangled or garroted (a brutal procedure in which a metal spike penetrated the throat) at the stake before the flames consumed their bodies. Many French witches were hanged before their bodies were burned. In the German principality of Ellwangen the princely prebend usually changed the sentence of burning to death by the sword, but he still had the corpse burned afterwards.[65] In similar fashion an entire group of witches in Ortenau were sentenced to death 'by the sword and burning' in 1630.[66] In Sweden it was standard practice to have condemned witches first beheaded and then their bodies burned.[67] Occasionally other methods of execution, such as drowning, were employed, but in the overwhelming majority of capital sentences either the witch or her corpse was burned.[68]

In some cases secular as well as ecclesiastical courts gave non-capital sentences. These were most common in England, where the witchcraft statutes made provision for such penalties when the crime was the first offence and did not result in the death of the wronged party. In Scotland and in some continental European countries there was a much closer correlation between the number of convictions and the number of executions, but non-capital sentences, usually banishment or imprisonment, were by no means rare.[69] In France the practice of appealing sentences to the provincial parlements often resulted in the commutation of death sentences, while in Geneva judges who could not determine guilt with certainty very often banished the accused.[70] Henri Boguet recommended banishment in cases when the prisoner withstood the torture but the judge remained convinced of his guilt.[71] The sentence of banishment does not necessarily imply that the judges viewed the crime of witchcraft as being any less spiritual in nature than heresy; in the few cases when German secular courts prosecuted heretics in the Middle Ages, the judges meted out the very same punishment.[72] But banishment does suggest, at least in cases of 'certain' guilt, that judicial authorities were more concerned with ridding their communities of socially marginal or dangerous individuals than with combating the forces of Satan. This was especially true in countries like Hungary, where there was more emphasis on the magical than on the diabolical aspects of witchcraft.[73]

No matter what its rationale, the use of banishment as a sentence in the secular courts should not be taken to indicate that these tribunals were more lenient than their ecclesiastical counterparts in the prosecution of witchcraft. Generally speaking, that was not the case. The secular courts at Geneva may have been especially reluctant to put witches to death, while the court of oyer and terminer at Salem did not execute anyone who made a confession.[74] But neither of these jurisdictions could match the standard of leniency that the Spanish Inquisition established in the early seventeenth century. In the largest witch-hunt in Spanish history, which involved more than 1,800 persons, only eleven individuals were condemned to the stake, and of these only one, a woman who had allegedly recruited other witches, transported toads to the sabbath, and had regular intercourse with the Devil, had actually made a confession.[75] In contrast to most secular courts, where a confession usually resulted in conviction and execution, in Spain it usually led to reconciliation with the Church. The original purpose of ecclesiastical justice was precisely such a reconciliation, and in Spain the Inquisition made sure that even in witchcraft cases only the unrepentant would suffer.

The Spanish example reveals, in a larger context, how absolutely crucial secular participation and eventually secular dominance was to the conduct of the European witch-hunt. If secular courts had not originally supplemented the ecclesiastical courts, if they had not fully cooperated with ecclesiastical authorities in the apprehension and execution of witches, if they had not filled a void that was created when church courts either became more lenient or abandoned the pursuit of witches, and if they had not been available for use in witchcraft cases by the clerics who presided over territorial states, then the great European witch-hunt would not have assumed the dimensions that it did.

Witchcraft and the early modern state

The assumption of secular control over most witchcraft prosecutions by the end of the sixteenth century raises the question of whether the prosecution of witches and the process of strengthening the state were related. One of the most significant developments in early modern European history was the growth in the powers of states, which are formal, public political entities that possess the highest legal authority within a specific territory. During the sixteenth and seventeenth centuries European states grew in size, wealth and military power. Rulers committed to the strengthening of their states engaged in a number of different enterprises. They brought the various and sometimes scattered territories over which they claimed jurisdiction within the ambit of effective and unified central governmental control. They established their sovereignty by reducing the power of rival authorities, such as the clergy and the nobility, within their dominions. They collected more taxes from their subjects, and they used much of the wealth derived from taxation to build large armies and navies. Most important, the rulers of these states established more direct, effective political and legal control over their subjects, making them more obedient and subordinate to central governmental authority.

There were many apparent links between the process of state-building and witch-hunting. Besides the assumption of jurisdiction over the crime of witchcraft by the secular courts (i.e. by the tribunals of the state rather than those of the Church), there is evidence that some rulers deliberately encouraged witch-hunting in order to make their rule more secure. In 1590 King James VI of Scotland, fearing that witches were engaged in a conspiracy against him, assumed a leading role in one of the largest witch-hunts in Scottish history.[76] Christian IV of Denmark not only promulgated a witchcraft ordinance in 1617 but actively encouraged the prosecution of witches who were under suspicion in Copenhagen and Elsinore in 1626.[77] The prince-bishop of Würzburg used witch-hunting to establish religious conformity in his electorate, while Duke Maximilian of Bavaria, who was determined to attain absolute power, prosecuted an entire family of wandering beggars to enhance his reputation as the guardian of the state and the moral order.[78] In seventeenth-century Hungary two Transylvanian princes, Gábor Bathlen and Mihály Apafy, brought charges of witchcraft against their aristocratic enemies, leading to a set of high-profile trials.[79] There are also some apparent connections between witchcraft theory and the theory of royal absolutism, especially in the writings of the demonologist and political theorist Jean Bodin.[80]

Nevertheless, it is misleading to establish a general correlation between state-building and witch-hunting. One reason for calling the connection into question is that the central or higher courts of most European countries – those that most directly represented the authority of the state – did more to restrict witch-hunting than to encourage it. These same central authorities were also primarily responsible for bringing witch-hunting to an end. It is true that rulers and royal councils did often pass legislation that facilitated the prosecution of witches, and it was not uncommon for the highest courts of European states to hold witchcraft trials. From time to time central authorities actually initiated witch-hunts, especially in the German principalities, and they sometimes gave local or regional officials the authority to hear witchcraft cases.[81] But most witch-hunts were actually conducted by the judicial officers of smaller administrative subdivisions of the state.[82] These judges of local or 'inferior' jurisdictions usually demonstrated much more zeal in prosecuting witches than did the central authorities, and when left to their own devices they generally executed more witches than when they were closely supervised by their judicial superiors.

There are two main reasons why local courts usually proved to be less lenient than central courts in the prosecution of witchcraft. The first is that the local authorities who presided over witch trials were far more likely than their central superiors to develop an intense and immediate fear of witchcraft. Central authorities might agree that witches were a threat to society and that they needed to be prosecuted, but they rarely knew the accused witches personally (as many local magistrates or the rulers of the smaller German states did) and they were not faced with the prospect of living in the same community with the witches should they be acquitted. They were, moreover, less likely to be affected by the panic that often engulfed towns and villages when witch-hunts occurred. Judges in the central courts of European states, therefore, would be more likely to proceed against witches on the basis of the evidence and avoid the prejudice that a local alarmed judge would naturally develop. The second reason is that judges in the central courts, having received legal training, were usually more committed to the proper operation of the judicial system and more willing therefore to afford accused witches whatever procedural safeguards the law might allow them.

The complex relationship between state-building and witch-hunting can best be illustrated in four countries, where efforts at state-building took different forms and where the intensity of witch-hunting varied greatly: France, Scotland, England and Germany.

France

The kingdom of France is often viewed as the most successful example of state-building in Europe during the early modern period. Historians often exaggerate the strength of the French state, even during the reign of its absolutist king, Louis XIV, in the late seventeenth century, but its administrative bureaucracy was large by contemporary European standards, and central control over the localities increased considerably during the seventeenth century. The history of witchcraft prosecutions in France can be written largely in terms of efforts by higher judicial authorities to review and in many cases modify or overturn the sentences promulgated by lower courts. This regulation of local justice was undertaken by the nine provincial parlements, staffed by men trained in the law. The most important of these parlements, and the one that handled the largest number of witchcraft cases, was the Parlement of Paris, which exercised an appellate jurisdiction over most of northern France and was to all intents and purposes a central court. Between 1588 and 1624 the Parlement of Paris gradually established its authority over these local tribunals, requiring that all capital sentences of witches be appealed to them.[83] An astonishingly high 36 per cent of cases reviewed by this parlement resulted in complete dismissal, while only 24 per cent of all cases were confirmed.[84]

The main reason for the greater leniency of the Parisian tribunal was that it adhered to a more demanding rule of proof than did the lower courts, refusing to sentence witches to death on the basis of a confession extracted under torture. Other considerations, however, including the remoteness of the judges from the actual environment of the witch-hunts and perhaps the scepticism of the *parlementaires* regarding the reality of witchcraft also played a part. Interestingly enough, the eight other provincial parlements in France, which could not, like the Parlement of Paris, be considered central institutions, had a much less lenient record in prosecuting witches and at the end of the seventeenth century had to be subjected to direct royal control in order to bring the witch-hunt to an end.

Scotland

The kingdom of Scotland, which is generally not known for its strong central government in the early modern period, provides a striking example of how a central government determined to control local justice failed to do so and, in an ironic way, actually contributed to intense witch-hunting in the localities. In Scotland almost all witchcraft trials took place in the secular courts under the provisions of the witchcraft statute passed by the Scottish Parliament of 1563. There were three main types of secular courts where Scottish witches could be tried. First, there was the Court of Justiciary, which sat in Edinburgh. Cases from all over Scotland could be heard there, but a disproportionate number came from the counties in the immediate vicinity of the capital. Next, there were the circuit courts, held in the various shires of the kingdom, over which judges from the central courts presided. These circuit courts did not function with much regularity until the late seventeenth century. Finally, there were local ad hoc courts that were commissioned either by the Privy Council or by Parliament to try witches in the areas where they were arrested. These courts, unlike the Court of Justiciary and the circuit courts, were not staffed by professionally trained judges from the central courts but by local landowners and magistrates.

In the wake of two particularly strong witch-hunts in the 1590s, in which the process of witch-hunting had spun out of control, the central government demanded that all witchcraft trials in the localities receive preliminary approval of the Privy Council or Parliament. In this way witchcraft became a 'centrally managed crime'.[85] It appeared, therefore, that this effort to establish central conciliar control over witchcraft would result in a reduction in the intensity of witch-hunting, just as the mandatory appeal of sentences to the Parlement of Paris resulted in the dismissal of charges against many witches. The difference between Scotland and France, however, is that the Scottish Privy Council did not give proper consideration to the petitions for local trials, especially during witch panics, when the number of requests to try witches was exceptionally high. To make matters worse, Scotland did not have a sufficiently large central judicial establishment to ensure that the cases would be heard in either the Court of Justiciary or the circuit courts. Therefore, the Privy Council often granted commissions of justiciary to the local magistrates routinely, and since there was no procedure for appeals or the review of the sentences of the local courts, the fate of many Scottish witches was entrusted to local magistrates who had no judicial training and who in most cases were determined to convict and execute them. Although we do not have complete statistics, it is apparent that the execution-rate in Scotland was significantly higher when unsupervised local authorities heard witchcraft cases than when judges from the central courts did so, either in Edinburgh or on circuit.[86] The presence of central judicial authorities, in other words, had a significant, negative impact on the number of executions. Scotland, therefore, stands as an example of how a relatively weak state with a small judicial establishment had difficulty guaranteeing due process in the great majority of cases. The contrast with the powerful French state could not be any clearer.

England

A very different situation from that in Scotland prevailed in its southern neighbour, England, where the country had a long tradition of judicial centralization. The English state, like the Scottish state, was not particularly strong by European standards, and the efforts of its Stuart kings to establish royal absolutism in the seventeenth century failed miserably. Nevertheless, England did have a long tradition of judicial centralization, the one respect in which the English state was stronger than any other in Europe. English judicial centralization had its origins in the establishment of the common law (a law for all English subjects) in the later Middle Ages. Royal judges of the three central common law courts at Westminster, appointed by the Crown, heard both civil and criminal cases at the county assizes – circuit courts over which they presided twice every year. The English tradition of legal central- ization had a significant bearing on the intensity of English witch-hunting. Although English courts tried a substantial number of witches, the conviction and execution rates were exceptionally low by continental European standards.

The strict prohibition of torture in England certainly helps to explain the low number of convictions, but even that feature of English witch-hunting can be related to the presence of central justices at almost all witchcraft trials. In an exceptional situation in 1645 during the English Civil War, when those justices failed to supervise the conduct of witchcraft prosecutions, the self- proclaimed witch-finders Matthew Hopkins and John Stearne succeeded in using forms of torture, mainly the *tormentum insomniae*, to extract confessions from suspected witches. Further evidence of the importance of central judges in preventing the use of torture comes from a comparison of the English situation with that of Scotland, which like England prohibited the use of torture unless the Privy Council had specifically authorized it in cases of treason. There is abundant evidence, however, that when Scottish witches were arrested many of them were illegally tortured to obtain confessions, thus giving Scotland the reputation for being more barbaric than England in its conduct of criminal procedure.[87]

Germany

The relationship between state-building and witch-hunting, especially with reference to judicial centralization, is most complex but at the same time most revealing in Germany, where about half of witchcraft prosecutions and executions took place. The complexity derives from the fact that during the period of witch-hunting there was no unified German state, such as was eventually established in the late nineteenth century. During the early modern period Germany consisted of more than 400 relatively autonomous territories of widely varying size, all of which were loosely included within the large Holy Roman Empire. Many of these small units were themselves states, and the larger units, such as the electorate of Brandenburg-Prussia and the duchy of Bavaria, were striving to become larger, wealthier and more powerful during the age of absolutism.

Compared with the large royal states in Europe, such as France, England and Scotland, the Holy Roman Empire was a highly decentralized political structure. The imperial *Reichstag* passed laws for all of the Emperor's subjects, but the extent to which any one of the German territories followed the law of the Empire and submitted to central control depended on a number of factors. The imperial cities were generally the most obedient, but even they manifested a strong streak of independence and in many ways were self-regulating. The autonomy of the German territories is most clearly evident in judicial affairs. Each territory had its own courts, and although these institutions enforced the imperial law codes to a greater or lesser extent, each had virtual autonomy over its own judicial life. There was no central judicial establishment to send judges on circuit or to supervise the conduct of local justice. There was a supreme imperial court, the *Reichskammergericht*, which sat in Speyer and heard cases on appeal, but there was no regular procedure for doing so.[88]

The decentralization of judicial life had profound effects on the prosecution of witches in Germany. Without effective control by imperial authorities, the judges and inquisitors of the smaller territories had enormous freedom to hunt witches as they wished. It should not surprise us that the largest witch-hunts took place within German territories; that the reports of the most barbarous tortures come from those same territories; and that the total number of executions for witchcraft within the Empire was greater than in all other areas combined. There are many reasons for the relatively high intensity of German witch-hunting, but the judicial situation must be considered the most important. The significance of these judicial factors becomes even more apparent when we realize that those jurisdictions that adhered strictly to the imperial code of criminal law, the *Carolina*, executed far fewer witches than those that blatantly ignored it.[89]

Once we focus our attention on the individual states within the Empire, however, the relationship between state-building and witch-hunting becomes more problematic. As mentioned above, some of the smaller German states were among the most zealous in prosecuting witches. In at least some of these jurisdictions witch-hunting served the clear political purpose of strengthening or legitimizing the ruler's authority and securing the obedience of the subjects.[90] In these smaller political units it was almost always the central courts of the duchies or the principalities, not the local courts that took the lead in prosecuting witches. There is not, however, a great inconsistency between this pattern and that which prevailed in the larger centralized states, since the central courts in these territories were for all practical purposes comparable in the scope of their jurisdiction to the local courts in the large royal states of Europe. Moreover, rulers of smaller German states were more likely to be aware of, and frightened by, the presence of witches in their midst.

The relationship between the size of the political units and the intensity of witch-hunting in Germany can be appreciated by comparing the intensity of the small ecclesiastical territories like Würzburg, Trier and Bamberg with the larger principalities like Bavaria in the south and Brandenburg-Prussia in the north. In those larger areas the prosecution of witches, while not minimal, was far more restrained than in the smaller prince-bishoprics. In Bavaria, for example, with a population of 1,400,000 in 1600, the number of witches executed was less than 1,000 during the entire early modern period.[91] One factor that kept this figure relatively low was the emergence of a faction in the central council that was reluctant to engage in witch-hunting. Such a faction was likely to emerge among people who were sufficiently removed from village tensions to view the charges against witches objectively.

Conclusion

On balance, therefore, the central judicial authorities of early modern European states did more to restrain the process of witch-hunting than to abet it. The real initiative in witch-hunting came from the localities, not the central government.[92] Almost all witches were initially apprehended by local officials, and in many cases they were tried by local tribunals. In the electorate of Trier, where witch-hunting took a terrible toll between 1589 to 1595, village committees actually seized the legal initiative from the council and started the hunt of their own volition.[93] The central authorities of the state usually became involved in witch-hunting at a subsequent stage of the judicial process, and sometimes not until sentence had been passed and submitted to them on appeal. Whenever central or higher courts became involved in the process, accused witches had a better chance of acquittal or a modification of their sentence than if their fate remained in the hands of local magistrates.

The fact that the highest courts of the state tended to treat witches with greater restraint than local judges and magistrates should not obscure the fact that the rise of the early modern European state still served as a necessary precondition of the great European witch-hunt.[94] Unless the state had acquired its immense judicial power, which was reflected in the adoption of inquisitorial procedure and which was turned against both traitors and witches with equally devastating effects, the hunt would never have taken place. It is no coincidence, therefore, that the great witch-hunt occurred during a period of extensive state-building throughout Europe.

At the same time, however, the European witch-hunt depended in a curious way on the failure of the late medieval and early modern state to realize its full potential. Most early modern European states – even those in which the rulers achieved absolute power – relied on local and regional authorities to prosecute crime and provide justice to the people. This delegation of state power meant that local courts conducted a large number of witchcraft prosecutions, and those courts were more likely than the superior courts to convict and execute witches. The growth of secular state power may have made the great European witch-hunt possible, but the ability of local courts to try and execute witches, sometimes with only the tacit approval of higher state authorities, explains why the number of executions for witchcraft was so high.

Notes

1. B. P. Levack, *Witch-hunting in Scotland: Law, Politics and Religion* (London, 2008): 16, 116, 179 n.2; Dupont-Bouchat, 'Répression', 106; Larner, *Enemies of God*, 114, 116, 119; Naess, 'Norway', 376. Remy interprets suicides as attempts to escape the Devil's powers; *Demonolatry*, 161.

2. W. Behringer, 'Lynching', in *Encyclopedia of Witchcraft*, III: 683; Soman, Witch-Hunting at Juniville', 15.

3. Henningsen, *Witches' Advocate*, 209. Levack, *Witch-Hunting in Scotland*, 145–91.

4. Baranowski, *Procesy Czarownic*, 178; J. Tazbir, 'Hexenprozesse in Polen', *Archiv für Reformationsgeschichte* 71 (1980): 299.

5. For a comprehensive study of witch-lynching both during and after the period of the witch trials see B. P. Levack, 'Witch Lynching: Past and Present', in *Swift to Wrath: Lynching in Global Historical Perspective*, ed. W. D. Carrigan and C. Waldrep (Charlottesville, 2013): 49–67. Soman suggests that lynchings were prevalent in France because the community could thereby avoid the cost of official justice. Soman, 'Parlement of Paris', 42–3.

6. For a brief discussion of the differences between Germanic and Roman forms see G. Bader, *Die Hexenprozesse in der Schweiz* (Affoltern, 1945): 11–12.

7. C. H. Lea, *The Ordeal*, ed. E. Peters (Philadelphia, 1973); J. Gaudemet, 'Les ordiales au moyen age: doctrine, législation et pratique canoniques', in *La Preuve* (Brussels, 1965): 99–135.

8. On this influence see B. Lenman and G. Parker, 'The State, the Community and the Criminal Law in Early Modern Europe', in *Crime and the Law*, ed. V. Gatrell, B. Lenman and G. Parker (London, 1980): 29–30.

9. On the growth of clerical opposition to the ordeal and the crucial role played by the papacy in suppressing it see R. Bartlett, *Trial by Fire and Water: The Medieval Judicial Ordeal* (Oxford, 1986): 70–102.

10. Some municipal jurisdictions, nevertheless, continued to use the ordeals into the seventeenth century. For the use of the hot water ordeal at Braunsberg in 1637 see Lea, *Materials*, III: 1234. Residents of some cities continued to clear their names by swearing to their innocence, but such instances were rare, and the courts accorded only secondary status to the older modes of proof. L. Stokes, *Demons of Urban Reform: Early European Witch Trials and Criminal Justice, 1430–1530* (Basingstoke, 2011): 84–7.

11. See J. Langbein, *Prosecuting Crime in the Renaissance* (Cambridge, MA, 1974): 130–1.

12. Some of the witchcraft cases tried in Schleswig-Holstein were initiated by private accusation, but the early modern accusatory process was not the same as that which was used in the Middle Ages, and it often followed the same course as an inquisitorial process. See D. Unverhau, 'Akkusationsprozess-Inquisitionsprozess: Indikatoren für die Intensität der Hexenverfolgung in Schleswig-Holstein?', in *Hexenprozesse: Deutsche und skandinavische Beitrage*, ed. C. Degn, H. Lehmann and D. Unverhau (Neumünster, 1983): 59–143, esp. 116.

13. On denunciation see Kramer and Sprenger, *Malleus Maleficarum*, 205–7; Bader, *Die Hexenprozesse in der Schweiz*, 15.

14. On the function of the fiscal see F. Merzbacher, *Die Hexenprozesse in Franken* (Munich, 1957): 78–80.
15. H. C. Lea, *Torture*, ed. E. Peters (Philadelphia, 1973): xiv.
16. Langbein, *Prosecuting Crime*, 130–1.
17. The English trial was, however, less adversarial than in the modern period. See J. Langbein, 'The Criminal Trial before the Lawyers', *University of Chicago Law Review* 45 (1978): 307–16.
18. See generally L. W. Levy, 'Accusatorial and Inquisitorial Systems of Criminal Procedure: The Beginnings', in *Freedom and Reform*, ed. H. Hyman and L. Levy (New York, 1967): 16–54.
19. For the weakening of the Scottish criminal jury in the late seventeenth century see I. D. Willock, *The Origins and Development of the Jury in Scotland* (Edinburgh, 1966): 218–21.
20. P. Sörlin, *'Wicked Arts': Witchcraft and Magic Trials in Southern Sweden, 1635–1754* (Leiden, 1999): 46–8; Ostling, *Between the Devil and the Host*, 91–2.
21. The resistance to the new procedures can be seen in the work of the eighteenth-century jurist M. Bodó, *Jurisprudentia criminalis secundum praxim et constitutiones Hungaricas* (Pozsony, 1751).
22. See Kieckhefer, *European Witch Trials*, 19.
23. See Cohn, *Europe's Inner Demons*, 215.
24. In Nuremberg, where a reception of Roman law led to the adoption of inquisitorial procedure in the late fourteenth century, torture was used regularly in criminal proceedings by end of the fifteenth century, and only after the publication of the *Carolina* did the courts begin to follow rules limiting its use. Stokes, *Demons of Urban Reform*, 90–9.
25. This requirement is known in Western jurisprudence as *corpus delicti*, which literally means 'body of a crime' and is defined as 'the fact of a crime having been committed'. The testimony of an accomplice does not qualify as corpus *delicti*.
26. See J. Langbein, *Torture and the Law of Proof* (Chicago, 1977): 14; M. Kunze, *Der Prozess Pappenheimer* (Ebelsbach, 1981): 216–22.
27. See Bodin, *De la Démonomanie des sorciers*, Book IV, ch. V; C. Larner, 'Crimen Exceptum?': The Crime of Witchcraft in Europe', in *Crime and the Law*, ed. V. A. C. Gatrell, B. Lenman and G. Parker (London, 1980): 49–74.
28. Langbein, *Torture*, 14.
29. For the discussion by Caesar Carena of this problem see Lea, *Materials*, II: 996.
30. Langbein, *Torture*, 15, 150.
31. Robbins, *Encyclopedia*, 256.
32. P. Carus, *The History of the Devil and the Idea of Evil* (New York, 1969): 331.
33. Oberman, *Masters of the Reformation*, 160–1.
34. *Newes from Scotland* (London, 1591): 18, 28.
35. Boguet, *An Examen of Witches*, 225, allows for three administrations of torture in such circumstances.
36. See Midelfort, *Witch Hunting*, 149.
37. For the failure of torture to produce convictions when it was applied by the Parlement of Paris see A. Soman, 'Trente procès de sorcellerie dans le Perche (1566–1624)', *L'Orne littéraire* 8 (1986): 44–5.
38. J. Tedeschi, 'Inquisitorial Law and the Witch', in *Early Modern European Witchcraft: Centres and Peripheries*, ed. B. Ankarloo and G. Henningsen (Oxford, 1990): 102–3.
39. See, for example, S. Clark, 'Protestant Demonology: Sin, Superstition and Society (c. 1520–c. 1630)', in *Early Modern European Witchcraft: Centres and Peripheries,*

ed. B. Ankarloo and G. Henningsen (Oxford, 1990): 49–50; Holmes, 'Popular Culture?', 92–3.

40. See Peters, *Magician, Witch and the Law*, 106.

41. Trevor-Roper, 'European Witch-Craze', 171, argues that the ideas of the clergy were extended to lay magistrates (but not to the 'independent laity') by the rather late date of 1600.

42. Kramer and Sprenger, *Malleus Maleficarum*, 194–205; A. Gari Lacruz, 'Variedad de competencias en el delito de brujería 1600–1650 en Aragón', in *La Inquisición española: Nueva visión, nueva horizontes*, ed. J. Perez Villanueva (Madrid, 1980): 319–21; Ginzburg, *The Night Battles*, 113–14.

43. See R. Kieckhefer, *The Repression of Heresy in Medieval Germany* (Philadelphia, 1980): 75–82.

44. G. Waite, *Heresy, Magic, and Witchcraft in Early Modern Europe* (Basingstoke, 2003): 36. The governor was Peter of Greyerz (Gruyères), and the trials were held at Boltigen in the Upper Simme Valley. A. Borst, *Medieval Worlds*, trans. E. Hansen (Chicago, 1992): 108–15.

45. The earliest of these secular laws was passed by the government of the town of Todi, which was in the hands of clerics, in 1426 against the casting of 'spells or any acts of witchcraft'. This ordinance was the basis of the prosecution of Matteuccia di Francesco two years later. Mormando, *Preacher's Demons*, 73.

46. The Polish legislative assembly, the *sejm*, was unusual in that it never defined witchcraft as a secular crime. A law of 1543 explicitly reserved jurisdiction over witchcraft to the ecclesiastical courts. See Ostling, *Between the Devil and the Host*, 47–8. Nevertheless the secular courts gradually acquired jurisdiction over the crime.

47. J. C. V. Johansen, 'Denmark: The Sociology of Accusations', in *Early Modern European Witchcraft: Centres and Peripheries*, ed. B. Ankaroo and G. Henningsen (Oxford, 1990): 341; Midelfort, *Witch Hunting*, 23; S. J. Fox, *Science and Justice: The Massachusetts Witchcraft Trials* (Baltimore, 1968): 37–43; Lea, *A History of the Inquisition of the Middle Ages*, III: 544. The English statute of 1604 declared it illegal to covenant with, entertain, feed, or reward any evil spirit. 1 Jac. I, c. 12.

48. On the problem of referring to the papal 'Inquisition' as an institution see Kieckhefer, *Repression of Heresy*, 3–8.

49. On the final loss of inquisitorial jurisdiction in Franche-Comté around 1600 see Monter, *Witchcraft in France and Switzerland*, 73.

50. See for example R. Houlbrooke, 'The Decline of Ecclesiastical Jurisdiction under the Tudors', in *Continuity and Change*, ed. R. O' Day and F. Heal (Leicester, 1976): 239–57.

51. For a classic case in England see the prosecution of the English cunning man John Walsh for magic in 1566. M. Gibson (ed.), *Witchcraft and Society in Early Modern England and America, 1550–1750* (Ithaca, NY, 2001): 19–24.

52. Lea, *Materials*, III: 1263.

53. Baranowski, *Procesy Czarownic*, 180.

54. Kieckhefer, *European Witch Trials*, 21–2.

55. Henningsen, *Witches' Advocate*, 387–8.

56. As the hunt developed, however, the clergy became less enthusiastic. Increase Mather and other members of the Massachusetts clergy wrote a letter urging the exercise of great caution in proceeding against witches. See Increase Mather, *Cases of Conscience concerning Evil Spirits Impersonating Men* (Boston, 1693); Boyer and Nissenbaum, *Salem Possessed*, 9–10.

57. Larner, *Enemies of God*, 72.

58. Muchembled, 'Witches of the Cambrésis', 259–60, 266–7. In Lorraine, however, the local priests generally did not become involved in the trials. See Briggs, *Communities of Belief*, 71–2.
59. Rothkrug, 'Religious Practices', 104–5.
60. The prince-bishop of Bamberg used a secular council staffed by doctors of civil law to prosecute witches in his diocese. Sebald, *Witchcraft*, 38–9.
61. Midelfort, *Witch Hunting*, 98, 143; Robbins, *Encyclopedia*, 35.
62. Witches were treated more severely than heretics, since they were usually executed after the first offence. See Lea, *Inquisition*, III: 515.
63. John 15:16.
64. The Danish witchcraft ordinance of 1617 specified that only those witches convicted of making a pact with the Devil should be burned. Johansen, 'Denmark', 341.
65. Midelfort, *Witch Hunting*, 99.
66. F. Volk, *Hexen in der Landvogtei Ortenau und der Reichsstadt Offenburg* (Lahr, 1882): 27. In 1628 four witches had been burned alive.
67. B. Ankarloo, 'Sweden: The Mass Burnings (1668–76)', in *Early Modern European Witchcraft: Centres and Peripheries*, ed. B. Ankarloo and G. Henningsen (Oxford, 1990): 295.
68. Schormann, *Hexenprozesse in Nordwestdeutschland*, 19, 24, 30–1, 34.
69. See the table in Monter, *Witchcraft in France and Switzerland*, 49.
70. Ibid., 51, 66.
71. Boguet, *An Examen of Witches*, 226.
72. Kieckhefer, *Repression of Heresy*, 76–8.
73. R. J. W. Evans, *The Making of the Habsburg Monarchy, 1550–1700* (Oxford, 1979): 411–12.
74. It is possible that the judges at Salem intended to execute all the confessing witches after they had provided evidence regarding the crimes of others. See P. Boyer and S. Nissenbaum (eds), *Salem Village Witchcraft: A Documentary Record of Local Conflict in Colonial New England* (Belmont, 1972), I: Introduction.
75. Henningsen, *Witches' Advocate*, 143–80, 397.
76. Levack, *Witch-Hunting in Scotland*, 34–41.
77. Johansen, 'Denmark', 341, 345–7; Henningsen, *Witches' Advocate*, 18. A period of intense witch-hunting followed the promulgation of the ordinance.
78. R. S. Walinski-Kiehl, 'Godly States: Confessional Conflict and Witch-Hunting in Early Modern Germany', *Mentalité-Mentalities* 5 (1988): 13–24; M. Kunze, *Highroad to the Stake: A Tale of Witchcraft*, tr. William E. Yuill (Chicago, 1987).
79. Gábor Klaniczay, 'Witch-Hunting in Hungary: Social or Cultural Tensions?', *Acta Ethnographica* 37 (1991–2): 75.
80. S. Clark, *Thinking with Demons: The Idea of Witchcraft in Early Modern Europe* (Oxford, 1997): 552–5, 670–4.
81. This was particularly true for Finland. See A. Heikkinen, *Paholaisen Liittolaiset* (Helsinki, 1969): 381.
82. See for example Evans, *Habsburg Monarchy*, 410. On the relationship between witch-hunting and state-building in Germany and elsewhere see J. Dillinger, 'Politics, State-Building and Witch-Hunting', in *The Oxford Handbook of Witchcraft in Early Modern Europe and Colonial America*, ed. B. P. Levack (Oxford, 2013): 528–47.
83. R. Mandrou, *Magistrats et sorcieres en France au XVII siècle* (Paris, 1968); Soman, 'Parlement of Paris'. For a discussion of the unregulated situation before 1588, see Soman, 'Witch Lynching at Juniville'.
84. Soman, 'Parlement of Paris', 36.
85. Larner, *Enemies of God*, 71.

86. C. Larner, C. H. Lee and H. V. McLachlan, *Source-Book of Scottish Witchcraft* (Glasgow, 1977): 237, table 2 gives the execution rates as 57 per cent for the Justicary Court, 16 per cent for the circuit courts, and 91 per cent for the local commissions. Goodare *et al.*, *Survey of Scottish Witchcraft*, gives 59 per cent for the Justiciary Court and 75 per cent for local commissions, but does not offer a figure for the circuit courts, choosing to group those executions with those sentenced by justice deputes assigned to a particular area. Only the figures for the Justiciary Court can be considered reliable, since the outcomes of more than half of trials in that court are known (102 out of 178 trials). By contrast, the outcomes of only 133 of the 1,936 trials by local commissioners are known. The figures for the circuit courts are exceptionally low, even when compared to the comparable figures for England, because most of those trials took place in the late seventeenth century as the witch-hunt was coming to an end.

87. B. P. Levack, 'Judicial Torture in Scotland during the Age of Mackenzie', in *The Stair Society Miscellany IV*, ed. H. L. MacQueen (Edinburgh, 2002): 185–98.

88. On the *Reichskammergericht* see Merzbacher, *Hexenprozesse*, 63–4; Midelfort, *Witch Hunting*, 114.

89. Monter, *Witchcraft in France and Switzerland*, 106.

90. On the political exploitation of witch-hunting in such territories see R. Voltmer, 'Hexenprozesse und Hochgerichte: zur herrschaftlich-politischen Nutzung und Instrumentalisierung von Hexenverfolgungen', in *Hexenprozesse und Gerichtspraxis*, ed. H. Eiden and R. Voltmer (Trier, 2002): 475–525.

91. Behringer, *Witchcraft Persecutions in Bavaria*, 35. The figure includes only documented executions. This number was about half as many executions per capita as in Scotland.

92. Henningsen, *Witches' Advocate*, 18; Trevor-Roper, 'Witch-Craze', 114; Briggs, *Communities of Belief*, 14; Naess, 'Norway', 379–80. On the lack of central state involvement in two German territories until the state was powerful enough to control the local population, see J. Dillinger, *'Evil People': A Comparative Study of Witch Hunts in Swabian Austria and the Electorate of Trier*, trans. L. Stokes (Charlottesville, 2009): chapters 1 and 6.

93. W. Rummel, *Bauern, Herren und Hexen: Studien zur Sozialgeschichte sponheimischer und kurtrierischer Hexenprozesse, 1574–1664* (Göttingen, 1991).

94. Larner, *Witchcraft and Religion*, 89, considers the rise of nation-states to be one of the 'crucial factors' in accounting for the rise of witch-hunting.

4

THE IMPACT OF
THE REFORMATION

The construction of the cumulative concept of witchcraft and the various legal developments described in the last chapter made the European witch-hunt of the fifteenth, sixteenth and seventeenth centuries possible. If these intellectual and legal developments had not occurred, then the hunt would not have taken place, at least not in the form and magnitude that it did. These preconditions do not, however, provide a complete causal explanation of the hunt. They were, in other words, necessary but not sufficient causes of the process that claimed the lives of thousands of Europeans. In order to achieve a fuller understanding of the hunt we must explore the religious, social and economic conditions that prevailed in early modern Europe. These conditions created an environment in which the hunting of witches was not merely possible but was likely to occur. They encouraged people to believe in witchcraft, created tensions that often found expression in witchcraft accusations, and strengthened the determination of both ruling elites and common folk to prosecute individuals for this crime. These conditions, therefore, occupy a second level of causation of the European witch-hunt. They were neither necessary preconditions nor sufficient causes, but they did intensify the process of witch-hunting. They also help to explain why intense witch-hunting occurred when it did.

The purpose of this chapter is to explore the ways in which the profound religious developments that took place in early modern Europe encouraged the growth of witch-hunting. The most important of these changes was the Reformation, the movement that shattered the ostensible unity of medieval Christendom. The main objective of the early Protestant reformers, such as Martin Luther, Jean Calvin, Huldreich Zwingli and Martin Bucer, was to restore the Church to its early Christian purity. In so doing, they denied the efficacy of indulgences, redefined the function of the sacraments, eliminated or drastically altered the Roman Catholic Mass, and changed the role of the clergy. They proclaimed the autonomy of the individual conscience and posited a direct relationship between a person and God, removing many of the clerical and angelic intermediaries that medieval Catholicism had

100

established between them. They developed the idea that each believer was a priest who by reading the Bible could acquire the faith that alone could bring him salvation. The incompatibility of these ideas with the doctrines of the Roman Catholic Church, the failure of that Church to reform itself, and the inability of the reformers to find scriptural support for papal authority led them to break with Rome and to establish independent Protestant churches. Millions of Europeans, in many cases encouraged by the establishment of Protestant state churches, left the Roman fold. Protestantism became the dominant religion in many parts of Germany, Switzerland and the Low Countries; in England, Scotland and the Scandinavian kingdoms; and in certain areas of France, Hungary and Poland.

The success of the Protestant Reformation encouraged the growth of a reform movement within Catholicism. This movement, which we refer to as the Counter-Reformation or Catholic Reformation, met a long-standing demand by Catholic clerics and laymen to bring about reform without destroying the structure of the Church. It cannot, therefore, be viewed simply as a negative response to the rise of Protestantism; indeed, its origins can be traced to the pre-Reformation period. The main goals of the Catholic reformers were to eliminate corruption within the Church, educate the clergy, inspire and strengthen the faith of the laity, and reclaim the allegiance of those individuals and communities that had been lost to Protestantism. The Counter-Reformation achieved a significant measure of success. Under the leadership of the papacy, the Church introduced a series of administrative and liturgical changes, many of which were authorized by the Council of Trent (1545–7, 1551–2, 1562–3). Missionaries from the newly formed Society of Jesus and other religious orders helped to reconvert Protestants in many parts of Europe, while ecclesiastical courts maintained theological orthodoxy and moral propriety in nominally Catholic areas. Military forces from Catholic countries waged war against Protestants in a number of internal and international conflicts, the most significant of which were the civil wars in France in the late sixteenth century and the Thirty Years War in the early seventeenth century. As a result of all this activity, parts of Germany, Austria, Bohemia, Poland, Hungary and the Low Countries returned to the Catholic fold, while other areas remained Protestant.

The period during which all of this reforming activity and conflict took place, the age of the Reformation, spanned the years 1520–1650. Since these years include the period when witch-hunting was most intense, some historians have claimed that the Reformation served as the mainspring of the entire European witch-hunt. It is certainly true that in some places the forces unleashed by the Reformation and Counter-Reformation did serve as the main catalyst to witch-hunting. It would be unwise, however, to attribute the entire European witch-hunt to these religious developments, since witch-hunting began almost one hundred years before Luther nailed his ninety-five theses to the castle church at Wittenberg. During the early years of the Reformation, moreover, from 1520 to 1560, there were relatively few witchcraft prosecutions in Europe, so it is difficult to establish a direct, causal connection between the two developments. And, at the other end of the European witch-hunt, in the first two decades of the eighteenth century, when hundreds of witches were still being prosecuted in Eastern Europe, it is difficult to speak of either the Reformation or the Counter-Reformation as a contemporary reality. It is more reasonable to claim, therefore, that the Reformation and Counter-Reformation served to intensify the process of witch-hunting, and perhaps helped the prosecutions spread from place to place.[1]

The question of course is exactly *how* the Reformation contributed to the growth of witch-hunting. In answering this question it is important that we study the effects of both the Protestant and the Catholic reformations. The main reason for adopting this comprehensive approach is that extensive witch-hunting took place in both Protestant and Catholic lands. Comparisons between the numbers of witches executed by Catholic and Protestant authorities can easily obscure this fundamental fact. It may be true that Catholics executed more witches in southwestern Germany than did Protestants, just as the opposite may be true in western Switzerland.[2] It may also be true that there are religious explanations for these discrepancies. The important consideration, however, is that large witch-hunts – significantly larger than any that had occurred before 1500 – took place in *all* of these areas during the Reformation era. The mere fact, moreover, that Protestants took the lead in prosecuting witches in some areas while Catholics did so in others recommends that we look at the effects of both reformations. As it is, the two reformations – which were to some extent different manifestations of the same general, European-wide religious revival – had many similar effects on witch-hunting.[3] Protestant and Catholic reformers did, after all, share many of the same witch beliefs and exhibited a similar desire to extirpate witchcraft.[4]

Approaching the subject in this broad way, we shall pursue three separate lines of enquiry. First, we shall study those changes in religious attitudes and practices during the age of the Reformation that encouraged the growth and persistence of witch-hunting. Some of these changes were more readily apparent in Protestant than in Catholic circles for the simple reason that the Protestant Reformation was more radical than the Catholic, but there is sufficient evidence that the changes were not confined to Protestant areas. Second, we shall explore the ways in which religious conflict between Protestantism and Catholicism, and to a lesser extent between the different denominations of Protestantism, inspired witchcraft prosecutions and executions. Finally, we shall see how the Reformation, while encouraging witchcraft prosecutions in various ways, also contributed in the long run to its decline.

The new religious outlook

The fear of the Devil

During the age of the Reformation, Europeans increased their awareness of the Devil's presence in the world and became more determined to wage war against him. One of the main sources of this heightened consciousness of, and militancy against, Satan was the thinking of the great Protestant reformers, Martin Luther and Jean Calvin. These men did not introduce a new and original conception of the Devil; their beliefs in who the Devil was and what powers he possessed were essentially the same as those of late medieval Catholic demonologists. This agreement with the Catholics is in itself somewhat perplexing. Since the reformers challenged so many other aspects of medieval Catholicism, and since they were so critical of scholastic theology, one assumes that they would have developed a distinctly Protestant demonology. Instead they merely adopted the traditional, late medieval view, modifying it only in some respects and placing it on a firmer scriptural foundation.

Although the great reformers did little to change traditional Catholic demonology, they did tend to emphasize the presence of the Devil in the world and exhibit a more profound fear of him. Martin Luther, who reported having active physical bouts with Satan, attributed to him a position in the world that borders on dualist heresy. 'We are all subject to the Devil, both in body and goods', wrote Luther, 'and we be strangers in this world, whereof he is the prince and god'. The Devil, according to Luther, 'liveth, yea and reigneth throughout the whole world'. The danger that Satan presented to a person was both physical and spiritual. Not only did he 'rehearseth sorcery among works of the flesh', but he deceived the mind with wicked opinions.[5] A number of late medieval writers had attributed similar intentions to Satan, but very few of them had described demonic power as being so pervasive. Everyone, even the most pious individual, could be deceived and ensnared by the cunning treachery of Satan. Luther was confident that the Kingdom of Christ would ultimately prevail over the forces of darkness, but the struggle against him would be difficult and continuous, and the individual was always vulnerable to deception and harm.[6]

Jean Calvin was no less preoccupied with diabolical power in the world and no less committed to counteracting it. For him the power of Satan was so strong and pervasive that the true Christian saint had to engage in an 'unceasing struggle against him'.[7] The militancy of Calvinism, which often found expression in actual physical battle, had its basis in the continuous campaign that the saint was enjoined to conduct against the Devil. Like Luther, Calvin was completely confident that the Devil would fail in his attempt to triumph over the forces of good. For him, no less than for scholastic theologians, the Devil operated only with the permission of God, whose creature he was. But the number of the Devil's earthly followers was so great that the saint could not afford to relax his or her efforts.[8]

Neither Luther nor Calvin was preoccupied with witchcraft as such. Although Luther said on one occasion that all witches were the Devil's whores and on another that they should all be burned, his concern was with any form of idolatry, which he considered to be a bewitching of God, rather than the traditional forms that witchcraft took.[9] Indeed, he believed that the witchcraft of the sorcerer was not as common as it had been in the past, before the truth of the Gospel had been revealed. Calvin said even less than Luther about witchcraft per se. On the basis of Exodus 22:18 he insisted that witches 'must be slain', but witchcraft was hardly of paramount importance to him.[10] Nevertheless, the preoccupation that both reformers had with satanic power made many of their followers more determined to take action against witches whenever their presence became apparent. The Lutheran and Calvinist concern with Satan also encouraged an emphasis on the heretical rather than the magical aspects of witchcraft, which in turn inspired a greater determination to extirpate it.

The attitudes of reformers such as Luther and Calvin towards demonic power were capable of having widespread influence because they and their disciples founded an active, preaching ministry, capable of reaching large numbers of people. The impact of the reformers must be measured not simply by the circulation of their published works but by the dissemination of their ideas from the pulpit. Protestants, owing mainly to their reliance upon the Bible as the source of religious truth, placed great emphasis on successful preaching. From the pulpit people of all social classes, not just a small literate elite, acquired, among other things, the sense of the immediacy of diabolical power that was so apparent in the writings of Luther and Calvin. This awareness and fear of the Devil's work in this world might not have stimulated many initial accusations of witchcraft; these continued to originate in peasant fears of *maleficium*. But the heightened consciousness of diabolical activity certainly made early modern European communities – and not just the members of the ruling elite – more eager to prosecute these witches as agents of the Devil whenever accusations of *maleficium* surfaced.

It was not just in Protestant circles that one detects a greater preoccupation with demonic power in the sixteenth and seventeenth centuries. To many Catholic reformers the Devil became just as frightening and omnipresent as he was to Lutherans and Calvinists. Indeed, the rise of Protestantism itself appeared to many Catholics to be the work of Satan, making them more aware of his capacity for bringing evil of all types into the world. Peter Canisius, the Jesuit missionary, actually mentioned Satan more often than Christ in the catechism he prepared.[11] Catholic priests often matched their Protestant colleagues in convincing their parishioners of Satan's omnipresence and in raising their fears of him.[12] They could also be equally effective in encouraging them to campaign ceaselessly against him. In both Catholic and Protestant quarters there arose a zealous commitment, sometimes strengthened by millenarian beliefs, to purify the world by declaring war against Satan. The war was to be waged both internally, by resisting temptation, and externally, by prosecuting witches and heretics.[13]

Personal sanctity, guilt and witchcraft

A second effect of the Reformation on witchcraft arose from the emphasis that both Protestant and Catholic reformers placed on personal piety and sanctity. One of the most salient characteristics of the Reformation era was the evangelical appeal of Protestant and Catholic preachers for all Christians, including the laity, to lead an exemplary moral life and to be responsible for their own salvation. Instead of merely encouraging conformity to certain standards of religious observance (such as attending church), the reformers of the sixteenth and seventeenth centuries instructed the people to lead a more demanding, morally rigorous life. This type of exhortation, which reflected the current preoccupation with the danger of diabolical temptation, helped to Christianize Europe in an unprecedented way. All people, including those in backward, rural areas, were exhorted to become active, morally conscious Christians. The process began with the clergy themselves, whose moral conduct was in many cases not much better than that of their parishioners, and then was spread, through them, to the laity.[14]

Among Calvinists there was a special premium placed upon personal sanctity because of their strong belief in predestination. If God had predetermined that certain persons would be saved and others would be damned, then it was especially important that one should lead a blameless personal life, for such holiness could easily be construed as a sign of election. Once assured that they were numbered among the elect, moreover, Calvinists would strive to achieve moral perfection, both to confirm their status as saints (which was always a source of at least residual doubt) and to thank God for their gift of salvation. The Calvinists' systematic, sustained search for salvation contributed to the development of a new personality type, a highly motivated, driven person whose moral energy could be diverted into political and economic activity.

The new emphasis on personal piety and the intense pursuit of salvation took a heavy psychological toll, for it brought with it a deep sense of sin. Whenever conscientious people sinned, whenever they failed to adhere to the demanding standards of behaviour that were being so loudly proclaimed, or whenever they experienced doubts about their own sanctity, they had to deal with what could be profound feelings of guilt and moral unworthiness. These feelings were especially strong among Calvinists who faced the frightening prospect that they were not among the elect, but no morally conscious Christian, Protestant or Catholic, could avoid such thoughts completely. When people experienced this type of guilt, they naturally sought to relieve it in any way possible, and one of the methods frequently employed was to transfer it to another person. Even the availability of auricular confession to Catholics and Anglicans did not prevent this process of projection from taking place. And the ideal object of such projection was the witch, a person who personified evil as it was defined at the time. In this indirect way the witch gave both the individual and the community the opportunity to gain reassurance regarding their own moral worth.

The relief of guilt through projection on to another person could easily lead to witchcraft accusations and prosecutions. Alan Macfarlane has shown, for example, that in sixteenth- and seventeenth-century England, many accusations arose when individuals refused to provide economic assistance to people who needed it and who came to one's door asking for it. In denying this aid, which both Catholic and Protestant moral teaching enjoined, the person naturally felt guilty, but by depicting the unaided person as a witch and therefore as a moral aggressor unworthy of support, he could rid himself of the guilt that he was experiencing. In a very real sense the guilty neighbour projected his guilt onto the witch.[15]

Another example of this type of projection comes from the Catholic Low Countries, where the Christianization of the populace, especially the rural populace, took place as part of the Counter-Reformation. In studying witch-hunts in the region of the Cambrésis, Robert Muchembled has observed that the local parish priests, who were the agents of this process, often found themselves backsliding in their adherence to the recently proclaimed stricter rules regarding moral conduct. In the case of the priests, their offence was often sexual incontinence. When the priests experienced the deep sense of moral guilt and weakness, they often projected their guilt on to witches, in whose apprehension and interrogation they took an active part. Since the witches were usually women, who in a certain sense served as symbols of sexuality, the projection was fairly clear. In proceeding against the witches, moreover, the priests did not act alone but in conjunction with many other members of the community, to whom the priests had been transmitting the instructional message of reformed Catholicism. The witches therefore became not only the objects of the priests' projected guilt but also 'expiatory victims' of an entire community that was striving to establish a new moral order.[16]

In the case of Salem, Massachusetts, there is further evidence of projected guilt in witchcraft accusations. Paul Boyer and Stephen Nissenbaum have shown that the people who made accusations against witches in Salem village clung desperately to a strict, Puritan set of social and moral values, while those who were accused subscribed to a new, secular, commercial ethic. The situation was, therefore, somewhat different from that which prevailed in the county of Essex, England, where the accusers appeared to be the ones affected by the values of a commercial society and the witches acted as the guardians of the old morality. Nevertheless, the accusers at Salem were not that different from their English counterparts, since they too were lured by the materialism of the new society and experienced guilt for such acquisitiveness. The witchcraft accusations that they made, therefore, were not only attempts to preserve the moral fabric of a model Christian community against corrupting influences, but also projections of their own guilt on to others. Once again, of course, the process was collective as well as individual.[17]

The religiously inspired guilt that lay at the root of many witchcraft prosecutions was not always projected. Sometimes witches themselves manifested a deep sense of sin and guilt. This was most obvious among those individuals who considered themselves to be witches or gradually came to that belief, but even when accused witches did not reach such a conclusion they sometimes seemed to be very much aware of their sinful enmity towards others. William Monter has claimed that in the Jura region witches were dominated by such feelings, so much so that one can draw a clear contrast between the morally superior English witch, whose guilt was projected onto her by others and whose act of revenge can in a certain sense be justified, and the Jura witch, whose guilt was internal and whose acts of vengeance were gratuitous.[18]

The attack upon superstition, paganism and magic

The Christianization of the European populace involved not only a demand that all Christians should lead exemplary lives but also that they learn the elements of the true Christian faith and the proper forms of worship. The process was, in other words, doctrinal and liturgical as well as moral, and the preaching and catechetical instruction of the reformed clergy served all of these related objectives. One of the main purposes of this instruction was to purify the faith by eradicating superstitious beliefs and practices, eliminating vestiges of paganism, and suppressing magic (the rival of true religion) in all its forms. The activities that came under attack included simple popular blessings and exorcisms that were modelled on medieval liturgical practice, the use of holy water, charms and amulets to protect oneself and one's possessions from evil power, and the practice of healing, divination and love magic, all of which could involve incantations and the recitation of prayers.[19]

The nature of this campaign against popular superstition and magic can be seen in a large body of demonological writings by Protestant pastors, most of which originated as sermons to their congregations. Unlike the theologians and jurists who wrote learned treatises on witchcraft and demonology, these pastors were just as concerned with charms, divination and healing as they were with maleficent witchcraft. Indeed, English Protestant writers like SOURCE BOOK William Perkins considered 'good witches' even more dangerous than their maleficent counterparts.[20] Since these Protestant pastors wished to alert their congregations to the moral and spiritual implications of magic and witchcraft, they emphasized the commerce with demons that all such activities involved, rather than the actual effects of magical actions. As good Protestants, they also drew on the Bible, especially the books of the Old Testament, to establish the different types of 'witchcraft' they were condemning.[21]

The determination of Protestant clergy to wipe out superstitious popular practices and thereby purify the faith finds its counterpart in the Catholic clergy of the Counter-Reformation, especially those who served as inquisitors in Mediterranean lands. Recognizing that the external practices reflected inner beliefs, inquisitors worked with local clergy to eradicate superstition and error and to standardize all devotional practices. Catholic reformers obviously did not label the official liturgy of the medieval Church as magical in the way that Protestants did, but they did try to eliminate many of the prayers, blessings and practices that had derived from that liturgy, as well as the various forms of white magic that were in popular use, especially healing and love magic.[22]

The campaign of reformers against these various forms of superstition and white magic led to an increase in witchcraft prosecutions in two very different ways. First, those individuals whom Protestant and Catholic reformers identified as practitioners of white witchcraft could easily incur the suspicion of having also engaged in maleficent witchcraft. It is true that white magicians and those guilty of superstitious practices were generally treated more leniently than maleficent witches, but that did not prevent the charges against white witches from being rewritten to include harmful deeds. Indeed, it was not uncommon for healers to be charged with maleficent witchcraft, since it was widely believed that those who could cure could also harm.[23] Even when the two types of charges were kept fairly distinct, the campaign against magic in general led to an increase in witchcraft prosecutions. In the 1580s, for example, the Roman Inquisition, acting in the spirit of the Counter-Reformation, turned its attention increasingly to cases of superstition, magic and sorcery. It prosecuted numerous cases of divination, love magic, therapeutic magic and spells, and at the same time it tried people for witchcraft.[24]

The second way in which the attack upon superstition and magic contributed to the intensification of witch-hunting was that it deprived the victims of sorcery of some of the weapons they customarily used to protect themselves from witches. Those who felt threatened or harmed by a witch, at least in Protestant lands, could no longer make the sign of the cross, sprinkle holy water on their houses, hang up medals of the saints, or perform many of the protective rituals that Europeans had traditionally employed when threatened with diabolical power. It is true that Protestant reformers never completely succeeded in eliminating popular forms of counter-magic, but they did manage to discourage their use in many godly communities. When that happened, the victims of witchcraft could easily have been led to the conclusion that the only way to deal with witches was to take legal action against them, thus leading to an increase in the number of prosecutions.[25]

It is interesting to note that both Protestants and Catholics continued to take action against various forms of white magic and superstition long after trials of maleficent witchcraft had ended. These prosecutions took place only in ecclesiastical courts, and they never resulted in executions, but they did proceed on the assumption that the accused had engaged in a forbidden relationship with the Devil. Thus in the Netherlands, which ended its trials for witchcraft in the early seventeenth century, trials for magic continued well into the eighteenth century.[26] The same was true in Scotland, where Presbyterian courts took action against 'charming' many years after the last witch had been executed. In 1728, for example, the synod of Merse and Teviotdale warned those within its jurisdiction that a particular type of charming known as 'scoring the brow', which was done when people imagined that they or their relatives had been 'ill done', was 'justly reckoned a sort and degree of witchcraft, not to be tolerated in a Reformed land'. It was also observed that such scorings, since they involved the 'effusion of human blood, may be called sacrifices to the Devil'.[27] In Catholic Spain and Italy the Inquisition continued to prosecute people for various forms of magic and superstition throughout the eighteenth century on the grounds that such practices involved either the adoration of the Devil or the abuse of the sacraments and thus were classified as 'manifest heresy'.

Witchcraft and the godly state

Another effect of the Reformation on witchcraft prosecutions was evident in the legislative process itself. As mentioned above, the entire process of religious reform was characterized by a zealous concern for purifying society and promoting individual morality. Preaching and catechetical training were the main methods used to achieve these ends, but reformers did not hesitate to use the legislative power of the state to facilitate the process. One sign of this new tactic was the passage of a considerable amount of legislation against moral offences. These crimes traditionally had been the exclusive preserve of the ecclesiastical courts, but the general decline of ecclesiastical jurisdiction, especially in Protestant countries, encouraged secular authorities to use the legislative and judicial authority of the state to achieve the same ends. Witchcraft was just one of the moral offences that came under attack; secular authorities also passed laws against sodomy, fornication, prostitution and adultery. But for our purposes it is significant that many of the laws against witchcraft, which as mentioned above constitute one of the main preconditions of the European witch-hunt, originated in a mentality that the Reformation helped to breed. This same mentality also found expression in a new emphasis on the responsibility of the secular magistrate to prosecute moral offences more determinedly. The end product of all this zeal was the creation of the godly state, a secular institution that assumed the obligation to preserve the moral purity of society. To some extent the medieval state had pursued this objective, especially in dealing with heresy, but the strength of the Church as an independent institution had made it unnecessary for the state to devote its energies to such a task. In the age of the Reformation, however, the state, often acting under clerical pressure, became a guardian of individual morality. The change was most evident in Scotland, where the clergy applied a number of pressures on the state to realize its new mission; in New England, where the clergy exercised exceptionally strong influence in civil government; and in Sweden, where the government took the advice of the clergy in deciding how to handle infractions of the Mosaic law. In all these areas civil authorities authorized and conducted large witch-hunts.[28]

The goal of establishing a godly state was not restricted to Protestant polities. Catholic rulers also pursued the same lofty ideal, and when they did, their efforts often found expression in witch-hunting. The clearest example occurred in German principalities governed by prince-bishops, rulers who epitomized the intersection of secular and clerical power. Some of the most intense witch-hunts in all of Europe took place in German principalities where bishops or abbots, using their secular power as rulers of these ecclesiastical territories, pursued witches in an effort to purify society as well as to promote their own image as the true defenders of Christian values. Thus small Catholic territories like Ellwangen, the site of a ferocious witch-hunt in 1611, and the larger prince-bishoprics of Würzburg and Eichstätt, became the Catholic counterparts of Protestant states that used campaigns against witches to SOURCE BOOK realize the ideal of a moral, devout Christian community.[29]

The Bible and witchcraft

This brief survey of the different ways in which the Reformation contributed to witch-hunting would not be complete without mentioning the effect of Protestant biblicism on the process. The Protestant Reformation not only established the Bible as the sole source of religious truth but also led to its translation into every major European language. At the same time, there was a new insistence upon the literal interpretation of those scriptures. The net effect of all this was that as the Reformation spread, increasingly large numbers of Europeans were able to read the Bible and to take those passages that refer to witchcraft literally. Of prime importance among those was Exodus 22:18, 'Thou shalt not suffer a witch to live'. It did not matter that the original Hebrew word translated as 'witch' in this passage meant a poisoner or 'someone who works in darkness and mutters things' rather than a sorcerer who makes a pact with the Devil and worships him. In this regard the efforts of scholars like Erasmus and Johann Weyer to prove that the Bible had little to say about sixteenth-century witchcraft fell on deaf ears.[30] Nor did it matter that some theologians could not accept the injunction as positive law, since Christ had declared that the old Mosaic law was annulled.[31] The important consideration is that the word was translated as 'witch' or its equivalent in all western European languages and that preachers and judges used the text to sanction an uncompromising campaign against witches.

'We have here', claimed Reverend James Hutchison of Killallan in Scotland in a sermon preached on this text, 'a precept of the law of God in reference to a certain sort of malefactor to be found within the visible church'.[32]

David Meder, the pastor of Nebra in Thuringia, gave no fewer than eight sermons on Exodus 22:18 in order to encourage secular magistrates to take action against witches.[33] Jean Bodin, the Catholic French judge and demonologist who was deeply attracted to Judaism, appealed to the text of Exodus in calling for the vigorous prosecution of witches in 1580.[34] The Bible also served to corroborate many people's belief in the reality of witchcraft, even in the late eighteenth century, when the belief in witchcraft was highly unfashionable in most intellectual circles. In 1768 John Wesley, the founder of Methodism, wrote that 'the giving up of witchcraft is, in effect, the giving up of the Bible'.[35] The celebrated English jurist, William Blackstone, writing at about the same time as Wesley, claimed no less credulously, 'To deny the possibility, nay, actual existence of witchcraft and sorcery is at once flatly to contradict the revealed word of God'.[36] The Hungarian Palatine Lajos Batthyány, also a contemporary of Blackstone, protested against Empress Maria Theresa's recently announced policy of leniency towards witches on the grounds that the Bible confirmed the existence of witches.[37] In 1760 the Danish jurist C. D. Hedegaard claimed that when one believes in scripture or the revealed word of God, the reality of sorcery cannot be denied.[38]

A different biblical inspiration to witch-hunting came from Revelation, the last book of the New Testament revealed to John of Patmos in the first century CE. Revelation consists of a description of the war in Heaven that drove the rebel angels into Hell and a prophecy of the apocalypse, the tumultuous events marking the end of the world that would be preceded by the appearance of the Antichrist, the Second Coming of Jesus Christ, the last Judgement, the conversion of the Jews, and the rapture of the saints into Heaven. Revelation has had a profound effect on the history of Christianity and has given rise to many movements proclaiming the imminence of Christ's coming and the belief it would usher in the millennium – a thousand-year period before the ascent into heaven in which Christ would rule with His saints on earth. Ever since the period of Christian antiquity, many theologians, including St Augustine, have interpreted Revelation in metaphorical terms, but most Protestants at the time of the Reformation took it literally. Many of them expected that the final battle in the cosmic struggle between God and the Devil was about to take place. During that struggle the faith of true Christians would be sorely tested.

Apocalyptic thought, whether millenarian or not, provided an inspiration to witch-hunting. Protestant preachers and demonologists often interpreted the *maleficia* of witches, and especially instances of demonic possession (which were often attributed to witchcraft), as signs that the Devil was engaged in his final attack on Christianity and the world was experiencing its last days.[39] In such circumstances the zealous Christian was expected to cleanse the world of these diabolical contaminants by prosecuting witches. This link between apocalyptic thought and witch-hunting was especially apparent in England and New England. In particular, it served as an inspiration to the witch-hunt conducted by Matthew Hopkins and John Stearne in the heavily Puritan county of Essex in 1645.[40] It played an even larger part in colonial Massachusetts. In 1689 the Puritan minister and demonologist Cotton Mather delivered an apocalyptic sermon on the text of Revelation 12:12 that served as a commentary on the possession of the Goodwin children in Boston the previous year, for which an Irish laundress had been executed for witchcraft.[41] That sermon also prepared the ground for the cases of apparent possession and witchcraft that erupted at Salem in 1692. The link between apocalyptic thought and witch-hunting could not have been made clearer.

SOURCE BOOK

Religious conflict

The Reformation and the Counter-Reformation not only changed many aspects of the religious outlook of both Protestants and Catholics but also led to bitter conflicts between them. Protestant efforts to establish the reformed religion throughout Europe encountered increasingly strong Catholic resistance and led eventually to attempts at reconversion. Conflicts also arose between the different Protestant denominations, especially Lutherans, Calvinists and Anabaptists. All of this confessional strife, which often erupted into domestic or even international warfare, played an important role in European witch-hunting. The role was, however, much more indirect than some scholars have argued.[42]

The uneven geographical distribution of witchcraft prosecutions throughout Europe suggests, in a very tentative way, that religious conflict had some connection with witch-hunting. A very rough correlation can be established between the intensity of witchcraft prosecutions on the one hand and the extent of religious divisions on the other. Witch-hunting was most severe in countries or regions where either large religious minorities lived within the boundaries of a state, or the people of one state or territory adhered to one religion and the residents of a neighbouring state adhered to another. As we have seen, witch-hunting was especially severe in some German territories and Swiss cantons. In Germany, which consisted of hundreds of political units within the weak Holy Roman Empire, the official religion of a particular area was in most cases determined by the religion of the local prince. Consequently, some areas, especially those in the north, became Lutheran, while others remained Catholic or became Calvinist. In Switzerland, which comprised thirteen loosely confederated cantons, six cantons became Protestant while the other seven remained Catholic.

In Scotland, where witch-hunting was far more intense than in England, religious divisions were less clear but nonetheless figured significantly in the pattern of witch-hunting. The Protestant national Church of Scotland, which was established by law in 1567, was essentially a Calvinist Church that acquired a Presbyterian form of Church government by the 1590s. At the same time, however, the episcopal structure of the Church, which derived from Catholic times and resembled the Protestant episcopal structure of the Church of England, survived in attenuated form and was strengthened and restored on a number of separate occasions by the king, who after 1603 was also the king of England. The Scottish Church was therefore divided between rival Protestant factions, and the pressure to prosecute witches came more from Presbyterians than their Episcopalian brethren. Even in England, where witch-hunting claimed relatively few victims overall, the uneven distribution of trials in the kingdom reveals that in areas where there were significant divisions between Puritans and their conformist brethren the urge to prosecute witches was much greater than in more religiously unified locations.[43]

If witch-hunting was more widespread and intense in areas that were religiously divided, then the converse was also true. Religiously homogeneous or monolithic states generally experienced only occasional witch-hunts and relatively low numbers of executions. The two best illustrations of this correlation are Spain and Italy, both of which remained solidly Catholic throughout the Reformation era. Neither country avoided witch-hunting completely. Spain experienced large hunts in the Basque country in the 1520s and again in 1609–11, and there also were a number of executions in the Spanish secular courts. Witch-hunts in Italy, especially in the north, took a significant number of lives in the fifteenth and early sixteenth centuries. But neither country had a rash of witch panics such as those that afflicted Germany, Switzerland and even Scotland in the late sixteenth and early seventeenth centuries, and the total number of executions in both countries, while impossible to measure precisely, was extremely low. A similar situation prevailed in Ireland, which, despite the arrival of Protestant English and Scottish settlers in Ulster, remained predominantly Catholic. There were only five witchcraft prosecutions and three executions in Ireland during the early modern period. In the Scandinavian kingdoms, which were solidly Lutheran, there were, once again, relatively few witchcraft prosecutions and executions.

We can therefore establish a very general correlation between religious disunity and conflict on the one hand and intense witch-hunting on the other. Such a correlation, however, does not necessarily indicate that there was any causal connection between the two phenomena. The reasons why more witches were prosecuted in some areas than in others are many and varied, some of them being of a legal or judicial nature, as we have seen. It is *possible* that religious tensions had very little or nothing to do with the prosecution of witches. Nevertheless, the general geographical correlation between religious conflict and intense witch-hunting is so close that *some* causal connection almost certainly exists between them.

But what is that connection? In answering that question we must rule out a number of possibilities. First, the adherents to the dominant faith in a religiously divided area generally did not use witchcraft prosecutions to dispose of their religious antagonists. This may have happened at Freudenberg, where Bishop Julius Echter von Mespelbrunn of Würzburg allegedly accused Protestants of witchcraft in order to consolidate the return to Catholicism that he had engineered.[44] But Erik Midelfort and Gerhard Schormann have shown that such patterns rarely occurred.[45] For the most part, individuals who were prosecuted for witchcraft belonged at least formally to the same faith as their prosecutors. Since witches usually came from the same communities or regions as their judges, one would expect that to be the case. Now, it is true that witches were usually considered to be heretics, a label that Catholics would just as readily apply to Protestants in their midst and Protestants might even use to describe Catholics. But the heresy of the witch was something quite different from the heresy of the Catholic or Protestant nonconformist. The witch was a heretic because she had completely abandoned her Christian faith and made a pact with the Devil; the religious nonconformist was a heretic because she rejected one or more doctrines of the established religion. The two might be prosecuted by the same authorities, and both could serve as scapegoats for the ills of society, but their crimes would only occasionally be confused. This was true in the fifteenth century, when the crime of witchcraft was in the process of definition, and it was even more true in the sixteenth and seventeenth centuries, by which time the stereotype of the witch was widely known.[46]

Occasionally, a Protestant reformer, such as Bishop Palladius in Denmark, would threaten to prosecute those who were 'backward' in religion as witches.[47] The threat illustrates the close connection that Protestants made between Catholic superstition and magic, but there is no evidence that Danish authorities used witchcraft trials to solve this religious problem. In Scotland the charges against many witches suggested they were still practising the old religion. Women like Agnes Sampson, for example, were accused of using Catholic prayers in their magical practices and also of praying in ruined churches.[48] These charges tell us much more about the concerns of Sampson's prosecutors than about her actual religious behaviour. There is no evidence that Sampson was actually a Catholic, but even if she were, it is unlikely that Scottish authorities would have resorted to a witchcraft trial to prosecute her. Reginald Scot claimed that some English witches were papists, but he did not thereby suggest that witchcraft prosecutions were a means of solving the Catholic problem.[49] The most that can be said about the connection between Protestant or Catholic nonconformity and witchcraft is that those persons who were suspected of, or had been prosecuted for, some form of religious nonconformity, just like those who had been prosecuted for immorality or petty crime, were more likely to be accused of witchcraft than others.

SOURCE
BOOK

114

In Massachusetts, for example, Anne Hutchinson was suspected of witchcraft after she had already been identified as an antinomian 'heretic'.[50] But this process is very different from the deliberate use of witchcraft accusations to prosecute religious nonconformists.[51]

We must also discount the possibility that religious wars between Protestants and Catholics inspired witch-hunting.[52] This simply is not true. The entire European witch-hunt may have coincided with the age of religious warfare, but the outbreak of hostilities in a particular locality usually had a negative impact on the process of witch-hunting. Luxembourg, for example, stopped the prosecution of witches just about the time that France entered the Thirty Years War, and both Franche-Comté and Württemberg experienced reductions in witchcraft prosecutions from the moment they went to war. Conversely, the most intense periods of witch-hunting in northern France and in Paris itself were times of religious peace.[53]

There are a number of reasons for this inverse relationship between religious warfare and witchcraft prosecutions. First, warfare very often impeded the operation of the regular judicial machinery that was used to prosecute witches. When foreign armies occupied a given area, they sometimes even took over the operation of that machinery, and since witchcraft did not present an immediate threat to the newly arrived authorities, they usually did not assign a high priority to its prosecution. The presence of soldiers in an area also gave local residents an alternative means of explaining misfortune. In more peaceful times members of a community often attributed the misfortunes of everyday life to witches, who thereby became scapegoats of society. In wartime, however, misfortunes – which usually became more frequent and severe in such disruptive times – could readily and persuasively be attributed to soldiers or, more generally, to the enemy. War, in other words, focused the hostilities of a community on people other than witches. It is true of course that in the long run war aggravated a number of social and economic problems that eventually encouraged witchcraft accusations. Warfare could upset the economic life of a community, drastically affect the size and composition of the population, and introduce disease. Eventually these effects of war helped to create situations in which witchcraft accusations and prosecutions became more likely. Even then, however, we must keep in mind that these long-term effects of war were in no way peculiar to religiously inspired conflicts. It is, in other words, difficult to attribute an increase in witch-hunting to religious warfare as such.

What effect then did religious conflict have on witchcraft prosecutions? In the most general terms it made communities more fearful of religious and moral change and more aware of the influence of Satan, who was considered the source of all moral and religious deviance. That fear of moral and religious subversion was stronger in those areas where the adherents of rival confessions or factions lived within the same communities or in close proximity to each other than in those that were religiously homogeneous. In such areas the demand for establishing a godly state or community by prosecuting witches was strongest, as it was among Puritans in England in the 1640s and Presbyterians in Scotland in 1649.[54] It was also strongest in the Catholic ecclesiastical territories within the Holy Roman Empire, where authorities also wished to establish a godly state as a bulwark against the nearby threat of Protestantism.[55]

Trying witches was not a direct means of dealing with the threat of rival religious groups, especially since witches were usually not members of rival confessions. But naming and prosecuting witches was the most readily available means of making war on Satan. Witch-hunting also strengthened the conviction of the community that they were among the godly. Just as the prosecution of witches allowed individuals to project their guilt on to other members of the community and thus vindicate their own moral superiority, so it also allowed Protestant or Catholic communities in religiously divided areas to prove that God was on their side, or more properly speaking, that they were on God's.

The prosecution of witches in a religiously divided area served, therefore, as an *alternative* to the prosecution of heretics or religious nonconformists. Both represented attempts to counteract the religious subversion that Satan was inspiring and abetting, and both were driven by religious zeal. The clearest evidence for their common cause and purpose comes from France, where trials for witchcraft often began precisely at the same time that trials for heresy stopped. In Germany a witch-hunt conducted by Count Ulrich of Helfenstein in 1566 followed on the heels of a campaign to purge the area of Anabaptist heretics. In similar fashion the Catholic bishop of Cologne stopped trials of Anabaptists and started trials of witches in 1605.[56] In Italy the Inquisition began trying witches in the late sixteenth century at the very same time that the percentage of heresy cases dropped more than 75 per cent.[57] Such neat patterns do not appear in all parts of Europe. In some areas witchcraft trials took place before heresy trials began, while in others they occurred at the same time.[58] In many areas, moreover, especially when the predominant religion was Protestantism, there were no heresy trials at all. The important consideration, however, is that in all these areas witchcraft trials served a function that was very similar to that of heresy trials: eliminating individuals who were believed to be in league with Satan and corrupting society. And the belief that such corruption was taking place was generally stronger in areas where the 'heretical' activities of either a Protestant or Catholic minority were close, visible and threatening.

The Reformation and the decline of witch-hunting

The Protestant Reformation, the Catholic Reformation and the bitter conflict between Protestants and Catholics during the sixteenth and seventeenth centuries did, therefore, have an effect upon the growth of the European witch-hunt. At the same time, however, these very same developments laid the foundation for its eventual decline. The Protestant emphasis on the sovereignty of God, the growth of biblical literalism, and the scepticism engendered by Catholic and Protestant exorcisms in cases involving witchcraft all had this negative effect on witch-hunting.

Christianity, being a monotheistic religion, has always insisted upon the sovereignty of God. It has accepted the existence of a supernatural evil power, the Devil, in the universe, but it has rejected as heretical the theological view of the Devil as a power co-equal to that of God. As mentioned above, some Protestant reformers, most notably Luther, seemed to exaggerate the extent of diabolical activity in the world, almost to the point of flirting with Manichaean or dualist heresy. The appearances, however, are deceptive, for Luther insisted that in the bitter struggle between God and Satan, the former would always prevail. Calvin emphasized even more strongly the majesty of God, arguing that the Devil could do nothing without God's permission and was little more than His servant or executioner. The insistence upon God's sovereignty led a number of Protestant writers and preachers to deny the Devil's ability to produce certain types of marvels, such as hailstorms, and this fostered a scepticism towards *maleficia* that involved such wonders. Consequently, Protestants were less likely than Catholics to accuse a witch of raising a hailstorm to destroy crops, a common form of *maleficium*.[59] During the main period of the European witch-hunt this Protestant tendency did not result in an overall reduction of witchcraft prosecutions and executions in Protestant lands, because it was to a large extent offset by a greater Protestant willingness to prosecute witches simply on the basis of the demonic pact. Eventually, however, the Protestant emphasis on God's sovereignty led to scepticism regarding the reality of *maleficia*, and that in turn developed into a more general scepticism regarding all aspects of witchcraft.

The way in which the Protestant conception of the sovereignty of God could undermine witch beliefs even at a fairly early date can be seen in the work of George Gifford, a Puritan clergyman in the English county of Essex who wrote two treatises on witchcraft in the late sixteenth century.[60] Gifford was by no means a complete sceptic when it came to witchcraft, and in typically Protestant fashion he cited Exodus 22:18 to justify the prosecution of witches who had made a pact with the Devil. But Gifford's main purpose was to bring an end to the recent rash of witchcraft prosecutions, which he thought were distracting people from the real danger that Satan would win their souls. The problem, as he saw it, was that people had lost their faith in God; hence the connection between witchcraft and the stubborn persistence of Catholicism. If people could only become fully aware of God's sovereignty, if only they would recognize that Satan operates as an agent of God and that *maleficia* occur only with His permission, then the punishment of witches for doing such things as destroying cattle would cease. And once people had faith in God, then He would no longer give permission to Satan and witches to exercise power in the world.[61]

A second aspect of Protestantism that originally abetted and then weakened witch-hunting was biblical literalism. Since the Hebrew Bible contained the lethal injunction, 'Thou shalt not suffer a witch to live', the close adherence to the letter of Scripture could and often did encourage authorities to put witches to death. In the long run, however, the increased reliance upon Scripture could give serious pause to witch-hunters. Not only did Scripture contain very few references to witchcraft, and none to Devil-worship, but it also gave an abundance of evidence regarding the restraints that God placed on diabolical power in the world. Calvin's firm belief in the sovereignty of God and his assurance that God would prevail over him was, after all, based on a firm scriptural foundation. Calvinism may have encouraged people to engage in an incessant war with Satan, but it also encouraged them eventually to define exactly what he could do and to see the danger he presented as purely spiritual. It is not surprising therefore that one of the most prominent critics of witch beliefs in the late seventeenth century was the Calvinist biblical scholar Balthasar Bekker.[62]

Even the conflict between Catholics and Protestants played a significant, albeit indirect role in bringing an end to witchcraft prosecutions. One of the interesting forms that this conflict took was the attempt by authorities to prove that they adhered to the true religion by exorcising demons from possessed persons. By using the Eucharist as one of the methods of such exorcism, for example, Catholics attempted to prove that Christ was really present in the Eucharist, a doctrine that Calvinists denied. Protestants, on the other hand, employing only the biblically prescribed measures of prayer and fasting, tried to drive out demons to prove that God favoured the cause of Protestant reform. These efforts were closely related to witch-hunting, for in the late sixteenth and seventeenth centuries many of those demoniacs who were exorcized accused witches of causing their possession. The problem, however, was that the possessions and the efforts of the exorcists, which attracted widespread publicity, engendered a great deal of scepticism. Many people became convinced that the possessions were fraudulent and that the exorcisms were shams. By extension, therefore, the accusations of witchcraft, which the exorcists had often encouraged, were discredited, as were the prosecutions that resulted from them. It was therefore partly the result of simple Catholic–Protestant rivalry in cases of possession that critics of witch-hunting acquired evidence to bolster their case.[63]

We must of course keep the negative effects of the Reformation on witch-hunting in perspective. The Reformation had more to do with the rise of witchcraft than with its decline. But the fact that the Reformation had a negative as well as a positive effect on European witch-hunting should make us pause before we blame the entire European witch-hunt on the Protestant Reformation, the Catholic Reformation, or both.

Notes

1. For the clearest statement of this argument see Trevor-Roper, 'Witch-Craze', 136 *et passim*.
2. See Midelfort, *Witch Hunting*, 33; Monter, *Witchcraft in France and Switzerland*, 106–7.
3. For the connection between witch-hunting and the Augustinian revival that was common to Protestantism and Catholicism see A. D. Wright, *The Counter-Reformation* (New York, 1982): 1–50.
4. For the influence of Catholic and Protestant writers on each other see N. Paulus, *Hexenwahn und Hexenprozesse, vornehmlich im 16 Jahrhundert* (Freiburg, 1910): 69.
5. M. Luther, *A Commentary on St. Paul's Epistle to the Galatians* (London, 1741): 146.
6. H. A. Oberman, *Luther: Man between God and the Devil*, tr. E. Walliser-Schwarzbart (New Haven and London, 1989): 104, claims that, according to Luther, the omnipotent God was hidden from man; the revealed God, incarnate in Christ, 'laid Himself open to the Devil's fury'.
7. Ibid., 204.
8. See M. Walzer, *The Revolution of the Saints* (Cambridge, MA, 1965): 64–5.
9. See Monter, *European Witchcraft*, 59.
10. On Calvin's statements about witchcraft see J. Teall, 'Witchcraft and Calvinism in Elizabethan England: Divine Power and Human Agency', *Journal of the History of Ideas* 23 (1962): 21–36, esp. 27–9.
11. Thomas, *Religion and the Decline of Magic*, 476.
12. See Muchembled, 'Witches of the Cambrésis', 259–73.
13. See W. Lamont, *Godly Rule: Politics and Religion, 1603–1660* (London, 1969): 98–100.
14. Larner, *Enemies of God*, 25.
15. Macfarlane, *Witchcraft in Tudor and Stuart England*, 192–9.
16. Muchembled, 'Witches of the Cambrésis', 259–60, 266–7.
17. Boyer and Nissenbaum, *Salem Possessed*, 179–216.
18. Monter, *Witchcraft in France and Switzerland*, 137.
19. For some of these practices see Thomas, *Religion and the Decline of Magic*, 27–50; R. Scribner, 'Ritual and Popular Religion in Catholic Germany at the Time of the Reformation', *Journal of Ecclesiastical History* 35 (1984): 47–77; E. Duffy, *The Stripping of the Altars* (New Haven, 1992): 277–87. On the process of the 'folklorization' of Christianity see J. Delumeau, *La Peur en occident XIVe–XVIIIe siècles* (Paris, 1978): 166–70.
20. Perkins, *Damned Art of Witchcraft*, 173–80.
21. Clark, 'Protestant Demonology', 45–81.
22. R. Martin, *Witchcraft and the Inquisition in Venice, 1550–1650* (Oxford, 1989): 246–50; M. O'Neil, 'Magical Healing, Love Magic and the Inquisition in Late Sixteenth-Century Modena', in *Inquisition and Society in Early Modern Europe*, ed. S. Haliczer (Totowa, 1987): 88–114.
23. See below, Chapter 5.
24. Parker, 'Some Recent Work', 529; W. Monter, *Ritual, Myth and Magic in Early Modern Europe* (Athens, OH, 1983): 66–8.
25. See Thomas, *Religion and the Decline of Magic*, 498.
26. M. Gijswijt-Hofstra, 'Witchcraft in the Northern Netherlands', in *Current Issues in Women's History*, ed. A. Angerman et al. (London, 1989): 77.
27. National Archives of Scotland, CH2/265/2, 165.
28. Larner, *Enemies of God*, 67–8, 71–5; B. Ankarloo, *Trolldomsprocesserna i Sverige* (Stockholm, 1971): 328.
29. Walinski-Kiehl, 'Godly States', 16.

30. Weyer, *De praestigiis daemonum*, in *Witches, Devils, and Doctors in the Renaissance*, 93–8. See also Sir Robert Filmer, *A Difference between an English and Hebrew Witch* (London, 1653).

31. For a survey of Protestant opinion on this difficult question see P. D. L. Avis, 'Moses and the Magistrate: A Study in the Rise of Protestant Legalism', *Journal of Ecclesiastical History* 26 (1975): 149–72.

32. A. L. Drummond and J. Bulloch, *The Scottish Church, 1688–1843* (Edinburgh, 1973): 12–13. See also J. Stearne, *A Confirmation and Discovery of Witchcraft* (London, 1648): 9.

33. Paulus, *Hexenwahn*, 82.

34. U. Lange, *Untersuchungen zu Bodins Démonomanie* (Frankfurt, 1970): 159–60.

35. John Wesley, *The Journal of the Rev. John Wesley, A. M.* (New York, 1906), III: 330. Wesley believed that if one account of witchcraft or ghosts could be proved true, deism, atheism and materialism would 'fall to the ground'. See Stephens, *Demon Lovers*, 366–7.

36. W. Blackstone, *Commentaries on the Laws of England* (Oxford, 1769), IV: 60.

37. G. Klaniczay, *The Uses of Supernatural Power* (Princeton, 1990): 171.

38. G. Henningsen, 'Witch Persecution after the Era of the Witch Trials', *ARV. Scandinavium Yearbook of Folklore* 144 (1988): 107.

39. Clark, *Thinking with Demons*, 380–8; Waite, *Heresy, Magic and Witchcraft in Early Modern Europe*, 58–60 *et passim*; Soman, 'Witch-Lynching at Juniville', 8–9.

40. Macfarlane, *Witchcraft in Tudor and Stuart England*, 141; M. Gaskill, *Witchfinders: A Seventeenth-Century English Tragedy* (London, 2005): 22, 85; Lamont, *Godly Rule*, 98–100; Elmer, 'Politics of Witchcraft', 109.

41. Cotton Mather, *Memorable Providences relating to Witchcrafts and Possession* (Boston, 1689).

42. For the classic statement of the argument see Trevor-Roper, 'Witch-Craze', 161. For the opposite point of view see Schormann, *Nordwestdeutschland*, 159. For a sustained treatment of this complex issue see Waite, *Heresy, Magic and Witchcraft in Early Modern Europe*, chapter 5.

43. Levack, *Witch-Hunting in Scotland*, 7–13; Elmer, 'Politics of Witchcraft', 107.

44. Midelfort, *Witch Hunting*, 138.

45. Ibid.; Schormann, *Nordwestdeutschland*, 159.

46. J. J. Marx, *L'Inquisition en Dauphiné* (Paris, 1914): 48; G. L. Burr, 'Fate of Dietrich Flade', in *George Lincoln Burr: Selections from His Writings*, ed. L. O. Gibbons (Ithaca, 1943): 229. There may have been some confusion between witches and secret Protestants who gathered in conventicles in Habsburg lands. See Evans, *Habsburg Monarchy*, 406.

47. See E. Cowan, 'The Darker Vision of the Scottish Renaissance', in *The Renaissance and Reformation in Scotland*, ed. I. B. Cowan and D. Shaw (Edinburgh, 1983): 128.

48. Ibid.

49. Scot, *The Discoverie of Witchcraft*, 4.

50. J. Demos, *Entertaining Satan: Witchcraft and the Culture of Early New England* (New York, 1982): 64.

51. For a different critique of witchcraft prosecutions as 'camouflaged heretic hunts' see Henningsen, *Witches' Advocate*, 16.

52. Trevor-Roper, 'Witch-Craze', 143–5.

53. Delumeau, *La Peur*, 356–8.

54. On the role played by Covenanters in Scotland and Puritans in England in the witch-hunts of the 1640s see Levack, *Witch-Hunting in Scotland*, 65–6, 75–6.

55. In Lorraine and the three archiepiscopal electorates in the Rhineland, all of which were close to Protestant lands, there was a 'combative' religious attitude and there were also many witch-hunts. Monter, *Ritual, Myth and Magic*, 84.

56. Monter, *European Witchcraft*, 35–6; Waite, *Heresy, Magic and Witchcraft*, 155.
57. Parker, 'Some Recent Work', 529.
58. At Trier the prosecution of heretics was still going on at the time of the great witch prosecutions of the late 1580s and early 1590s. See Burr, 'Fate of Flade', 228–9.
59. Monter, *Witchcraft in France and Switzerland*, 151–7.
60. G. Gifford, *A Discourse of the Subtle Practice of Devils by Witches* (London, 1587); idem, *A Dialogue Concerning Witches and Witchcraftes* (London, 1593).
61. J. Hitchcock, 'George Gifford and Puritan Witch Beliefs', *Archiv für Reformationsgeschichte* 58 (1967): 90–9; Teall, 'Witchcraft and Calvinism', 21–36.
62. In Finland, the opposition came from bishops. See Heikkinen, *Paholaisen Liittolaiset*, 394.
63. Levack, *The Devil Within*, Chapter 4.

5

THE SOCIAL
CONTEXT

In order to provide a satisfactory explanation of the European witch-hunt, we must consider not only the religious changes and conflicts of the early modern period but also the broader social environment in which accusations arose. In studying any crime, of course, we can profit from this type of investigation, for by acquiring knowledge of the social setting of the crime and the relationship between the criminal and his victim we can more fully understand the motivation of the criminal. In the case of witchcraft, however, which was to a great extent an imagined crime, a social investigation can be even more revealing, since it can help to explain why the alleged victims of the crime, or their kin, singled out innocent persons for prosecution. The social history of this crime, therefore, becomes more than a study of deviant behaviour. In dealing with witchcraft the historian must explain not only why the witch acted in a certain way but also why the witch's neighbours suspected and accused her. The witch may have been responding to social or economic pressures when she cursed at her enemies or used sorcery against them, but her neighbours, by denouncing the witch and testifying against her, were being no less responsive to the social conditions in which they lived. Witchcraft accusations allowed members of early modern European communities to resolve conflicts between themselves and their neighbours and to explain misfortunes that had occurred in their daily lives.

In establishing the social context of European witch-hunting, historians confront a number of problems. The first of these is a dearth of information regarding the lives and activities of those who were accused of witchcraft and those who accused them. Although trial records usually give the names of those who were tried for witchcraft and, less commonly, the names of those who testified against them, they very often do not tell us much more. They carefully catalogue the various *maleficia* that the witches allegedly committed, and they often describe in lurid detail the various acts of diabolism that they engaged in. But the records only rarely tell us how old the witches were, what their marital statuses were, what occupations they or their spouses engaged in, and what kind of dealings they had with their neighbours. Sometimes the court records contain the depositions of witnesses against the accused, and since these statements mention conflicts that had arisen between the deponents and the witch, we can learn from them a limited amount of information about the social status of the individuals involved and the circumstances surrounding the prosecution. All too often, however, these depositions have been lost or, in some cases, never even taken. Especially during large witch-hunts, when many witches were named as accomplices by persons who had already been convicted, the legal record contains nothing but the mere allegation of Devil-worship. Faced with such lacunae in the sources, historians of witchcraft must base their interpretation of the social dynamics of witchcraft accusations on a very small sample of cases.

A further problem arises in trying to generalize about the social context of witchcraft prosecutions throughout Europe over an extended period of time. Although many cases of witchcraft arose out of similar socio-economic circum-stances, conditions obviously varied from place to place and from time to time. Even when we concentrate our attention on a particular geographical area during a relatively brief period of time, we find that witchcraft accusations and prosecutions often reflected a wide variety of social conflicts. For this reason it is impossible to provide a single socio-economic interpretation of European witch-hunting. The most that we can do is to describe the most typical environments in which witchcraft accusations arose, establish the most com-mon social characteristics of the individuals who were singled out for prosecu-tion, and explore some of the reasons why these individuals were particularly vulnerable to the charge of witchcraft. This technique will allow us to draw some general conclusions about the identity of the 'typical' European witch without failing to appreciate the variety of circumstances that could have led to her accusation and prosecution.

In addition to these problems of insufficient evidence and geographical and temporal diversity, the social investigation of witchcraft raises two substantive issues. The first deals with the relative importance of social and economic factors in explaining the great witch-hunt. It should be clear from the preceding chapters that the hunt had long-term intellectual and legal causes and more immediate religious ones. It is possible that in some witch-hunts these factors, taken together, provide a sufficient explanation of the prosecutions that took place. This was most commonly the case when witch-hunts were initiated from above (i.e. by magistrates or inquisitors), when torture was used to obtain the names of accomplices, and when charges of diabolism took clear precedence over those of *maleficia*. In these situations religious ideology very often became the driving force of the hunt, the only social dynamic being the interaction between the official who belonged to a ruling or administrative elite and the accused, who usually came from the lower ranks of society. When witch-hunting was initiated from below, however, when the initial reason for bringing charges against a person was the determination of her neighbours to punish her for causing a personal misfortune, then social and economic considerations assumed paramount importance. In most cases, of course, there was extensive involvement of both magistrates and villagers in witch-hunting. When prosecutions were initiated from above, neighbours were called upon to testify regarding alleged *maleficia*; when they originated from below, magistrates eventually assumed control of the proceedings and emphasized the diabolical nature of the crime. For this reason one can rarely neglect the social context of witch-hunting. At the same time, however, one must be careful not to exaggerate the importance of that context. There were many reasons for accusing a person of witchcraft, and not all of these were conditioned by general social and economic circumstances.

The second substantive issue concerns the importance of social and economic *change* in explaining the rise of witch-hunting. Since the European witch-hunt was a time-bound phenomenon, beginning in the fifteenth century and ending by the early eighteenth, it is tempting to see it as the product of the profound social and economic changes that occurred during those very same centuries. Between 1520 and 1640 the population of Europe increased dramatically after a centuries of stagnation and decline; prices of all commodities rose at an unprecedented pace; towns grew in size and number; and both mercantile and agricultural capitalism were introduced in many areas. Periodic visitations of the plague and other epidemic diseases affected entire communities, while more than the usual number of bad harvests, especially in the 1580s and 1590s, led to widespread famine.

There is little question that all of these developments played a role in witchcraft prosecutions. They engendered conflict within communities and, perhaps even more importantly, contributed to a general mood that encouraged witch-hunting. Historians such as Keith Thomas, Wolfgang Behringer, Robert Muchembled, Paul Boyer and Stephen Nissenbaum have all shown how witchcraft accusations reflected the tensions that were generated by these changes. The problem, however, is that many of the specific social and economic conditions that lay at the basis of witch-hunting were not all that new. Many of the social conflicts that gave rise to witchcraft accusations were common to pre-capitalistic, medieval communities and do not appear to have been exacerbated by novel developments. Some witchcraft accusations may have occurred in communities that were in a state of transition or economic crisis, but many others arose in villages that were still part of a relatively static, traditional world.[1] In these areas the interpersonal conflicts that led people to accuse others of witchcraft were not any more intense in the early modern period than they had been during the Middle Ages. The reasons why these conflicts resulted in witchcraft prosecutions in the early modern period, whereas they had failed to do so before, had more to do with changes in the nature of witch beliefs, the growing awareness of witchcraft in all segments of society, the possibility of successful legal prosecution, and the impact of the Reformation than with the realities of social and economic change.

In dealing with the social and economic context of witchcraft prosecutions, therefore, we must recognize that the environment we are describing was not necessarily new and that the social conflicts that led to or reinforced prosecutions were not always the product of broad socio-economic change. It may be true that some witch-hunts occurred at critical periods in early modern European history, when a new set of values and a new way of life clashed with the old. It may also be true that all witch-hunting was to some extent a by-product of the anxiety engendered by rapid social change. But if we assume that every witchcraft accusation and every prosecution can be directly attributed to a process of social change, we run the risk of reading too much into the documents and of failing to recognize that the personal conflicts that often found expression in witchcraft accusations could occur in a relatively static as well as in a rapidly changing world.

The geographical and social setting

In establishing the social context of witchcraft prosecutions it is important first to determine the type of communities in which the hunts took place. In most parts of Europe during the early modern period witchcraft was essentially a rural phenomenon.[2] A large majority of witches appear to have come from small agricultural villages that were part of a peasant economy. This localization of witchcraft in the countryside is usually attributed to two characteristics of rural life: the strength of superstitious beliefs among an uneducated and conservative peasantry and the small size of these communities. We know from anthropological studies of preliterate societies today not only that magical beliefs are especially durable among an uneducated population but also that accusations of sorcery tend to arise when people live in close-knit, face-to-face communities, where everyone knows everyone else and where undesirable people cannot easily be ignored.[3] Since similar conditions prevailed in the agricultural villages of early modern Europe, witchcraft has come to be regarded as a peculiarly rural phenomenon.

Although a great majority of early modern European witches came from the countryside, witchcraft accusations and prosecutions in the towns and cities cannot be ignored. Indeed, some of the largest and most famous witch-hunts took place in an urban environment. In some cases, of course, the urban setting of witchcraft is deceptive, since the witches were brought from the countryside to the towns for trial. In the records of Scottish witchcraft, for example, there are occasional references to witches coming from Edinburgh, Aberdeen or Dalkeith, but on close examination it appears that they actually lived in rural villages near those cities or towns. In Geneva, where a number of witch-hunts took place in the sixteenth and seventeenth centuries, roughly half of the victims came from the rural hamlets that surrounded the city but supplied only about 20 per cent of that tiny republic's population.[4]

Even if we discount all of the urban trials in which the accused witches came from the surrounding countryside, we still are left with a substantial number of strictly urban cases, especially in Germany. The two phases of intense prosecution in the prince-bishopic of Eichstätt in the seventeenth century, for example, identified witches mainly among residents of the town rather than the surrounding countryside.[5] Exactly what percentage of the accused in such urban witch-hunts were townspeople is impossible to determine. There is good reason to believe, however, that the percentage was higher than that of the urban component of the entire population. In other words, the number of urban witchcraft cases may have been disproportionately high. In Poland, for example, 19 per cent of those accused of witchcraft lived in urban areas, a small proportion to be sure, but far greater than the relative size of the urban population of that country, which was almost certainly less than 5 per cent.[6] In Finland, which was no less rural than Poland, the proportion of urban witches was an even higher 26 per cent.[7] We must not forget that despite their enormous economic and political importance, towns did not contain a very large percentage of the early modern European population. Even if we use the low figure of 2,000 inhabitants to define the minimum size of a town, the urban population of neither Germany nor England was more than 10 per cent at the beginning of the sixteenth century.[8]

In some cases of urban witchcraft the social environment was not much different from that of the rural villages. Towns served different economic functions from those of villages, and they also had a distinct identity, but their size was often only marginally greater. Some of the smaller towns in the early modern period had a population of little more than 2,000 souls and were, therefore, just as much face-to-face communities or 'small-scale societies' as their rural counterparts.[9] It should not surprise us, therefore, to learn that the overwhelming majority of urban Polish witches came from small towns or that in Essex, England, where witchcraft was largely a rural affair, the few urban witches came from market towns like Chelmsford or cloth towns like Braintree, Coggeshall and Dedham. In these small communities it would be difficult to establish the existence of any peculiarly urban characteristics of witchcraft accusations.[10]

In larger towns and cities, however, we are dealing with a completely different type of environment. In these communities, which had more than 5,000 inhabitants, one could usually ignore, or at least avoid, one's neighbours. The occurrence of witchcraft accusations in these urban areas, therefore, must be attributed to factors other than inevitable social interaction or, for that matter, peasant superstition. One reason why such an urban environment might have proven to be fertile ground for witchcraft accusations and prosecutions was that the practice of politically inspired sorcery, either at royal courts or within city councils, where members of urban elites accused their rivals, or more often their wives, to gain political advantage.[11]

In addition to serving as an arena for the practice of political sorcery, towns were the only places where plague-spreaders (*engraisseurs*) were prosecuted as witches. Plague-spreaders were persons who allegedly had succeeded in distilling the essence of the plague in the form of an unguent, which they then used to infect various parts of towns.[12] Like other sorcerers, plague-spreaders were accused of worshipping the Devil and of acting collectively, and for that reason they readily became identified with witches. Their prosecution also resembled that of witches, for a visitation of the plague could trigger a plague-spreader panic, in which a large number of *engraisseurs* were accused and tried. Geneva experienced no fewer than three of these hunts in the sixteenth century, while another one took place at Milan in 1630.[13] Because outbreaks of the plague in the sixteenth and seventeenth centuries were almost entirely restricted to the towns, plague-spreader panics represented a peculiarly urban form of witchcraft prosecution.

Another predominantly, although not exclusively, urban form of witchcraft was the use of magical powers to cause collective demonic possession. Although incidents of group possession were reported in rural areas during the period of the great witch-hunt, as in the village of Mattaincourt in Lorraine between 1627 and 1631, the largest and most famous cases of multiple or collective possession involving witchcraft occurred in towns, especially in France.[14] The main reason for this concentration may have been the simple fact that collective demonic possession often took place in convents and hospitals, which were often located in cities and towns. Cities were also capable of supplying the large crowds of observers upon which such episodes thrived, as we know from the thousands that flocked to witness the exorcism of Ursuline nuns at Loudun in 1634.[15]

There are two other reasons why towns proved to be surprisingly fertile ground for witchcraft prosecutions. One is that a hunt, once it had begun, was more likely to take a heavier toll in the more densely populated towns than in the countryside, especially since the number of potential victims was limited. It is for this reason that rural witchcraft panics tended to move from village to village by means of rumour and occasional accusations of non-villagers, whereas urban panics developed more quickly and took a heavier toll. This was especially clear in the ecclesiastical territories of Bamberg, Würzburg and Eichstätt, where many of the witches named as accomplices in the large witch panics there in the early decades of the seventeenth century came from the cathedral cities rather than the rural villages in the prince-bishoprics. Another reason is that urban life generated a number of tensions that could find expression in witchcraft accusations. It may have been easier to ignore one's neighbours in the cities and become convinced that they had no magical power over others, but at the same time the problem of urban residents in adjusting to urban life may have led them to suspect their neighbours of witchcraft more readily than if they had been living in the countryside.

We may conclude, therefore, that there was more than one 'world of the witches' in early modern Europe. There was, to be sure, a peasant world in which witchcraft suspicions and accusations formed a staple of everyday life and periodically resulted in isolated trials and occasionally large panics. This was a world in which peasant beliefs could combine in a lethal manner with the interpersonal conflicts that arose regularly in a face-to-face society. But there was also an urban world of witchcraft in which the political sorcerer, the ritual magician, the possessed nun and the plague-spreader played a part and in which accusations and chain-reaction hunts could spread rapidly. This urban world was also the destination of many rural witches, the place where the illiterate peasant who had been accused by her neighbours confronted an urban, literate magistrate or cleric as her inquisitor. When this confrontation occurred, the witch found herself accused not only by neighbours who believed she had harmed them magically but also by a judiciary determined to place the testimony they heard in a demonological context. The trial, therefore, became the place where elite and popular culture interacted and where the countryside came in contact with the town.

Who were the witches?

In order to understand the social tensions that underlay witchcraft prosecutions, it is necessary to determine which groups of people were most commonly tried as witches and explain why these groups were more vulnerable to such charges than others. The dearth of information regarding the witches as well as the motivation of their accusers makes this type of investigation somewhat speculative. Even when a fair amount of information can be collected, it is still difficult to determine which characteristics of the witch's personality and which conflicts between her and her neighbours led to her accusation. There are, however, enough data available to establish some general patterns of accusation and offer some possible reasons why these persons were accused.

Sex

The most well-documented characteristic of those persons who were prosecuted for witchcraft is that they were predominantly, if not overwhelmingly, female. As Table 5.1 indicates, the percentage of female witches exceeded 75 per cent in most regions of Europe, and in a few localities, such as the county of Essex, England, the bishopric of Basel, and the county of Namur (in present-day Belgium), it was more than 90 per cent.[16] These figures suggest that the predominant stereotype of the European witch as female has a solid foundation, or at least finds confirmation, in the actual prosecutions of the early modern period.

The table also shows, however, that in at least four regions or countries – Normandy, Russia, Estonia and Iceland – men constituted a solid majority of all accused witches, while in Finland the sex distribution was close to even. In a few other locations, such as in the kingdom of Aragon, men constituted a large percentage, although not a majority, of the witches who were brought to trial. These figures, together with the fact that as many as 25 per cent of European witches were male, make it impossible to dismiss the male witch as a mere exception to the rule or to claim that only men who were related to female witches were prosecuted.[17]

The prosecution and execution of a significant number of men as witches should not surprise us. There was nothing in the legal definition of a witch that excluded males. Men could, just like women, practise harmful magic, make pacts with the Devil, and attend the sabbath. In some of the woodcuts and engravings produced during the sixteenth and seventeenth centuries, especially those illustrating the pact with the Devil, male and female witches are shown in equal numbers.[18] Demonologists often used the masculine form for the word witch in their treatises and sometimes specifically referred to witches of both sexes.[19] Willem de Blécourt has argued that there was a stereotype of the male witch that coexisted with the more common female stereotype.[20]

Table 5.1 Sex of accused witches.

Region	Years	Male	Female	% Female
Holy Roman Empire (1648 boundaries)	1530–1730	4,575	19,050	76
South-western Germany	1562–1684	238	1,050	82
Rothenburg ob der Tauber	1549–1709	19	46	71
Prince-bishopric of Eichstätt	1617–1631	27	155	88
Bishopric of Basel	1571–1670	9	181	95
Franche-Comté	1559–1667	49	153	76
Geneva	1537–1662	74	240	76
Pays de Vaud	1581–1620	325	624	66
County of Namur	1509–1646	29	337	92
Luxembourg	1519–1623	130	417	76
City of Toul	1584–1623	14	53	79
Dept of the Nord, France	1542–1679	54	232	81
Normandy	1564–1660	278	103	27
Castile	1540–1685	132	324	71
Aragon	1600–1650	69	90	57
Venice	1550–1650	224	490	69
Finland	1520–1699	316	325	51
Estonia	1520–1729	116	77	40
Wielkopolska, Poland	1500–1776	21	490	96
Russia	1601–1701	367	128	26
Hungary	1520–1777	160	1,482	90
County of Essex, England	1560–1675	23	290	93
New England	1620–1725	75	267	78
Iceland	1625–1685	110	10	8

We still must explain, however, under what circumstances men were just as likely as women to be accused of witchcraft. One of these occurred when witch trials were closely linked to prosecutions for other forms of heresy. William Monter has shown that in the Jura region in the fifteenth century, when prosecutions for witchcraft took place in conjunction with those for Waldensian heresy, far more males were prosecuted than females.[21] The reason for the large percentage of males in these trials is that heresy, unlike witchcraft, was not generally sex-related. Women were, to be sure, well represented in medieval heretical sects, and their prominence in these groups might have reinforced their later identification as witches, but men were even more active in these sects and for that reason could easily be suspected in connection with the new 'heresy' of witchcraft.[22] It is significant that in these early witchcraft trials, most of which were conducted in ecclesiastical courts, the judges were much more concerned with the diabolical or heretical aspects of witchcraft than with *maleficium*.[23]

The fact that heresy was not sex-linked may also explain why the Spanish and Roman inquisitions tried a higher percentage of male witches than most other European courts. As Table 5.1 indicates, the percentage of male witches tried by the Inquisition in both Castile and Venice was well above the European average. In the kingdom of Aragon, where almost all the witches prosecuted in the secular courts were female, 72 per cent of the witches tried by the Inquisition during the first half of the seventeenth century were male.[24] Just like the ecclesiastical courts in the Jura in the late fifteenth century, the Inquisition in Italy and Spain prosecuted witchcraft mainly as a form of heresy and displayed little or no concern with *maleficium*.[25] With the crime defined in this way, men were likely to be prosecuted in large numbers.

Another situation in which men tended to be prosecuted for witchcraft was when the crime involved political sorcery. During the Middle Ages a number of men had actually practised ritual magic in order to advance their political careers.[26] It was in connection with such practices that many witch beliefs were developed. As the magician was gradually transformed into the witch, the sex and social status of the malefactor changed, but during the early period of witch-hunting this transition was not complete. Many early trials for witchcraft, therefore, involved treasonous activities, and consequently a higher number of men were prosecuted during the early stages of the hunt than at its peak. In the most famous early witch-hunt in Scotland, for example, which took place in 1590 and 1591 and involved accusations of treason against the king, the ringleader of the witches was believed to be the earl of Bothwell, and one of the most prominent of the witches was a schoolmaster, Dr Fian.[27]

The most persuasive explanation for the accusation and prosecution of significant numbers of male witches in certain localities was the existence of a tradition of male magic. A good number of the men accused of witchcraft were known to be practitioners of village magic. Some of these men were believed to have powers similar to those of shamans – magicians or healers who could commune with spirits. The herdsman Chonrad of Oberstdorf in the duchy of Bavaria fits into this category, as do many of the witches from Russia, Finland, Estonia and Iceland.[28] W. F. Ryan has argued that the male magicians in these regions, who often had an importance in village life rivalling that of the local priest, probably descended from early Russian shamans.[29] In Normandy, which had a higher percentage of male witches than in any part of western Europe, the typical witch was a male shepherd who practised a particular type of magic that employed venom taken from toads and stolen communion wafers.[30] In the Saar region in Germany the men who were accused of witchcraft were known to be proficient in conducting magical rituals that did not involve pacts with the Devil.[31] In England, where very few witches were men, a charge of killing animals and a child by means of witchcraft was brought against William Godfrey, a farmer from a village in Kent, in 1613.[32]

A fourth situation that led to the prosecution of substantial numbers of male witches occurred when witch-hunts got out of control and confessing witches were forced to name accomplices, who after being tortured and convicted were forced to name more accomplices themselves. In these chain-reaction hunts, which did not occur very frequently but which account for a significant number of executions, the pressure to name accomplices and the hysterical mood of the populace led to the almost indiscriminate naming of witches. In such circumstances the stereotype of the witch broke down and many persons who did not conform to the model of the typical witch, including men of high social standing, found themselves accused. At Würzburg in 1629, so it was reported, confessing witches implicated some 400 witches 'of every rank and sex', including clerics, electoral councillors and doctors, city officials, court assessors and law students.[33] At Salem, where more than 160 witches were accused, some of the most prominent merchants in Boston as well as Nathaniel Saltonstall, who was a member of the Governor's Council and had sat as a judge of the witchcraft court, were all named as accomplices.[34]

Recognizing that men could be and were prosecuted for witchcraft, sometimes in significant numbers, we are still left with the task of explaining why in most situations, and certainly in all prosecutions taken together, witches were predominantly female. It will not suffice to say that the stereotype of the witch in both popular and learned culture had always been female and that consequently those who believed they were victims of witchcraft instinctively accused women rather than men.[35] To some extent, of course, this was true. Since the prototype of the witch in ancient and early medieval culture and in both literature and art was female (e.g. Hecate, Medea and Diana), people familiar with those literary and artistic traditions were probably predisposed to think that witches were female. The early modern stereotype of the female witch was, however, more the product than the source of witchcraft accusations and prosecutions. If women had not been much more

SOURCE
BOOK

readily accused of witchcraft than men, then the image of the witch that prevailed in early modern Europe and has been passed down to modern times would not be predominantly female.

Explanations for the predominance of women as witches often focus on the treatises written by demonologists, many of which comment on the fact that most witches were women. This literature is in most cases intensely misogynistic, in the sense that it is demeaning, if not blatantly hostile, to women. The common theme in these demonological treatises is that women were more susceptible to demonic temptation because they were morally weaker than men and more likely, therefore, to succumb to diabolical temptation. This idea, which dates from the earliest days of Christianity, is expressed most forcefully in the *Malleus maleficarum*, but it can be found in many places, even in the sceptical demonological treatise of Johann Weyer.[36] The *Malleus* relates this weakness not only to women's intellectual inferiority and superstitiousness but also to their sexual passion, and concludes that 'all witchcraft comes from carnal lust, which is in women insatiable'.[37]

The image of women as the more carnal and sexually indulgent members of the species was pervasive in medieval and early modern European culture; only in the eighteenth century did it begin to give way to the alternative depiction of women as sexually passive.[38] The image received its strongest endorsement from clerics, especially monks, who viewed women as sexual temptresses, but it was by no means restricted to clerical circles. Jean Bodin, a lay jurist and magistrate, referred to the 'bestial cupidity' of women in a manner similar to that of Kramer, while Henri Boguet, a secular judge, claimed that the Devil had sexual relations with all witches because he knew that 'women love carnal pleasures'.[39] Another lay judge, the French *parlementaire* Pierre de Lancre, who took a leading role in the large witch-hunt in the Pays de Labourd in 1609, emphasized the erotic content of their dances and their promiscuous sexual activity at the sabbath, while Nicolas Remy, the lawyer who served as *procureur générale* in the duchy of Lorraine, dwelt on the way in which witches experienced the coldness of the Devil's phallus during intercourse.[40]

The view that women were driven by lust was especially pertinent to the crime of witchcraft, for it was believed that the witch often made a pact with the Devil as a result of sexual temptation and then engaged in promiscuous sexual intercourse at the sabbath. Male witches also took part in these orgies, but the assumption that women were more eager to satisfy their lust in this way simply reinforced the image of the female witch. That image received strong visual reinforcement in the engravings of Hans Baldung Grien, who depicted witches as the embodiment of female sexual power[41] (see Figure 5.1). This erotic literature and art, which could be published only because it condemned the activities of the women it depicted, can legitimately be considered the pornography of its day.

SOURCE
BOOK

The problem with basing an explanation of female witchcraft on miso-gynistic excerpts from witchcraft treatises is that this literature did not have very much to do with the original identification of women as witches. The people who determined who would be prosecuted for witchcraft were almost always the witches' neighbours, who brought the original accusa-tions to the attention of the court. When confessing witches named their accomplices, they selected people whom they knew rather than names that judges suggested to them. Even when judges proceeded *ex officio* and initiated prosecutions by their own authority, they depended upon ill-fame or rumour within the community to identify suspects. The only time when the literary stereotype of the witch as morally weak and sexually charged might have influenced the initial identification of women as witches was when members of the clergy who were engaged in a programme of religious or moral reform denounced or otherwise singled out as witches women who were morally suspect.[42]

We must turn our attention, therefore, to the witches' neighbours to determine why the overwhelming majority of people identified as witches were women. These villagers and townfolk may have shared some of the negative, clerically inspired views of women, but being more concerned with the magical than with the diabolical aspects of witchcraft, they tended to suspect women because their customary roles in society gave them more opportunities to practise harmful magic. Women in early modern European communities generally served as the cooks, healers and midwives, and each of these functions made them vulnerable to the charge that they practised harmful magic. As cooks they not only had the opportunity to gather herbs for magical purposes, but they also had the skill to turn them into potions and unguents. It is no accident that witches are often portrayed standing over cauldrons, for it was in such vessels that many of the agents of sorcery were allegedly concocted (see Figure 1.2). The image of a man engaged in this type of activity is at the very least implausible.

Women also acted as healers in early modern European villages. Often known as 'wise women', these persons used a variety of folk remedies – mainly herbs and ointments – in their work. Many of these treatments should be regarded as magical, if only because natural ingredients were usually supple-mented with magical formulae or superstitious prayers. Since wise women served a useful function in their communities, their neighbours generally tolerated them. They were, however, vulnerable to the charge of practising white magic, and when villagers contracted a disease or died unexpectedly, they might be accused of using their magical arts for maleficent purposes. The *Malleus* makes specific reference to those witches who could cure as well as injure, and in 1499 a woman from Modena reassured the Inquisition that 'who knows how to heal knows how to destroy'.[43] Studies of witchcraft depositions in France, Switzerland, Austria, Hungary, Schleswig-Holstein,

England, Scotland and New England reveal that many of those who were prosecuted for witchcraft were in fact wise women.[44] The same was true in France, where roughly one-half of the witchcraft cases that reached the Parlement of Paris on appeal involved accusations of magical healing.[45]

Like cooks and healers, midwives were also vulnerable to charges of sorcery. Until the eighteenth century, when male midwives and doctors began to assist in the process of childbirth, the delivery of infants was entrusted entirely to women. A number of these midwives – although probably not as many as was once believed – were prosecuted for witchcraft.[46] The main reason for their susceptibility to charges of this nature was that they could easily be blamed for the death of infants. In an age when as many as one-fifth of all children died either at birth or during the first few months of life, and when infanticide was by no means a rare occurrence, the charge that a midwife had killed a child by sorcery was both functional and plausible, and it offered the bereaved parents a means of revenge. In some cases the midwife became the victim of years of accumulated suspicion. In the German town of Dillingen a licensed midwife by the name of Walpurga Hausmännin was accused in 1587 of having caused the death of forty children, some of them as early as twelve years before, by witchcraft.[47]

SOURCE
BOOK

Once the midwife had been accused of various *maleficia*, demonological theory, which was admittedly of greater importance to judges than to common folk, gave added plausibility to her crime. Witches, it will be recalled, were allegedly eager to obtain unbaptized babies so that they could sacrifice them to the Devil, feast upon their flesh at the sabbath meal and use their remains in the production of magical ointments. As midwives, witches were ideally situated to procure the necessary infants, and they also had a perfect opportunity to baptize them into the Devil's service. In 1728 a Hungarian midwife from Szeged who was burned at the stake for witchcraft was charged with baptizing 2,000 children in the Devil's name.[48]

More numerous than midwives among the accused were women who were engaged in caring for other women's children. Lyndal Roper has shown that many of the witchcraft accusations in Augsburg in the late sixteenth and early seventeenth centuries arose out of conflicts between mothers and the lying-in maids who provided care for them and their infants for a number of weeks after birth.[49] It was not unnatural for the mothers to project their anxieties about their own health, as well as the precarious health of their infants, on to these women. When some misfortune did occur, therefore, the lying-in maids were highly vulnerable to charges of having deprived the baby of nourishment or of having killed it. What is interesting about these accusations is that they originated in tensions among women rather than between men and women. The same can be said regarding many other accusations made against women for harming young children.[50] The origin of these tensions in female circles helps to explain why a large number of witnesses in witchcraft trials were in fact women.[51]

The women who accused and testified against women for allegedly harming their children imagined that the witch was the inverse of both the good wife and the good mother. She was the person who, instead of providing sustenance for her family, contaminated the food supply with her poisons and powders and who, instead of nurturing and caring for young children, caused their sickness or death.[52] This interpretation of witchcraft accusations is applicable only in cases where young children were the victims of the alleged *maleficia*, and it is more persuasive in explaining the accusations that came from women than from men. Even if it cannot provide a comprehensive explanation of the preponderance of women as witches, it serves the important function of showing that the villagers and townspeople who accused witches were just as likely to fantasize about the witches' alleged activities as the judges who imagined that they were flying off to the sabbath and worshipping the Devil.[53]

A final explanation of the preponderance of female witches is that women, who generally had none of men's physical or political power, were believed to be able to use sorcery as an instrument of protection and revenge. The power to bring about harm by magical means was one of the few forms of power available to women in early modern Europe. Even if women did not actually have recourse to the magical arts for such purposes, they were naturally suspected of doing so. This popular view of the witch as a powerful woman reminds us that although the witch was often a scapegoat for the ills of society and a victim, many of her neighbours viewed her as both powerful and threatening.[54] By having her tried and executed, her neighbours were not simply picking on a helpless old woman but counteracting a form of female power that they believed had placed them, their children and their domestic animals in considerable danger.

Age

There is very little evidence relating to the age of witches, but the limited data that we do have regarding age, which are summarized in Table 5.2,[55] suggest that a solid majority of witches were older than fifty, which in the early modern period was considered to be a much more advanced age than it is today.[56] It appears, moreover, that the typical witch was significantly older than fifty. In two locations, Geneva and the English county of Essex, the median age of witches was just about sixty, while four of the six witches examined at Musselburgh in Midlothian, Scotland, on 29 July 1661 were identified as being in their sixties.[57] Reginald Scot was on solid ground, therefore, when he claimed that 'Witches are women which be commonly old'.[58]

Bearing in mind their fragmentary statistical foundation, there is good reason to treat these generalizations regarding the age of witches with caution. In analysing the data for Rothenburg ob der Tauber, Alison Rowlands has discovered a pattern of accusation in which people from a wide range

Table 5.2 Ages of accused witches.

Region	Years	Witches of known age	Number 50 or over	% 50 or over
Geneva	1537–1662	95	71	75
Dept of the Nord, France	1542–1679	47	24	51
County of Essex, England	1645	15	13	87
Württemberg	1560–1701	29	16	55
Salem, Mass.	1692–1693	118	49	42
Scotland	1563–1736	166	68	41
Saarland	1575–1634			56
Rothenburg	1561–1652	48	17	40
Würzburg	1550–1650	190	112	59
Siena	1580–1721	79	41	52

of age groups, including children, were prosecuted.[59] Many of the depictions of witches in early modern art lend support to her argument. Young attractive females clearly outnumber older ones in the engravings of Hans Baldung Grien, Albrecht Dürer and Filipino Lippi (see Figure 5.1).

Even after making these qualifications, however, we are still faced with the question of why so many old people, especially old women, were prosecuted for witchcraft. The percentage of old witches becomes even more striking when we consider that because of low life expectancies, people in the age group of fifty or older constituted a very small percentage of early modern populations. The most plausible explanation for this statistical pattern is that witches were often suspected of witchcraft for many years before they were tried in a court of law. When villagers first suspected a person of witchcraft, they generally did not denounce her to the authorities but either attempted a reconciliation with her or took informal countermeasures against her. They also sought confirmation from neighbours that they too suspected that the person was a witch. Legal proceedings were generally taken as a last resort, when efforts at reconciliation or countermeasures had failed.[60] Consequently, most witches were fairly old when they were brought to trial, although not when they were first suspected.

The reluctance to take legal action when witches were first suspected explains why, when witches were eventually tried, depositions of witnesses against them included events that had transpired decades before. In Lorraine, for example, the witnesses testifying against Françatte Camont, who was about fifty-four years old, reported incidents that had transpired twenty years and in some cases thirty years before.[61] These depositions were not the product of recovered memory, triggered only at the time of the witch's arrest. They were statements of long-standing suspicion that grew over the years and contributed to Camont's reputation as a witch. Since suspicions of Camont began only when she reached adulthood, she was of necessity 'old' when she was finally brought to trial. The same can be said of the midwife Walpurga Hausmännin,

Figure 5.1 Hans Baldung Grien's engraving of witches, young and old, playing leapfrog.

who had been practising as a midwife for more than thirty years before she was accused of witchcraft.[62]

An equally plausible explanation for the relatively advanced age of witches is that healers, lying-in maids and other women entrusted with the care and nourishment of young children – the very occupational groups that were most vulnerable to accusations – were almost always well along in years. The typical female witch was an older, postmenopausal woman who had borne children and who wished to strengthen her ties with her community by caring for young children. Such older women could easily be suspected of envying the young mothers whose children were placed in their care. Lyndal Roper has argued that it was not the appearance of old age as such but the ending of fertility that made a woman especially vulnerable to witchcraft accusations.[63]

An additional factor that might have contributed to the suspicion that older women were witches is that women who were over sixty years of age often manifested signs of eccentric or antisocial behaviour, which tended to make neighbours uncomfortable and invite accusations of witchcraft.[64] In a few isolated instances this behaviour might be attributed to senility. The seventeenth-century French dramatist Cyrano de Bergerac apparently had the senile witch in mind when he wrote:

> She was old: age had weakened her reason. Age makes one gossipy: she invented the story to amuse her neighbors. Age weakens the sight: she mistook a Hare for a Cat. Age makes one afraid: she thought she saw fifty instead of one.[65]

A final reason for the accusation of people whom we would term senior citizens today is that they were physically less powerful than younger persons and more likely, therefore, to use sorcery as a means of protection or revenge. Younger women, who are often depicted in Renaissance art as capable of violence, might have been able to defend themselves against some of their enemies,[66] but older women were forced to rely upon the tenuous authority they had acquired by virtue of either their longevity or the alleged control that they exercised over the occult forces of nature.[67]

The image of the old, postmenopausal witch was by no means incompatible with the prevailing view of the witch as a woman driven by sexual desire. It might strike us that beautiful, young women, who often appear as witches in contemporary paintings and engravings,[68] would have been considered more sexually voracious than old crones, but contemporaries did not always see it that way. It is true that the authors of the *Malleus maleficarum* distinguished between the 'honest matrons who are little given to carnal vice' and young girls, who were 'more given to bodily lusts and pleasures', but other writers did not agree with them.[69] The Englishman Robert Burton, in his popular book, *Anatomy of Melancholy* (1621), while complaining that girls sought sex as soon as they reached puberty, emphasized that older women were just

Figure 5.2 The Devil seducing a woman into making a pact with him. The Devil was
often described as having appeared to a woman in a man's clothing and seduced
her into his service. From Ulrich Molitor, *De Lamiis* (1589).

as lustful. 'Yet whilst she is so old a crone', wrote Burton, 'she caterwauls
and must have a stallion, a champion; she must and will marry again, and
betroth herself to some young man.'[70] Even today, in the Spanish province of
Andalusia, widows are 'commonly believed, even in cases of apparent
implausibility, to be sexually predatory upon young men'.[71]

Underlying the depiction of the old, sexually voracious hag was a deep male
fear of the sexually experienced, sexually independent woman. The young
maiden, lustful though she may have been, was at least still assumed to be
sexually inexperienced until she married, at which time she became strictly
subordinated to her husband. There was much more to be feared from the
sexually experienced, mature woman, whose passion had not subsided,
especially if she was no longer married and no longer able to conceive a child.
Perhaps it was this fear that lay at the basis of the frequent condemnation and
ridicule of female, postmenopausal lust.[72] An added source of male anxiety in
this regard was the widespread recognition that men were not only less ardent
but also less sexually capable than women as they entered old age.[73]

It was the old witch, therefore, and especially the old widow, who became
the primary object of male sexual fear, male hostility and male accusations of
witchcraft. The designation of such women as witches also made sense in the

context of demonological theory, since the Devil, who was known for his sexual prowess, was believed to appear to prospective witches in the form of an attractive young man and make sexual advances to them (see Figure 5.2). Since older women were considered to be driven by lust and yet were often unable to find sexual partners, they would be ideal prey for the Prince of Darkness. In a witchcraft treatise written in about 1540, Arnaldo Albertini, the bishop of Patti in Sicily, argued that witches were mostly old women who could not find lovers and who therefore became *striges*.[74]

Although the great majority of witches were old or middle-aged, younger persons were by no means immune to prosecution. Those witches who were originally accused of performing love magic, for example, tended to be in their twenties or early thirties, since it was customary for relatively young women to practise that particular trade. This probably explains why the Venetian Inquisition, which was particularly concerned with the practice of love, tried more witches who were in their twenties and thirties than in their forties and fifties.[75]

Occasionally children and adolescents were tried and executed for witch-craft.[76] Children are probably more famous as the source than the object of witchcraft accusations, but in some hunts they were prosecuted in large numbers, especially in the seventeenth and early eighteenth centuries.[77] One set of circumstances in which they appeared in fairly large numbers was when the process of making accusations got out of control. At Würzburg, for example, more than 25 per cent of the 160 witches executed between 1627 and 1629 were children, all of them having been implicated in the later stages of the hunt.[78] Occasionally the children of witches were suspected of and charged with witchcraft, for it was widely believed that witches could acquire their powers from their parents, usually by instruction but sometimes by heredity.[79] In one case in Saxony in 1660 the two children of a magician were summarily executed upon the conviction of their father.[80]

Children also figured prominently in witch-hunts when the fertile imaginations of youth were given encouragement and credence. In the famous witch-hunt in the Basque country in 1609–11, when witches were given freedom to confess with impunity, more than 1,300 of the some 1,800 individuals who confessed were minors. In another well-known hunt, which began at Mora in Sweden in 1668, a combination of youthful imagination and the naming of accomplices resulted in the production of a dispropor-tionately high number of child witches. The hunt began when a fifteen-year-old boy accused a young girl and several others of stealing children for the Devil. In the trials that followed, a number of children were condemned to death, while many others were given non-capital punishments on the basis of testimony by confessing witches that the children had accompanied them to the sabbath.[81]

The prosecution of children as witches themselves rather than as victims or accusers of their elders and parents tended to occur mainly in the seventeenth century, after prosecutions had peaked. It can reasonably be assumed, therefore, that the increased prosecutions of children played a significant role in the decline and end of witchcraft.[82] It is no coincidence that child witches figured prominently in the last large witch-hunts in Sweden, Augsburg and Austria. The conviction and especially the execution of children for criminal behaviour causes concern in any society, and the miscarriages of justice involving child witches contributed to a general doubt that those accused were guilty. As we shall see in Chapter 8, this scepticism eventually developed into an uncertainty whether any person at all could be proven guilty of the crime.

Marital status

The marital status of accused witches varied greatly from place to place and from time to time, as the scant evidence summarized in Table 5.3 indicates.[83] In most regions, however, the percentage of unmarried witches (i.e. those who were either widowed or who had never married) was higher than the percentage of such people in the general female population. In six of the ten regions represented in the table, married witches did not even form a majority of those accused, and in some areas, such as the English county of Kent and the city of Toul in Lorraine, the percentage of married witches was astonishingly low.[84] Among the unmarried witches, the widows were the most numerous, but we cannot ignore the single witches, for without them we would not be able to claim that the typical European witch was unmarried.

It is difficult to determine how much the unmarried status of witches made them vulnerable to witchcraft accusations. Villagers and townspeople may have suspected widows and elderly spinsters of witchcraft mainly because they were old and poor rather than because they were unmarried.[85] There is reason to believe, however, that the single status of many witches contributed at least indirectly to their plight. In a patriarchal society, the existence of women who were subject neither to father nor husband was a source of concern, if not fear, and it is not unreasonable to assume that both the neighbours who accused such women and the authorities who prosecuted them were responding to such fears.[86] These same accusers might also have come to the conclusion that unmarried women, regardless of age, were more likely than their married counterparts to have been seduced by a demon impersonating a man.

The fears of authorities regarding unmarried women acquired greater urgency during the early modern period both because their numbers were increasing and because their position in towns and villages was changing. The percentage of widows in the female population, which usually ranged from 10 to 20 per cent, rose at times and in certain places to 30 per cent.[87] These increases usually occurred after visitations of the plague, which often caused more deaths among men than women, and after periods of warfare, when men suffered greater casualties than women.[88] At the same time, the number of

Table 5.3 Marital status of accused female witches (status known).

Region Married	Dates	Married	Widowed	Single	% Married
City of Toul	1584–1623	17	29	7	36
Basel	1571–1670	110	60	11	61
Montbéliard	1555–1661	31	25	11	50
County of Essex, England	1645 only	22	21	8	43
County of Kent, England	1560–1700	11	24	19	25
Scotland	1560–1727	245	67	7	70
Salem, Mass.	1692–1693	68	22	40	52
Sweden	1668–1676	49	19	32	49
Geneva	1537–1662	104	81	50	44
Venice	1550–1650	170	71	32	62

women who never married increased from about 5 per cent in the late Middle Ages to 10 per cent, and in some places to as much as 20 per cent by the seventeenth century, a development that coincided with an increase in the age at first marriage.[89] As this change was taking place, the institutions that had accommodated a large proportion of the single female population in the Middle Ages – the convents – either experienced a decline in membership or were dissolved as a result of the Reformation. This meant that early modern European communities not only contained more unmarried women than they had during the Middle Ages but also had greater difficulty accommodating them. Many unmarried women, to be sure, found places in the patriarchal households of masters, brothers or adult children, but others opted for an independent existence. To make matters worse, most of these unmarried women were fairly poor, and thus represented a serious social problem. Unmarried women, like many others suspected of witchcraft, were perceived as a threat to the social order.

Unlike the single and widowed witches, married witches generally did not become vulnerable to charges of witchcraft by virtue of their marital status. Other factors relating either to their sex or economic position appear to have been much more important in arousing suspicion of them. There were, however, two situations in which the marital status of a witch contributed at least indirectly to the charges against her. The first was when conflicts between her and her spouse or children gave rise to accusations of witchcraft. One of the attractions of accusing someone of witchcraft was that it allowed a person to express hostile feelings that did not have any other socially approved means of expression. Generally speaking, hostilities among family members were not allowed to result in violence or legal action. We might expect, therefore, that witchcraft accusations would occasionally surface within family units, and with the notable exception of England, they often did.[90] Since witchcraft was generally viewed as a crime committed by adult females, wives and mothers were more vulnerable to such charges than other members of the family. Not only did husbands occasionally name their wives as witches, but children sometimes accused their mothers.[91] In a number of cases children and their spouses used witchcraft accusations to retaliate against a mother who disapproved of their marriage. Indeed, witchcraft accusations became one of the many weapons that were used to attack the custom of arranged marriage, a practice that underwent a gradual loss of popularity during the early modern period as religious reformers insisted upon marital fidelity and as the age at first marriage increased.[92]

The second situation in which a woman's marital status led to her accusation as a witch was when she became involved in conflicts over her husband's property. Although married women had no independent wealth or property at this time, they very often assisted their husbands in their work. All too often, therefore, they found themselves involved in disputes over rents, labour or even the possession of land, and we know that many of these disputes led to witchcraft accusations. One of the charges against Margaret Allan, a Scottish woman from Musselburgh tried for witchcraft in 1661, originated in a conflict between her husband and one of his creditors, William Tate. After Tate had Allan's goods seized in order to repay a debt, Tate's horse and oxen died, a misfortune later interpreted as an act of witchcraft. Margaret was also accused of using sorcery to 'distract him of his wits' because he had taken some of her husband's land.[93]

Social and economic status

Although very little hard evidence regarding the social, occupational and economic status of witches has survived, we can be fairly certain that the great majority of those prosecuted came from the lower levels of society. The general comments made by the authors of witchcraft treatises, the allegation that witches made pacts with the Devil in exchange for very little material gain, the motives attributed to witches for taking action against their neighbours, and the mere fact that so many witches were unattached women of no apparent social distinction all point to this conclusion. Witches were not necessarily the very poorest members of society. Vagrants, for example, do not appear to have figured very prominently in the trials, except in Russia and Austrian Habsburg lands,[94] and many witches owned some property.[95] Witches did, however, often live on the margin of subsistence, and some of them did in fact have to resort to begging to survive.[96] Indeed, the Italian physician Girolamo Cardano described witches as 'miserable old women, beggars, existing in the valleys on chestnuts and field herbs', while Nicolas Remy, in his treatise of 1595, claimed that witches were 'for the most part beggars, who support life on the alms they receive'.[97] In New England, the great majority of women accused of witchcraft before the Salem episode of

1692 were dependent members of the community who qualified for poor relief.[98] The witches imprisoned within the presbytery of Dunfermline, Scotland, in 1649 were reported to be so impoverished that they could not provide for themselves in gaol.[99] In Norway, where large numbers of accused witches were described in the trial records as extremely poor, most of those who were actually convicted were beggars.[100]

One reason why the people who filled the lower ranks of society incurred accusations of witchcraft is that poor people, especially poor women, were the weakest and most vulnerable members of society. 'Witches', wrote Johann Weyer, 'are poor ignorant creatures, old and powerless'.[101] Because of this impotence, they were most readily chosen as scapegoats for the ills of society. As individuals in dire financial straits, moreover, they were the persons most likely to resort to the selling of magical cures in order to survive, or to use sorcery as a means of revenge against those who threatened to deprive them of their already meagre resources. Even if they did not actually practise maleficent magic, they would be the ones most readily suspected of doing so. In a similar vein, poor people were the most likely members of society to try to make pacts with the Devil in order to improve their economic situation, and even though very few of them did so, a charge to that effect was eminently plausible. Finally, and perhaps most importantly, poor people, being dependent upon the community, easily aroused feelings of resentment and (when assistance was not forthcoming) guilt among their neighbours for not fulfilling their Christian duty. The naming of poor people as witches in these circumstances represented attempts either to retaliate in a legitimate fashion against those who imposed on them or to project their own guilt on to the same persons.

Since the poverty of witches appears to have been of no little importance in encouraging people to accuse them of this crime, it is reasonable to assume that some of the economic changes of the early modern period played a part in causing the great European witch-hunt. There is no doubt that the most intense period of witch-hunting occurred at a time when poverty was becoming more severe and widespread. The main reason for this unkind development was a dramatic increase in the European population from the early sixteenth to the early seventeenth century. Because labour was in abundant supply, real wages declined sharply. At the same time, unprecedented inflation, caused mainly by the pressure of an expanding population on a limited supply of resources, had a more serious impact on the poor than on the rich. The net result was a decline in the standard of living, a process that began in the late fifteenth century and continued well into the eighteenth.[102] This decline was widely felt, but it most seriously affected the most marginal elements of society, the very people who became the main victims of the witch-hunt.

If economic change deepened the predicament of the poor, making them more willing to contemplate sorcery as a solution to their problems, it also made their accusers more willing to make witchcraft accusations. Since almost all people were at least frightened by the prospect of economic decline, they became less accommodating and tolerant in their dealings with the poor and more willing to use witchcraft accusations to maintain their tenuous position in society. In some cases, as in many English witchcraft prosecutions studied by Alan Macfarlane, they became less willing to give the poor the assistance that medieval social and religious theory demanded. In other cases, the accusers of witches became more intolerant of the poor and more willing to take legal action against them because they reminded them all too easily of what they themselves might have become in such times.

Although the great majority of witches lived in straitened economic circumstances, a few were relatively well off. Sometimes these wealthier witches were accused in the later stages of chain-reaction hunts, just as men and children were, as the stereotype of the witch broke down. At other times, however, prominent and wealthy men became the early targets of witchcraft accusations. This happened most frequently at the beginning of the European witch-hunt, when a number of witches in high places were accused, usually in connection with some sort of real or imagined political conspiracy. When charges of this nature arose, they bore a close resemblance to the charges of politically inspired sorcery that occurred frequently in the fourteenth and fifteenth centuries. Even in seventeenth-century accusations, however, political motives could come into play, such as when members of town councils accused their rivals or their wives of witchcraft.

Another motive for accusing wealthy and prominent persons was the desire of either relatives or magistrates to acquire a witch's property upon conviction. In colonial New England inheritance played a particularly important role in the accusation of witches. Carol Karlsen has shown that most of the New England women named as witches had either inherited property or stood to inherit it. The wealth of these women varied greatly, but as mothers without sons or as women without brothers they all 'stood in the way of the orderly transmission of property from one generation of males to another'.[103] Thus conflicts between men and women over economic resources played a central role in determining the pattern of New England witchcraft accusations.

The personality of the witch

As we turn to the personal, as opposed to the social and economic characteristics of the witch, we encounter a picture of broad diversity. As one might expect, witches did not all conform to one single personality profile. They did, nevertheless, often exhibit certain behavioural characteristics that explain why they, rather than others, were singled out for accusation and prosecution. First and most commonly, witches were often described as sharp-tongued, bad-tempered and quarrelsome, traits that naturally involved them in disputes with their neighbours and directed non-specific, communal resentment against them.[104] Witches were very often the village scolds who, among other things, were prone to cursing, a habit that could easily be interpreted as an act of sorcery and the cause of a neighbour's misfortune. In colonial New England those women accused of witchcraft had a reputation for their threatening and 'disorderly' speech.[105] Witches were, in other words, people one did not enjoy having as neighbours.

Since witches were a group of predominantly old persons, they often manifested signs of dementia. It is of course such persons who very often exhibit the signs of contentiousness and irritability that we have just referred to. The dementia of witches, moreover, best explains the widespread but erroneous belief that witches were mentally unbalanced.[106] Witches certainly had vivid imaginations, as the details of free confessions clearly reveal, and some of them may have been mythomaniacs.[107] Whether any significant number of them suffered from the disorder that early modern physicians called melancholy, which was believed to cause anxiety, depression, sorrow and chronic fatigue, is much more doubtful.[108] The sixteenth-century sceptic Johann Weyer thought that the 'silly and miserable' women who believed they had made pacts with the Devil and rode out at night with Diana had contracted melancholy, and it is possible that some witches were depressed. But on the basis of what we know today regarding the mental effects of old age, the women about whom Weyer was writing, as well as the great majority of 'mentally unbalanced' witches, were probably exhibiting the signs of nothing more than dementia.[109]

Another personal characteristic of many witches was their reputation for various forms of religious or moral deviance. Witches were, by definition, intrinsically evil creatures, and consequently their neighbours assumed that their acts of *maleficium* and Devil-worship formed only part of a poor moral record. Conversely, the reputation of witches for other moral transgressions made them more vulnerable to the charge of witchcraft. In determining the moral reputation of those persons accused of witchcraft we cannot rely upon the references to their recurrent sinfulness that often appear in the formal charges against them, since magistrates might have deliberately inserted such statements, regardless of their veracity, into the record in order to present the witch in the worst possible light. But there is independent judicial evidence, usually contained in church court records, of the fact that many witches had in fact been suspected of and occasionally prosecuted for other manifestations of immoral behaviour.[110] Witches were surely not hardened criminals, and no more than a small percentage of them had ever been prosecuted for serious crimes like theft.[111] A number of witches, however, had been named in ecclesiastical courts for such crimes as non-attendance at church, Sabbath-breaking, cursing, fornication, prostitution, abortion and even adultery, while some male witches had been suspected, if not formally accused, of homosexuality.[112] An English woman tried for witchcraft in 1613 had given birth to three illegitimate children, while some of the women accused of witchcraft in Lucerne were known to have spoken openly about sexual matters or to have displayed their sexuality publicly.[113] It is also clear that women who were suspected of religious nonconformity or who had no religion at all were vulnerable to charges of witchcraft.[114] On the basis of all this evidence it may be too strong to suggest that witches were deviants,[115] a word that often connotes criminality, but they certainly had displayed 'inappropriate female behaviour' and had failed to protect their reputations.[116]

Witches as rebels

The witch was viewed by authorities as a rebel – an apostate rebel against God and a conspirator against the political, social and moral order of humankind. As we have seen, the fear of rebellion in late medieval and early modern European society played a significant role in creating the fantasy of the witches' sabbath and in arousing fear and hatred of the witch. It remains to be determined, however, to what extent witches conformed in reality to this learned stereotype. Since an actual sect of witches almost certainly did not exist, it is difficult to depict them, in the tradition of nineteenth-century French historiography, as rebellious peasants who gathered secretly to protest the economic and social injustices of their world.[117] It is possible to interpret some of their confessions, in which they described a world turned upside down, as symbolic protests against the established order, as Emmanuel Le Roy Ladurie has claimed.[118] But since many of these confessions were adduced under torture, the symbols contained in them usually reflect the projected fears of magistrates more than they do the protests of the poor. As long as we see witches as scapegoats and victims, which in the great majority of cases they were, it is difficult to depict them as protesters or rebels, even if it can be shown that some of them came from rebel families.[119] Only in colonial Peru, where witches became identified as the defenders of native Andean culture against the Spanish regime, could witches be considered actual political subversives, encouraging disobedience to both the parish priests and local political authorities.[120]

In a certain sense, however, European witches did play the part of rebels. All too often the witch, in her determination to survive in a hostile environment, registered a protest against her male social and political superiors. Sometimes it took the form of a curse or an act of sorcery, the witch's only weapons against the villagers and officials who victimized her. At other times it took the form of a heroic protest against the courts that investigated her. Some witches, to be sure, submitted meekly to the pricker and the torturer in the naive confidence that they would be vindicated. Sometimes, almost inconceivably, they expressed gratitude to their torturers.[121] At other times, however, they submitted reluctantly, voicing threats against their inquisitors. At Salem, for example, the witches who were punished most severely were those who refused to recognize the authority of the court that was trying them.[122] Such individual protests did not turn the witch into a conspiratorial rebel, but they do suggest that the image of her as a totally passive victim must be seriously qualified. In the duchy of Württemberg, witches displayed an aggressiveness that was regarded as inappropriate for their sex, while in the Pays de Labourd they were known for their 'effrontery'. In Russia a group of witches showed disrespect or insubordination for their superiors, thereby challenging the hierarchical social order.[123]

If we need one word to describe the witch of the early modern period, we might refer to her as a nonconformist. The witch was usually not a foreigner or stranger in her community, but she was hardly a typical villager. Older and poorer than average, and more often than not unmarried, she did not adhere to the traditional behavioural standards of her community or of her sex. By her actions and her words she defied contemporary standards of docility and domesticity and inverted the ideal of the good Christian wife and mother.[124] Cranky, acerbic, and often angry about her plight, she attracted attention, hostility, suspicion and fear. Sometimes, but by no means always, she possessed physical characteristics that made her appear even more different from the norm. For Reginald Scot, witches were 'commonly old, lame, blear-eyed, pale, foul and full of wrinkles . . . lean and deformed, showing melancholy in their faces to the horror of all that see them'.[125] By prosecuting such persons, members of the ruling elite may not have been eliminating rebels in the traditional sense of the word, but they were, perhaps unconsciously, making their communities more homogeneous and possibly even more harmonious. They also were upholding conventional standards of female conduct.

Social and economic change and witch-hunting

Although social and economic factors certainly played an important role in prompting witchcraft accusations and in determining which individuals were blamed for personal misfortune, it is more debatable whether the European witch-hunt, taken as a whole, should be considered the product of social and economic *change*. There is no question that some of the economic, social and demographic developments that occurred in early modern Europe aggravated the personal tensions that underlay many witchcraft accusations. As mentioned above, inflation, an increase in poverty, pressure by a growing population on a limited supply of resources, the growth of the unattached female population, and changes in the structure of the family all played some part in encouraging witchcraft accusations. Some women may have been accused of witchcraft because they were most adversely affected by such change or, with respect to the advent of capitalism, most resistant to it.[126] In addition, specific economic crises, such as famine, outbreaks of epidemic disease, and dislocations caused by war, may have helped to trigger many individual witch-hunts. Wolfgang Behringer has demonstrated a correlation between intense periods of witch-hunting and harsh climatic conditions that produced widespread famine.[127]

The large witch-hunts that he studied in Bavaria conform fairly closely to this pattern, but in other parts of Europe, especially in Scotland, the connection between economic change and witch-hunting is far less apparent. Moreover, many of the personal conflicts that led to witchcraft accusations, as well as the misfortunes that triggered them, such as the illness or death of a young child, were a constant feature of village life and could just as easily have developed in good times as in bad.[128] In many cases the charges against witches provide little evidence that they or their neighbours were responding to social or economic change, and in the few instances when magistrates or inquisitors initiated and directed the prosecutions, the connections often become even more elusive.

There was, however, a more general and indirect way in which social change contributed to witch-hunting. When combined with the religious and political changes of this period, social and economic change created a mood of anxiety in all segments of society that made people more aware of the danger of witchcraft in the world and more eager to counteract it. The anthropologist Adam Ashforth detected a similar fear of witchcraft among South Africans in Soweto during the 1990s. Ashforth claims that the sense of insecurity caused by a combination of poverty, disease, violence and political oppression in everyday life led Sowetans to attribute their many misfortunes to evil forces in the world, namely witchcraft.[129] It might be objected that all historical ages are periods of change and anxiety among those who either experience or witness it. That may very well be true, but the period of the witchcraft trials, just like the 1990s in South Africa, was a special case. During these years Europe not only experienced unprecedented inflation and a decline in the standard of living, but also the growth of capitalism, the emergence of the modern state, a rash of rebellions and civil wars, international conflict on an unprecedented scale, and the destruction of the ostensible unity of medieval Christendom. The changes that took place were more fundamental, rapid and extensive than at any other time in European history before the advent of the Industrial Revolution. These changes took a heavy psychic toll. For a population that believed in the fixed order of the cosmos and society, the trans-formation of almost every aspect of their lives was a disconcerting experience. It may have produced the mood of gloom, pessimism and sadness that contemporaries and historians have detected in late medieval and early modern Europe, and it certainly created deep fear among those who were unable to cope with the instability and uncertainty of the new world.[130] It was the prevalence of such fear throughout Europe and in all social classes that has led to the designation of this period as one of the 'most psychically disturbed periods in human history'.[131]

The prevalence of this anxiety created a mood both among the elite and the common people that greatly encouraged the process of witch-hunting. Among the learned and ruling classes it encouraged a tendency to attribute the turmoil, instability and confusion that they saw everywhere around them to the influence of Satan in the world, a process which in turn suggested the activity of witches. Many of the concrete signs of social disintegration – religious dissent, popular rebellion, the apparent spread of poverty, and even the emergence of the spirit of capitalism – were in fact often attributed to Satan and his allies. Convinced that the Devil was loose, members of the administrative elite could easily come to the conclusion that one of the best ways to counteract him and his destructive influence was to prosecute those individuals who had made pacts with him. In this way the world could be purified of its diabolical contaminants and the order of society restored. By conducting a witch-hunt, moreover, administrative authorities could heal, at least temporarily, potentially dangerous divisions in society by focusing the attention of the entire community on a common enemy, and so distract them from more serious (and more real) concerns.[132]

Among the common people an attack on witches also helped to relieve anxiety. The individuals who brought the initial charges against witches were of course doing this in a very specific way, since by denouncing witches they were explaining misfortunes that had befallen them and gaining revenge against those who had harmed them. But in a more general way the entire community, by assisting in the apprehension of witches, testifying against them and flocking to their execution, was responding to an emotional need. Faced with inflation, increased competition for a limited amount of land, periodic famine and visitations of the plague, and an often bewildering set of religious and political changes, peasants and labourers found in witch-hunting a release from the psychic turmoil they were experiencing. Witch-hunting, in other words, became one of the ways by which people could maintain their equilibrium at a time of great stress. Witches became the scapegoats not simply of those who had experienced misfortune but of entire communities.

The role played by witch-hunts in relieving anxiety becomes even more obvious when we consider the moral or spiritual anxiety that many villagers were experiencing at the time of the Reformation. As a result of the moral instruction and exhortation of religious reformers – both Protestant and Catholic – European villagers and townsmen of the sixteenth and seventeenth centuries were made highly conscious of their need to attain salvation. This process was naturally accompanied by widespread feelings of guilt for moral transgressions and anxiety regarding one's ultimate destination, especially since the standards of moral behaviour were themselves being transformed. In such circumstances the prosecution of individuals who by definition were intrinsically evil and who were allegedly undermining the entire moral order provided a certain amount of reassurance to troubled souls. Support for witchcraft trials provided a means by which the members of European communities could acquire confidence in their own moral sanctity and ultimate salvation.

The moral dimension of early modern European anxiety reveals how difficult it is to separate the effects of social and economic change from those of religious change. The malaise that early modern Europeans experienced may be vague and difficult to analyse, but it certainly resulted as much from the process of religious change as from the transformation of society and the economy. Once a general mood conducive to witch-hunting had been established, then much more specific social and economic concerns came into play and led to the identification of certain individuals – usually poor, old women – as witches.

Notes

1. In this regard a contrast between England and such areas as southeastern Scotland, Lorraine, and Franche-Comté is instructive. Levack, *Witch-Hunting in Scotland*, 92; Delumeau, *La Peur*, 375.

2. Tausiet, *Urban Magic in Early Modern Spain*, 7, 143–4, 157–8; Schormann, *Deutschland*, 72; R. Muchembled, 'Satan ou les hommes? La chasse aux sorcières et ses causes', in M. Dupont-Bouchat *et al.*, *Prophètes et sorciers dans les Pays-Bas XVIᵉ–XVIIIᵉ siècles* (Paris, 1978): 19; Monter, *Witchcraft in France and Switzerland*, 128, 200; Larner, *Enemies of God*, 199.

3. See Mair, *Witchcraft*, 9–10; M. J. Swartz, 'Modern Conditions and Witchcraft/Sorcery Accusations', in *Witchcraft and Sorcery*, ed. M. Marwick, 2nd edn (New York, 1982): 391–400.

4. Monter, *Witchcraft in France and Switzerland*, 65. See also Blauert, *Frühe Hexenverfolgungen*, 14.

5. J. Durrant, *Witchcraft, Gender and Society in Early Modern Germany* (Leiden, 2007): 245.

6. Baranowski, *Procesy Czarownic*, 180. That figure is consistent with Michael Ostling's calculation that about two-thirds of Polish trials in the town courts originated in villages. Village magistrates could not try capital cases but had to send the accused to a Saxon law court in a nearby town. M. Ostling, 'Witchcraft in Poland', in *The Oxford Handbook of Witchcraft in Early Modern Europe and Colonial America*, ed. B. P. Levack (Oxford, 2013): 325.

7. Heikkinen, *Paholaisen Liittolaiset*, 386.

8. See F. Braudel, *The Structures of Everyday Life* (New York, 1981): 482–4. If we use the figure of 10,000, the percentage drops to just over 3 per cent. J. De Vries, *European Urbanization* (Cambridge, MA, 1984).

9. Schormann, *Deutschland*, 72, uses 2,000 as the minimum population of a medium-sized town and 500 as the minimum size of a small town. D. Herlihy and C. Klapisch-Zuber, *Tuscans and their Families* (New Haven, 1985): 54, use 700–800 inhabitants as the dividing line between a village and a small city.

10. Macfarlane, *Witchcraft in Tudor and Stuart England*, 149, 325–30.

11. Kieckhefer, *European Witch Trials*, 95.

12. W. G. Naphy, *Plagues, Poisons and Potions: Plague Spreading Conspiracies in the Western Alps c. 1530–1640* (Manchester, 2002).

13. See Monter, *Witchcraft in France and Switzerland*, 207.

14. M. de Certeau, *The Possession at Loudun*, trans. M. B. Smith (Chicago, 1996): 4, sees a fundamental distinction between the essentially rural phenomenon of sorcery and the urban milieu of possession. One of the few group possessions in Germany began in the small town of Brakel in 1657. See R. Decker, *Witchcraft and the Papacy*, trans. H. C. E. Midelfort (Charlottesville, 2008): 157–73.

15. For the narrative of the case see R. Rapley, *A Case of Witchcraft: The Trial of Urbain Grandier* (Montreal, 1998).

16. Sources for Table 5.1: R. Schulte, *Hexenmeister: Die Verfolgung von Männern in Rahmen der Hexenverfolgung von 1530–1730 im Alten Reich* (Frankfurt, 1999): 81; Midelfort, *Witch Hunting*, 281; Rowlands, *Witchcraft Narratives in Germany*, 12n.; Durrant, *Witchcraft, Gender and Society*, xiv; W. Monter, 'Toads and Eurcharists: The Male Witches of Normandy, 1564–1660', *French Historical Studies* 20 (1997): 563–95; Monter, *Witchcraft in France and Switzerland*, 119–20; P. Kamber, 'La Chasse aux sorciers et sorcières dans le Pays de Vaud: Aspects quantitatifs (1581–1620)', *Revue historique vaudoise* 90 (1982): 22–3; Dupont-Bouchat, 'La Répression', 138; A. Denis, *La Sorcellerie a Toul aux XVIe et XVIIe siècles* (Toul, 1888): 177–8; Gari Lacruz, 'Variedad de competencias', 236; Martin, *Witchcraft and the Inquisition in Venice*, 226; Heikkinen and Kervinen, 'Finland', 321; Madar, 'Estonia I', 266–7; Kivelson, *Desperate Magic*, 83, 119; Klaniczay, 'Hungary', 222; Wyporska, 'Poland', 908; Macfarlane, *Witchcraft in Tudor and Stuart England*, 160; Karlsen, *The Devil in the Shape of a Woman*, 47; Larner *et al.*, *Source-Book*, 240, Table 6.

17. For the argument that witchcraft is universally specific to women see R. Briffault, *The Mothers* (New York, 1927), II: 556. See also M. Hester, *Lewd Women and Wicked Witches: A Study of the Dynamics of Male Domination* (London, 1992): 109–23. For an effective critique of the argument that witch-hunting was a disguised form of woman-hunting see R. Briggs, 'Women as Victims? Witches, Judges and the Community', *French History* 5 (1991): 438–50.

18. See, e.g., the illustrations in Guazzo, *Compendium Maleficarum* (Figures 2.4–2.6).

19. L. Apps and A. Gow, *Male Witches in Early Modern Europe* (Manchester, 2003). The witches described in Nider's *Formicarius* (1436–37) were both male and female. See Ginzburg, *Ecstasies*, 70.

20. Blécourt, 'The Making of the Female Witch', 298.

21. Monter, *Witchcraft in France and Switzerland*, 23–4. See also S. Burghartz, 'The Equation of Women and Witches: A Case Study of Witchcraft Trials in Lucerne and Lausanne in the Fifteenth and Sixteenth Centuries', in *The German Underworld*, ed. R. J. Evans (London, 1988), 64.

22. Russell, *Witchcraft in the Middle Ages*, 281; B. Easlea, *Witch Hunting, Magic and the New Philosophy: An Introduction to the Debates of the Scientific Revolution 1450–1750* (Brighton, 1980): 35–6.

23. Burghartz, 'Equation of Women and Witches', 64. The percentage of female witches was much higher in the trials conducted in the secular courts, such as at Lucerne, during the same period of time. In these trials, in which the demonological stereotype of the female witch was not very well established, more attention was given to *maleficium* than diabolism. Ibid., 62–4.

24. See Gari Lacruz, 'Variedad de competencias', 326.

25. On the preoccupation of the Venetian Inquisition with forms of magic that savoured of manifest heresy and their lack of interest in *maleficium* see Martin, *Witchcraft and the Inquisition in Venice*, 254–7.

26. See Peters, *Magician, Witch and the Law*, 120–5.

27. P. G. Maxwell-Stuart, *Satanic Conspiracy: Magic and Witchcraft in Sixteenth-Century Scotland* (East Linton, 2001), Chapter 6.

28. W. Behringer, *Shaman of Oberstdorf: Chonrad Stoecklin and the Phantoms of the Night*, trans. H. C. E. Midelfort (Charlottesville, 1998).

29. W. F. Ryan, 'The Witchcraft Hysteria in Early Modern Europe: Was Russia an Exception?', *Slavonic and East European Review* 76 (1998): 73–80. The fact that after 1716 witches were prosecuted mainly by the ecclesiastical courts and by the military courts helps to explain why a majority of the Russian witches, being either priests or soldiers, were men.

30. Monter, 'Toads and Eucharists', 563–95.

31. E. Labouvie, 'Männer im Hexenprozess: Zur Sozialanthropologie eines "männlichen" Verstandnisses von Magie und Hexerei', in *Hexenverfolgung in der dörflichen Gesellschaft*, ed. W. Schieder (Göttingen, 1990): 56–78.

32. M. Gaskill, 'The Devil in the Shape of a Man: Witchcraft, Conflict and Belief in Jacobean England', *Historical Research* 71 (1998): 142–78. One possible reason for the reluctance to prosecute men for witchcraft was the fear that conviction might undermine the patriarchal order of society. Prosecution was more likely when men violated traditional masculine roles or violated the ideal of the good head of their household. See A. Rowlands, 'Not "the Usual Suspects": Male Witches, Witchcraft and Masculinities in Early Modern Europe', in *Witchcraft and Masculinities in Early Modern Europe*, ed. A. Rowlands (Basingstoke, 2009): 1–30.

33. G. L. Burr, *The Witch Persecutions* (Philadelphia, 1902): 28.

34. Boyer and Nissenbaum, *Salem Possessed*, 32.

35. Holmes, 'Popular Culture', 95, argues that the association of maleficent power with women was 'a perdurable component of popular belief'.

36. *Malleus maleficarum*, 41–7; Lea, *Materials*, II: 449; P. de Lancre, *Tableau de l'inconstance des mauvais anges et démons*, ed. N. Jacques-Chaquin (Paris, 1982): 89–93; Remy, *Demonolatry*, 56; James VI, *Daemonologie*, 43–4; Weyer, *Witches, Devils and Doctors*, 181–3.

37. *Malleus maleficarum*, 47.

38. For the strength of the old image in the late seventeenth century see R. Thompson, *Unfit for Modest Ears* (London, 1979): 97.

39. Bodin, *Démonomanie*, 386; Boguet, *An Examen of Witches*, 29.

40. de Lancre, *Tableau*, 189–90; Remy, *Demonolatry*, 13–14.

41. C. Zika, *Exorcising Our Demons: Magic, Witchcraft and Visual Culture in Early Modern Europe* (Leiden, 2003): 237–67.

42. J. Klaits, *Servants of Satan: The Age of the Witch Hunts* (Bloomington, 1985): 65–85, argues that the novelty of the 'new misogyny' was its connection to ideologically based movements for reform. On the identification and prosecution of women as part of a clerically driven programme of Catholic reform see Durrant, *Witchcraft, Gender and Society*, xxi–xxii.

43. *Malleus maleficarum*, 99; Ginzburg, *The Night Battles*, 78. See also Monter, *Witchcraft in France and Switzerland*, 179; T. Dömötör, 'The Cunning Folk in English and Hungarian Witch Trials', in *Folklore Studies in the Twentieth Century*, ed. V. J. Newall (Woodbridge, 1978): 183. In Russia healers who treated male impotence were sometimes suspected of having actually caused it. V. A. Kivelson, 'Through the Prism of Witchcraft: Gender and Social Change in Seventeenth-Century Muscovy', in *Russia's Women: Accommodation, Resistance, Transformation*, ed. B. E. Evans, B. A. Engel and C. D. Worobec (Berkeley, 1991): 89.

44. R. A. Horsley, 'Who Were the Witches? The Social Roles of the Accused in the European Witch Trials', *Journal of Interdisciplinary History* 9 (1979): 700–12; Dömötör, 'Cunning Folk', 183–6; R. C. Sawyer, '"Strangely Handled in All her Lyms": Witchcraft and Healing in Jacobean England', *Journal of Social History* 22 (1989): 461–85; Larner, *Enemies of God*, pp. 138–42; Demos, *Entertaining Satan*, 81–4; Kivelson, *Desperate Magic*, 118–22.

45. Soman, 'Parlement of Paris', 43. See also Briggs, *Communities of Belief*, 16.

46. At Lucerne only one of forty-five women tried for witchcraft can be identified as a midwife. Burghartz, 'Equation of Women and Witches', 67. D. Harley, 'Historians as Demonologists: The Myth of the Midwife-Witch', *Social History of Medicine* 3 (1990): 1–26, establishes that midwives, contrary to widespread belief, were not

widely prosecuted as witches, especially in England, where only one midwife was known to have been tried as a witch. But midwives remain one of the few female occupational groups mentioned in most judicial records. The inquisitorial tribunal at Siena investigated seven midwives for witchcraft, the second largest occupational group identified in the record after prostitutes, who numbered twenty. O. Di Simplicio, 'Giandomenico Fei, the Only Male Witch: A Tuscan or an Italian Anomaly', in *Witchcraft and Masculinities in Early Modern Europe*, ed. A. Rowlands (Basingstoke, 2009): 128. On midwives as witches in Russia see Ryan, 'Witchcraft Hysteria', 79. On the prosecution of the town midwife in Nördlingen in 1478 see Behringer, *Witchcraft Persecutions in Bavaria*, 78.

47. Monter, *European Witchcraft*, 75–81. In Hungary, competing midwives from different localities often accused each other of witchcraft, leading to the execution of both women. Klaniczay, 'Hungary', 254.

48. *Malleus maleficarum*, 66; Lea, *Materials*, III: 1255.

49. L. Roper, *Oedipus and the Devil: Witchcraft, Sexuality and Religion in Early Modern Europe* (London, 1994): Chapter 9. See also Kivelson, *Desperate Magic*, 129.

50. Roper, *Oedipus and the Devil*; J. Sharpe, 'Witchcraft and Women in Seventeenth-Century England: Some Northern Evidence', *Continuity and Change* 6 (1991): 179–99.

51. C. Holmes, 'Women: Witnesses and Witches', *Past and Present* 140 (1993): 45–78,

52. Purkiss, *The Witch in History*, Chapter 4; D. Willis, *Malevolent Nurture: Witch-Hunting and Maternal Power in Early Modern England* (Ithaca, NY, 1995). See also S. Brauner, *Fearless Wives and Frightened Shrews: The Construction of the Witch in Early Modern Germany* (Amherst, MA, 1995).

53. On the fantasies of accusers about witchcraft see Rowlands, *Witchcraft Narratives in Germany*, Chapter 5; Roper, *Oedipus and the Devil*, Chapter 9.

54. On the power of witches see Sharpe, 'Witchcraft and Women', 185–6.

55. Sources for Table 5.2: E. Bever, 'Old Age and Witchcraft in Early Modern Europe', in *Old Age in Pre-Industrial Europe*, ed. P. Stearns (Princeton, 1983): 181; J. P. Demos, 'Underlying Themes in the Witchcraft of Seventeenth-Century New England', *American Historical Review* 75 (1970): 1315; Macfarlane, *Witchcraft in Tudor and Stuart England*, 161; E. Labouvie, *Zauberei und Hexenwerk: Ländlicher Hexenglaube in der Frühen Neuzeit* (Frankfurt, 1987): 172–3; Labouvie, 'Männer', 69; A. Rowlands, 'Stereotypes and Statistics: Old Women and Accusations of Witchcraft in Early Modern Europe', in *Power and Poverty: Old Age in Pre-Industrial Past*, ed. S. Ottaway, L. A. Botelho and K. Kittredge (Westport, 2002); Goodare *et al.*, *Survey of Scottish Witchcraft*; L. Roper, *Witch-Craze: Terror and Fantasy in Baroque Germany* (New Haven, 2004): 160; Di Simplicio, 'Giandomenico Fei', 127.

56. Historians have set the age at which old age begins anywhere from 40, the age of menopause in early modern Europe, to 65. See Bever, 'Old Age and Witchcraft', 165. For the use of the age of sixty in New England see Demos, *Entertaining Satan*, 67.

57. National Archives of Scotland, JC 26/27/2, item 6. Agnes Loch was sixty, Janet Daill sixty-three, Janet Lyle sixty, and Agnes Thomson sixty-five. The ages of the other two suspects were not given.

58. Monter, *Witchcraft in France and Switzerland*, 123; Macfarlane, *Witchcraft in Tudor and Stuart England*, 176; Scot, *The Discoverie of Witchcraft*, 4.

59. Rowlands, 'Stereotypes and statistics'; idem, 'Witchcraft and Old Women in Early Modern Germany', *Past and Present* 173 (2001): 50–89

60. Larner, *Witchcraft and Religion*, 134; Briggs, *Communities of Belief*, 63; Macfarlane, *Witchcraft in Tudor and Stuart England*, 103.

61. Levack, *Witchcraft Sourcebook*, 179–84.

62. Ibid., 75.
63. Roper, *Witch-Craze*, 160–1. The percentage of witches who were postmenopausal would be higher than the percentage over fifty, since menopause usually came during the early forties in the early modern period.
64. In Rothenburg, however, most accused witches had tried to be helpful and friendly towards their accusers and became irritable and angry only when they were accused of witchcraft. See Rowlands, 'Witchcraft and Old Women', 50–89.
65. Quoted in Monter, *European Witchcraft*, 115.
66. C. Merchant, *The Death of Nature: Women, Ecology and the Scientific Revolution* (New York, 1980): 132–36.
67. On the power of older New England women see Demos, *Entertaining Satan*, 68.
68. Hans Baldung Grien, *Prints and Drawings*, ed. J. H. Marrow and A. Shestack (Chicago, 1981): 116–19.
69. *Malleus maleficarum*, 97.
70. R. Burton, *Anatomy of Melancholy* (New York, 1932), III: 55–6.
71. J. Pitt-Rivers, 'Honour and Social Status', in *Honour and Shame: The Values of Mediterranean Society*, ed. J. G. Peristiany (Chicago, 1966): 69.
72. For some of these statements see Bever, 'Old Age and Witchcraft', 175 n.112. The sexual appetites of postmenopausal women were related to their dryness and desire for seminal fluid. See Roper, *Oedipus and the Devil*, 208.
73. See Easlea's discussion of Montaigne's views on this subject in *Witch Hunting, Magic and the New Philosophy*, 28.
74. Lea, *Materials*, II: 449.
75. Martin, *Witchcraft and the Inquisition in Venice*, 228.
76. See, for example, F. Byloff, *Hexenglaube und Hexenverfolgung in den österreichischen Alpenländern* (Berlin and Leipzig, 1934): 117; Monter, *Ritual*, 104; L. Roper, *The Witch in the Western Imagination* (Charlottesville, 2012): 132–4.
77. W. Behringer, 'Kinderhexenprozesse: zur Rolle von Kindern in der Geschichte der Hexenverfolgung', *Zeitschrift für Historische Forschung* 16 (1989): 31–47; L. Roper, 'Evil, Imaginings and Fantasies: Child Witches and the End of the Witch Craze', *Past and Present* 167 (2000): 107–39.
78. See Midelfort, 'Witch-Hunting and the Domino Theory', in *Religion and the People, 800–1700*, ed. James Obelkevich (Chapel Hill, 1979): 283.
79. Henningsen, *Witches' Advocate*, 34; Bader, *Hexenprozesse*, 209; Karlsen, *Devil in the Shape of a Woman*, 3, 71; Perkins, *Damned Art of Witchcraft*, 202–3; Mandrou, *Magistrats et sorciers*, 115–16; W. G. Soldan and H. Heppe, *Geschichte der Hexenprozesse*, ed. M. Bauer (Munich, 1912): I, 483–5; Remy, *Demonolatry*, 92; D. Sabean, *Power in the Blood: Popular Culture and Village Discourse in Early Modern Germany* (Cambridge, 1984): 107.
80. Lea, *Materials*, II: 902.
81. Robbins, *Encyclopedia*, 348–50.
82. Roper, 'Evil, Imaginings and Fantasies'.
83. Sources for Table 5.3: Denis, *Toul*, 177; Macfarlane, *Witchcraft in Tudor and Stuart England*, 164; A. Pollock, 'Social and Economic Characteristics of Witchcraft Accusations in Sixteenth- and Seventeenth-Century Kent', *Archaeologia Cantiana* 95 (1979): 41, table 3 (excluding those listed as 'married and spinster' in the indictments); Larner *et al.*, *Source-Book*, 241, table 8; Karlsen, *Devil in the Shape of a Woman*, 72; Ankarloo, 'Sweden', 311; Monter, *Witchcraft in France and Switzerland*, 121; Martin, *Witchcraft and the Inquisition in Venice*, 229.
84. The validity of the statistics for Scotland in Table 5.3, which reveal a high percentage of married witches in that kingdom, has been questioned on the grounds that the

marital status of the overwhelming majority of accused witches was not recorded and that married women were much more likely than single ones to offer that information. J. Goodare, 'Women and the Witch-Hunt in Scotland', *Social History* 23 (1998): n.8. It is unclear whether the same objection can be raised against the figures for other locales. If so, the proportion of unmarried witches in other regions would be even higher than those given in Table 5.3.

85. Burghartz, 'Equation of Women and Witches', 65–6, argues that in Lucerne age was a more important distinguishing characteristic of witches than widowhood.

86. Women who had left their husbands were particularly vulnerable to suspicion of witchcraft. Martin, *Witchcraft and the Inquisition in Venice*, 229–30. See also Karlsen, *Devil in the Shape of a Woman*, 73.

87. In Tuscany in the early fifteenth century the proportion of widows ranged from 16 per cent in the country to 25 per cent in the towns. Herlihy and Klapisch-Zuber, *Tuscans and their Families*, 216–17.

88. In some communities, such as Mora, Sweden, where a large witch-hunt took place in 1668, the number of adult men was less than half the number of adult women, mainly as a result of warfare. See Ankarloo, 'Sweden', 316.

89. See S. C. Watkins, 'Spinsters', *Journal of Family History* 9 (1984): 315–16; P. Laslett, *The World We Have Lost*, 3rd edn (New York, 1984): 111.

90. For England see M. MacDonald, *Mystical Bedlam: Madness, Anxiety and Healing in Seventeenth-Century England* (Cambridge, 1981): 110; Thomas, *Religion and the Decline of Magic*, 561.

91. See for example Midelfort, *Witch Hunting*, 101–2; E. Delcambre, 'La psychologie des inculpes Lorrains de sorcellerie', *Revue historique de droit français et étranger*, ser. 4, 32 (1954): 517; R. Briggs, *Witches and Neighbours: The Social and Cultural Context of European Witchcraft* (Harmondsworth, 1996): 228–9.

92. See S. Ozment, *When Fathers Ruled* (Cambridge, MA, 1983): 27–8, for a discussion of parental control of marriage.

93. National Archives of Scotland, JC 26/27, process against Musselburgh witches, 14 Nov. 1661, items 4 and 6.

94. Kivelson, *Desperate Magic*, 115–16; Evans, *Habsburg Monarchy*, 412–13. In Russia 15 per cent of the accused fell into this category as either primary defendants or those who had taught them magic.

95. See, for example, Pollock, 'Social and Economic Characteristics of Witchcraft Accusations', 45.

96. Heikkinen, *Paholaissen Liittolaiset*, 388, 390, shows that even some of those Ostrobothnian witches who were not classified as beggars often found it necessary to beg.

97. G. Cardano, *De rerum varietate* (Basel, 1557), cited in Lea, *Materials*, II: 446; Remy, *Demonolatry*, 159. On Remy's exaggeration in this regard see Briggs, *Communities of Belief*, 75.

98. Weisman, *Witchcraft, Magic and Religion*, 76–91. See also Thomas, *Religion and the Decline of Magic*, 562–3.

99. E. Henderson, *Annals of Dunfermline* (Glasgow, 1879): 319.

100. Naess, 'Norway', 377.

101. Lea, *Materials*, II: 491.

102. F. Braudel and P. Spooner, 'Prices in Europe from 1450 to 1750', in *Cambridge Economic History of Europe*, IV (Cambridge, 1967): 429.

103. Karlsen, *Devil in the Shape of a Woman*, 111–16.

104. Thomas, *Religion and the Decline of Magic*, 530. Macfarlane, *Witchcraft in Tudor and Stuart England*, 158–60; Monter, *Witchcraft in France and Switzerland*, 136–7; Demos,

Entertaining Satan, 54–6; J. Kamensky, 'Words, Witches and Woman Trouble: Witchcraft, Disorderly Speech and Gender Boundaries in Puritan New England', *Essex Institute Historical Collections* 128 (1992): 286–307.

105. Kamensky, 'Words, Witches, and Woman Trouble', 288.

106. G. Zilboorg, *The Medical Man and the Witch during the Renaissance* (New York, 1941): 204–20.

107. Delcambre, 'Psychologie, 391–2.

108. Early modern physicians often attributed the symptoms of demonic possession to melancholy. See Levack, *The Devil Within*, 117–23.

109. See S. R. Burstein, 'Aspects of the Psychopathology of Old Age Revealed in the Witchcraft Cases of the Sixteenth and Seventeenth Centuries', *British Medical Bulletin* (1949): 63–72.

110. Two witches prosecuted for witchcraft in the great Scottish witch-hunt of 1661–2 – Helen Cass and Helen Concker – had been previously brought before the kirk session of Inveresk for sexual offences. National Archives of Scotland, CH 2/531/1.

111. In New England, 10 out of 118 witches had been prosecuted for theft. See Demos, *Entertaining Satan*, 77. In Norway, 40 persons accused of witchcraft had been previously brought before local courts for other crimes. See Naess, 'Norway', 378. See also Monter, *Witchcraft in France and Switzerland*, 136.

112. Delcambre, 'Psychologie', p. 105; Levack, *Witch-hunting in Scotland*, 91; Karlsen, *Devil in the Shape of a Woman*, 138; Byloff, *Hexenglaube*, 117; E. W. Monter, 'La sodomie à l'époque moderne en Suisse romande', *Annales* 29 (1974): 1031–2.

113. *Witches Apprehended, Examined and Executed* (London, 1613), sig. B; Burghartz, 'Equation of Women and Witches', 68–9.

114. Scot, *The Discoverie of Witchcraft*, 4; Delcambre, 'Psychologie', 105.

115. Muchembled, 'Witches of the Cambrésis', 222, rejects the use of the term. On deviance see K. Erikson, *Wayward Puritans* (New York, 1966); C. McCagy, *Deviant Behavior* (New York, 1976): 2–4; N. Ben-Yehuda, *Deviance and Moral Boundaries* (Chicago, 1985).

116. C. Garrett, 'Women and Witches: Patterns of Analysis', *Signs* 3 (1977): 466; Karlsen, *Devil in the Shape of a Woman*, 119, 127, argues that in New England witches were women who refused to accept the place in society assigned to them by men.

117. See, for example, J. Michelet, *Satanism and Witchcraft*, tr. A. R. Allison (New York, 1939).

118. Le Roy Ladurie, *Les Paysans de Languedoc*, 407–13.

119. Muchembled, 'Witches of the Cambrésis', 264, insists that the witches of that region were not rebels but passive victims.

120. I. Silverblatt, *Moon, Sun, and Witches: Gender Ideologies and Class in Inca and Colonial Peru* (Princeton, 1987): 195–6.

121. Delcambre, 'Psychologie', 87–8.

122. D. Konig, *Law and Society in Colonial Massachusetts* (Chapel Hill, 1980): 173–4.

123. E. W. M. Bever, 'Witchcraft in Early Modern Württemberg' (Princeton PhD thesis, 1983); N. Davis, *The Return of Martin Guerre* (Cambridge, MA, 1983): 32; Kivelson, *Desperate Magic*, 123.

124. S. Brauner, 'Martin Luther on Witchcraft: A True Reformer?' in *The Politics of Gender in Early Modern Europe*, ed. J. R. Brink, A. Coudert and M. C. Horowitz, Sixteenth-Century Essays and Studies 12 (Kirksville, MO 1989): 29–42; A. P. Coudert, 'The Myth of the Improved Status of Protestant Women: The Case of the Witchcraze', in Brink, *The Politics of Gender in Early Modern Europe*, 61–94.

125. Macfarlane, *Witchcraft in Tudor and Stuart England*, 158; Scot, *Discoverie*, 320.

126. Macfarlane, *Witchcraft in Tudor and Stuart England*, 161; Thomas, *Religion and the Decline of Magic*, 562.
127. W. Behringer, 'Weather, Hunger and Fear: Origins of the European Witch-Hunts in Climate, Society and Mentality', *German History* 13 (1995): 1–27. In addition to the correlation between specific hunts and agrarian crises, Behringer sees a close correlation between the entire period of intense witch-hunting from 1560 to 1630 and the 'little ice age' of those years.
128. Briggs, *Communities of Belief*, 74.
129. A. Ashforth, *Witchcraft, Violence, and Democracy in South Africa* (Chicago, 2005): 7–15. Ashforth interprets the fear of bewitchment in these years as a non-specific, free-floating anxiety that arises when suffering and misfortune become acute, rather than a reaction to specific crises.
130. One dimension of this general mood was melancholy, which was the subject of Burton's book and the art of Albrecht Dürer. For the argument that melancholy was central to Renaissance culture, see A. Gowland, 'The Problem of Early Modern Melancholy', *Past and Present* 191 (2006): 77–120.
131. Lynn White, Jr, 'Death and the Devil', in *The Darker Vision of the Renaissance*, ed. R. S. Kinsman (Berkeley, 1974): 26.
132. For the extreme view that the ruling class deliberately used witch-hunting to create insecurity among the lower classes and to divert latent revolutionary energy see M. Harris, *Cows, Pigs, Wars and Witches* (New York, 1974): 225–40.

6

THE DYNAMICS
OF WITCH-HUNTING

The prosecution of witches in early modern Europe is usually viewed in monolithic terms. We commonly refer to *the* European witch-hunt or witch-craze of the fifteenth, sixteenth and seventeenth centuries. There are legitimate reasons for viewing the pursuit of witches in this general, comprehensive fashion. The various ecclesiastical and secular authorities that prosecuted witches from Spain to the Baltic and from Scotland to Transylvania were in a sense participating in a common enterprise: the destruction of a particularly dangerous heresy and form of rebellion that had spread throughout Europe. The intensity of their campaign varied greatly from place to place and from time to time, but their reasons for prosecuting witches, the charges they brought against them and the methods they used to discover them had a great deal in common. In a certain sense, therefore, there *was* a large hunt or campaign that began in the fifteenth century, became much more intense in the second half of the sixteenth century, reached a peak around 1600 and then slowly declined in the late seventeenth and eighteenth centuries. It is this large, pan-European hunt that has been the main focus of this book so far.

However valid the concept of a single European witch-hunt may be, it can be misleading. Not only can it encourage the formulation of general statements about European witchcraft that ignore national and regional variations (which will be the subject of the next chapter), but it can also obscure the fact that the hunt was an amalgam of hundreds, if not thousands, of separate hunts that occurred at different places and at different times. Each of these hunts, like the larger composite phenomenon, has its own history, and each is capable of detailed analysis. Some of these individual hunts, such as the series of trials at Trier in the 1580s and 1590s, the campaign against witchcraft in the Basque country in 1609–11, the hunt conducted by Matthew Hopkins and John Stearne in England in 1645–7, the great Scottish witch-hunt of 1661–2, and the episode that occurred at Salem, Massachusetts, in 1692, have been the subjects of detailed research. Many others, of varying size, still await scholarly investigation. We have enough information, however, to explore the many different ways these hunts got started, the different forms they took as they developed, and the different ways they came to an end. The picture that emerges is of such wide diversity that it becomes difficult to describe a 'typical' witch-hunt.

The preconditions

Before any witch-hunt could take place it was necessary for certain preconditions to have been satisfied. These preconditions, which roughly parallel those of the broader, European hunt, concern the witch beliefs of the local population, the laws and judicial institutions of the area, and the mood of the entire community. Concerning witch beliefs, it was necessary that both the ruling elite and the common people had some knowledge of the various activities that witches allegedly engaged in. This does not mean that all the residents of those communities that experienced witch-hunts had a full knowledge of the cumulative concept of witchcraft. It does mean, however, that the people in general believed in the reality of harmful magic and that the magistrates and clergy were at least vaguely familiar with the demono-logical theory that intellectuals had been developing since the late Middle Ages to explain that magic. If the common people did not believe in the reality of *maleficia* and the existence of witches, they would not have been inclined to testify that their misfortunes were attributable to witchcraft. Reluctance of this sort could thwart the efforts of even the most determined prosecutor and might even lead to popular opposition to the trials. It was essential, therefore, to have a witch-believing populace before a witch-hunt could start. In most instances this precondition was easily satisfied. Popular witch beliefs pre-dated the formation of the cumulative concept of witchcraft and were easily rekindled by preachers when they became convinced that witches were loose in the community. On the other hand, there were parts of Europe where such beliefs were weak, notably in southern Spain, and the low incidence of witchcraft prosecution in that area can be attributed at least in part to that fact.[1]

Much more important than popular beliefs were those of the ruling and administrative elite. Because these men controlled the judicial process, their belief in witchcraft was essential to the conduct of a witch-hunt. As we know from the events of the late seventeenth century, by which time scepticism had begun to penetrate the upper levels of society, popular beliefs were incapable of generating a witch-hunt if they met with bureaucratic disbelief and judicial inaction. In order for a witch-hunt to take place, therefore, it was necessary for this group of officials to believe in the reality of witchcraft and to harbour deep fears of it. It was also necessary for these men to be sufficiently familiar with the contemporary demonological theory of witchcraft, according to which the essence of the crime was the pact with the Devil. And if a large hunt was to take place, in which accomplices would be sought, it was necessary

160

for these men to believe in witchcraft as a collective, conspiratorial activity. As the ruling elite in Europe became more educated, as more literature, including witchcraft treatises, began to reach small communities and as news of witchcraft spread by word of mouth among provincial elites, witch-hunts became much more likely to occur. In the Cambrésis region the rise of witchcraft prosecutions accompanied the spread of literacy among the local elites, and in the outlying regions of Europe, such as in Scandinavia and Transylvania, witch-hunting never took place until after the introduction of learned witch beliefs.[2]

A second set of preconditions for specific witch-hunts concerns the laws and the judicial machinery that operated in the area where the hunts took place. In order for such hunts to begin it was necessary for the courts that operated in that particular locality to have possessed both a clearly defined jurisdiction over the crime of witchcraft and the procedural tools necessary to prosecute witches successfully. The need for clear definition, which usually was obtained through the passage of a witchcraft statute, the promulgation of a witchcraft edict, or the publication of a new legal code that made reference to witchcraft, was most clearly evident in England, where virtually no trials took place until the passage of the witchcraft statute of 1542. In similar fashion, witchcraft trials in Denmark reached a peak only after King Christian IV issued a 'Decree concerning Sorcerers and their Accomplices' in 1617.[3] Looking back to an earlier period, one can argue that the prosecution of witchcraft by papal inquisitors was not possible until sorcery was specifically classified as heresy.[4] Even then, however, it was necessary for Pope Innocent VIII to issue his famous bull, *Summis desiderantes*, to give his two inquisitors, Heinrich Kramer and Jacob Sprenger, authority to proceed against witches in Germany in 1484.

SOURCE BOOK

In addition to possessing clear jurisdiction over witchcraft, European courts had to have adopted certain procedures in order to prosecute witches successfully. At the very least they had to have abandoned the rule by which the accuser was liable to a charge of false accusation, the *lex talionis*, in the event that the accused proved his innocence. If a large hunt were to develop, it was also necessary for the judicial authorities to have the right to accuse and interrogate individuals on their own authority and to use coercive measures, usually torture, to obtain confessions. In most cases courts acquired these rights when inquisitorial procedure was introduced, a process that had taken place in most European jurisdictions by the middle of the sixteenth century. In England, of course, inquisitorial procedure had not been adopted, and torture could not be used in witchcraft cases. This meant, in effect, that large witch-hunts were unlikely to occur in that kingdom, and indeed very few did. Nevertheless, the use of public prosecutions initiated by grand juries acting in the name of the community after a private complaint was entered, coupled with a certain amount of judicial coercion, could result in successful witchcraft prosecutions, with or without confessions. And although torture could not be employed in England, the ability of the jury to reach verdicts on the basis of circumstantial evidence meant that the English judicial system was capable of facilitating a witch-hunt.

The final precondition of witch-hunting in European communities was the presence of a crisis mentality that heightened the fear of witchcraft and encouraged people to take action against it. We have already seen how a general mood of anxiety throughout Europe provided the emotional setting for the entire witch-hunt. In the towns and villages where witch-hunts occurred this mood became readily apparent, either among a small group of villagers or magistrates or, more commonly, among the entire populace. The insecurity and fears that these people shared could arise either from the discussion of witchcraft or, somewhat more indirectly, from economic, political or religious developments.

Probably the most common source of an atmosphere that was conducive to witch-hunting was the public discussion of witchcraft itself. In many cases the sermons of a zealous preacher prepared the minds of his parishioners to look for witches among their daily associates. The role of the clergy, both Protestant and Catholic, in raising consciousness of witchcraft has long been recognized,[5] and the sermons of Samuel Parris at Salem prior to the witch-hunting that began there in 1692 provide a good case in point. Occasionally contemporaries made observations about the role that preaching played in starting witch-hunts. Referring specifically to the preaching of Fray Domingo Sardo in the village of Olagüe during the Basque witch-hunt of 1609–11, the inquisitor Alonso de Salazar Frías observed that 'there were neither witches nor bewitched in a village until they were talked and written about'.[6]

Preachers were not the only individuals who were responsible for the talking and the writing. The news of witch-hunts and executions in other parts of a country could easily fan popular and elite fears and create a mood that was conducive to witch-hunting in a village or town. It was because of such communications that many hunts spread from village to village, even when confessing witches did not implicate accomplices outside their communities or when witch-hunters did not move from place to place. Sometimes the dissemination of pamphlets or treatises discussing witchcraft cases served the same purpose, while official pronouncements regarding the danger of witchcraft could also raise fears that might otherwise have been dormant. One witch-hunt in Franche-Comté in the first decade of the seventeenth century began shortly after the publication of Henri Boguet's *Discours des sorciers* (1602), while another in the same province in 1657 started only after inquisitors proclaimed a *monitoire* in each province requiring anyone with information about acts of witchcraft to make it known to them.[7]

In a somewhat more indirect way, the experience of economic, religious or political crisis often produced a mood in which the hunting of witches could easily begin. In a number of instances a succession of bad harvests and near famines appears to have encouraged the growth of witch-hunting. At Trier, for example, a combination of many different natural calamities succeeded in destroying all but two harvests between 1580 and 1599, during which time a ferocious epidemic of witch trials took place.[8] In similar fashion a couple of bad harvests in the northern portions of Franche-Comté set the stage for the witch-hunt that took place there in 1628–9.[9] Epidemics of disease, including the plague, often had a similar effect, such as at Ellwangen in 1611.[10] In certain areas of Europe there appears to have been a rough correlation between periods of dearth, famine and pestilence on the one hand and periods of intense witch-hunting on the other. In Germany, for example, the years witnessing the most serious agrarian crises between 1562 and 1630 were also the years in which large witch-hunts began.[11] Similar patterns can be seen in Switzerland throughout the fifteenth century and in the Pays de Vaud between 1581 and 1620.[12] It would be misleading to explain individual witch-hunts entirely in such terms, but agrarian crises and epidemics of disease did apparently contribute to the creation of an atmosphere in which accusations of witchcraft arose.

Religious crises, especially the experience of recent, current or impending religious change, also had great potential for creating the type of communal anxiety that led to witchcraft accusations, and, as we have seen, this might explain why witch-hunting most commonly occurred in religiously volatile areas. Another religious sentiment that could have a similar effect was millenarianism, the belief that the Antichrist had appeared and that the rule of Christ was imminent. Witches were not identified as the Antichrist, but the desire to cleanse the world to prepare the way of the Lord could easily encourage the pursuit of them, for they were, after all, the agents of the Devil.[13] The prevalence of millenarian sentiment in East Anglia in 1645 might very well have made communities there receptive to the witch-hunting activities of Matthew Hopkins.[14]

The role that political crises played in preparing the ground for witch-hunting is more subtle than that of famine, disease or religious change. Political crises usually had a greater impact on the ruling elite than on the general population and for that reason probably created profound anxieties only within the upper levels of society. Political crises could, moreover, have an immediate negative impact on witch-hunting by disrupting the operation of the judicial machinery. Nevertheless, the experience of political turmoil could create unease among magistrates that might lead them to begin a witch-hunt, especially in the immediate aftermath of the crisis. In those circumstances witch-hunting would offer the elite an opportunity to suppress what they considered to be a dangerous challenge to the order of society, and perhaps even to punish malefactors who might have eluded the arm of the law in the midst of more pressing political change or as the result of judicial paralysis. It was partly for such reasons that large witch-hunts took place in Scotland in 1661–2 after the end of English rule and two years of judicial inactivity; in Lorraine in 1658 after the end of French rule; and at Salem in 1692 after years of constitutional turmoil and judicial uncertainty.[15]

The final factor that played a significant role in preparing people psychologically for witch-hunting was war, which because of its profound and far-reaching effects had an enormous capacity for generating communal anxiety. Here again, however, we must not make unwarranted assumptions. The direct and immediate effect of armed conflict on witch-hunting, just like the effect of the political crises that often accompanied war, was usually negative. The experience of war was so disruptive, the effects so pervasive, that communities where battles were fought or where troops were quartered had little time to be concerned with the activities of maleficent sorcerers or even apostates. In the towns and villages of France, Germany, Switzerland, Austria and the Low Countries, witchcraft trials were relatively rare during periods of actual warfare and even during the period of exhaustion that followed. Witch-hunting was for all intents and purposes a peacetime pursuit.[16] Nevertheless, the actual experience of war, which entailed a disruption of social life for years after hostilities had ceased, could contribute to the communal anxiety that was central to the process of witch-hunting. It was no coincidence that a priest at Besançon in 1657 thought witchcraft had reached epidemic proportions 'because the troubles of the late wars had been so great and had caused such disorders in the province'.[17] The same circumstances may explain why witchcraft prosecutions in Hungary tended to increase a few years after a war or internal uprising had come to an end and after the country had begun to experience its long-term effects.[18] There is also a fairly clear connection between the long-term effects of war in Poland and the beginning of intense witch-hunting in the late seventeenth century.[19]

In dealing with the psychological foundations of witch-hunting it is important to note that in most cases no single factor produced a mood that made people eager to pursue witches. Usually a combination of circumstances, such as war, plague and famine, or bad harvests, coupled with the promulgation of an official edict against witchcraft, was responsible. There was, moreover, no necessary causal connection between a mood that is conducive to witch-hunting and the actual occurrence of such a hunt. We should not be surprised, therefore, when one combination of factors seems to have 'caused' a witch-hunt in one locality while a virtually identical situation produced not one official prosecution in another. The mood of a community was merely one precondition of witchcraft, and those preconditions simply made witch-hunting possible, not inevitable.

The triggers

Witch-hunts did not start spontaneously in those communities that were intellectually, legally and psychologically prepared to experience them.

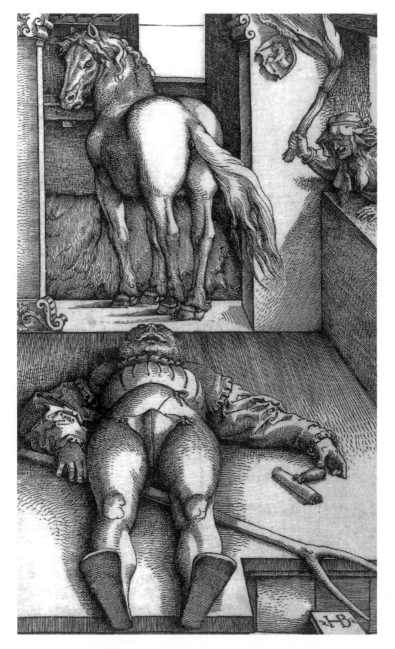

Figure 6.1 Hans Baldung Grien's early sixteenth-century depiction of the death of a stable
groom by witchcraft. The witch, depicted as a crone with her breast exposed,
appears in the top right corner.

Someone – either a private citizen, a group of villagers or a magistrate – had to get the ball rolling by accusing or denouncing someone or by citing a person who was rumoured to be a witch. That being the case, we must ask what specific events prompted these initial accusations. In most cases the catalyst was a personal misfortune that an individual and his neighbours interpreted as an act of maleficent magic (see Figure 6.1). The sudden death of a child or family member, the contraction of a disease (especially one for which there was no known cause), the loss of a farm animal, sexual impotence, romantic failure, fire, or even theft led the victim of such misfortune, in an effort both to explain what had happened and to wreak vengeance upon the alleged malefactors, to attribute the harm to witchcraft and to bring the witch to justice. In some cases, especially in larger hunts, a number of individuals, each seeking satisfaction for his own personal misfortune, brought their complaints to the proper authorities.

Most of the misfortunes that triggered witch-hunts were individual in nature, but occasionally they were communal, and in those cases the magistrates, as representatives of the community, took the initial action against the witches. Hailstorms, which could destroy an entire crop within a few minutes, were probably the most frequent of such communal misfortunes, and in many instances, most notably at Wiesensteig in Germany in 1562, they provided the initial impetus for a round-up and eventual execution of all the suspected local witches.[20] Less frequently, fire, which was very difficult to control in early modern times, could lead its victims to think of witchcraft as its source, while in coastal communities storms at sea, which often destroyed life as well as property, could have the same effect. A storm in the North Sea in the spring of 1590 when King James VI of Scotland was bringing his new bride, Anne of Denmark, to his native land was the first of many events that led to witch-hunts in both kingdoms.[21]

Somewhat surprisingly, the plague, which ravaged whole communities during the entire period of the European witch-hunt, did not very often serve as the catalyst for specific witch-hunts. Like many of the other epidemics that affected Europe at this time, the plague heightened social tensions and probably contributed to a mood that encouraged witch-hunting, but it did not lead directly to many accusations. This may have been because the disease was known to spread from place to place and was not therefore likely to be the work of local witches. In a few cases, however, individuals were accused of spreading the plague by capturing its essence in an ointment that they smeared on houses. These plague-spreaders were accused of both magic and Devil-worship and were prosecuted as witches. Plague-spreading panics took place at Geneva in 1530, 1545, 1567–8, 1571 and 1615; at Chambéry in 1577; at Vevey in 1613; and at Milan in 1630.[22]

The process of scapegoating in response to misfortune was probably the most common trigger of European witch-hunts, but it was by no means the only one. Sometimes, for example, individuals deliberately and maliciously brought charges of witchcraft against their antagonists – political rivals, economic competitors, and sometimes even family members with whom they were in conflict – in order to resolve their differences and bring vengeance upon them. At other times they actually saw the accused party practise some sort of magical ritual or cast a spell on someone and therefore brought the action to the attention of the authorities.

Although alleged *maleficia* were responsible for precipitating most witch-hunts, accusations of Devil-worship could also provide the stimulus to prosecution. Since it is unlikely that sabbaths ever took place, we do not hear of witch-hunts beginning when unsuspecting travellers chanced upon cannibalistic orgies or saw witches flying to or from such gatherings. Less dramatic meetings of small numbers of women did, however, occasionally start witch-hunts. In Neuchâtel, for example, a woman named Jehanne Berna was arrested for witchcraft after she was seen dancing around a fire with several other women; one assumes that the gathering was thought to be the sabbath.[23] In the county of Essex, England, the notorious witch-hunt of Matthew Hopkins and John Stearne began when Hopkins concluded that Elizabeth Clarke and other women were gathering at regular assemblies in a home near Hopkins's residence in Manningtree.[24] A charge of diabolism also sparked the great Swedish witch-hunt in 1668. That episode began when a fifteen-year-old boy accused a number of other children and a seventy-year-old woman of stealing children for the Devil.

Some witch-hunts began when individuals made free confessions to diabolical activity, either with the coaxing of their confessors or in the context of an investigation for another crime. It appears that some of the earliest witch-hunts occurred when inquisitors who were investigating Waldensian heresy in France and Switzerland came across some women who confessed to riding out at night with Diana. More commonly, some women did actually attempt to make pacts with the Devil, and their free confessions to such arrangements served as prima facie evidence of witchcraft. In similar fashion the 'dream epidemic' that apparently ran wild in the Basque villages of northern Spain in 1610 provided the original stimulus to the witch-hunt of that year.

One trigger of a number of witch-hunts, demonic possession, deserves special consideration. Some of the afflictions that demoniacs were reported to have endured, such as violent fits or convulsions, skin lesions, muscular rigidity, paralysis and temporary blindness or deafness, were considered to have been caused by witchcraft. There was, however, no necessary connection between witchcraft and possession, even though both involved the exercise of demonic power, and throughout this period many possessions did not result in witchcraft accusations. One reason for this is that many of the symptoms of possession, such as the demonstration of preternatural strength, speaking in previously unknown foreign languages, and uttering blasphemies, were not harmful and could not be classified as *maleficia*. Also, the Devil was perfectly capable of entering a demoniac's body by his own power, without involving a witch in the assault. This capability explains why a large number of demonic possessions, especially those reported before 1590, made no reference to witchcraft whatsoever.

Most of the witchcraft cases that did originate in incidents of demonic possession involved the prosecution of a single individual for witchcraft. That was certainly true in the five cases of collective possession in France for which witches were held responsible.[25] The possession of nuns at Aix-en-Provence in 1611 led to the brutal torture, confession and execution of Father Louis Gaufridi the following year, and in 1634 another priest, Urbain Grandier, was tried and executed for causing the possession of a convent of Ursuline nuns in the religiously divided town of Loudun (see Figure 6.2).[26] A majority of the witchcraft trials in Calvinist Geneva in the seventeenth century began with people displaying the symptoms of possession, and there were numerous similar cases in England and Franche-Comté.[27] A few of these cases involved the trial of more than one person for witchcraft, and in the German

Figure 6.2 The execution of Urbain Grandier, who was accused of causing the possession of Ursuline nuns at Loudun, 1634. In the top left corner an exorcism of one of the nuns is taking place, and a black demon is seen leaving her body. From *Effigie de la condemnation de mort et execution d'Urbain Grandier* (1634).]

university town of Paderborn a wave of possessions and exorcisms between 1656 and 1659 led to a large witch-hunt that resulted in about fifty executions.[28]

A series of possessions linked to witchcraft occurred in Calvinist Scotland and New England towards the end of the seventeenth century, when witch-hunting in most areas of Europe was in a state of decline. A strong dose of apocalyptic thinking, which had always been strong in Britain and colonial America, led many religious communities to look for signs that the Devil was loose and that the world had entered its final days.[29] A case of possession in Boston, Massachusetts, in 1688, in which the four children of John Goodwin manifested classic symptoms of possession, led to the witchcraft trial and execution of an Irish laundress working in the Goodwin household. The case received wide publicity and was placed within an apocalyptic explanatory **SOURCE BOOK** framework when the Boston minister Cotton Mather published a treatise, *Memorable Providences Relating to Witchcrafts and Possessions*.[30] The publication of this pamphlet certainly helps to explain why the afflictions experienced by a group of young girls in Salem village four years later were interpreted as symptoms of possession and why witches were identified as their source.[31]

The witch-hunt at Salem received wide publicity in America and also in England and Scotland, where a number of cases of demonic possession arose in the households of English and Scottish presbyterians.[32] The most remarkable of these occurred near Paisley in the west country of Scotland in 1697, when Christian Shaw, the eleven-year-old daughter of the laird of Bargarran, experienced fits, performed bodily contortions, and regurgitated a variety of alien substances, including pins, bones, straw and the feathers of fowl. After the local clergy and authorities concluded that she was possessed, Shaw accused a maid in her household, Katherine Campbell, of causing her possession. She later extended the charges to seven other people, all of whom **SOURCE BOOK** were tried and executed at Paisley in 1697.[33] This was the last large witch-hunt not only in Scotland but in all of western Europe.

Whenever one deals with the origins of witch-hunts, the question arises of whether the prosecutions came from 'above' or 'below', that is, from the judges and other members of the ruling elite or from the common people. There is wide agreement among scholars that in England, where judges could not initiate cases by themselves, the pressure to prosecute came from the witches' neighbours.[34] Justices of the Peace might have occasionally encouraged people to make accusations, but the nature of the judicial process prevented them from taking the first steps. In continental Europe, however, and to a lesser extent in Scotland, judicial authorities could take the initiative, and this has led to the assumption that most witchcraft prosecutions outside England came from above. One historian has suggested that the common people were so tolerant of witchcraft suspects that they had to be prodded by officials into testifying against them.[35] That some magistrates decided on their own initiative to start a witch-hunt – and not simply when they themselves were the witches' alleged victims – cannot be denied. In these cases the judges drafted the charges against the witches and then summoned villagers to court to testify against them. But in most cases the original pressure to prosecute came, just as in England, from the common people.[36]

The large witch-hunt that took place in the electorate of Trier between 1581 and 1595 illustrates how even in small German states the pressure to prosecute witches came from below rather than above. For many years historians assigned responsibility for these trials to the prince-archbishop, Johann von Schönenburg, his deputy and notary, and the suffragan bishop, the demonologist Peter Binsfeld. There is little doubt that these members of the ruling elite directed the interrogation, torture and execution of the hundreds of witches who perished during these years. The original impulse to prosecute, however, came not from the these authorities but from local communities that were responding to the dire agrarian crisis of those years.[37] Local committees actually seized the initiative by wresting control of the judicial machinery and beginning the judicial process by their own authority. This pattern was repeated in many villages throughout the entire region of Saarland.[38]

Once villagers did decide that the witch should be prosecuted, they would denounce the suspect before a local court or ask the members of the governing body of the village, such as the elders of the church or the local magistrates, to take action against her. These men generally belonged to what we might call the village elite, a social group that lay between the peasantry on the one hand and the aristocracy and the central court justices on the other.[39] Only occasionally would villagers apply pressure directly on the members of that higher group. One such instance occurred in Scotland in 1661, when the tenants of the earl of Haddington threatened to leave his lands in Samuelston if the local witches were not prosecuted. Haddington, an influential nobleman, then petitioned Parliament to delegate a commission to try the malefactors, thus beginning the largest witch-hunt in Scottish history.[40]

The members of the local elite who responded to popular pressure were usually responsible for the arrest and initial interrogation of the accused. These men were often familiar with demonological theory, so it was at this stage of the judicial process that notions of the pact and the sabbath were often introduced.[41] The members of the local elite were also the ones who pricked the witch to see if she had the Devil's mark, and they sometimes applied judicial torture, thereby facilitating the imposition of their demonological notions. In most circumstances, however, these men did not actually try the accused witch. In order to do that it was usually necessary to obtain approval from higher levels of government. In Scotland, for example, the elders in the kirk sessions often referred the witchcraft cases they heard to the civil magistrate, or they requested that the Privy Council authorize certain men to try the witch locally. Securing the cooperation of higher judicial officials was not always as easy as it may seem. At Mora in Sweden in 1669, the parents of numerous bewitched children, the elders of the parish and the vicar all put pressure on the local bailiff in order to get him to start legal proceedings against the accused witches when the county sheriff would not visit the area. Later in the hunt the same parties found it necessary to appeal to the royal government in Stockholm in order to bring the witches to trial.[42]

The development of hunts

Once judicial officials agreed to hear witchcraft cases, they assumed complete control of the witch-hunting process. Judges have been referred to as the gatekeepers of witch-hunts, in that they decided which cases to prosecute and which ones to ignore. They decided which witnesses to call, which persons should be tortured, and which alleged accomplices of the witches should be pursued. In most cases they determined the guilt or innocence of the accused, and they also determined what sentences the witches were to receive. Even when the original impetus to prosecute had come from below, the way in which hunts developed was determined mainly from above. The common people played only a supporting role, by testifying against those implicated in the process and maintaining a popular mood that was conducive to witch-hunting.

Individual prosecutions and small hunts

Once the first suspects were brought to trial, the hunt would develop according to one of three different models. The first, which was by far the most common, involved the prosecution of usually one and not more than three persons. To use the word 'hunt' to describe such a process is in a sense inappropriate, since that term usually connotes the search for, and the prosecution of, a large group of persons who share similar beliefs and personal characteristics.[43] But since even this type of operation involved the search for witches and the attempt to impose fantasies upon innocent persons, it merits classification as a hunt. The main feature of the small hunt is that the search for malefactors was limited to the individuals who were originally accused. It was most common in England, where charges for witchcraft usually had a solid foundation in *maleficia* and where judges could not use torture to obtain the names of accomplices. Throughout Europe, however, the prosecution of individuals for isolated acts of sorcery was not at all uncommon. Even in Germany, which is notorious for its large, chain-reaction hunts, there was a steady stream of individual prosecutions.[44] Most of these operations had the potential for developing into larger hunts, since charges of attending the sabbath could easily have arisen in almost any continental trial, and those charges could in turn have led to a search for accomplices. Very often, however, a chain-reaction hunt of this sort did not develop, perhaps because of judicial preoccupation with other matters or because of the failure of the mood of the community to reach a state of panic. Many continental hunts may have failed to grow because the populace or the authorities were determined only to rid themselves of specific individuals, and once that was achieved, they felt no pressing need to pursue the matter further.

Medium-sized hunts

When authorities were not content to restrict their investigation of witchcraft to those persons who had initially been accused, then witch-hunts that conformed more closely to the stereotype could develop. One of the forms that such hunts took was that of the medium-sized hunt, a process that claimed somewhere between five and ten victims. William Monter has found that this type of hunt, which he calls a 'small panic', often occurred in French-speaking Switzerland, and other examples can be adduced from Germany and Scotland. The main characteristic of the medium-sized hunt is that torture was employed and a second round of accusations took place, but the process did not get out of hand. In some of these hunts, such as the prosecutions that occurred in Neuchâtel in 1583 and in Fribourg in 1634, restraint was achieved through the spare use of torture and the grant of non-capital sentences. Other hunts may have ended after the naming of the first set of accomplices because the supply of stereotypical witches had dried up. Technically, of course, anyone could be a witch, and in some of the larger hunts virtually everyone was vulnerable. But in most communities there was a fairly small number of individuals whom people instinctively suspected of witchcraft. Witches were those people whom 'everybody knew to be witches by common reputation'.[45] When such persons were disposed of, it was necessary to have recourse to less discriminating standards of witchcraft if the hunt was going to continue. In communities where medium-sized hunts occurred, there may not have been a sufficient degree of popular hysteria for the less rigorous standards to be invoked. In the final analysis, therefore, the reason for the limited development of the medium-sized hunt might very well have been the absence of full-scale panic among either the judicial authorities or the people in general.

Large hunts

The large witch-hunts of the sixteenth and seventeenth centuries, those that claimed anywhere from ten to hundreds of victims and were characterized by a high degree of panic, were the prototypes of the classic 'witch-hunt'. These hunts were most common in Germany, but almost all European countries, including England, Spain and Sweden, experienced at least one such episode.[46] Many of these mass prosecutions were chain-reaction hunts, in which the first witches who were tried gave the names of accomplices, who in turn were arrested, tried, convicted and forced to denounce others. The largest of these hunts took place in Trier, where a total of 306 witches named about 1,500 different accomplices, each accused witch offering an average of 20 names.[47] Other well-known chain-reaction hunts took place at Ellwangen in 1611, Würzburg in 1627–9, Bamberg in 1630, and the Pays de Labourd in Guienne in 1609. The chain reaction was not, however, the only means by which large hunts developed. In some cases a single accuser or group of accusers served as the main source of names throughout the hunt. Demoniacs, such as the afflicted girls at Salem, could do this relatively easily since they, not being guilty of witchcraft themselves, were not executed during the course of the hunt. Even when there was no demonic possession, a small number of accusers could be responsible for the entire progress of the hunt. At Rouen, for example, a group of nine persons provided a total of 525 accusations in 1670.[48] Another variation in the mechanics of the large hunt occurred when a small group of magistrates summoned large numbers of suspects before them on the basis of information they had gathered by various means. When this scenario unfolded, the hunt took the form of a general round-up of witches, very often from a few small villages, rather than a steadily growing snowball.

Our picture of large-scale witch-hunting becomes even more variegated when we realize that many large witch-hunts were in fact composites of a number of small hunts. This was especially true when the defined area of the hunt was very large or when the period during which the hunt took place was very long. In Scotland, for example, we speak of the great witch-hunt of 1661–2, since during those years there were hundreds of accusations, trials and executions throughout the country, especially in the southeastern counties. These prosecutions were not completely divorced from each other. The Privy Council or Parliament approved all of the trials; a solid number of the cases were heard before the same judges; some of the villages hired the same men to search suspects for the Devil's marks; and in a few instances the witches from one village implicated accomplices from another. But for the most part the individual hunts that comprised this larger campaign were discrete operations, separate manifestations of a general, national panic regarding witchcraft. The same could be said about the Swedish hunt of 1668–76 and the English prosecutions of 1645–7, although in the latter case the travels of Matthew Hopkins and John Stearne to various towns and villages in Essex and Suffolk provided more structural unity than the Scottish hunt possessed. In a rather curious way the English witch-finding movement of 1645–7 resembled the campaigns that papal inquisitors often conducted on the Continent, moving from town to town to try cases of witchcraft.[49]

Even when officials or witch-hunters remained stationary and heard cases brought before them, large witch-hunts could lack the cohesion that they appear to have had. Not only did judges often hear cases from many different areas within their jurisdiction, but they did so over a long period of time. Witch-hunts very often occurred in waves, each rash of trials having its own dynamic. When a witch-hunt spanned a two- or three-year period, marked by intervals when there were no trials at all, it became problematic whether there was one large campaign or a succession of smaller operations conducted by the same court or the same judge. A close examination of the witch-hunt that took place in the imperial city of Offenburg during the period 1627–30 reveals the complexity of what may be described as a single large hunt. The campaign began in 1627 as an offshoot of a hunt that took place in Ortenau, the larger territorial unit in which Offenburg was situated. On the basis of denunciations made by witches in Ortenau, the members of the Offenburg council began a hunt that took the lives of twelve witches between November 1627 and January 1628. After a respite of five months the council, receiving further information regarding the children of one of the witches executed in January, started a new round of trials that resulted in the execution of seven more witches and the death of another during torture. Then, after another interval of four months, the council began a long series of trials that lasted until January 1630 and claimed an additional forty lives. The hunt, in other words, really comprised three distinct operations, each of which had its own dynamic.[50]

Although many large hunts were in fact composites of smaller hunts, the intensity of fears regarding witchcraft provided a unity to all of the trials that occurred in places like Offenburg. Indeed, one of the main characteristics of the large witch-hunt was the prevalence of a mood of profound fear or panic while the hunt was going on. It is this mood that gives substance to the use of the words 'mania' or 'craze' that are used to describe the process of witch-hunting. Appearances suggest that communities involved in witch-hunting sometimes experienced a form of mass hysteria. We must be careful, however, to distinguish this collective psychic development from the physiological illness that became the most common medical diagnosis of demoniacs in the early modern period. That form of hysteria, which was originally classified as a female disease originating in the uterus, has been redefined in more recent years as a dissociative or a conversion disorder whose symptoms include paroxysms, contortions, stiffness of the limbs, paralysis and temporary deafness or blindness.[51] The hysteria manifested by communities during witch-hunts was different in kind from such personality disorders. It should more properly be referred to as 'collective obsessional behaviour', a term that can be applied to various group phenomena ranging from fads or booms to the frenzy of the riot. In the case of witch-hunting it was the product of the general anxiety that served as a precondition of virtually all witch-hunting. Like the terrified Londoners who learned about the Popish Plot in 1678 and the Americans who experienced the Red Scares of 1919–20 and 1947–54, these villagers and townspeople, learning that more and more of their neighbours and even some of their rulers were being denounced as witches, became terrified – terrified that their closest friends and neighbours were witches, terrified that their communities would be made totally captive of diabolical power, perhaps even terrified that they themselves might be falsely accused. This terror led them to support the trials, bring suspects to the attention of the proper authorities, and even imagine that they witnessed people flying through the air or attending sabbaths. In the same mood, people who harboured deep feelings of guilt may have even been led to confess freely to acts of witchcraft. The 'dream epidemic' in which hundreds of persons admitted that they had attended *aquelarres* in the Basque country in the early seventeenth century can be interpreted in these terms. So too can the depositions of French peasants in Normandy that they had seen naked people flying through the air and hundreds of others dancing naked at the sabbath after local doctors concluded that witchcraft was the source of widespread illness in the region.[52]

In all of this we must be careful to distinguish between the mass hysteria of some witch-hunts and the apparent psychological problems of some of the individual participants in these hunts. The sadistic judge or hangman, the compulsive witch-finder, or the 'melancholic' witch might be subjected to modern psychological diagnosis, but these speculative retrospective diagnoses should not be confused with efforts to understand the psychology of entire communities in the past. Within the context of specific witch-hunts we can legitimately – although at the same time hypothetically – talk about collective obsessional behaviour during witch panics.[53]

The end of witch-hunts

Witch-hunts usually did not last for very long periods of time. The large witch-hunts often spanned a period of two, three or four years, and occasionally they lasted even longer, but they never went on indefinitely. In most cases, moreover, they ended rather abruptly and their termination usually signalled the end of witch-hunting in that area for many years, sometimes for generations. The end of small and medium-sized hunts does not require detailed analysis. The small hunts were isolated prosecutions that ended when the prisoner was either executed, given a non-capital sentence or acquitted. The medium-sized hunts came to an end for pretty much the same reasons that they had been restricted in their scope: the tight control that magistrates retained over the process of investigation, the restriction of accusations to stereotypical witches, and the absence of a mood of panic. The end of large hunts, however, is more problematic, for they had the potential for indefinite extension. The mass hysteria that underlay them, the willingness of authorities to use torture freely, and the determination of those same authorities to elicit the names of accomplices meant that the trials could go on and on. Contemporaries were fully aware of the open-ended character of the large hunts. In the German town of Rottenburg, for example, authorities worried that the witch-hunt of 1585 would eliminate all the women in the town. Their fears were not exaggerated: in that very year two villages had been left with only one female inhabitant apiece in the aftermath of witch-hunts.[54] In most cases, however, witch-hunts ended before they took such a heavy toll. Indeed, one of the most perplexing features of the larger witch-hunts is the number of individuals who were implicated by confessing witches but were never tried. In the Scottish witch-hunt of 1661–2, for example, a total of 664 persons were named as witches, but apparently not even half that number were actually prosecuted. At Salem some 162 individuals were accused, but only seventy-six were actually tried and only thirty were convicted. At Trier only a small number of the 1,500 witches named by accomplices were ever prosecuted.

The reasons for the suspension of the judicial process in these large hunts were many and varied, and responsibility for the suspension could be attributed either to the officials who conducted the trials, the general populace, or officials in the central government. In most cases the hunts ended when some or all of these people came to the conclusion that innocent people were being accused and executed, or that the social effects of the hunt were more detrimental than beneficial. In all of these hunts there was a loss of confidence in the process of witch-hunting, and in many cases this was a result of the breakdown of the stereotype of the witch. As mentioned above, the great majority of witches were old, poor women, and the frequency of their prosecution led to the creation of a stereotype of the witch that was accepted both by villagers and members of the elite. In many large witch-hunts, especially in Germany but also in Massachusetts, the stereotype broke down as accusations and implications became more indiscriminate and as motives of political and economic advantage came increasingly into play. In the early stages of most large witch-hunts the victims conformed to the stereotype, but as the hunts progressed a higher percentage of wealthy and powerful individuals, children and males were named. At Würzburg in 1629 the chain of accusations led to the naming of numerous children, law students, clerics, and eventually the bishop's chancellor and the bishop himself. At Trier a similar pattern emerged, while at Bamberg the burgomaster, Johannes Junius, was named.[55] This breakdown had the effect of arousing suspicions that innocent persons were being accused and of making men aware that the procedures of torturing confessed witches to obtain the names of accomplices could not be trusted. When the accusations reached into very high places the breakdown of the stereotype had the added effect of prompting the implicated officials to put an end to the trials. This is exactly what the bishop of Würzburg did in 1629, and a similar motive may have been at work when Governor William Phips helped to end the Salem trials after his own wife had been accused.[56]

Although the breakdown of the stereotype sowed the seeds of doubt in some large hunts, it did not occur very frequently. In the five major Scottish witch-hunts of the late sixteenth and seventeenth centuries, the great majority of witches conformed fairly closely to the stereotype throughout the period of the trials. The same pattern prevailed in most French and Swiss hunts and even in some German ones, such as the large witch-hunt in the prince-bishopric of Eichstätt. How then did these hunts come to an end? In some cases judges became sceptical as they tried an ever-increasing number of suspects. We must remember that although judicial officials placed great

SOURCE BOOK

SOURCE BOOK

credence in confessions adduced under torture, they did not always conduct careful analyses of all the evidence brought before them. As witch-hunts developed, this evidence became sparser and weaker, if only because specific evidence of *maleficia* was usually not forthcoming when witches were named by their accomplices. This dearth of evidence might help to explain the acquittals that occurred in the midst of even the most intense hunts. Another reason for acquittals was the occasional endurance of torture. Whatever their reasons, acquittals could have a profound effect on the development of the hunts themselves, because they strengthened the conviction that at least some of the accusations were false and possibly even malicious, thereby encouraging greater judicial caution. Acquittals also broke the chain of accusations and may even have contributed to a popular scepticism regarding the trials.

Perhaps the most dramatic end to witch-hunts occurred when conscious fraud or deceit was discovered. The most famous of these was the so-called Pendle Swindle of 1633 at Hoarstones in Lancashire, England. In that episode an eleven- or twelve-year-old boy, Edmund Robinson, deposed that a woman had taken him to a witches' assembly where some sixty participants were producing meat, butter and milk by pulling on ropes that were attached to the top of a barn. He also claimed that the witches had sexual intercourse with demonic familiars. Upon his father's suggestion the boy named a number of witches, nineteen of whom were convicted. Doubts about the guilty verdicts led the justices of the peace to request an investigation by the Privy Council, and during an interrogation conducted by the bishop of Chester the boy admitted that he had fabricated his story and that the names had been suggested by his father 'for envy, revenge, and hope of gain'.[57] Upon this admission all those who had been convicted were released, and one of the few large witch-hunts in English history came to an abrupt end. A number of smaller English hunts ended in similar fashion, and the suspicion of fraud may have even led to the end of the great witch-hunt conducted by Hopkins and Stearne.[58] In Scotland the large national hunt of 1661–2 collapsed when two witch-hunters, John Kincaid and John Dick, were prosecuted by the Privy Council for fraud and deceit in their work of pricking witches for the Devil's mark.[59]

Occasionally financial considerations were responsible for bringing witch-hunts to an end. Historians have exaggerated the role of private gain in witchcraft.[60] There is no question that throughout Europe at this time lawyers and officials welcomed and may have even encouraged business in order to make money, which in most cases came from fees that were paid either directly to lawyers or indirectly to the officials of the court. In criminal cases the confiscation of the guilty party's property often paid these fees and provided additional revenue for the prince. Among the various types of cases that they might have to argue or adjudicate, however, witchcraft cases were probably the least lucrative, if only because the economic status of witches was usually so low. In some cases, however, especially those in which wealthy and powerful people were accused, the chance to profit from witch-hunting contributed to the zeal of the prosecutors. It is perhaps for this reason that in Germany, where confiscation was the accepted procedure in witchcraft cases, and where prosecutions often reached high up the social ladder, the financial motive for prosecutions was most powerful.

Another group that could profit from witchcraft prosecutions were the witch hunters and witch finders who offered their services to local communities to help them to identify witches in their midst. When such financial motives were operative, a reduction of fees resulting either from the general impoverishment of the community or from the reluctance of communities to pay for the services of a witch-hunter could help to bring a hunt to an end. It was reported that the mass witch trials at Trier in the 1580s and 1590s, which brought considerable wealth to the judicial establishment, came to an end when the population, drained of its resources, could no longer support this costly judicial extravagance and when the fees that officials collected were reduced.[61] Another financial motive for ending witch-hunts, which may have led directly to the general impoverishment reported at Trier, was the cost of keeping suspects in prison. If witches were not able to pay the cost of their maintenance in gaol, then the town or village had to foot the bill until the trial. Sometimes those trials did not take place for weeks or months after arrest. In the case of one Scottish witch in 1661, who languished in prison for eight months at public charge, a local laird petitioned the Privy Council to have her either tried or set at liberty.[62] When one considers the number of suspects who were held in gaol at any one time during large witch-hunts, the burden of prison maintenance becomes a plausible explanation for opposition to the continuation of the hunt.

The responsibility for ending witch-hunts varied from place to place, as did the methods of termination. Sometimes popular pressure, arising from either a recognition that innocent persons were being accused, appreciation of the costs of the hunt, or a realization that the witch-hunt was destroying the equilibrium of daily life, served as the main stimulus to ending the affair. In this situation the common people had surprising power. Not only could they refuse to denounce or testify against their neighbours, but they could also express their disapproval by boycotting executions and making protests to the appropriate authorities. In England and Scotland they had the decisive power of returning not-guilty verdicts, a tactic that clearly helped to bring the Scottish hunt of 1661–2 to a close. Finally, the more articulate members of society, especially the clergy, could formulate a critique of the trials, a risky though not unusual tactic. The turning point in the Salem witch-hunt of 1692 occurred in October of that year when Increase Mather, with the support of fourteen other ministers, challenged the court that had been conducting the trials, insisting that the evidence used to convict the witches must be as solid as any other capital crime evidence.[63] The largest witch-hunt in Scandinavian history ended when a young doctor in Stockholm demonstrated that the entire panic was the result of imagination, mental confusion, pure malice, or a desire to attract attention.[64]

The men who had the greatest opportunity to bring witch-hunts to an end were the magistrates and inquisitors themselves. They might have done so because they themselves or their wives had been accused, because they had developed serious doubts about the guilt of many of the accused or, more practically, because they realized that the hunt was causing popular discontent or social chaos. Whatever their motivation, they had control of the judicial machinery and therefore were capable of terminating the hunt at any stage of the proceedings. They could acquit the witches whose cases were still pending or, more commonly, simply refuse to interrogate those who were implicated by others or any other persons whose names might be brought before them.

When hunts were not terminated by the action of either the general populace or the men entrusted with local judicial power, higher political or judicial authorities often intervened in the process. As we saw in Chapter 3, men who held positions of prominence in the higher levels of government tended to be more restrained, if not more sceptical, in dealing with witchcraft. This was both because they were usually not involved in the local tension that produced witch-hunts and because they tended to be more committed to the maintenance of official standards of criminal procedure. We also saw that whenever such authorities played a regular role in the prosecution of witches, either as officials of a central court or as circuit judges, witch-hunting was more restrained. It stands to reason, therefore, that the same men might be more disposed than local officials to admit that some large witch-hunts had got out of control and to bring them to an end. Their intervention could take one of two forms. Either they could overturn negative witchcraft verdicts on appeal or they could issue edicts that forbade further prosecutions or established more rigid procedures for conducting them.

The effect of appeals in stopping witch-hunts can most readily be observed in the Pendle Swindle discussed above and in a number of French witch-hunts. In France it was customary, and eventually obligatory, for witchcraft verdicts to be appealed to one of the nine parlements.[65] Although these parlements often confirmed the verdicts of the lower courts, they also did not hesitate to overturn or reduce the sentences of many witches.[66] Even when these reconsiderations did not bring about an abrupt end of one of these hunts, they certainly helped to reduce their intensity and may have even encouraged the judges of the lower courts to proceed more cautiously in handling subsequent witchcraft cases. In the Parlement of Paris the sceptical attitude of the jurists was so influential that they not only interrupted a series of small hunts but actually contributed to a long-term decline in all witchcraft prosecutions.[67]

The promulgation of edicts or the establishment of tougher standards of judicial interrogation could have a much more dramatic and sudden impact

179

on witch-hunts. One example of this effect comes from Scotland in 1597, when the country was engaged in one of its largest national hunts. In some communities, especially Aberdeen, an almost uncontrolled epidemic of witch-hunting had erupted. Once the Privy Council became aware of the fact that innocent persons had been executed, it recalled all the commissions of justiciary it had granted to local authorities and insisted upon a policy of reviewing individual commissions before authorizing individual trials. The Privy Council's policy helped to terminate the hunt of 1597, although it still had the potential (which was later realized) of allowing witch-hunts to occur with governmental support.[68]

A second example of the effects of edicts on witch-hunting comes from Spain, where the supreme council of the Inquisition played a key role in ending the Basque hunt of 1609–11. The turning point in that hunt came when Salazar, the inquisitor at Logroño, investigated the thousands of confessions that had been made and concluded that no act of witchcraft had ever taken place. Salazar's reconsideration of the evidence in this hunt is a good example of the loss of confidence that prosecuting judges themselves often experienced, but his investigation was not decisive in ending the hunt, since any action on the basis of his conclusions had to come from Madrid. After a long delay Madrid acted, adopting Salazar's recommendations for a set of new, stricter guidelines for the prosecution of witches. This action, like that of the Parlement of Paris, not only ended the great Basque hunt but had the added effect of greatly reducing the intensity of witch-hunting in Spain.[69]

A third example comes from France, where in 1669–70 a very large hunt took place in Normandy. Unlike the Parlement of Paris, the Parlement of Normandy at Rouen had confirmed the first twelve death sentences and was still to consider an additional twenty-four when the families of the twelve convicted witches appealed directly to King Louis XIV for a pardon. Partially motivated by a determination to curb regional judicial autonomy, Louis issued the pardon, and despite subsequent pleas from the officials at Rouen, he refused to rescind his decree. Twelve years later, in fact, Louis took a more decisive action by issuing an edict banning all witchcraft cases in France. Like the other cases discussed, therefore, the action of Louis had an impact not only on the particular hunt at Rouen but on the entire process of witch-hunting in France.[70]

On the basis of all this we may draw a number of simple, if not self-evident, conclusions. First, witch-hunts were highly contingent operations. Their beginning, development and continuation depended on a number of variables and therefore they could be limited or terminated – sometimes very abruptly – by any one of many factors. Second, witch-hunts were enormously complex historical phenomena, involving the interaction of intellectual, legal, social and psychological trends. Third, witch-hunts varied greatly in their size and dynamics, so much so that we really cannot speak of a typical witch-hunt. Nevertheless, witch-hunts possessed enough common features that a stereotype has in fact emerged, and that stereotype has been used to define various campaigns against deviants in the modern world. All witch-hunts, then and now, involve the pursuit of a secret enemy of society, an assumption that this enemy was not alone but part of a broader movement (if not an actual conspiracy), and the use of extraordinary legal measures to uncover what is not only a secret but also an ideological or religious crime. All witch-hunts, therefore, involve a high degree of judicial and communal anxiety, and it is this mood that both justifies the exceptional legal procedures and reinforces the fear that accomplices or other malefactors lie undiscovered. When, therefore, in the modern world various courts, commissions or investigatory panels conduct open-ended inquiries into allegedly subversive political, ideological or religious movements on the assumption that such an investigation will reveal the names and activities of the enemies of society, we are witnessing a phenomenon that bears a striking resemblance to the hundreds of witch-hunts that took place in early modern Europe.

Notes

1. G. L. Kittredge, *Witchcraft in Old and New England* (Cambridge, MA, 1929): 357; Henningsen, *Witches' Advocate*, 389.
2. Muchembled, 'Witches of the Cambrésis', 256–7.
3. G. Henningsen, 'Witchcraft in Denmark', *Folklore* 93 (1982): 135.
4. The first step was taken by Pope Alexander IV in 1258. See Kors and Peters, *Witchcraft in Europe*, 116–18.
5. See, for example, Trevor-Roper, 'Witch-Craze', 137–9; Clark, 'Protestant Demonology', *passim*; Naess, 'Norway', 374.
6. G. Henningsen (ed.), *The Salazar Documents: Inquisitor Alonso de Salazar Frías and Others on the Basque Witch Persecutions* (Leiden, 2004): 342.
7. Monter, *Witchcraft in France and Switzerland*, 72–3, 81. For an illustration of the effects of rumours on witch-hunting see Ankarloo, *Trolldomsprocesserna*, 338–9.
8. See Robbins, *Encyclopedia*, 202.
9. Monter, *Witchcraft in France and Switzerland*, 77, 86.
10. Midelfort, *Witch Hunting*, 122.
11. Behringer, 'Erhob sich das ganze Land', 141–3. The plague did not always have such an effect. See Midelfort, *Witch Hunting*, 122.
12. Blauert, *Frühe Hexenverfolgungen*, 20–3; Kamber, 'La Chasse', 26–8.
13. Stearne, *A Confirmation and Discovery*, 60, argues that when the millennium arrived, there would be no witches. See also Trevor-Roper, 'Witch-Craze', 172–3.
14. Macfarlane, *Witchcraft in Tudor and Stuart England*, 141, 223; Lamont, *Godly Rule*, 14, 99; Gaskill, *Witchfinders*, Chapters 1–3.
15. Levack, *Witch-hunting in Scotland*, 81–4, 96–7; Trevor-Roper, 'Witch-Craze', 160.
16. Monter, *Witchcraft in France and Switzerland*, 81; Kamber, 'La Chasse', 27; Byloff, *Hexenglaube*, 160. Robin Briggs has argued that in those few instances when witchcraft prosecutions can be related to warfare, it was 'usually on the fringes of conflict or when its impact was less overwhelming'. Briggs, *Witches and Neighbours*, 308–9.
17. Monter, *Witchcraft in France and Switzerland*, 81.
18. Klaniczay, 'Hungary', 224
19. Baranowski, *Procesy Czarownic*, 178.

20. Monter, 'Witch Trials in Continental Europe', 18–21; Midelfort, *Witch Hunting*, 88–90.
21. See Larner, 'James VI and Witchcraft', 80–1. An earlier storm at sea also sank a ship laden with wedding gifts for the royal couple and killed 40 passengers in November 1589. Witches later confessed to having caused the storms by throwing a christened cat into the North Sea. *Newes from Scotland*, 116–17.
22. Monter, *Witchcraft in France and Switzerland*, 44–7; Naphy, *Plagues, Poisons and Potions*.
23. Monter, *Witchcraft in France and Switerland*, 92–3.
24. M. Hopkins, *The Discovery of Witches* (London, 1647): 50.
25. Only five of the forty-five group possessions taking place in French convents resulted in accusations of witchcraft. M. Sluhovsky, 'The Devil in the Convent', *American Historical Review* 107 (2002): 1380.
26. On these French cases see S. Ferber, *Demonic Possession and Exorcism in Early Modern France* (London, 2004); Rapley, *A Case of Witchcraft*; Certeau, *The Possession at Loudun*; Waite, *Heresy, Magic and Witchcraft*, 217–23.
27. Monter, *Witchcraft in France and Switzerland*, 59–60, 70–2; J. Sharpe, *Instruments of Darkness: Witchcraft in England, 1550–1750* (London, 1996): chapter 8.
28. R. Decker, *Die Hexen und ihre Henker* (Freiburg, 1994).
29. Clark, *Thinking with Demons*, chapter 27.
30. Mather, *Memorable Providences*, 1–41.
31. Their afflictions might have technically been cases of obsession rather than possession, since it was unclear whether the Devil had actually entered their bodies. This distinction, however, was rarely made in the twentieth century, and possession was used to describe a number of mysterious assaults upon the human body. See D. Harley, 'Explaining Salem: Calvinist Psychology and the Diagnosis of Possession', *American Historical Review* 101 (1996): 307–30.
32. The most notable English cases were described in *The Second Part of the Boy of Bilson, or a True and Particular Relation of the Impostor Susanna Fowles* (London, 1698); *The Surey Demoniack: or, An Account of Satan's Strange and Dreadful Actings in and about the Body of Richard Dugdale of Surey, near Lancashire* (London, 1697).
33. The case of Shaw and the prosecution of the witches were recounted in *A True Narrative of the Sufferings and Relief of a Young Girle* (Edinburgh, 1698), reprinted in J. Millar (ed.), *A History of the Witches of Renfrewshire* (Paisley, 1877): 93. The account is modelled closely – sometimes word for word – upon the account of the Salem witches by Robert Calef. The legal documents can be found in National Archives of Scotland, JC 10/4. See Levack, *Witch-Hunting in Scotland*, chapter 7.
34. Thomas, *Religion and the Decline of Magic*, 457–8; A. Gregory, 'Witchcraft, Politics and "Good Neighbourhood" in Early Seventeenth-Century Rye', *Past and Present* 133 (1991): 31–66.
35. Horsley, 'Who Were the Witches?', 713.
36. C. Baxter, 'Jean Bodin's *De la Démonomanie des sorciers*: The Logic of Persecution', in *The Damned Art: Essays in the Literature of Witchcraft*, ed. S. Anglo (London, 1977): 78; Muchembled, 'Witches of the Cambrésis', 241; Soman, 'Parlement of Paris', 42–3; Schormann, *Deutschland*, 109–10; Henningsen, *Witches' Advocate*, 1; Ankarloo, 'Sweden', 308–9.
37. Rummel, *Bauern, Herren und Hexen*, 317–21; Dillinger, *Evil People*, 15–16.
38. Labouvie, *Zauberei und Hexenwerk*, 82–95. Dillinger sees local committees of common folk and city councillors as the driving force of witch-hunts in Swabian Austria as well as Electoral Trier. *Evil People*, chapters 4 and 5.
39. Briggs, *Communities of Belief*, 36; Soman, 'Witch Lynching at Juniville', 15.

40. P. H. Brown (ed.), *Register of the Privy Council of Scotland*, 3rd ser., I (Edinburgh, 1908): 11–12.
41. Briggs, *Communities of Belief*, 136.
42. Ankarloo, 'Sweden', 308.
43. On the modern connotations of the word see Larner, *Witchcraft and Religion*, 88.
44. Roper, *Oedipus and the Devil*, 199–200; A. Rowlands, 'Eine Stadt ohne Hexenwahn. Hexenprozesse, Gerichtspraxis und Herrschaft im frühneuzeitlichen Rothenburg ob der Tauber', in *Hexenprozesse und Gerichtspraxis*, ed. H. Eiden and R. Voltmer (Trier, 2002): 331–47.
45. Garrett, 'Women and Witches', 464.
46. In Bavaria there were fourteen large hunts, each claiming twenty or more lives, between 1586 and 1631. These hunts accounted for more than half of the witchcraft executions in that region. Behringer, *Witchcraft Persecutions in Bavaria*, 60–5.
47. Robbins, *Encyclopedia*, 515.
48. Ibid., 318.
49. For a full account and analysis of this witch-hunt see Gaskill, *Witchfinders*; Sharpe, *Instruments of Darkness*, chapter 5.
50. Volk, *Hexen*, 58–88; Midelfort, *Witch Hunting*, 128.
51. On the diagnosis of demonic possession as hysteria see Levack, *The Devil Within*, 123–9. On the broader history of hysteria, see A. Skull, *Hysteria: The Biography* (Oxford, 2009).
52. Robbins, *Encyclopedia*, 317.
53. G. Rosen, 'Psychopathology of the Social Process: (I) A Study of the Persecution of Witches in Europe as a Contribution to the Understanding of Mass Delusion and Psychic Epidemics', *Journal of Health and Human Behavior* 1 (1960): 13–44.
54. Midelfort, *Witch Hunting*, 192; Lea, *Materials*, III: 1075.
55. Levack, *Witchcraft Sourcebook*, 198–202; Burr, *The Witch Persecutions*, 23–8.
56. Midelfort, 'Witch Hunting and the Domino Theory', 277–88.
57. Sharpe, *Instruments of Darkness*, 126, 164; R. Seth, *Children against Witches* (New York, 1969): 164–9; W. Notestein, *A History of Witchcraft in England* (Washington, DC, 1911): 146–63.
58. Notestein, *A History of Witchcraft in England*, 140–3; Hopkins, *The Discovery of Witches*, 9–10.
59. Brown, *Register of the Privy Council of Scotland*, 3rd ser., I: 187, 210.
60. See, for example, E. P. Currie, 'Crimes without Criminals: Witchcraft and its Control in Renaissance Europe', *Law and Society Review* 3 (1968): 21–8.
61. Kors and Peters, *Witchcraft in Europe*, 315.
62. Brown, *Register of the Privy Council of Scotland*, 3rd ser., I: 78.
63. Mather, *Cases of Conscience*, 62.
64. Robbins, *Encyclopedia*, 350.
65. On the resistance of lower courts to the appeal procedure in witchcraft cases and the insistence on automatic appeal to the Parlement of Paris in 1624 see Mandrou, *Magistrats et sorciers*, 343–8.
66. Soman, 'Parlement of Paris', 36.
67. Mandrou, *Magistrats et sorciers*, 313–63.
68. J. Goodare, 'The Scottish Witchcraft Panic of 1597', in *The Scottish Witch-Hunt in Context* (Manchester, 2002): 51–72. The edict that marked the new, more cautious policy was promulgated on 12 August 1597. Brown, *Register of the Privy Council of Scotland*, V: 409–10.
69. Henningsen, *Witches' Advocate*, 357–93.
70. Mandrou, *Magistrats et sorciers*, 425–86.

7

THE CHRONOLOGY
AND GEOGRAPHY OF
WITCH-HUNTING

One of the most difficult tasks facing historians of European witchcraft is to account for the variations in the intensity of witch-hunting at different times and places. Why, for example, did more European prosecutions take place between 1560 and 1630 than between 1520 and 1560? And why was witch-hunting so much more intense in Germany than in Spain, or in Scotland than in England? To answer such questions we must pursue two separate lines of enquiry. On the one hand, we must establish the general chronological patterns of witch-hunting throughout Europe, suggesting various reasons for the waxing and waning of prosecutions over the entire period. Then we must survey the history of witchcraft prosecutions in the various states and regions of Europe, an enterprise that will also take into account chronological patterns within those particular areas. Both investigations will provide further illustration of the complexity and the diversity of the general phenomenon.

Chronological patterns

Prior to the 1420s, the concept of witchcraft as a crime involving both harmful magic and Devil-worship was in the process of formation. Therefore, it is problematic to speak of the prosecutions that took place during those years as witchcraft trials. Most such trials before 1420 were prosecutions either for simple *maleficium* or for ritual magic. These early trials can be grouped into three fairly distinct periods, each involving different types of charges against the accused. From 1300 to 1330, most of the 'witches' were ritual magicians who attempted to harm political rivals or to advance their careers. In the second period, from 1330 to 1375, the trial of politically related cases almost ceased, but there were numerous trials for sorcery. Whether these sorcerers were being prosecuted for simple *maleficium* or ritual magic is difficult to determine, but in either case the most noteworthy feature of the trials is the absence of diabolism. During the third period, from 1375 to 1420, the number of prosecutions increased and charges of diabolism became more common, mainly in Italy. This development, which was facilitated by the adoption of inquisitorial procedure in local courts, reflected the gradual assimilation of charges of diabolism to those of *maleficium*.[1]

The first period of witch-hunting, 1420–1520

Beginning around 1420 the history of European witchcraft prosecutions entered a new and distinct phase. Not only did trials for sorcery increase in number but charges of diabolism were more frequently grafted on to them, and witch-hunting began to assume the characteristics it maintained throughout the period of prosecution. During the 1420s and 1430s the full stereotype of the witch, complete with descriptions of the witches' sabbath, emerged, most notably in trials in the western Alps. For all intents and purposes, these fifteenth-century trials denote the beginning of the European witch-hunt. It was during this period, moreover, that the first witchcraft treatises appeared – most notably Johannes Nider's *Formicarius* [The Anthill, written 1436/7; published 1475], Heinrich Kramer's *Malleus maleficarum* [The Hammer of Witches, 1486], and Ulrich Molitor's *De lamiis et phitonicis mulieribus* [Concerning Witches and Female Soothsayers, 1489]. The publication of these works, which emphasized the diabolical as well as the magical dimensions of the witch's crime, corresponded to the increase in the number of prosecutions. Some of these early witch-hunts, including a large number of panics in Italian lands, took a heavy toll in human life.[2]

The period of limited prosecutions and small hunts, 1520–1560

At this point the history of European witch-hunting began to follow a somewhat surprising course. Instead of slowly gathering strength and leading into the large panics of the late sixteenth and early seventeenth centuries, the number of trials levelled off during the early sixteenth century and in certain areas actually declined.[3] The decline did not escape the notice of contemporaries. Martin Luther, writing in 1516, claimed that although there had been many witches and sorcerers in his youth, they were 'not so commonly heard of anymore'.[4] As might be expected, there were some areas where Luther might have heard much more about witches during these years. There were a number of trials in the Basque country between 1507 and 1539; in Catalonia in 1549; in the diocese of Como and in other parts of northern Italy in the 1510s and 1520s; in the northern parts of Languedoc between 1519 and 1530; and in Luxembourg, Namur, Douai and other parts of the Low Countries throughout the first half of the sixteenth century.[5] There also were occasional prosecutions in places like Nuremberg.[6] But it is difficult to avoid the conclusion that the early sixteenth century was a period of relative tranquillity as far as witch-hunting was concerned.[7]

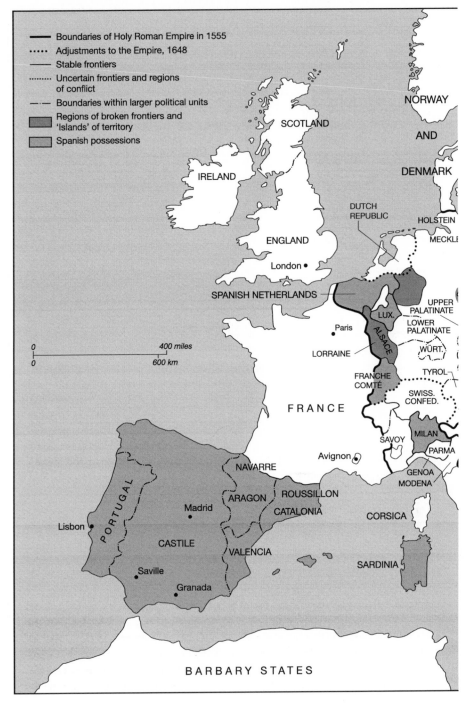

Europe in the early seventeenth century

The levelling off or reduction in the intensity of witch-hunting during the first half of the sixteenth century was reflected in, and to some extent even caused by, an interruption in the publication of witchcraft treatises and manuals. The *Malleus maleficarum*, for example, while enormously popular between 1486 and 1520 and again between 1580 and 1650, was not reprinted at all between 1521 and 1576. In similar fashion, none of the other fifteenth-century witchcraft treatises found a market during these years. And after the publication of Grillandus's *Tractatus de hereticis et sortilegiis* [Treatise on Heretics and Sorcerers] in 1524 there was very little written in support of witch-hunting until the 1570s. In other words, if the production of witchcraft literature serves as a gauge of the intensity of witch-hunting, there was definitely an early sixteenth-century gap, lagging a little behind the actual reduction in the number of trials. Instead of one continuous European witch-hunt, there were really two separate campaigns: an early, geographically limited hunt in the late fifteenth century and a much more intense and widespread series of prosecutions in the late sixteenth and early seventeenth centuries.

The lull in witch-hunting during the early sixteenth century can be attributed both to the development of scepticism among the learned elite and to the preoccupation of both ecclesiastical and secular authorities with the confessional disputes and prosecutions of the Reformation. This period witnessed the spread of Renaissance humanism throughout Europe, and although the humanists failed to undermine the cumulative concept of witchcraft, they did attack parts of it as well as the scholastic mentality that proved receptive to it. For a brief period of time the critiques of witch beliefs and prosecutions that one finds in the writings of men like Erasmus, Andre Alciati, Pietro Pomponazzi and Cornelius Agrippa may have shaken the resolve of various authorities to pursue witches in great numbers.[8] Their insistence that magic could be performed naturally, without the aid of demons, and that witches were harmless creatures victimized by delusion had at least the effect of raising doubts about the practice of the crime. At the same time a belief developed in Germany, especially in the work of the preacher Martin Plantsch of Tübingen, that God was directly responsible for many of the natural disasters like hailstorms that were often attributed to witchcraft.[9] This early sixteenth-century scepticism found its most articulate and forceful expression in the work of the tolerant humanist physician, Johann Weyer, during the 1560s.

The role that the Protestant Reformation played in the early sixteenth-century reduction of witchcraft prosecutions is more complex and problematic. There is little doubt that the combined efforts of the Protestant and Catholic reformations did much to encourage witchcraft prosecutions in the late sixteenth and seventeenth centuries. During the early years of the Reformation, however, the confessional disputes between Protestants and Catholics (who considered each other heretics but not the same type of heretics as witches) served to distract European elites from the task of witch-hunting. More specifically, the Protestant rejection of Roman Catholicism naturally led to a desire on the part of reformers to formulate their own theories of witchcraft rather than to rely on the work of fifteenth-century Catholic demonologists and inquisitors. This rejection of Catholic witchcraft theory thus contributed to a decline in the demand for the older, fifteenth-century treatises. Finally and most importantly, the Protestant rejection of the Inquisition, its drastic overhaul of all ecclesiastical jurisdiction, and its transfer of much ecclesiastical jurisdiction from the ecclesiastical to the secular courts involved extensive alterations in the judicial machinery that was used to prosecute witches. Even within Catholic areas the assumption of secular jurisdiction over witchcraft required both the passage of specific legislation to facilitate it and the acceptance by secular magistrates of the necessity to use it.

The period of intense prosecutions and large hunts, 1560–1630

During the 1560s and 1570s there were many signs that Europe was poised on the threshold of a new outbreak of witch-hunting, one that was much more intense and widespread than the initial assault of the fifteenth century. In the southwestern German town of Wiesensteig some sixty-three witches were executed in 1562, and during the winter of 1562–3 the Parlement of Toulouse heard on appeal about three dozen cases of witchcraft from the diocese of Couserans.[10] A series of trials in the Low Countries offered further evidence that witchcraft was once again on the rise, as did the passage of witchcraft statutes in both England and Scotland in 1563. A number of small panics occurred during the 1570s in the wake of a serious agrarian crisis. The resumption of the printing of the *Malleus maleficarum*, the appearance of Lambert Daneau's *Dialogue of Witches* in 1574, and the refutations of Weyer's sceptical arguments by Thomas Erastus (1572) and Jean Bodin (1580) also signalled a renewal and an intensification of witch-hunting zeal.[11]

Most European territories experienced the full force of the European witch-hunt between 1580 and 1630. Large-scale prosecutions involving hundreds of victims occurred throughout western and central Europe, most notably in the diocese of Trier in the late 1580s and early 1590s, Scotland in 1590–1 and 1597, Lorraine in the late 1580s and early 1590s, Ellwangen in the 1610s, and Würzburg and Bamberg during the 1620s. Without complete statistics it is difficult to determine which decade between 1580 and 1630 was the time of the most intense witch-hunting. The 1580s were especially bad in Switzerland and the Low Countries; the 1590s in France, the Low Countries, Scotland and in many German territories; the 1600s in the Jura region and in many German states; the 1610s in Spain; and the 1620s and 1630s in Germany.

This period of intense witch-hunting between 1580 and 1630 was related, as both cause and effect, to the proliferation of witchcraft treatises. The well-known works by Peter Binsfeld (1591), Nicolas Remy (1595), King James VI of Scotland (1597), Martín Del Rio (1599), Henri Boguet (1602), Francesco Maria Guazzo (1608) and Pierre de Lancre (1612) were all written during these years, and the power of the rapidly developing printing industry made their works available to an increasingly large literate European population.[12] These witchcraft treatises all used the evidence of late sixteenth-century trials to confirm the reality of witchcraft, deepen elite fears of the crime, and provide guidance for its effective prosecution.

The unprecedented intensification of witch-hunting in the late sixteenth century reflected not only the resolution of learned doubt, but also the impact of both the Protestant and Catholic reformations. By this time the Bible, with its literal death sentences for witches, was being widely circulated in the vernacular; preachers had heightened people's awareness of the immediacy of Satan; reformers had declared war on magic in all its forms; and the process of Christianization had helped to cultivate the feelings of both moral superiority and guilt that played such an important part in witch-hunting.[13] To make matters worse, the conflict between Protestantism and Catholicism on the one hand and between various forms of Protestantism on the other began to reach its peak, a development that reinforced a fear of the Devil and hostility towards witchcraft.[14]

A final and perhaps decisive factor in the intensification of witch-hunting in the late sixteenth century was the onset of one of the most economically volatile and politically unstable periods in European history. During the years from 1580 to 1630 Europe experienced unprecedented inflation, a series of harsh climatic changes, periodic famines (the worst being in the 1590s), depressions in trade (especially in the 1620s), and a more general crisis of production.[15] Real wages declined sharply, while the condition of the poor and unemployed reached critical proportions. These developments aggravated the personal conflicts that often found expression in witchcraft accusations, and they also heightened the fears of many members of the ruling and literate elite that witches were complicit in a diabolical campaign to bring dearth and famine to European communities.

The period of decline, 1630–1770

The prosecution and execution of witches did not end in 1630, but it entered a new phase marked by a general decline in the number of trials. There were notable exceptions to this pattern: in the Dutch Republic the prosecutions came to almost a complete end shortly after 1600, while in Spain the Inquisition stopped executing witches in the wake of the great Basque witch-hunt of 1609–11. In France the procedural measures introduced by the Parlement of Paris resulted in a dramatic reduction in the number of executions by the 1620s. In England prosecutions tapered off significantly after 1612, although the largest single witch-hunt in its history occurred in 1645–7, thus interrupting this period of decline. Scotland also had its last and largest witch-hunt in 1661–2, shortly after it had experienced a significant reduction in the number of prosecutions in the 1650s. These late witch panics in England and Scotland, as well as similar episodes in Sweden and Finland in the 1660s and early 1670s, make it even more difficult to establish universal patterns of decline. What is more, a few countries on the periphery of Europe – Hungary, Transylvania, Poland and New England – did not bear the full brunt of witchcraft prosecutions until the late seventeenth and early eighteenth centuries.[16]

Nevertheless, for most of Europe, especially the core witchcraft area that included the Germanic territories, the Swiss cantons and the predominantly French-speaking lands on the eastern borders of the French kingdom, the period from 1675 to 1750 was a time of contraction in the prosecution of witches. Those trials that did take place, moreover, usually involved only one or two defendants. It took some time, however, before *all* witchcraft prosecutions came to an end. Many courts discouraged prosecutions in the late seventeenth and early eighteenth centuries, but only seven European countries (France in 1682, Prussia in 1714, Great Britain in 1736, the Habsburg Monarchy in 1766, Russia in 1770, Poland in 1776 and Sweden in 1779) took legislative action either declaring that witchcraft was no longer a crime or seriously restricting the scope of earlier witchcraft laws. The limited number and late dates of those legislative acts, coupled with the determination of individuals to accuse their neighbours of witchcraft, explains why witchcraft trials, and even some executions, continued to take place well into the eighteenth century. In England, for example, the ability of grand juries to indict criminals and petty juries to convict them explains why the last execution took place in 1685 and the last conviction in 1712. In Scotland, where juries had less influence on the outcome of the trials but where authorities were more inclined to allow charges to be brought against witches, the trials continued until 1727. In France the royal edict of Louis XIV ended almost all witchcraft prosecutions, but the failure of the edict to end prosecutions for acts of blasphemy allowed isolated trials until 1745. Within the German territories a number of late executions took place, most notably in Würzburg in 1749 and in Württemberg the same year. The last execution in Europe occurred in the Swiss canton of Glarus (which was also the last territory to ban torture) in 1782. An execution in Poland in 1793, which occurred during a period of great jurisdictional uncertainty, was probably illegal.

Geographical patterns

Any attempt to establish the broad chronological patterns of European witch-hunting is complicated by regional variations. Some clear patterns are evident, but witch-hunting began, peaked and declined at different times and in different places. To make matters even more complex, the sum total of prosecutions, convictions and executions varied greatly in the different states and regions of Europe. A full study of these regional patterns, broken down by individual provinces, counties and towns would be impossible to undertake in a study of this nature. We can, however, establish some of the broader geographical patterns. Choosing the most appropriate geographical units for such comparison presents some difficulty. If we were to use the political boundaries of sovereign states we would have to deal separately with each of the individual states of Germany and Italy and with the various kingdoms of Spain, and we would also have to take into account the changes in sovereignty that occurred in many European areas during the early modern period.

If we use the criterion of language, we would be unable to discuss Switzerland or, for that matter, Scotland as distinct units. Medium-sized geographical regions are perhaps the most sensible units of analysis, and in this category we have some very fine studies by Midelfort on southwestern Germany, Schormann on northwestern Germany, Behringer on Bavaria, Muchembled and Dupont-Bouchat on the Low Countries, Monter on the Jura region, and Godbeer on New England. It is often difficult, however, to find other regions with which these regions can be conveniently and legitimately compared, and even when such areas can be defined, there is often not sufficient data available to make meaningful comparisons.[17] For the purposes of this study we shall discuss five very large areas of Europe: (1) western and west-central Europe: Germany, France, Switzerland and the Low Countries; (2) the British Isles and Britain's overseas possessions: England, Scotland, Ireland and colonial America; (3) the Nordic countries: Denmark, Norway, Sweden, Finland and Iceland; (4) east-central and eastern Europe: Poland, Hungary, Transylvania and Russia; and (5) southern Europe: Italy, the Iberian Peninsula, and the Spanish and Portuguese overseas empires. We shall exclude the area effectively controlled by the Ottoman Empire, with the exception of the relatively autonomous provinces of Moldavia and Wallachia, since no witchcraft prosecutions occurred in that area. Within each of these large areas there were some pronounced regional and national differences with regard to witch-hunting. There were, for example, significant differences between France and Germany, England and Scotland, Norway and Sweden, Poland and Russia, and Spain and Italy. But these large geographical areas, in addition to being fairly cohesive geographically, exhibit enough similarities regarding witch-hunting to make the broader comparisons worthwhile. These similarities are rooted in various religious, legal and political characteristics that the countries in these large areas shared.

Western and west-central Europe

The overwhelming majority of witchcraft prosecutions – perhaps as many as 75 per cent – occurred in Germany, France, Switzerland and the Low Countries, an area that comprised roughly one-half of the entire population of Europe. Not surprisingly, this was also the area where most large hunts and panics took place, and it is mainly because of these panics that the total number of prosecutions and executions was disproportionately high. During the early years of the hunt most prosecutions took place in France, especially in those areas in the eastern part of the country that bordered on Swiss and Burgundian lands. By the late sixteenth century, however, when the hunt had entered its most intense stage, Germany had become the centre of prosecutions. Trials continued in France, especially in the southern borderlands, and a number of urban cases of demonic possession led to witchcraft prosecutions. But the largest panics of the late sixteenth and seventeenth centuries took place in German-speaking lands.

More than half of the territory in the western and west-central area lay within the Holy Roman Empire. In 1559 the Empire extended so far in the west and the south that it included all of the Netherlands and Franche-Comté (which were under Spanish control), the Swiss Confederation, and even parts of northern Italy, while to the east it embraced Bohemia, Austria and Silesia. By 1648 its boundaries had shrunk considerably, as both the northern provinces of the Netherlands and the Swiss Confederation had established their identity as sovereign states, while the duchies of Savoy, Milan, Genoa and Tuscany no longer were included within the Empire. The shifting boundaries of the Empire make it difficult even to attempt any sort of estimate of the total number of witch trials held there, but it is not unreasonable to assert that the number was significantly greater than for all other parts of Europe combined.[18] If we restrict ourselves to German-speaking lands within the Empire, the number of executions was probably somewhere between 20,000 and 25,000.[19]

The political weakness of the Empire may have been the single most important reason for the high concentration of witchcraft trials in this part of Europe. The Empire was a very loose confederation of numerous small kingdoms, principalities, duchies and territories that acted either as sovereign or near-sovereign states. Some of these territories, such as the Spanish Netherlands, were possessions of foreign rulers. Others were dependencies of larger units within the Empire, such as Montbéliard, which was technically under the sovereignty of the duke of Württemberg. Still others were ecclesiastical territories under the control of a prince-bishop or abbot. There were, moreover, a number of imperial cities which, while having a direct relationship to the imperial structure, operated with relative autonomy. The judicial effects of all this political diversity and decentralization was to give virtual judicial autonomy to relatively small political units. The Empire itself provided very little legal unity and exercised very little judicial control over the activities of the various tribunals that heard witchcraft cases. It supplied a legal code, the *Constitutio Criminalis Carolina* of 1532, for the entire Empire, but it did not provide effective mechanisms for enforcing it. There were no itinerant imperial judges to ensure that the code was upheld and no procedure for regular appeals to the imperial chamber court, the *Reichskammergericht*, at

Speyer. Consequently only 247 witchcraft cases were litigated there between 1500 and 1800. Even the larger political units within the Empire, being either weak patrimonial estates or themselves confederations of smaller entities, often failed to exercise effective judicial control over the various courts within their territories. In most cases, therefore, the trial of witches in Germany was entrusted to courts that exercised jurisdiction over a relatively small geographical area.

The prevailing pattern of jurisdictional particularism in Germany meant that witch-hunting could easily go unchecked. It would be an exaggeration to claim that this situation gave every lord, parson or magistrate the freedom to 'burn to his heart's content', but German judges did have a latitude in handling witchcraft cases that zealous witch-hunters in other parts of Europe would certainly have envied.[20] One of the most striking examples of this type of jurisdictional independence was the principality of Ellwangen, a fairly small Catholic territory in southwestern Germany which was almost completely independent of outside political and ecclesiastical control and never permitted appeals to higher courts. Not surprisingly, Ellwangen was the location of one of the most severe witch-hunts in German history, an operation that took the lives of almost 400 individuals between 1611 and 1618.[21]

The distribution of witchcraft prosecutions within the Empire provides additional support for the thesis that the size of German jurisdictional units had a great deal to do with the intensity of witch-hunting. Without over-simplifying an immensely complex situation, we can divide Germany into two regions, one of which experienced much more intense witch-hunting than the other. The lands that exercised relative restraint for the most part lay to the north and to the east, the one notable exception to this rule being the northeastern duchy of Mecklenburg, which was a particularly black spot in the history of German witchcraft. The main centres for witch-hunting, however, lay to the south and to the west, a large area that included Würzburg, Bamberg, Eichstätt, Württemberg and Ellwangen, to name only a few sites of famous witch-hunts. As Gerhard Schormann has shown, there are a number of differences between these two regions, but one of the most significant is that the northern and eastern areas consisted of much larger, less fragmented political units than in the south and the west.[22] In keeping with this thesis, Schormann classifies the large, southeastern principality of Bavaria with the northern and eastern lands, for it executed a relatively small number of witches for a political unit of its size.[23] If we include the even larger countries of Austria and Bohemia (both of which were in the Empire) in this scheme, the relationship between the size of autonomous political units and the intensity of witch-hunting becomes even clearer. The total number of executions in Austria was probably about 900 and in Bohemia about 400. The great majority of these prosecutions took place in the late seventeenth and eighteenth centuries, somewhat later than the bulk of other German prosecutions.[24]

Although local German courts usually did not have to deal with appeals to imperial tribunals or with supervision by imperial judicial authorities, they were required to consult with the universities in witchcraft cases. This requirement, which was included in Article 109 of the *Carolina*, was intended to help local judges deal with the complexities of criminal procedure in an area of the law with which they were often unfamiliar. Before proceeding with torture and before sentencing they would send reports to the law faculty of the neighbouring university (there were twenty-three within the Empire by the early seventeenth century) to request advice. Instead of leading to greater restraint and caution in witchcraft prosecutions, such as often resulted from the intervention of central authorities, this practice usually had the opposite effect. Indeed, since the universities were the centres for the development and dissemination of demonological theory, consultation with learned jurists helped to introduce diabolical ideas to local magistrates whose beliefs were sometimes no different from those of simple peasants.[25] In this case, therefore, local determination to eliminate witchcraft was strengthened rather than weakened by the intervention of 'higher' judicial authorities.

Once we leave the Holy Roman Empire we can still witness the importance of jurisdictional factors in determining the intensity of witch-hunting within the 'heartland' of witchcraft. In Switzerland, where as many as 10,000 witches were tried and more than 5,000 executed,[26] the picture is extremely complex, since the Confederation was religiously, culturally and linguistically pluralistic. The cantons were also jurisdictionally autonomous, a situation that not only encouraged diversity in witch-hunting patterns but also made uncontrolled witch-hunting possible. The severity of Swiss witch-hunting is best illustrated in the Pays de Vaud, where more than 90 per cent of those tried for witchcraft were executed and the total number of victims exceeded 3,000. On the other hand, Geneva, while experiencing a few severe plague-spreading panics from time to time, had a very mild record of witch persecutions.[27]

As we move north from Switzerland we encounter a whole string of territories which, while technically within the Empire, were virtually autonomous, such as Franche-Comté, Lorraine and the Low Countries. In all of these areas witch-hunting was encouraged by de facto jurisdictional independence, although in the case of the Spanish possessions it was aggravated by the attempts of royal agents to define witchcraft as a crime and encourage its prosecution. In these areas there was in fact a lethal combination of central and local involvement in witch-hunting, with the king of Spain, the Holy Roman Emperor, or the archduke of Burgundy providing the legislation and sometimes the initial inspiration to witch-hunting and the small duchies or states possessing the freedom to proceed as they wished.[28] As might be expected, prosecutions for witchcraft took a heavy toll in these small territories. In Lorraine, where Nicolas Remy sent more than 800 witches to their deaths between 1586 and 1595 (and more than 2,000 during his entire career), travellers could see 'thousands and thousands of the stakes to which witches

SOURCE BOOK

are bound'.[29] During the entire period of the witch-hunt, approximately 3,000 witches were executed in that duchy.[30] In Luxembourg there were 358 executions between 1509 and 1687 and in the other parts of the Spanish Netherlands there were many more.[31]

The only political units in this part of Europe that did not conform to this general pattern of intense prosecution were the northern Netherlands. In this region, later known as the Dutch Republic, which had more than one million inhabitants, fewer than 150 witches were executed. Executions for witchcraft also ended earlier in this region than in any other part of Europe. The Netherlands did experience a few large hunts in the provinces of Groningen, Utrecht and North Brabant, but none of these areas executed as many witches as the region of Limburg, which at that time was not part of the Republic.[32]

It is unlikely that jurisdictional factors, which account for the intense persecutions in so many parts of Germany, can be used to explain the pattern in the Netherlands. The entire judicial system was highly decentralized – a situation which elsewhere often facilitated prosecutions – and the degree of central control within each province varied widely.[33] It is noteworthy, however, that in the province of Friesland, where justice was centralized, there were virtually no prosecutions, while in the province of Groningen, where local courts were given considerable freedom of action, two fairly large witch-hunts took place in the sixteenth century.[34]

The Dutch system of criminal procedure may have played a role in keeping the total number of prosecutions low. Although Dutch courts followed inquisitorial procedure and allowed the use of torture, torture was never employed excessively, and in 1594 the central court in the province of Holland forbade the use of torture as well as the swimming test in witchcraft cases. This decision made prosecutions very difficult and certainly contributed to the early decline and end of prosecutions throughout the Republic. A further procedural explanation of the relatively low number of witchcraft convictions and executions was the opportunity that accused witches had to bring counter-suits of slander against their accusers. These too played a role in bringing Dutch witch-hunting to an early end.[35]

The main explanation for the tameness of Dutch witch-hunting appears to be more ideological than judicial. Although Dutch judges had all the procedural tools for conducting massive witch-hunts, including the right to use torture, they never believed that witches were engaged in the activities described in the demonological literature. The cumulative concept of witchcraft developed slowly in the Netherlands, and even when it finally appeared, it never found fertile ground.[36] Magistrates accepted the reality of the pact with the Devil, but they never subscribed to the notion of a vast diabolical conspiracy. Without that frightening belief, they were more likely to respect the rules for judicial caution that were readily available to them.

In accounting for the weakness of Dutch witch-hunting, two other possible explanations deserve consideration. The first was the intense preoccupation of the country with the struggle for independence from Spain, a conflict that was all-consuming between 1568 and 1609 and not formally resolved until 1648. As mentioned in Chapter 5, witchcraft prosecutions did not generally occur during periods of war or domestic political crisis, and in this case the conflict with Spain covered the entire period of witch-hunting. The second explanation was the reluctance of either Catholic or Protestant ecclesiastical authorities to engage in campaigns against magic and superstition. Those same authorities were also reluctant to assist secular authorities in the detection and prosecution of witches.

Turning finally to France, the question arises as to whether political and jurisdictional factors played as much of a role in determining the intensity of witch-hunting as in the Empire. The overall pattern of witchcraft prosecutions, especially after secular courts assumed the main burden of prosecution in the sixteenth century, suggests that they did. The areas within France that were most heavily affected by witchcraft were situated on the frontiers of the kingdom: the north, the east, Languedoc, the southwest and (belatedly) Normandy. All of these areas were resistant to the efforts of the French monarchy to establish a centralized, absolutist state.[37] It is possible that this situation led royal judges to prosecute witches as part of a general programme of disciplining and Christianizing the population and of curbing rebellion in these outlying regions. As we have seen, contemporaries made associations between witchcraft and rebellion in Languedoc, and they may have been at least partially correct. But the main reason for intense witch-hunting in the peripheral regions of France is that courts in these regions operated with greater independence from central governmental control than did those in the centre of the country. And, as we know from the late seventeenth-century trials in Rouen, the right of particular localities to prosecute witches without interference from the central government was one of many issues that pitted Louis XIV against the various provinces in his kingdom.[38]

The struggle between the centre and the periphery in France did, therefore, have a great deal to do with witchcraft prosecution in that kingdom, and the greater success that France had in establishing a powerful central monarchy in the sixteenth and seventeenth centuries goes a long way towards explaining why far fewer witches were executed within its boundaries than in Germany. Another factor, not unrelated to this process of centralization, was the regular system of appeals from local courts to the nine provincial parlements. In some cases, as in Normandy in the 1590s, when the provincial Parlement of Rouen fully supported the trials and confirmed sentences that were appealed to it, this system of provincial control did little to discourage prosecutions by local authorities. But the reversal of many sentences by the Parlement of Paris, which exercised an appellate jurisdiction over most of northern France, and which set the standards for the other provincial parlements, did have a negative effect on the entire process of witch-hunting in France. More than any one factor it explains why France, with a population only marginally smaller than that of the Empire, prosecuted far fewer witches. Until more work is done on the records of the provincial parlements most estimates will remain a matter of guesswork, but it would not be unreasonable to suggest a figure of 3,000 prosecutions and perhaps only 1,000 executions for the areas that actually came within the king's jurisdiction.[39] The numbers of illegal executions, such as the 300 that occurred at Ardennes in the early seventeenth century, might swell this figure some more.[40] Even so, this larger figure would not denote a persecution much more intense than took place in England, provided we take into account the relative size of the population of the two countries.[41]

The concentration of the great majority of witchcraft prosecutions in the west-central core of Europe had religious as well as political and judicial causes. There is no question that this was the most ecclesiastically volatile region in all of Europe. It was a hotbed of heresy in the late Middle Ages and the very centre of the Protestant Reformation. After the Reformation the region became ecclesiastically unstable, with certain areas changing their religious affiliation more than once and others becoming religiously pluralistic. In Germany each prince determined the religion of his lands after 1556, while in France a period of qualified religious toleration occurred from 1598 to 1685. Throughout France, therefore, there were many religiously divided areas, and in both France and Germany there was extensive religious conflict. All of this religious dissent, instability and diversity encouraged the prosecution of witches. The mere tradition of dissent, of course, made authorities conscious of the possibility of witchcraft, since witchcraft was, after all, a new and particularly virulent strain of heresy. The close proximity of adherents to a rival faith may also have strengthened the consciousness of the Devil in these areas, while the frequency and intensity of outright religious conflict contributed to the mood of anxiety that lay at the foundation of witchcraft prosecutions.

The British Isles

Once we leave the west-central area of Europe and survey witchcraft prosecutions on its periphery, we confront a general pattern of witch-hunting that is relatively mild and restrained. All of these peripheral areas had their witch panics, but they were far more limited in size and in number than those in the European heartland. Looking first at England, Scotland and England's overseas possessions, we find a pattern that varies considerably but which as a whole stands in stark contrast to that which prevailed in west-central Europe. England, to be sure, experienced a major witch-hunt in the 1640s, while Scotland had a number of national panics in the late sixteenth and seventeenth centuries, and Salem, Massachusetts, was the site of the notorious hunt of 1692, but few of these hunts can compare in size or intensity to the holocausts that occurred at Ellwangen, Würzburg or Bamberg. The total number of British trials, moreover, probably did not exceed 6,000, and the number of executions was less than 2,500 and may have been as low as 2,000.

The main reason for the relative tameness of witch-hunting in Britain was the belated and incomplete reception of the cumulative concept of witchcraft. The failure of the great medieval heresies to cross the Channel and the absence of papal inquisitors to extirpate them made both Englishmen and Scots less paranoid about the introduction of a new heresy like witchcraft in the fifteenth century. And when the cumulative concept of witchcraft began to spread throughout all of Europe in the sixteenth century, it did not find very fertile ground in Britain. It received only reluctant and half-hearted support from the administrative and ruling elite in England, and even in Scotland, where the new ideas were more eagerly embraced, the concept was never fully developed. The witch belief that was most responsible for the development of large witch-hunts – the belief in the sabbath – worked its way into a number of English trials in the seventeenth century and also into the major Scottish hunts, but it was never embellished as it was on the Continent. English and Scottish sabbaths were relatively tame affairs, where witches dined with the Devil but did not usually engage in cannibalistic infanticide, participate in orgies, or fly to and from their gatherings. The belief in the sabbath, when it found acceptance, was sufficient to provoke a search for accomplices, but the number of participants was invariably small and the general picture did not inspire the type of horror that the standard continental nightmare did.

The slow and incomplete acceptance of the cumulative concept of witchcraft in Britain had a great deal to do with the second main reason for the mildness of witch-hunting in this region: the spare use of torture in witchcraft cases. In both England and Scotland torture could be used only at the specific command of the Privy Council and only when matters of state were involved.[42] In England this prohibition was strictly enforced, with the result that only once, during the disruptive period of the Civil War, was torture used illegally in witch-hunting. In Scotland, where central control of local justice was less effective than in England, torture was used without warrant more frequently, very often during pre-trial investigations.[43] It was also used by official order in one very important witch-hunt, when King James VI was considered to be the intended victim of witchcraft.[44]

The relatively spare use of torture in Britain had a two-fold effect on witch-hunting. On the one hand, it weakened the reception of continental witch beliefs, for it was mainly through confessions to such activities as attending the sabbath and flying through the air that judicial officials, let alone the common people, accepted such beliefs. It is certainly worthy of notice that the British hunts in which the idea of the sabbath was most fully developed were those in which torture was in fact employed, legally or illegally. On the other hand, the infrequent use of torture prevented the development of chain-reaction hunts. There were only two of these in Britain, the Scottish hunts of 1590–1 and 1661–2, and in both cases torture was used. Even in these hunts, however, the majority of prosecutions originated independently of the others and could not be considered part of any sort of judicial chain.

A further legal reason for the relative mildness of British witch-hunting was the practice both in England and in Scotland of trying witches by jury. Although juries were not bound by the strict laws of evidence that prevailed on the Continent, and although they could convict a witch on the basis of either reputation or circumstantial evidence, in practice they proved to be relatively lenient, returning a number of acquittals in both countries. The presence of juries, moreover, reflected another characteristic of British justice: the absence of inquisitorial procedure, which of course is the system that led to the use of torture. Scottish justice, being influenced by Roman law, did incorporate some features of inquisitorial procedure, but until the late seventeenth century the Scottish system remained essentially English in its character. Not only did juries retain their independence, but another feature of inquisitorial procedure, the initiation of prosecutions by the courts themselves, occurred only rarely in Scotland, and never in England.

Although witch-hunting throughout Britain was much tamer than in Germany, France and Switzerland, prosecutions in Scotland were much more intense than in England. When we consider the fact that as many as three Scottish witches were executed for every one in England and that England had a population four times that of Scotland, we can appreciate how great the differences between the two countries were in this regard. The main reasons for these differences were the reception of some continental witch beliefs in the northern kingdom and the more frequent illegal use of torture. Another Scottish practice, of possibly even greater consequence, was the custom of granting commissions to local magistrates to try witches without the supervision of itinerant judges. In those cases the conviction-rate and the execution-rate were higher than when cases were heard before the central judges in Edinburgh or on circuit. In England almost all witchcraft cases were heard before circuit judges at the county assizes.

A number of other legal and religious factors contributed to the greater intensity of Scottish witch-hunting. Scottish juries required only a majority to convict a criminal, whereas English juries required unanimity. It is hard to determine the precise effect of this difference on the total number of convictions, but we do know that many Scottish convictions were majority decisions. The differences in the sentencing provisions of the witchcraft statutes of the two kingdoms may also have led to a higher number of Scottish executions (although not convictions). Whereas the English statutes of 1542, 1563 and 1604 provided for non-capital sentences in certain types of cases for the first offence, the Scottish statute of 1563 called for death in all cases, a grim example of the notorious severity of Scottish justice. In fact, some Scottish witches were given non-capital sentences, but the number was far lower than in England.

Religious factors may also have played a part in the different results of English and Scottish witch-hunting. Both countries were Protestant after 1560 and both countries had their fair share of religious conflict, but there were significant religious differences between them. The greater strength of Calvinism in Scotland does not appear to have encouraged witch-hunting, but the Scottish clergy did play a more active part in the religious life of their country than their English counterparts. Not only did Scottish ministers assist in the initial interrogation of witches by virtue of their status as members of the kirk sessions of their parishes, but as members of the General Assembly they also applied constant pressure on the government to establish a godly state by prosecuting witches. This type of pressure stands as one of the clearest examples of the way in which religious reformers influenced secular governments to redouble their efforts at hunting witches.[45]

Witchcraft in England's overseas possessions deserves special comment. In Ireland, where the fourteenth-century trial of Dame Alice Kyteler had marked an important stage in the development of the cumulative concept of witchcraft, witch trials in the early modern period were surprisingly rare. Although the land was believed to abound in sorcerers and warlocks, and although the Irish Parliament passed a witchcraft statute in 1586, the number of trials does not appear to have been very large. It is possible that this low number reflects the incompleteness of the judicial record, but the absence of literary evidence regarding witch-hunts suggests that neither Catholics nor Protestants (who settled mainly in the northern province of Ulster in the seventeenth century) lodged formal accusations against suspected witches. The unsettled state of Irish justice, the conflict between English law and native Gaelic or Brehon law, and a general reluctance to use the law courts to resolve social conflicts may help to explain the absence of significant witch-hunting in the country.[46]

In any event, the evidence that we have regarding witchcraft accusations and prosecutions makes it clear that continental ideas of diabolism did not penetrate Ireland to any appreciable extent. The statute of 1586, which was passed at least to some extent to remedy the legal difficulty encountered in 1578 when judges had to resort to the natural law to convict two witches, resembled the English statutes of 1563 rather closely, and the charges brought against Irish witches resembled those raised against their typical English counterparts rather than German or French witches. One of the few cases that we know about, that of the Protestant clergyman John Aston in 1606, involved charges of digging for treasure, an activity with which English witchcraft cases were occasionally concerned. The most famous case of the seventeenth century – that of Florence Newton, 'the witch of Youghal', in 1661 – also conforms closely to an English model. Newton's problems began when she demanded a piece of beef from the household of John Pyne and upon being refused went away cursing. Shortly thereafter she violently kissed one of Pyne's servants, Mary Longdon, and when Longdon subsequently experienced fits, trances, and vomiting of pins and nails, she named Newton as the cause of her afflictions. (Kissing was often cited as a method of bewitchment.) Newton's predicament worsened while in prison, for she allegedly kissed the hand of David Jones, the prison warden, through the grate, thereby causing his death. The case, which resembled that of two English witches executed for witchcraft at Bury St Edmunds in the following year, did not involve continental ideas of diabolism. Nor should we expect such charges to have been made, since torture was not used in this or in any other Irish cases. Witchcraft in Ireland, as in England, was essentially the crime of *maleficium*, not Devil-worship.[47]

Turning to the English colonies in America, we find a somewhat different situation from that which existed in Ireland. In the middle and southern colonies witch-hunting was either restrained or non-existent. There were about forty known cases of witchcraft in these mainland colonies, and only one of these, a prosecution in Maryland in 1685, ended with an execution.[48] In Bermuda witch-hunting was more intense, with twenty-one cases and five executions between 1651 and 1696.[49] These figures, however, pale in comparison with those for New England, where 234 New Englanders were indicted or presented for this crime in the seventeenth century, and of these thirty-six were executed. When we realize that the population of New England was on average only about 100,000 at this time, we can appreciate the intensity that witch-hunting reached in that locale. It was significantly more intense than in the county of Essex, England, and perhaps even more intense than in Scotland. New England, moreover, exhibited many of the signs of a witch panic. Continental European witch beliefs were current there, and a large witch-hunt, claiming more than half of the total number of victims for all of New England, occurred at Salem in 1692.[50]

The presence of 'continental' witch beliefs in New England should not strike us as highly unusual, for such notions did exist, at least in literary form, in England by the early seventeenth century and were readily available in New England by the time of the Salem hunt (see Figure 7.1). Nor should the conduct of a large witch-hunt in an 'English' world prove incapable of explanation. Not only did an extraordinary combination of political and social tensions provide a foundation for the panic that developed at Salem, but the court's decision to allow spectral evidence in what was originally a case of demonic obsession allowed the afflicted girls to implicate a larger number of suspects than might normally be expected in an English hunt. In one case, moreover, a mild form of torture was used in order to obtain the names of accomplices.[51]

The real problem connected with New England witchcraft is why the entire population was more fearful of witchcraft and more eager to prosecute it than in the southern colonies, Ireland or even England itself. The explanation is almost certainly religious rather than social or economic. The New England

Figure 7.1 The Devil and witches flying on broomsticks. This woodcut appeared in Cotton Mather, *Wonders of the Invisible World* (1693), written during the Salem witch-hunt. The belief that witches flew never gained acceptance in England but was given greater credence in colonial Massachusetts.

colonies were, at least in their inception, theocratic institutions whose purpose was to create a New Jerusalem. The same urge to create a godly state that was evident in Scotland also existed in New England, and in both cases the mission entailed the prosecution of witches as God's enemies. Witchcraft in Massachusetts, just as in England, was a secular crime tried in a civil court, and most of the charges brought by villagers against their neighbours were mainly for *maleficia*. The clergy, however, and the magistrates whom they advised, viewed witchcraft exclusively in terms of a demonic compact and interpreted the Massachusetts witchcraft law of 1641 in those terms.[52] For these influential men, who directed the witch-hunt at Salem, the prosecution of witches was part of a general assault upon diabolical power, not an attempt to punish the perpetrators of harmful magic.[53] The belief that Indians, with whom the colonists had been engaged in a series of wars on the Maine frontier, worshipped the Devil, only deepened the fear of witchcraft that gripped the area and made it more imperative to identify the Devil's confederates in their communities.[54]

The Nordic countries

Witch-hunting in the Nordic countries was somewhat more intense than in the British Isles. The total number of prosecutions in Denmark–Norway and Sweden–Finland was roughly 5,000, of which somewhere between 1,700 and 2,000 resulted in executions. These figures are roughly equivalent to those for the British Isles, but they denote a more intense prosecution since the population of the Nordic lands was only about 40 per cent of Britain's.[55] In other respects Nordic witch-hunting bore a close resemblance to its British counterpart. In both areas the cumulative concept of witchcraft met with an incomplete and belated acceptance, entering Sweden and Finland only in the middle of the seventeenth century. Throughout the Nordic countries, moreover, there was a general reluctance to use torture in order to obtain the confessions of accused witches or the names of their accomplices. The combined effect of ideological weakness and judicial restraint explain the relative mildness of Nordic witch-hunting, but as in Britain, these characteristics were not universal and large witch-hunts took place in certain areas at specific times.

Denmark was the first of the Nordic countries to engage in witch-hunting. As early as the 1540s Peter Palladius, the Lutheran bishop of Sealand, urged the prosecution of witches, arguing that those who exhibited Catholic tendencies were culpable of the crime. Palladius reported in 1544 that a fairly large chain-reaction hunt had claimed the lives of fifty-two persons. In 1547, however, the government declared that the testimony of those who had been convicted of infamous crimes, including sorcery, could not be used to convict another person. It also forbade the application of torture until after a death sentence had been pronounced.[56] These two laws, taken together, prevented the development of large witch-hunts, kept the total number of convictions at a fairly low level, and also prevented notions of Devil-worship from being fully received. This is not to suggest that beliefs in diabolism were absent in Denmark. A number of Danish witches were in fact accused of making pacts with the Devil and of worshipping him collectively.[57] In 1617 a royal ordinance defined witchcraft for the first time in terms of diabolical compact and specified that those convicted of such charges would be burned.[58] But the legal reforms of 1547, together with the mandatory appeal of all death sentences to the county courts after 1576, kept Denmark from going the way of many German states. According to the most reliable estimates, there were approximately 2,000 witchcraft trials in Denmark and about 1,000 executions.[59] These totals are roughly proportional to those from Scotland, which had a population almost twice as large as that of Denmark.[60]

Witchcraft prosecutions in Norway, which during this period was governed by Denmark, were slightly less intense than those in the southern kingdom. With a population about three-quarters the size of Denmark's in 1650, Norway tried more than 900 witches between 1566 and 1747, but only about 25 per cent of those tried were executed. A disproportionately high number of prosecutions and a higher percentage of executions of took place in the northern province of Finnmark, where 91 of the 135 witches brought to trial were executed.[61] As in other countries where witch-hunting was relatively mild, a combination of legal and ideological factors provides an explanation. The main form of criminal procedure in Norway was accusatorial, according to which the testimony of two eyewitnesses to any crime was required for conviction. Public prosecutions based on rumour could, however, be used in witchcraft cases, since witchcraft was a *crimen exceptum*. Torture was allowed in Norwegian trials, but it was used only occasionally, and this probably explains why charges of diabolism figured in less than one-fifth of all cases. Notions of diabolical conspiracy did penetrate Norway, mainly from Danish sources, and were apparent as early as the 1590s, but they did not predominate in the trials whose records are extant.[62] There was, to be sure, a widespread belief in Norway, both among common folk and elites, that witches frequently assembled with the Devil in the northern parts of the country. Because of the remoteness of such assemblies a belief in the ability of witches to fly also gained currency, and this belief was closely connected to a belief in metamorphosis. In the actual trials, however, charges of attending the sabbath appeared only occasionally, and such accusations usually did not become central to the case against the accused.[63] The belief remained much more a part of popular legend than of demonological theory. The related beliefs in metamorphosis and flight, however, often did become central to the trials and were grafted on to traditional charges of *maleficium*. Those persons who, for example, were accused of causing storms at sea – a frequent charge in all seafaring countries – were often accused of working their craft while airborne, and others were accused of having performed *maleficia* after having taken the form of a wolf, raven, dog or cat.

The most famous case of Norwegian witchcraft was that of Anne Pedersdotter Absalon, who was executed at Bergen in 1590. The case owes its fame to a Norwegian play by Hans Wiers-Jenssen, an English translation by John Masefield, and a brilliant film by Carl Theodor Dreyer, *Day of Wrath*.[64] Although the play and film possess little historical accuracy, the actual trial throws a great deal of light on the nature of Norwegian witchcraft. Anne Pedersdotter Absalon was the wife of Norway's most famous humanist scholar, the Lutheran minister Absalon Pedersen Beyer. The charges against Anne arose out of the opposition that had developed in Bergen to the efforts of Absalon and the clergy to destroy the holy images that had been prominent in the pre-Reformation Church. The impetus for witch-hunting was therefore different from that in Denmark fifty years earlier, where the Lutheran clergy apparently took the initiative in spreading the fear of witchcraft and perhaps even in drafting accusations. In this Norwegian case the reforming clergy were the victims, although since they themselves were too highly placed to be attacked successfully, their wives served as their surrogates. This was a pattern of witchcraft accusations that occurred frequently in German towns, where members of political factions used charges of witchcraft against their rivals' wives in order to advance their own political careers. It is also important to note that the court in which Anne was tried was a civil tribunal and not, as both the play and the film suggest, a Lutheran church court.

Although Anne was exonerated when the charges were first brought against her in 1575, the year of Absalon's death, the case was reopened in 1590. The most interesting aspects of this second trial were the charges brought against Anne. Most of them were traditional charges of *maleficia*: putting into a coma a man who had refused her prior payment for a weaving frame; inflicting sickness on a man who had refused to give her wine, beer and vinegar; and causing the death of a four-year-old boy by giving him a bewitched biscuit. As so often happened in cases that began with accusations of *maleficia*, charges of diabolism were introduced. Anne's servant testified that Anne had turned her into a horse and had ridden her to the sabbath at a mountain called Lyderhorn in Bergen, where a number of witches plotted a storm to wreck all ships arriving at Bergen and then, on subsequent occasions, to burn the town and cause it be flooded. The sabbath, however, was dispersed by a man in white who said that God would not allow it. On the basis of the testimony by Anne's servant and others, Anne was burned as a witch.[65]

The trial of Anne Pedersdotter Absalon reveals how charges of collective Devil-worship influenced but did not dominate Norwegian witchcraft trials. The sabbath that allegedly took place at Lyderhorn derived mainly from Norwegian belief, not demonological theory, and it lacked most of the distinctive features of German, French and Swiss assemblies. There was, for example, no infanticide or cannibalism, and although Anne and her servant allegedly took the sacrament on their journey home, there was no alleged demonic administration of that sacrament. The sabbath was in fact a more restrained affair than those that allegedly occurred in Scotland or even in England. In fact, Anne was convicted mainly on the basis of her individual and collective *maleficia*, the occurrence of a storm in Bergen at the time of the sabbath proving to be the conclusive evidence. Her burning as a witch reflects a belief that witchcraft was a crime of heresy rather than sorcery, but the charges upon which she was convicted reflected her putative status as a magician, not a person who made a pact with the Devil and worshipped him.

Two other features of Anne's trial provide us with insights into the nature of Norwegian witchcraft. First, although the testimony of two women previously executed for witchcraft was introduced at her trial – a procedure that would not have occurred in Denmark – this testimony did not have a decisive impact on the outcome of the trial. Second, Anne was apparently not tortured during her trial, and her confession was not required for conviction. Nor was she tortured to secure the names of accomplices. While torture was not unknown to Norwegian law, it was apparently used as sparingly as in Denmark, and this restraint prevented both the full imposition of demonological theory upon a body of native folklore and the development of large chain-reaction hunts. It also probably explains the relatively low number of Norwegian executions, which on a proportionate basis was as low as in England.

Sweden originally followed a pattern of witch-hunting which resembled that of Norway, but in the late seventeenth century it experienced a large panic that was, by Scandinavian standards, quite exceptional. Prosecutions for witchcraft had begun in the 1580s, but most of those early trials were for simple *maleficium*, and very few of them resulted in executions. A law of 1593 requiring either the testimony of six witnesses or a confession for a capital conviction, together with a requirement that all death sentences be appealed to a royal court in Stockholm after 1614, were in large part responsible for holding witch-hunting in check. Charges of diabolism were not absent from these trials, however, and since torture was often allowed in witchcraft cases, the potential for large-scale witch-hunting clearly existed. Soldiers returning from Germany from the Thirty Years War may have introduced more extreme diabolical ideas during the 1640s.[66]

Queen Christina, who put an end to the witch trials that were being conducted in Sweden's German territory of Verden during the Thirty Years War, claimed many years after her abdication that in 1649 she had forbidden the death penalty in all Swedish witchcraft cases except those involving murder. She also said that she had attributed the confessions of witches to female disorders or diabolical illusions. There is reason to doubt the queen's honesty in this claim to leniency in such matters, but whatever action she did take was insufficient to prevent a major hunt from occurring during the reign of Charles XI. The hunt began in 1668 in the northern Swedish province of Dalecarlia (now Dalarna) and eventually spread throughout the entire northern part of the country and even spilled over into the Swedish-speaking sections of Finland. The hunt was unusual in that a large number of both the accusers and the accused were children. Drawing on a body of Swedish legend about witches visiting a mythical site called Blåkulla (Blue Mountain), where they allegedly feasted, danced and married demons, a number of children accused parents, neighbours and older children of having taken them to this Swedish version of the sabbath.

Charles appointed a number of royal commissions to investigate the matter in the localities and try the accused witches. To make matters worse, the first wave of trials, which took place in the vicinity of Mora, encouraged parents and magistrates in many small villages to demand the prosecution of witches in their communities, a task that was entrusted to newly appointed commissions. The commissioners were forbidden to use torture, but it appears that in the hysterical mood that prevailed they did not always follow that policy. These royal commissions pronounced a number of death sentences, including more than a hundred in 1675, the year marking the height of the panic. The hunt did not end until after it had spread to the south and affected Stockholm. Two new commissions, appointed in 1676, acted more cautiously than their predecessors and exercised a moderating influence on a panic-stricken population. At the same time the Court of Appeal, which had confirmed many of the sentences during the past eight years, began interrogating witnesses directly. When many of the children began to confess that their charges were groundless, the court reviewed all the evidence and set the most recently condemned witches free.[67]

More than 200 persons were executed during the north Swedish hunt of 1668–76. Like Matthew Hopkins's hunt in England in the 1640s, the entire episode reveals that even countries not known for their severe treatment of witches could occasionally experience large panics. All that was required was a belief in the sabbath, a relaxation of judicial restraint and a popular mood that pressured authorities to take action.

Finland at this time was a part of Sweden, and the two provinces in which the largest number of Finnish witch trials took place were Swedish-speaking. For these reasons witch-hunting in Finland must be considered in connection with the Swedish experience. Indeed, a large number of Finnish prosecutions occurred as a part of the panic that began in Dalecarlia. On the other hand, the history of witchcraft in Finland followed a course that differed in large measure from that of Sweden. Among all the Nordic countries, Finland was the last to begin its prosecutions for witchcraft. Witch beliefs, including reports of Devil-worship, were not unknown in Finland in the late sixteenth and seventeenth centuries. They entered the country both from the northern, Swedish-speaking provinces and from the lower Baltic countries of Estonia and Livonia, which were part of the Swedish state and had extensive cultural contacts with both Finland and Germany.[68] Despite these influences, however, Finland did not concern itself with witchcraft until 1640, when the Swedish bishop, Isaac Rothovius, became the vice-chancellor of the first Finnish university, Turku Academy. Rothovius, who was a champion of the Lutheran cause against both Catholics and Calvinists, did not express concern over witches attending the sabbath, but he did encourage the extirpation of sorcery (which he regarded in an old-fashioned way as a form of residual pagan superstition) and he also inaugurated a campaign, which was joined by other officials and his successor, against the practice of demonic magic in Turku Academy. In this respect Finland was beginning an operation in 1640 that other European countries had started more than two centuries earlier.

It was not until the 1660s that the full concept of witchcraft appeared in Finnish trials, and the person most responsible for the introduction of these ideas was Nils Psilander, a judge of the civil court in the Swedish-speaking province of Ahvenanmaa. Psilander had been educated in the Baltic area at Tartu Academy, where he had become familiar with current German juridical thought regarding witchcraft. Between 1666 and 1674 he conducted a protracted chain-reaction hunt in which original accusations of soothsaying and sorcery were overlaid with demonological theory and were also fused with Swedish legend concerning trips to Blåkulla. In many of these trials the Devil's mark was located and torture was used, but sceptical juries and a somewhat less sceptical court of appeal at Turku kept the hunt from getting out of control. Although the first suspect, Karin Henriksdoteer, denounced thirteen accomplices, only four of them, together with Karin and one later suspect, were executed.

In Finland's other predominantly Swedish-speaking province of Ostrobothnia, a large number of witch trials took place between 1665 and 1684. This hunt, in which at least 152 persons were accused of witchcraft, resulted in twenty death sentences (most of which were probably confirmed on appeal) and the execution of another eight persons for whom trial records are missing. These trials were inspired by the great northern Swedish witch-hunt of 1668–76. Somewhat surprisingly, however, these trials did not centre on charges of Devil-worship. With the charges of witchcraft coming mainly from below, and in the absence of a counterpart to Psilander to introduce learned theories of witchcraft, the charges against the accused remained essentially those of *maleficia*. Only when children and one servant denounced their elders for taking them to Blåkulla, a charge that occurred only in a small percentage of cases, did charges of Devil-worship surface, and even then they did not form the basis of the case against the accused.

All in all, the Ostrobothnian witch-hunt of 1665–84 was a relatively tame affair. Since only about one-third of the witches were denounced by others, it was not primarily a chain-reaction hunt. The denunciations, moreover, were not extracted under torture. Those denunciations that did not spring from juvenile imagination either arose out of malice or were elicited by zealous clergymen. Nor were the sentences especially harsh. More than half (57 per cent) of those accused were acquitted or released, while a smaller number were given ecclesiastical punishments, fined, or sentenced to prison or hard labour. The death-sentence rate was only 13 per cent, and some of these sentences may have been reduced on appeal.[69]

Looking at Finland as a whole, one is led to the conclusion that witchcraft prosecutions never got out of control. The total number of trials probably did not exceed 1,000;[70] notions of Devil-worship were never fully received and only occasionally became the focal point of witch trials; torture was used sparingly; juries tempered the zeal of witch-hunters; and the execution-rate was lower than in other Nordic countries. Among Finnish-speaking people the process of witch-hunting was even more restrained. At least one-half of the Finnish trials took place in the province of Ostrobothnia and only one execution is known to have taken place outside of the two Swedish-speaking provinces of Ostrobothnia and Ahvenanmaa.

East-central and eastern Europe

It is difficult to make many broad generalizations about witchcraft prosecutions in eastern European lands – those that lay to the east of the Holy Roman

Empire and north of the uncontested boundaries of the Ottoman Empire. In all of these areas witch-hunting began much later than in western Europe and it also lasted much longer, until the middle of the eighteenth century. The intensity of this witch-hunting, however, varied from region to region. In certain parts of Poland, where the cumulative concept of witchcraft found fertile ground, prosecutions were most intense, although not on the scale of the prosecutions in many German states. In Hungary, where learned notions of witchcraft were only partially and reluctantly received, there was a substantial but by no means exceptionally large number of trials and only a few large hunts. In Transylvania, Wallachia and Moldavia, where demonological ideas were weak or non-existent, prosecutions were much less common. In the most general terms, we can say that those areas that were closest to Germany, had cultural contacts with Germany or were populated by German-speaking people prosecuted far more witches than those that were more exclusively Slavic. It is also readily apparent that those regions which followed the rites of Orthodox Christianity did not engage in intensive witch-hunting. We can no longer claim that witchcraft prosecutions were entirely absent from these areas, since there were a number of Russian trials and also some in the Orthodox and Uniate sections of Lithuania.[71] But there is little question that the lands in the easternmost parts of Europe did not participate in the European witch-hunt with the same degree of enthusiasm as their western and Latinized neighbours.

The only eastern or east-central European country that acquired a reputation for intense witch-hunting was the kingdom of Poland, and that reputation is not fully deserved. Because of the incompleteness of the judicial record (most of the trial records were destroyed during the Second World War), the total number of trials and executions in that country cannot be determined with any degree of accuracy. It appears, however, that Bohdan Baranowski's original estimate of 10,000 legal executions was too high; even he later scaled back his original estimate to a few thousand executions, and more recent estimates have been as low as 2,000.[72] These revised figures would make Poland's record of witch-hunting not much more intense than that of the Nordic countries. Witchcraft in Poland also resembled its northern neighbours in its witch beliefs. Polish theories of diabolism were not any more elaborate than those in the Nordic countries, and they appeared in the trials only somewhat more frequently. Just as Norwegian witches were believed to assemble at Lyderhorn and Swedish witches at Blåkulla, Polish witches allegedly gathered at a similar site named Lysa Góra (Bald Mountain). The activities at Polish gatherings were not much different from those that transpired in Norwegian and Swedish assemblies. The main distinction between Polish and Nordic witch-hunting is that prosecutions in Poland reached a peak much later and lasted much longer. More than half of the Polish executions took place between 1676 and 1725, the worst years being those of the early eighteenth century.

The greater intensity of Polish witch-hunting in relation to other eastern European countries can be attributed to three related factors: the presence of theories of diabolism, the absence of effective central control over prosecutions, and the unrestricted use of torture. The theories of diabolism were mainly a foreign import, just as they were to a large extent in Britain and the Nordic countries. Poles had long believed in *maleficium*, and the early witchcraft trials reflected that belief almost exclusively. Learned witch beliefs were received first in those parts of Poland that were close to Germany, had a large German-speaking population, and had close commercial or cultural links with German lands. From there these ideas spread to the other provinces of the country, a process that was greatly facilitated by the translation of the *Malleus maleficarum* into Polish in 1614. Charges of making pacts with the Devil and attending the Sabbath began to appear in the trials the late seventeenth century, and in the early eighteenth century the Devil began to 'take centre stage' in the trials.[73] The only areas where these beliefs did not take root were the far eastern section of Lithuania (which became fully integrated into the Polish state in the sixteenth century) and Galicia to the south. It should come as no surprise that these sections of Poland did not experience the full force of the European witch-hunt.

The majority of Polish witchcraft cases took place in the municipal courts, despite the fact that a law passed by the *sejm* in 1543 had entrusted jurisdiction over witchcraft to the ecclesiastical courts. Although Bishop Czartoryski of Leslau made an effort to enforce the Church's jurisdictional monopoly in 1669 and demanded that he authorize all prosecutions, the municipal courts continued to hold the trials. Royal edicts of 1672 and 1713 – themselves evidence of the failure of the bishop's efforts – also failed to control the jurisdictional appetite of the local courts. Since the Polish state was exceptionally weak at this time, it is not surprising that these efforts did not succeed. In any event, the success of the municipal courts in ignoring central edicts had a profound effect upon the progress of the witch-hunts, since the municipal courts, which adopted many features of inquisitorial procedure in the seventeenth century, repeatedly violated the procedural rules that were designed to protect the accused. We know from the instructions of Bishop Czartoryski himself that these courts were withholding the proofs from the accused, denying them counsel and, most importantly, torturing them without restraint to obtain both their own confessions and the names of accomplices. In Poland, therefore, all of the conditions that encouraged large-scale witch-hunting – diabolical theories, secular prosecutions, local autonomy and the unrestricted use of torture – were present, and consequently the number of victims was higher than in other eastern European countries.[74]

The problem still remains why witch-hunting in Poland began so much later than in Germany. Theories of a slow transmission of ideas, which might be used to explain Sweden's belated adoption of demonological theory, are less applicable in a country where German influence was more direct and immediate. It seems as if Poland, despite the availability of advanced witchcraft theories, was simply not disposed to engage in witch-hunting in the early seventeenth century, but then rather suddenly began a significant legal campaign in the later period. One reason for this delayed inauguration of witch-hunting was the sudden and unprecedented devastation caused by the wars of the mid-century. During the sixteenth and early seventeenth centuries, Poland experienced neither civil war nor invasion. In the middle of the seventeenth century, however, a Cossack rebellion (1648) and the first northern war against Sweden and Russia (1655–60) signalled the beginning of 'the deluge', during which hostile forces ravaged the country and paralyzed the government. As in other parts of Europe, the wars did not lead to an immediate intensification of witch-hunting, but the long-term effects of the deluge created the necessary social, economic and psychological preconditions for witch-hunting, which had not been present before.

A second, less tangible cause of the belated seventeenth-century inauguration of witch-hunting in Poland was a change in the religious atmosphere. The Reformation ran an unusual course in Poland. The growth of Protestantism and the successful efforts of the Counter-Reformation to reclaim its converts led neither to religious warfare nor suppression but to the establishment of a policy of toleration that had no parallel in Europe.[75] For a variety of practical reasons (including the weakness of the central government and the attitude of an unzealous and religiously divided nobility), Poland became a 'state without stakes', in which a Protestant minority coexisted with a Catholic majority. In the seventeenth century, however, especially after 1648, Catholic intolerance increased and led to a number of restrictions of Protestant freedom. It is possible that this new spirit of intolerance towards religious dissent encouraged witchcraft prosecutions. Religious dissent and witchcraft were of course different phenomena, but since they were both forms of religious rebellion they also shared many similarities, and intolerance towards one *could* lead to harsher treatment of the other. It is probably no coincidence that the burning of Polish witches coincided with the rise of a more militant, uncompromising Catholicism and the ostensible decline of toleration, even if this did not involve the actual burning of heretics. One might even speculate that the burning of witches was one of the means by which an intolerant Catholic majority expressed its will to impose religious uniformity on a country which, even in the late seventeenth and early eighteenth centuries, remained religiously pluralistic.

A final reason for the slow development of the witch-hunt in Poland was the prolonged maintenance of ecclesiastical jurisdiction over the crime of witchcraft. As we have seen, the intensification of witch-hunting in Europe was encouraged by the decline of ecclesiastical jurisdiction and the transfer of jurisdiction over witchcraft to much more ruthless secular courts. In the late sixteenth century Polish ecclesiastical courts were, like so many of their European counterparts, restricted in their jurisdiction, but they were not deprived of their traditional jurisdiction over *maleficium*.[76] Throughout the late sixteenth and early seventeenth centuries, therefore, the church courts, which adopted a rather tolerant attitude towards witchcraft, continued to prosecute cases of malefic witchcraft. Only in the second half of the seventeenth century did the municipal courts establish their jurisdictional predominance. In this way the rise of Polish witchcraft prosecutions did in fact reflect a decline in ecclesiastical jurisdiction, even if the decline occurred much later than in other parts of Europe.

Witch-hunting in Hungary was less intense and took a lower toll than in Poland, although the total number of trials and executions was by no means insignificant. Between 1520 and the 1777, just under 1,500 individuals were tried for witchcraft, of whom some 450 are known to have been executed (most by burning), while at least 225 suffered non-capital punishments.[77] Most of the trials took place in the kingdom of Hungary, the only part of the country to remain independent of the Ottoman Empire after King Louis II was defeated at the battle of Mohács in 1526. There were also a number of prosecutions in the southeastern province of Transylvania, which remained an autonomous province within the Ottoman Empire between 1526 and 1699 and which did not become fully reintegrated into the kingdom of Hungary (which was ruled by the Habsburgs) until 1711.

Although witchcraft has a long history in Hungary, it took a long time for intense witch-hunting to develop. As early as the fifteenth century sorcery was defined as a form of heresy, and in 1421 the *Stadtrecht* of Buda decided that sorcerers were obliged to wear the Jew's hat. Western demonological ideas, however, took a long time to penetrate the country, except in areas inhabited by Germans, and they were never fully developed. A few copies of the *Malleus maleficarum* circulated in the sixteenth century, but there was no significant volume of witchcraft literature, and the few Hungarian intellectuals who addressed such questions tended to take a sceptical position.[78] It was not until Benedict Carpzov's *Practica rerum criminalium* was codified for Austria in 1656 and incorporated into the body of Hungarian law in 1696 that Western demonological ideas were made readily available to Hungarian judges. Those judges succeeded in extracting confessions to most of the charges of diabolism that were commonplace in the West. The way in which this process worked can be seen in a series of trials in 1728–9 in Szeged, where thirteen witches were executed and another twenty-eight were spared by the intervention of Emperor Charles VI. This hunt began with accusations of destroying vineyards with hailstorms, but these charges easily led to the further charges of making explicit pacts with the Devil, receiving his mark (usually in the shape of a chicken's foot) and attending the sabbath.[79]

In addition to these standard demonological ideas, a variety of native Hungarian folk beliefs found expression at the trials. One of the most interesting of these beliefs, which dates back at least to 1656 and which was present in the Szeged trials, was that the witches were organized in military fashion, with the Devil as commander-in-chief. There may be some connection between this belief and that of the *benandanti* in the Friuli, who were likewise organized militarily to fight against the witches.[80] Many native Hungarian beliefs dealt with the *táltosok*, shaman-like magicians and healers whose souls left their bodies in a trance and went out to fight with other *táltosok*.

The slow reception of learned witch beliefs in Hungary was matched by a belated adoption of inquisitorial procedure, which was not introduced into the kingdom of Hungary until the 1650s. Predictably, the first significant trials and convictions did not take place until that decade. In the province of Transylvania, which had a separate legal system, inquisitorial procedure arrived even later. Until 1725 all accusations in Transylvania were made publicly and under the threat of the talion; witnesses were presented on behalf of both parties; and the main method of probation was the water ordeal, the purpose of which was to produce a confession. Torture was used only if there was strong suspicion of witchcraft and if the water ordeal failed. It was also used on one occasion to secure the names of accomplices.[81] This system was in large part responsible for keeping the number of convictions in Transylvania at a minimum. Most of the Transylvanian trials about which we have information occurred in Siebenburgen, an area originally settled by Germans in the twelfth century. The witch trials that took place in this region were all conducted by secular authorities, although local pastors often played an important part in the process.[82]

The chronological pattern of witch-hunting in Hungary resembles that of Poland. Beginning in the 1580s there was an irregular succession of isolated trials and an occasional small panic, such as in 1615, when a number of witches allegedly attempted to destroy all of Hungary and Transylvania with hailstorms, a danger that somewhat ironically emerged when the country was suffering from a drought.[83] The great majority of witchcraft prosecutions, however, did not occur until the eighteenth century. The reasons for this belated intensification of witch-hunting in Hungary cannot be explained simply in terms of heightened German and Austrian political and legal influence after 1699. It is much more likely attributable to a more general historical pattern by which the social, economic and cultural conditions that facilitated witch-hunting in the west did not develop until much later in eastern regions.[84]

In Russia the most distinctive feature of witch-hunting, apart from the high proportion of men among the accused, was the weakness of Western demonological theory. Prosecutions for harmful magic have a long history in Russia. During the eleventh, twelfth and thirteenth centuries, when prosecutions in the West for simple *maleficium* were rare and executions even rarer, Russian men and women who allegedly used magic to cause droughts were executed in sufficient numbers to attract the notice of chroniclers and foreign travellers. The clerical interpretation of these acts of sorcery was not much different from that which prevailed in the West at that time: they were vestiges of pagan superstition and in that sense were demonic. But whereas in the West this interpretation of demonic magic gradually gave way to a belief that sorcerers were allies of Satan and adherents of a new form of heresy who worshipped him at nocturnal assemblies, in Russia the old interpretation prevailed. Prosecution for the crime increased somewhat in the fifteenth and sixteenth centuries, including a mass burning of twelve female witches at Pskov in 1411, but the theory upon which the prosecutions were based did not change.[85]

In 1551 Ivan IV, being concerned about the practice of magic at the royal court, summoned a church council to condemn a variety of magical practices. This council also resulted in bringing the crime under the jurisdiction of secular as well as ecclesiastical courts.[86] Prosecutions in substantial numbers did not begin, however, until the early seventeenth century, and most of these trials took place between 1625 and 1700, with the heaviest concentration of prosecutions taking place between 1645 and 1660. [87] The most prominent of these were the prosecutions in the small town of Lukh between 1656 and 1659, which resulted in the accusation of twenty-five persons, five of whom were executed.[88] These numbers indicate that there was something resembling a 'witch-scare' in seventeenth-century Russia, but no 'witch-panic'.[89] Witch-hunting was probably more common in Russia than in the province of Transylvania, but more restrained than in Poland, which for reasons of proximity and comparable size is the most appropriate standard of comparison.

It is unlikely that the Russian system of criminal procedure had very much to do with the relatively low number of convictions and executions in that country. It is true that all criminal prosecutions in Russia were supposed to come from the local community rather than the officers of Church or state. This requirement, however, did not prevent local officials from bringing charges against suspected witches when private parties failed to do so. Once the original accusation was lodged, the state took over all prosecutions, thus making the Russian system essentially inquisitorial.[90] Torture, sometimes in the most severe form, was freely used, both to secure confessions and to obtain the names of accomplices. The torture of the male healer Tereshka Malakurov during the Lukh witch-hunt was so severe that he incriminated his wife, who was promptly arrested and tortured until she confirmed her husband's testimony.[91] Judgment could be reached without the participation of lay jurors. Indeed, the only procedural rule that served as a restraint on unlimited witch-hunting in Russia was the requirement of referring cases to Moscow. Between 1622 and 1700 the reports of forty-seven trials, involving ninety-nine defendants, were referred to Moscow for confirmation and sentencing. Of the forty-one of these witches whose fates are known, ten were sentenced to death, five were exiled, three died during torture and interrogation, and twenty-one were acquitted. These figures represent a fairly low execution-rate, comparable to that in countries that provided for appeals or confirmation of witchcraft sentences.[92]

SOURCE BOOK

The main reason Russian witch-hunting never developed into a major witch-craze was the absence of Western demonological theory. If the witch beliefs that flourished in German intellectual circles had penetrated Russia and had been embraced by local and central authorities, Russia would probably have had a witch-hunt similar to that in western Poland. But the ideas simply did not become available. The Devil was not unknown in Russia, and references to the Devil or other demons occasionally made their way into witchcraft trials, such as when one male witch, Ivan Zheglov, allegedly renounced Christ and made an oath of allegiance to Satan. But Orthodox Russian clergy and writers did not make the connection between the Devil and the practice of magic, which became a central tenet of Western demonology. Nor did they develop a belief in the sabbath, cannibalistic infanticide or flight. Russian witchcraft, even more than English witchcraft, remained a crime of practising harmful magic, not Devil-worship. As Valerie Kivelson has shown, the Devil cast a 'pale shadow' over the charges of *maleficium* that remained the main basis for witchcraft accusations.[93] Fear that maleic witchcraft would undermine the hierarchical social order explains the substantial number of Russian prosecutions, but the main reason Russia did not experience a massive witch-hunt was the failure of Orthodox Christianity to develop the same demonological world-view as the Latin Church did in the late Middle Ages.

Southern Europe

It may seem inappropriate to consider the Mediterranean region last in this survey of European witchcraft, for it was in Spain, Portugal and Italy that the most durable symbol of witchcraft prosecutions – the Inquisition – maintained its strength longer than in any other parts of Europe. It was in Italian lands, moreover, that some of the earliest witchcraft prosecutions took place.[94] Yet if we use the total number of executions as a standard for evaluating the relative intensity of witchcraft prosecutions, then these southern countries deserve to be treated last. About 600 witches were executed in Italian lands, and another 500 or so in the Iberian kingdoms. Most of the Spanish executions were ordered by secular courts rather than the various tribunals of the Inquisition.[95] In the Spanish and Portuguese American colonies there were very few executions.[96] We must not conclude from this, however, that witchcraft was of little concern to Italian, Spanish and Portuguese authorities. The total number of prosecutions in these countries was in fact fairly substantial. In Spain, for example, the Inquisition tried more than 3,500 persons for various types of magic and witchcraft between 1580 and 1650.[97] In Italy, where the records of the Inquisition are still being researched, the numbers were even higher: the tribunal in Venice alone tried more than 700 persons.[98] In Portugal, where work on the records is also incomplete, a total of 291 witches were tried in the southern part of the kingdom alone.[99] The mildness of Iberian and Italian witchcraft, therefore, derives mainly from the reluctance of Spanish, Portuguese and Italian courts to put witches to death. This reluctance can in turn be explained by the way in which inquisitors viewed the crime they were prosecuting, the procedures they followed and the careful supervision of their work by central authorities.

One of the most striking features of Italian and Iberian witchcraft prosecutions was the rarity of charges of collective Devil-worship. The belief in such assemblies was not unknown in either peninsula, and in a few large hunts it appeared in a rather dramatic form. The confessions of the Basque witches of 1610 provide us with some of the richest descriptions of the witches' sabbath in all of Europe.[100] But in the large majority of cases heard by Spanish, Portuguese and Roman inquisitors, especially in the southern parts of both peninsulas, these charges are completely absent. In Portugal the demonic pact figured in most witchcraft prosecutions, but not the sabbath.[101] In colonial Brazil, where beliefs regarding the pact with the Devil, familiars, and metamorphosis were prevalent, the legal record makes no mention of sabbaths.[102] Peasants and town-dwellers in Mediterranean lands were accused of performing various types of magic, including love magic and healing, and their magic was considered to be heretical, but this was not taken to mean that they had worshipped the Devil collectively. Some of the magical practices of these people were considered to be maleficent, but charges of *maleficium* were usually not amplified by charges of collective Devil-worship. The practitioners of magic were to be prosecuted, of course, but the purpose was to correct error and purify the faith, not to protect society from a conspiratorial menace.[103] The end result, therefore, was the frequent administration of non-capital sentences by the Inquisition in the traditional manner of ecclesiastical justice.[104]

There is no single explanation for the prevalence of this view of witchcraft in Spain, Portugal and Italy. One important factor was the widespread belief in classical forms of witchcraft. Both the Spanish and the Italian witch were very often viewed in the manner of Horace's Canidia or the even more widely known sorceress Celestina, a woman depicted in Fernando de Rojas's play, *Tragicomedy of Calisto and Melibea* (1499), who engages in love magic, fortune-telling and divination. Such women were believed to use the flesh of children to make their spells and to acquire the power to summon up the Devil, but they had little in common with the German and Swiss witches who flew to the sabbath. As Julio Caro Baroja has shown, this type of witch tended to flourish in urban rather than rural environments, not only because such women actually plied their trade there but also because the Renaissance culture that supported the belief in such figures was predominantly urban to begin with.[105] It is no coincidence that the areas of both Italy and Spain in which the cumulative concept of witchcraft was widely known and in which a majority of the prosecutions took place were both rural and northern, subject to northern (i.e. either German or French) influences.

A survey of Italian, Spanish and Portuguese witchcraft literature reinforces the conclusion that the stereotypical view of the witch never gained widespread acceptance in the Mediterranean world. It is true that in the late Middle Ages Italian and to a lesser extent Spanish intellectuals had made important contributions to the cumulative concept of witchcraft,[106] while the papacy itself was largely responsible for equating magic and heresy. Once the full concept of diabolical witchcraft had been constructed, however, very few Spanish, Portuguese or Italian writers provided explicit support for the definition of witchcraft that had emerged or contributed to its further development. The overly credulous Italian judge Paulus Grillandus did subscribe to most of the learned notions of witchcraft in his *Tractatus de hereticis et sortilegiis*, drawing upon cases that he had adjudicated in Rome and southern Italy, but after that time the only Italian author who fully subscribed to the cumulative concept of witchcraft was Francesco Maria Guazzo, a Milanese friar who based his popular *Compendium maleficarum* not only on numerous French and German sources but also on his own experience as a witchcraft prosecutor in the Rhineland.[107] It can be argued, therefore, that at the height of the great witch-hunt the most extreme and credulous Italian witch beliefs had northern rather than native sources.

SOURCE BOOK

The same can be said for Spain, where the demonological ideas that prevailed during the Basque trials can be traced to southern France and the work of the demonologist Pierre de Lancre.[108] Overall, the cumulative concept of witchcraft did not become firmly established in Spain, especially in the south.[109] Nor was it widely held in Portugal. Reports of night flight and sabbaths were not unknown in that kingdom, but Portuguese inquisitors tended to treat such stories with extreme scepticism. There were hardly any demonological treatises written in Portugal during the period of the trials, and the only European works cited by Portuguese authorities in discussing witchcraft were the *Malleus maleficarum* and Martín Del Rio's *Disquisitionum Magicarum*. Neither of these works was primarily concerned with the sabbath, and both were intended as manuals for inquisitors.[110]

The failure of many learned witch beliefs to take hold among Italian, Spanish and Portuguese inquisitors may have had something to do with the popularity of Nicholas Eymeric's *Directorium Inquisitorum* (1376), the inquisitorial manual most widely used in Italy throughout the period of the great witch-hunt. The form of witchcraft described in Eymeric's manual was ritual magic, which Eymeric considered in true scholastic fashion to be a form of heresy, since it involved a pact with the Devil. Eymeric had nothing to say about the sabbath or, for that matter, *maleficium*. By relying on Eymeric's definition of witchcraft, therefore, Italian inquisitors perpetuated an earlier view of the crime that excluded many of the elements that had been added to the cumulative concept of witchcraft after he wrote the manual.[111]

Another reason for the relative tameness of witchcraft prosecutions in Italy, Spain and Portugal was the adherence of the Inquisition in each country to fairly strict procedural rules. In the Middle Ages papal inquisitors had become notorious for their unrestrained use of torture and the many other ways in which they had prejudiced the case against the accused. By the time the European witch-hunt began, however, inquisitors had produced a large body of cautionary literature, and two of the early modern institutions that succeeded the medieval inquisition – the Spanish and the Roman inquisitions – demonstrated exceptional concern for procedural propriety. Indeed, the Roman Inquisition has been referred to as 'a pioneer in judicial reform'.[112] Unlike many secular courts, it made provision for legal counsel; it furnished the defendant with a copy of the charges and evidence against him; and it assigned very little weight to the testimony of a suspected witch against her alleged confederates.[113] One of the most noteworthy features of both Spanish and Roman inquisitorial procedure is that torture was rarely employed. In Spain it was used only when there was strong circumstantial evidence but no proof, and it was applied towards the end of the trial, just before judgement was pronounced.[114] Even in the great Basque witch-hunt of 1609–11, which involved thousands of suspects, the Inquisition tortured only two of the accused, and since the torture actually allowed their sentences to be commuted from death to banishment, it can be legitimately considered an act of mercy.[115] The only pressure to use torture as a deliberate means to extract confessions came from local secular authorities and local mobs, groups whose extra-legal tactics the Inquisition sought to restrain. In Italy there was no less of a reluctance to use torture.[116] Even the *benandanti*, the members of an ancient fertility cult in Friuli whom the Inquisition gradually convinced they were witches, were never put to torture.[117]

The restraint shown by both the Spanish and the Roman inquisitions in the use of torture had a predictable effect upon witch-hunting in the Mediterranean world. It did not completely prevent large witch-hunts from taking place, since local panics and dream epidemics were by themselves capable of supplying large numbers of suspects. But without the unrestricted use of torture the hunts that developed did not produce as many convictions or result in as many executions as the large hunts that occurred in Germany and Switzerland. Even more importantly, the reluctance to use torture prevented the development of extreme, diabolical witch beliefs. Without torture the potential for transforming simple acts of superstition into crimes of diabolical conspiracy was greatly limited, since only through confessions adduced under torture could diabolical beliefs gain the widespread legitimacy that was necessary to sustain further witch-hunting. Without torture it was certain that the learned as well as the popular view of witchcraft would remain essentially an individual moral transgression, not a large-scale attack upon Christian civilization.

In explaining the relative tameness of Spanish and Italian witch-hunting one additional factor – the strength of central control – must also be mentioned. Although medieval inquisitors had always received their commissions from Rome, they had never been subject to central regulation or coordination. In the sixteenth and seventeenth centuries, however, inquisitors lost this autonomy. The loss was most apparent in Spain, where a new national institution under the king was established in 1478, superseding the medieval inquisition that had operated only in Aragon. The main organ of this new institution was the Supreme Council at Madrid, which exercised strict control over a large number of regional tribunals (eventually twenty-one) throughout Spain and its overseas possessions. In the early sixteenth century some of these regional courts had managed to exercise a large measure of local autonomy, but by 1550 the Supreme Council had established its superiority over all local tribunals.[118] The effect of this assertion of central control on the process of witch-hunting became evident in Barcelona in the 1530s, when the council put an end to a witch-hunt by establishing its right to confirm all sentences.[119] Even more dramatically, the council put an end to the great Basque witch-hunt of 1609–11 when, upon the recommendation of Salazar, it issued a very strict set of procedural rules for the prosecution of witches throughout the country. The authority and influence of the council was even evident in secular witchcraft prosecutions. In a number of seventeenth-century cases, most notably in northern Vizcaya in 1621, the council managed to bring about modifications of very severe sentences.[120]

The various inquisitorial tribunals that operated in Italy outside the Papal States were not subject to the same degree of central control as those in Spain. Some of the regional bodies, such as the Inquisition in Venice, which included lay members representing the secular government, operated with a certain measure of independence from the Congregation of the Holy Office in Rome.[121] Nevertheless, the Roman Inquisition achieved some success in its efforts to standardize procedure and sentencing practices throughout Italy. It gave prior approval to all sentences and, what was even more important, occasionally demanded that provincial inquisitors should conduct further investigation of cases that it believed required such action.[122] Even the Venetian tribunal of the Roman Inquisition, which jealously defended its independence, often consulted with Rome on matters of procedure and sometimes extradited suspects to Rome for trial.[123]

Before leaving the subject of Mediterranean witchcraft we must consider H. R. Trevor-Roper's thesis that witchcraft prosecutions in Spain were relatively mild because the Spanish directed all their hostility towards Jews instead of witches. This thesis is based upon the assumption that the prosecution of witches was just one manifestation of a more general need of society to find scapegoats for its problems and to release social tension by prosecuting them. Witches and Jews (and for that matter heretics and any other minority groups) were in a certain sense interchangeable. Either of them could serve as an object of social fear and discrimination; it simply was a question of which group appeared more threatening. One of the corollaries of this argument is that the elimination of the fear of one group can lead to the prosecution of the other, as society finds new scapegoats after the old ones are dispensed with. Another corollary is that judicial officials have only so much time to devote to the prosecution of deviant groups and that it is likely therefore that only one such group would be prosecuted at one time.[124]

This thesis has only limited value in explaining the mildness of Spanish witch-hunting. It can help us to understand why relatively few Spanish witches were prosecuted in the late fifteenth and early sixteenth centuries. Although Spanish inquisitors had been concerned with ritual magic in the fourteenth and fifteenth centuries, they did not maintain their vigilance as such magicians in France and the Rhineland were transformed into witches. Instead they turned their attention almost exclusively to Jews, who were the main reason for the establishment of the Inquisition in 1478 and who bore the full brunt of its force until about 1540. It is difficult, however, to attribute the mildness of Spanish witch-hunting *after* 1540 to the presence of Jewish scapegoats, since by that time the problem had been largely resolved and the Inquisition had turned its attention to other matters. Now, one might argue that the increase in the number of Spanish witches after 1540 was in fact a result of the decline of the Jewish threat; that would be consistent with the general tenor of Trevor-Roper's argument. But it is impossible to explain the *mildness* of Spanish witch-hunting – which as we have seen is not to be measured by the number of trials but by the number of executions – in this way. There is simply no way we can attribute the 'moderate wisdom' of Spain in handling witches after 1540 to the presence of Jewish scapegoats in Spanish society. The fact of the matter is that Jews were *not* being prosecuted during this period and witches were. The reasons for the lenient treatment of witches had a great deal to do with the nature of the Inquisition and the way in which the crime of witchcraft was perceived at the time, and precious little to do with the Jews.

Conclusion

In describing the general patterns of European witch-hunting, historians frequently compare the European continent with England, showing how the prohibition of torture and the incomplete reception of demonological theory in England prevented witchcraft prosecutions from becoming as intemperate and extensive as they were in places like Germany and Switzerland. The comparison is both valid and instructive, but its frequent use can lead to an oversimplified view of the geography of European witchcraft. On the one hand, it can lead to the unwarranted conclusion that England was the only European country in which authorities prosecuted witches in moderate numbers. On the other hand, it can lead to the equally false assumption that there was a common 'continental' European pattern of witchcraft prosecutions. The foregoing regional survey of witchcraft should make the invalidity of those assumptions readily apparent. England, with its distinctive body of national law and its failure to adopt either Roman law or inquisitorial procedure, may have been very different from France and the various states of Germany in the way it dealt with witches (just as it was different from them in many other ways), but it was by no means the only exception to the prevailing European norm. One can just as easily claim that witchcraft prosecutions in Denmark, Norway, Russia and Spain were 'exceptional' by German or Swiss standards.

There were in fact so many regions in Europe where demonological ideas were only partially received, where the application of torture was effectively restricted, where the conviction- and execution-rates in witchcraft cases were kept fairly low, and where mass witch-hunts occurred only on rare occasions, that one must seriously question whether there really was a general European witch panic. There was certainly a general European witch-*hunt* in which various countries participated to a larger or somewhat smaller extent. But a witch panic, characterized by an unrestrained and paranoid pursuit of large numbers of witches, really only took place in west-central Europe. Although we shall never have complete statistics, those that are available suggest that as many as 75 per cent of all witchcraft prosecutions occurred in that large and populous area. Within that area we can define the boundaries of intense witch-hunting even more narrowly, since the number of trials in the kingdom of France was relatively small. The real centre of the witch-hunt was the area that encompassed the Holy Roman Empire, Switzerland and the various French-speaking duchies and principalities that bordered German and Swiss lands. By comparison to this area, all other regions were temperate in their pursuit of witches and mild in their treatment of them.

There are of course no simple explanations for the rather uneven geographical pattern of prosecutions we have traced in its broader outline. Generally speaking, however, four separate but related variables had the greatest effect. The first was the nature of witch beliefs in a particular region and the strength with which they were held. Wherever witchcraft was defined primarily as *maleficium* and not as Devil-worship, witch-hunts tended to remain limited in scope, mainly because the suspicion that one person practised sorcery did not usually lead to a search for accomplices. The contrast between Germany, where the belief in diabolism was widespread, and Russia, where it was virtually absent, could not be more pronounced. In many areas, however, the crime of witchcraft could be defined in either way, with theories of diabolism receiving only occasional expression and commanding only limited subscription. This was certainly the situation in England, the Nordic countries and Spain, and in each of these countries the pattern of witchcraft prosecutions included both a number of individual trials for *maleficium* and a few larger hunts for Devil-worship.

The second major factor in determining the relative intensity of witchcraft prosecutions was the system of criminal procedure that was used in the courts. Although we tend to assume that all European courts, with the exception of those in England, followed 'inquisitorial' procedure and used torture freely, we have seen that witchcraft trials were conducted in a wide variety of ways. Methods of initiating cases, rules regarding the use of torture, customs regarding the appointment of advocates and procedures for appealing sentences all differed from place to place. Differences in procedures had profound effects on the process of witch-hunting, since they greatly influenced the chances of conviction and execution. Legal procedures also had an effect upon the reception of witch beliefs among judicial authorities, for it was often only under torture that certain witch beliefs could be legitimized through confessions.

The third major determinant of the intensity of witchcraft prosecutions was the degree of central judicial control over the trials. Central control did not necessarily serve as a restraining force in witchcraft cases, since some rulers were often very eager to see witchcraft eliminated and occasionally even initiated witch-hunts. But in most cases local authorities (the magistrates of a particular town or village or the judicial officers of a small region) were more determined to detect, prosecute and execute witches than those who occupied higher positions of authority in Church or state, and more likely to violate the procedural rules formulated by central governments while doing so. The relative mildness of English, Swedish, Russian and Spanish witch-hunting, as well as that which took place in the central areas of France, can be attributed at least in part to the success of central secular or ecclesiastical authorities in restraining the enthusiasm of local authorities for waging a full-scale war against Satan's allies.

The final factor that must be taken into account in explaining regional patterns is the degree of religious zeal manifested by the people of a particular region. It is of course difficult to measure religious zeal, and it is even more difficult to demonstrate its effects upon witchcraft prosecutions. But it did inspire many judicial authorities to pursue, interrogate and convict witches, and those jurisdictions that convicted and executed witches in great numbers were known for their Christian militancy, their religious intolerance and their vigorous participation in either the Reformation or the Counter-Reformation. Differences between witch-hunting in New England and the other North American colonies, between England and Scotland, between Poland and Russia, and between Italy and Germany can all be attributed in some measure to these elusive differences in religious 'enthusiasm' among those who conducted witch-hunts. These differences can in turn be linked to the religious stability of the countries in question, for it was areas that had experienced religious change or felt threatened by it that tended to pursue witches with the greatest determination. These areas were, moreover, much more likely than others to become preoccupied with diabolical witch beliefs and to allow their magistrates to use torture to protect the Christian faith. In this way religious zeal tended to reinforce other reasons for intense witch-hunting, just as its absence allowed public officials to develop a more 'enlightened' and moderate attitude towards the whole process.

Notes

1. This early chronology, with some minor alterations, is taken from Kieckhefer, *European Witch Trials*, 10–26.
2. For a detailed treatment of the fifteenth-century trials in Switzerland and a discussion of some of the treatises see Blauert, *Frühe Hexenverfolgungen*. For a list of the trials in Italy during this period, most of which were conducted by papal inquisitors see T. Herzig, 'Witchcraft Prosecutions in Italy' in *The Oxford Handbook of Witchcraft in Early Modern Europe and Colonial America*, ed. Brian P. Levack (Oxford, 2013): 250.
3. Compare the numbers of trials and executions for 1450–1500 and 1500–1550 in Hansen, *Quellen*, 68–262; in Foucault, *Les Procès de sorcellerie dans l'ancienne France devant les jurisdictiones séculières* (Paris, 1907): 297–306; and in Midelfort, *Witch Hunting*, 201–2.
4. Luther, *St. Paul's Epistle to the Galatians*, 397.
5. H. Kamen, *Inquisition and Society in Spain in the Sixteenth and Seventeenth Centuries* (Bloomington, 1985): 210–12; E. W. Monter, *Frontiers of Heresy: The Spanish Inquisition from the Basque Lands to Sicily* (Cambridge, 1990): 255–67; G. Bonomo, *Caccia alle Streghe* (Palermo, 1959): 143; Lea, *Materials*, III: 1112–13; Le Roy Ladurie, *Paysans*, 408; J. Delumeau, *Catholicism between Luther and Voltaire: A New View of the Counter-Reformation* (London, 1977): 170–1.
6. H. H. Kunstmann, *Zauberwahn und Hexenprozesz in der Reichsstadt Nürnberg* (Nuremberg, 1970): 39–73.
7. Trevor-Roper, 'Witch-Craze', 136.
8. Evans, *Habsburg Monarchy*, 402, attributes the absence of Austrian witch prosecutions at this time to 'an atmosphere of Humanism, tolerance and comparative urbanity'.
9. Oberman, *Masters of the Reformation*, 158–83.
10. Monter, 'Witch Trials in Continental Europe 1560–1660', 1–52.
11. For the disappearance of scepticism in Luxembourg see Dupont-Bouchat, 'Répression', 87.
12. On the impact of printing on all aspects of European culture see E. L. Eisenstein, *The Printing Revolution in Early Modern Europe* (Cambridge, 1983).
13. See Chapter 4 above.
14. Trevor-Roper, 'Witch-Craze', 137–40.
15. See E. Hobsbawm, 'The Crisis of the Seventeenth Century', in *Crisis in Europe, 1560–1660*, ed. T. Aston (New York, 1967): 5–62.
16. Byloff, *Hexenglaube*, 160; Evans, *Hapsburg Monarchy*, 404–5. Baranowski, *Procesy Czarownic*, 179.
17. For a valuable comparison of two German-speaking regions – electoral Trier and Swabian Austria – see Dillinger, *Evil People*.
18. E. W. Monter, 'The Pedestal and the Stake: Courtly Love and Withchcraft', in *Becoming Visible. Women in European History*, ed. R. Bridenthal and C. Koonz (Boston, 1977): 130, claims that more than one-half of the executions took place there.
19. See Schormann, *Deutschland*, 71; Behringer, *Hexenund Hexenprozesse*, 193.
20. Lea, *Materials*, III: 1231.
21. Midelfort, *Witch Hunting*, 98–100.
22. Schormann, *Deutschland*, 65–6. The topography of the two regions is also different. The north and east are mainly lowlands, whereas the south and west are characterized by medium altitude mountains.
23. Behringer, *Witchcraft Persecutions in Bavaria*, 64, estimates there were 1,000–1,500 executions in the entire region of south-east Germany. Most of these came within the old duchy of Bavaria (after 1623 a principality and then an electorate), which

had a centralized system of justice. For comparisons between the entire south-eastern region and other parts of Germany see Behringer, 'Erhob sich das ganze Land', 163–5.

24. Behringer, *Witchcraft Persecutions in Bavaria*, 401; Evans, *Habsburg Monarchy*, 402–17. Byloff, *Hexenglaube und Hexenverfolgungen*, 159–60, estimates that 1,700 individuals were accused in Austria but admits that the number may have been as high as 5,000.

25. See H. C. E. Midelfort, 'Heartland of the Witchcraze: Central and Northern Europe', *History Today* 31 (1981): 30; Lea, *Materials*, III: 1229, 1246, 1251; Schormann, *Nordwestdeutschland*, 158–9; S. Lorenz, *Aktenversendung und Hexenprozess: Dargestellt am Beispiel der Juristenfakultäten Rostock und Greifswald (1570/82–1630)* (Frankfurt, 1982).

26. Bader, *Hexenprozesse in der Schweiz*, 211ff., counted 8,888 accusations and 5,417 executions. Behringer, *Witches and Witch-Hunts*, 150, gives a more conservative estimate of 4,000 executions.

27. Monter, *Ritual*, 47.

28. For the efforts of Philip II and the Council of Luxembourg to introduce new legal procedures and to encourage general inquisitions for witchcraft see Dupont-Bouchat, 'Répression', 86–99.

29. Boguet, *Examen*, p. xxxiii. Remy, *Demonolatry*, 56, refers to no fewer than 800 executions and 'nearly as many more' who have fled or endured torture. For the estimate of 2,000–3,000 total executions, see C. Pfister, 'Nicolas Rémy et la sorcellerie en Lorraine la fin du XVI siècle', *Revue historique* 93 (1907): 239.

30. Briggs, 'Witchcraft and Popular Mentality in Lorraine', 338.

31. Dupont-Bouchat, 'Répression', 127.

32. M. Gijswijt-Hofstra, 'Six Centuries of Witchcraft in the Netherlands', in *Witchcraft in the Netherlands*, ed. M. Gijswijt-Hofstra and W. Frijhoff (Rotterdam, 1991): 25–30.

33. A. F. Soman, 'Decriminalizing Witchcraft: Does the French Experience Furnish a European Model?', *Criminal Justice History* 10 (1989): 17, sees the Netherlands, where a decentralized judiciary achieved a very early decline of witch-hunting, as an exception to the rule that prevailed in most European jurisdictions.

34. Gijswijt-Hofstra, 'Six Centuries', 31–2.

35. H. de Waardt, 'Prosecution or Defense: Procedural Possibilities following a Witchcraft Accusation in the Province of Holland before 1800', in *Witchcraft in the Netherlands from the Fourteenth to the Twentieth Centuries*, ed. Marijke Gijswijt-Hofstra and W. Frijhoff (Rotterdam, 1991): 71–90.

36. M. Gielis, 'The Netherlandic Theologians' Views of Witchcraft and the Devil's Pact', in *Witchcraft in the Netherlands from the Fourteenth to the Twentieth Centuries*, ed. Marijke Gijswijt-Hofstra and W. Frijhoff (Rotterdam, 1991): 37–52.

37. Muchembled, 'Satan ou les hommes?', 18.

38. Mandrou, *Magistrats et sorciers*, 449–62.

39. For the area within the jurisdiction of the Parlement of Paris there are records of 1,288 appeals and 554 cases that never reached that stage. Soman, 'Trente procès de sorcellerie dans le Perche', 42–7. The Parlement of Rouen, which had jurisdiction over Normandy, confirmed 97, or 44 per cent, of the 219 death sentences appealed to it between 1560 and 1660. Monter, 'Toads and Eucharists', 572.

40. Soman, 'The Parlement of Paris', 40. Muchembled, 'The Witches of the Cambrésis', notes that with the exception of Lorraine, which was not in France at this time, the numbers of French witches were counted in the hundreds rather than the thousands. The *Parlement* of Paris confirmed only 115 death sentences between 1565 and 1640. See Soman, 'Parlement of Paris', 26. There were, however, some fairly severe hunts in the outlying regions of the country. For de Lancre's report of 400 executions at Toulouse in 1577 see Mandrou, *Magistrats et sorciers*, 92.

41. Briggs, *Communities of Belief*, 12.
42. For the English torture warrants, which number 81 for the period 1540–1640, see Langbein, *Torture*, 94–123. The Scottish Privy Council and Parliament together issued 39 warrants between 1590 and 1689. See Levack, 'Judicial Torture in Scotland', 191.
43. See, for example, B. Whitelocke, *Memorials of the English Affairs* (London, 1682): 252. One of the reasons for the use of torture was that the Privy Council required a confession in order to approve a local witchcraft trial. Mackenzie, *Laws and Customes*, 88.
44. *Register of the Privy Council of Scotland*, IV, 680.
45. Larner, *Enemies of God*, 67–8, 71–5. For a full discussion of the differences between English and Scottish witch-hunting, see Levack, *Witch-Hunting in Scotland*, 1–14.
46. There are records of only four trials, resulting in three executions, and one lynching. A. Sneddon, 'Witchcraft Belief and Trials in Early Modern Ireland', *Irish Economic and Social History* 39 (2012): 16–17. Including the case of the Anglican minister John Aston, who was prosecuted for treasure –hunting on the basis of the Elizabethan statute, would bring the number of trials to five. E. C. Lapoint, 'Irish Immunity to Witch-Hunting: 1534–1711', *Eire-Ireland* 27 (1992): 76–92, argues that the Catholic, Gaelic-Irish population was reluctant to bring formal accusations in courts controlled by England. Presbyterian settlers were reluctant to turn cases of witchcraft over to civil authorities. See Sneddon, 'Witchcraft Belief', 15. R. Gillespie, 'Ireland', in *Encyclopedia of Witchcraft: The Western Tradition* (Santa Barbara, 2006), II: 568, argues that the Irish population viewed the law as a means of negotiating social relationships rather than an adversarial system.
47. St John Seymour, *Irish Witchcraft and Demonology* (Dublin, 1913): 105–13; Mary McAuliffe, 'Gender, History and Witchcraft in Early Modern Ireland: A Re-Reading of the Florence Newton Trial', in *Gender and Power in Irish History*, ed. M. A. Gialenella Valiulis (Dublin, 2009): 39–58; Sneddon, 'Witchcraft Belief', 17–18. The similarity with the prosecution of the two Bury St. Edmunds witches, Rose Cullender and Amy Duny, lies mainly in the use of spectral evidence to identify Newton. The only diabolical component of the case was the charge that Longford had displayed a few of the symptoms of demonic possession, including falling into fits and vomiting pins. Technically, Longford was obsessed rather than possessed, since the Devil, at the command of Newton, allegedly attacked her externally rather than entering her body. The Bury St Edmunds witches and the bewitched girls at Salem in 1692 were also obsessed rather than possessed. In no way can the case cannot be considered a classic case of possession, as Sneddon argues.
48. F. N. Parke, 'Witchcraft in Maryland', *Maryland Historical Magazine* 31 (1936): 284, 290. There was also an unauthorized execution at sea when the captain of a ship hanged Katherine Grady for causing violent storms by means of witchcraft.
49. M. Jarvis, 'Bermuda', in *Encyclopedia of Witchcraft: The Western Tradition*, II: 111–12.
50. Demos, *Entertaining Satan*, 11–13.
51. Hansen, *Witchcraft at Salem*, 284.
52. *The Colonial Laws of Massachusetts*, ed. W. H. Whitmore (Boston, 1889): 55. The wording of the law was based on Mosaic language.
53. One of the reasons for the extraordinarily low conviction-rate in Massachusetts before the Salem trials was that charges brought by the witches' neighbours usually referred only to *maleficia*, whereas the judges required evidence of diabolical compact. See Richard Godbeer, *The Devil's Dominion: Magic and Religion in Early New England* (Cambridge, 1992); Weisman, *Witchcraft, Magic and Religion*, Chapter 7.
54. On the importance of the Indian wars on the Salem witch-hunt see M. B. Norton, *In the Devil's Snare: The Salem Witchcraft Crisis of 1692* (New York, 2002).

55. In 1600 the population of Britain was approximately 5.4 million persons, that of Scandinavia approximately 2 million. De Vries, *European Urbanization*, 36.

56. Johansen, 'Denmark', 340.

57. Henningsen, 'Witchcraft in Denmark', 134, argues that neither the sabbath nor the pact was ever figured prominently in the charges against Danish witches. See also Johansen, 'Denmark', 343.

58. Johansen, 'Denmark', 341–7. Most of the executions after this time, however, were still based upon charges of *maleficium*.

59. Henningsen, 'Witchcraft in Denmark', 135. See also Johansen, 'Denmark', 344–5.

60. The population of Denmark in 1650 was 580,000, whereas that of Scotland was approximately one million. A. Lassen, 'The Population of Denmark in 1660', *Scandinavian Economic History Review* 13 (1965): 29.

61. Naess, 'Norway', 371, calculates an execution-rate of 38 per cent on the basis of those cases in which the fates of the accused are known. His calculation of executions for all trials, 372, is only 25 per cent of those tried. B. Alver, *Heksetro og Trolddom* (Oslo, 1971): 63, also estimates an execution-rate of 25 per cent. The data base compiled by the University of Oslo lists 924 trials dating from 1566 to 1747, with all but a few of them occurring in the seventeenth century. For the statistics on Finnmark, where 135 persons were tried for witchcraft, and 91 were convicted and executed see L. H. Willumsen, *The Witchcraft Trials in Finnmark Northern Norway*, tr. K. Edwardsen (Bergen, 2010): 11.

62. In Finnmark the source of diabolical beliefs may have been the Scotsman John Cunningham, who served as governor of the province in the 1620s. L. H. Willumsen, *Witches of the North: Scotland and Finnmark* (Leiden, 2013): 361–6.

63. See Robbins, *Encyclopedia*, 361–2. The case of 1680 appears to have been an exception to this rule.

64. H. Wiers-Jenssen, *Anne Pedersdotter: A Drama in Four Acts*, tr. John Masefield (Boston, 1917).

65. R. Bainton, *Women of the Reformation: From Spain to Scandinavia* (Minneapolis, 1977): 128–33.

66. Ankarloo, *Trolldomsprocesserna i Sverige*, 326–8; K. Baschwitz, *Hexen und Hexenprozesse* (Munich, 1963): 321.

67. Ankarloo, 'Sweden', 285–317; Lea, *Materials*, III: 1282–5; Heikkinen, *Paholaisen Liittolaiset*, 375–7.

68. On Estonian witchcraft see Madar, 'Estonia I'; J. Kahk, 'Estonia II: The Crusade against Idolatry', in *Early Modern European Witchcraft: Centres and Peripheries*, ed. Bengt Ankarloo and Gustav Henningsen (Oxford, 1990): 257–84.

69. Heikkinen, *Paholaisen Liittolaiset*, 386–9.

70. Heikkinen and Kervinen, 'Finland', 320.

71. See Schormann, *Hexenproesse in Deutschland*, 6 for the traditional view.

72. Baranowski, *Procesy Czarownic*, 178; epilogue to K. Baschwitz, *Czarownice. Dzieje procesów o czary* (Warsaw, 1963). For recent estimates see Wyporska, 'Poland', III: 907–8.

73. The prominence of diabolism in the trials was most evident in the trials at Grodzisk in Greater Poland between 1702 and 1756. W. Wyporska, *Witchcraft in Early Modern Poland, 1500–1800* (Basingstoke, 2013): 35–6.

74. Torture was used in virtually every trial in Wielkopolska, including those involving children. Wyporska, 'Poland', 907–8. See also Ostling, *Between the Devil and the Host*, 76–80.

75. J. Tazbir, *A State Without Stakes* (Wydawniczy, 1973): 92.

76. Ibid., 169, 208.

77. Klaniczay, 'Hungary', 222. The fates of only 932 are known.
78. Ibid., 233–4, 249–50.
79. Ibid., 230, n.30.
80. Ginzburg, *The Night Battles*, 7, 13. For beliefs similar to those of the *benandanti* in Hungary see G. Klaniczay, 'Benandante-kresnik-zduhac-táltos', *Ethnographia* 94 (1983).
81. Lea, *Materials*, III: 1264–5.
82. Ibid., III: 1271–3.
83. Ibid., III: 1254.
84. Klaniczay, 'Hungary', 221–35.
85. R. Zguta, 'Witchcraft Trials in Seventeenth-Century Russia', *American Historical Review* 82 (1977): 1189.
86. Ibid., 1191–2. On the *Stoglav* Council of 1551, whose decrees did not specifically refer to witchcraft, see W. F. Ryan, *The Bathhouse at Midnight: Magic in Russia* (University Park, 1999), 411.
87. Kivelson, *Desperate Magic*, 31.
88. Kivelson, 'Through the Prism of Witchcraft', 75–8.
89. On this question R. Zguta, 'Was There a Witch Craze in Muscovite Russia?', *Southern Folklore Quarterly* 40 (1977): 119–27, and Ryan, 'The Witchcraft Hysteria in Early Modern Europe', 49–84. Kivelson, *Desperate Magic*, 37–8, takes the position that although the number of trials and executions was low by Western standards, Russian courts proved to be as zealous and as cruel in their pursuit of witches as any courts in the West.
90. For a description of Russian criminal procedure in witchcraft cases see Kivelson, *Desperate Magic*, 38–51.
91. J. Baissac, *Les Grands jours de la sorcellerie* (Paris, 1890): 154–5; Kivelson, 'Through the Prism of Witchcraft', 81. On the excesses of torture in witchcraft cases, see Kivelson, *Desperate Magic*, 17, 155.
92. Zguta, 'Witchcraft Trials', 1196. The requirement could easily be ignored.
93. Kivelson, *Desperate Magic*, Chapter 3.
94. Herzig, 'Witchcraft Prosecutions in Italy', 250–2.
95. Henningsen, 'The Papers of Alonso de Salazar Frías', 104, estimates a few hundred executions for all of Spain. Behringer's estimate of only 300 executions for all of Spain is almost certainly too low. Behringer, *Witches and Witch Hunts*, 150. On the executions by the Barcelona tribunal in the early 17th century see W. Monter, 'Witchcraft in Iberia', in *The Oxford Handbook of Witchcraft*, 272–3. For the hundreds of trials in the secular courts see G. W. Knutsen, *Servants of Satan and Masters of Demons: The Spanish Inquisition's Trials for Superstition, Valencia and Barcelona, 1478–1700* (Turnhout, 2009): 86–8. On the reluctance of the regional tribunals of the Inquisition to execute witches after 1550 see Knutsen, *Servants of Satan*, 64–6, and Tausiet, *Urban Magic*, 137. In Portugal secular courts were responsible for all but one execution for witchcraft. F. Bethencourt, 'Portugal: A Scrupulous Inquisition', in *Early Modern European Witchcraft: Centres and Peripheries*, ed. Bengt Ankarloo and Gustav Henningsen (Oxford, 1990): 405.
96. Monter, *Ritual, Myth and Magic*, 98–107; R. E. Greenleaf, *Zumarraga and the Mexican Inquisition, 1536–1543* (Washington, 1962), 111–21; idem, *The Mexican Inquisition of the Sixteenth Century* (Albuquerque, 1969), 173. For Brazil see L. de Mello e Souza, *The Devil and the Land of the Holy Cross* (Austin, 2003): 277–378. On the distinction that colonial Spanish made between *hechicería* (sorcery) and *brujería* (witchcraft), the latter being the more serious offence meriting death, see I. Gareis, 'Merging Magical Traditions: Sorcery and Witchcraft in Spanish and Portuguese America', in *The Oxford*

Handbook of Witchcraft in Early Modern Europe and Colonial America, ed. Brian P. Levack (Oxford, 2013): 414–15. Portuguese trial records made no distinction between sorcery and witchcraft.

97. Parker, 'Some Recent Work on the Inquisition', 529.
98. Martin, *Witchcraft and the Inquisition in Venice*, 226.
99. Bethencourt, 'Portugal', 405.
100. Henningsen, *The Witches' Advocate*, 69–94.
101. J. P. Paiva, *Bruxaria e Superstição num País sem 'Caça às Bruxas', 1600–1774* (Lisbon, 1997): 36–42.
102. Souza, *The Devil and the Land of the Holy Cross*, 163–6. The only references to collective Devil-worship in Brazil came from three African slaves who had spent time in Brazil but were tried in Lisbon. All three confessed under torture.
103. In Siena 22 per cent of prosecutions for magic were for *maleficium*, but only 1 per cent of the total involved charges of diabolical witchcraft. O. di Simplicio, *Inquisizione Stregoneria Medicina: Siena e il Suo Stato* (Siena, 2000): 22, 25. The cases of witchcraft brought before Ventian Inquisition also were concerned almost exclusively with *maleficum* rather than diabolism. Martin, *Witchcraft and the Inquisition in Venice*, 5, 192–3, 254. See also O'Neil, 'Magical Healing', 88–114.
104. Tedeschi, 'Inquisitorial Law and the Witch', 94.
105. Caro Baroja, *World of the Witches*, 99–102.
106. F. Mormando, 'Bernardino of Siena, Popular Preacher and Witch-Hunter: A 1426 Witch Trial in Rome', *Fifteenth-Century Studies* 24 (1998): 84–118.
107. Robbins, *Encyclopedia*, 236–7; E. W. Monter, 'French and Italian Witchcraft', *History Today* 30 (1980): 33.
108. Henningsen, 'The Papers of Alonso de Salazar Frías', 88–96.
109. Henningsen, *Witches' Advocate*, 22–3.
110. Paiva, *Bruxaria e superstição num país sem 'caça às bruxas'*.
111. Martin, *Witchcraft and the Inquisition in Venice*, 50–66, 253–5.
112. J. Tedeschi, 'Preliminary Observations on Writing a History of the Roman Inquisition', in *Continuity and Discontinuity in Church History*, ed. F. F. Church and T. George (Leiden, 1979): 42.
113. Ibid., 242–3.
114. Henningsen, *Witches' Advocate*, 44, 170.
115. Ibid., 170–1. Salazar proposed that the same procedure be used with the other accused witches, 179–80.
116. Tedeschi, 'Inquisitorial Law and the Witch', 97–104; Martin, *Witchcraft and the Inquisition in Venice*, 26–8.
117. For the threat of torture against one of the *benandanti* see Ginzburg, *The Night Battles*, 105.
118. E. Peters, *Inquisition* (Berkeley, 1989): 90, 101. For conflict with local tribunals in Saragossa in 1535 and Barcelona in 1548–49 see Monter, *Frontiers of Heresy*, 264–6.
119. H. Kamen, *The Spanish Inquisition* (New York, 1965): 145.
120. Henningsen, *Witches' Advocate*, 387–9.
121. Peters, *Inquisition*, 109–19.
122. Ginzburg, *The Night Battles*, 125–6.
123. Peters, *Inquisition*, 117.
124. Trevor-Roper, 'Witch-Craze', 110–12.

8

THE DECLINE AND END
OF WITCH-HUNTING

During the seventeenth and eighteenth centuries, prosecutions and executions
for the crime of witchcraft declined in number and eventually came to an end.
The decline occurred in all European countries where witch-hunts had taken
place, as well as in the colonial possessions of Spain, Portugal, England and
France. The decline was marked by an increasing reluctance to prosecute
witches, the acquittal of many who were tried, the reversal of convictions
on appeal, and eventually the repeal of the laws that had authorized the
prosecutions. By 1782 the last officially sanctioned witchcraft execution had
taken place, and in many jurisdictions witchcraft, at least as it had been defined
in the sixteenth and seventeenth centuries, had ceased to be a crime.
Individuals continued to name their neighbours as witches, and in some cases
they took violent action against them, but they did so illegally and at the risk
of being prosecuted themselves.

The reduction and eventual end of witch-hunting occurred at different
times in the various kingdoms and regions of Europe. In some countries, such
as the Dutch Republic, the decline in prosecutions became evident before the
end of the sixteenth century, while in others, like Poland, it did not begin
until the middle of the eighteenth century. The length of time that the entire
process took also varied greatly from place to place. In Scotland, for example,
the initial reduction in the number of prosecutions was followed by more than
fifty years of trials, whereas in Franche-Comté and colonial Massachusetts
witch-hunts came to a complete end only a few years after the courts started
to discourage prosecutions.

This long, gradual reduction in the number of trials, just like their rise in
the fifteenth century, had multiple causes. These include the introduction of
new rules governing the procedures used in the trial of witches, a shift in the
way that educated people viewed the supernatural realm, a pronounced change
in the religious climate in most European countries, and the abatement of
some of the social and economic conditions that had encouraged witchcraft
prosecutions.

Judicial procedure and legal caution

The main cause of the decline in witchcraft prosecutions in the seventeenth and eighteenth centuries was the establishment of new rules for conducting witchcraft trials and the application of new, more demanding standards of evidence for the conviction of witches. The pressure to make these changes originated in the objections that judges and legal writers had to the ways in which the trials were being conducted. As a consequence of these changes in judicial procedure, witchcraft trials resulted in a larger number of acquittals, the mass panics in which scores of witches perished no longer recurred, and the courts became increasingly reluctant to initiate prosecutions in the first place.

The judges, inquisitors, magistrates and writers who responded to the trials in this critical way can best be defined as judicial sceptics. In the context of witchcraft the word 'scepticism' usually denotes the attitudes of those who doubt or deny the existence of witches or the possibility of their crime. Judicial sceptics did not necessarily adopt such a stance. The essence of their intellectual position was a genuine doubt whether those persons who were being pro-secuted were actually guilty as charged, and this concern led in turn to a more general uncertainty as to whether the crime could ever be proved at law. Some judicial sceptics may have also harboured a more fundamental, philosophical doubt whether witchcraft even existed. But judicial scepticism could, and in most cases did, coexist with a firm belief in the reality and possibility of the crime.

The three most significant changes in the conduct of witchcraft trials that led to a decline in prosecutions were the regulation of local witchcraft trials by higher authorities, the restriction or prohibition of torture, and the demand for more persuasive evidence to support the conviction of witches.

The regulation of local justice

The decline in witchcraft prosecutions in most European countries began when higher judicial authorities, very often the judges who staffed the central institutions of the state, took steps to control the prosecution of witches by local judges or inferior courts. These efforts usually began in response to large witch-hunts that had spun out of control.

The classic example of the way in which higher judicial authorities contained the witch-hunting zeal of local officials comes from the large portion of northern France that was subject to the jurisdiction of the Parlement of Paris, the royal courts that exercised an appellate jurisdiction over most of northern France. In 1587–8 a large witch panic broke out in the Champagne–Ardennes region, which fell within the jurisdiction of the Parisian tribunal. In this local panic, which claimed hundreds of lives, all semblance of due process appears to have vanished. In an effort to discover the identity of witches, village judges were using the popular method of swimming those who had been named, a vestige of the medieval ordeal by cold water that was now illegal. Local officials were also torturing suspects without restraint and executing them in summary fashion. In response to this crisis the Parlement demanded that henceforth all sentences of death in witchcraft cases be reviewed by the Parlement, a step that constituted an unprecedented imposition of central judicial authority on the French localities. This policy, which involved the punishment of local officials for violating procedural norms, was formally adopted in 1604 and published as an edict in 1624. The Parlement's reversal of many of the sentences, coupled with the difficulty of defending the lower court's decision, led to a precipitate decline in the number of sentences within the area of the Parlement's jurisdiction. By the 1640s the number of appeals itself had declined precipitately.[1]

A similar regulation of local justice by higher authorities took place at about the same time in Spain, where witchcraft was considered a crime of mixed jurisdiction and could be prosecuted either by the Spanish Inquisition, an ecclesiastical institution that was under the authority of the king, or the secular courts. The Inquisition was a highly centralized, national institution, consisting of nineteen (ultimately twenty-one) regional tribunals that reported to, and were supervised by, a central council, *La Suprema*, in Madrid. One of the functions of this Supreme Council, which was headed by the Inquisitor General, was to enforce procedural rules in the trial of the crimes brought before it. The first set of guidelines, which were issued in 1526 in the wake of a witch-hunt in Navarre, was intended to govern the activities of inquisitors who tried witches in the regional tribunals. These guidelines restricted the practice of confiscating a witch's property, required consultation with the Supreme Council before convicting a witch a second time, and forbade the arrest or conviction of a witch solely on the basis of another witch's confession. These rules, coupled with a tradition of leniency that they encouraged, were in large part responsible for keeping executions for witchcraft in Spain at very low levels during the remainder of the sixteenth century. Indeed, on a number of occasions the Inquisition succeeded in acquiring jurisdiction over cases of witchcraft that had originated in the secular courts and reversed the sentences of death that had been pronounced on the victims.[2]

The Spanish Inquisition's impressive record of tight regulation and judicial leniency in witchcraft cases did not remain unblemished. A major lapse occurred in the great Basque witch-hunt of 1609–11. As we have seen, however, the inquisitor Alonso de Salazar Frías succeeded in returning the Inquisition to its traditional posture of judicial restraint. The new instructions that Salazar drafted and the Inquisition issued in 1614 stand as a testament to the efforts of central authorities to regulate the conduct of officials in lower courts in order to contain the spread of witch panics. In addition to restating many of the guidelines that had been put in place in 1526, and issuing new instructions regarding the taking and recording of confessions and denunciations, the Inquisition also dissociated itself from the tactics followed by local authorities who had, 'without any legal authority, exposed the subjects to such abuses in order to make them confess and witness against others'. Moreover, as in France, the Inquisition took steps to punish the parties that had been responsible for these miscarriages of justice, turning them over to the High Court of Navarre and promising that in the future the Inquisition itself would proceed against them with the greatest severity.[3]

The conflict between the Supreme Council at Madrid and local authorities continued after the publication of the new instructions. In a number of cases, most notably in northern Vizcaya, the Inquisition found it necessary to intervene in local witch-hunts conducted by secular authorities, reversing sentences and preventing executions. In a few other localities, most notably in Catalonia and Aragon, it chose to intervene belatedly, if at all, and consequently hundreds of witches were executed.[4] But in the long run the Supreme Council, which was the most highly centralized judicial institution in Spain, succeeded in enforcing a policy of judicial caution that not only kept executions for witchcraft at a minimum after 1614 but also brought about their ultimate termination.

The Spanish pattern was in many respects mirrored in Italy, where a centralized Roman Inquisition, which had been established in 1542, maintained control over witchcraft prosecutions long after ecclesiastical tribunals in northern European lands had deferred to secular courts in prosecuting witches. The record of the Roman Inquisition regarding witchcraft is even more impressive than that of its Spanish counterpart. Not only did it develop a strong tradition of leniency in sentencing witches, but it also insisted upon adherence to strict procedural rules in the conduct of witchcraft trials.[5] As in Spain, the enforcement of these rules was entrusted to the highest tribunal in the inquisitorial organization, the Congregation of the Holy Office in Rome. Thus, once again, as in France and Spain, a centralized institution assumed the role of regulating justice on a lower level.

The quintessential statement of the judicial caution that characterized the Roman Inquisition was a set of instructions for proceeding against witches and sorcerers drafted by Cardinal Desiderio Scaglia in the early 1620s during the pontificate of Gregory XV. This document circulated widely in manuscript until 1655, when Cesare Carena, fiscal of the Roman Inquisition, annotated and published it as an appendix to his treatise on the Inquisition.[6] Reflecting the influence of the Spanish Inquisition's new instructions of 1614, Scaglia's instructions dealt with all aspects of criminal procedure, establishing strict rules for examining accused witches, calling for restraint in the administration of torture and recommending particular care in the evaluation of witches' confessions. The most revealing part of this document, however, is the preface, which explains why the instructions had been drafted to begin with. The author referred to the grave errors that were committed daily by ordinaries, vicars and inquisitors in witchcraft trials, including the use of defective forms

233

of process, the administration of excessive torture, conviction on the most slender evidence, and the turning over of suspects to the secular courts. As Carena observed in his commentary, the atrocity of the crime had led inferior judges to disregard all the rules.[7] Scaglia's instructions were intended to remedy this problem.

In Germany the higher judicial authorities that helped to apply the brakes to local witch-hunting were the law faculties of the German universities. The imperial code promulgated by Charles V in 1532, the *Constitutio Criminalis Carolina*, required that when local courts confronted difficult cases they would consult with the jurists in the law faculty of a nearby university. These consultations, which dealt with the successive stages of arrest, torture and judgment in the criminal process, served as one of the few mechanisms that could prevent local German courts from violating due process and conducting large witch-hunts.[8]

During most of the period of witch-hunting, consultation with the law faculties in cases of witchcraft did little to restrain witch-hunting. Indeed, the consultations probably did more to facilitate than to hamper the prosecution of the accused and to spread learned witch beliefs throughout Germany.[9] In the late seventeenth century, however, the consultations began to have the opposite effect, as jurists started to advise the use of extreme caution in the prosecution of the crime and to secure acquittals rather than executions.[10] This change was particularly evident at the University of Tübingen, which began to recommend against torturing witches and in favour of acquitting them in a majority of cases in the 1660s.[11] A similar but less dramatic change occurred at the University of Helmstedt in the 1660s, and that change contributed to the striking decline in the percentage of executions for witchcraft in the principality of Braunschweig-Wolfenbüttel, which consulted with the Helmstedt jurists on a regular basis. Between 1648 and 1670 the number of acquittals in witchcraft cases in that principality exceeded the number of capital sentences for the first time.[12]

The restriction and prohibition of torture

When superior judicial authorities took steps to remedy the procedural abuses that occurred in local jurisdictions, they were almost always concerned, at least in part, with the improper administration of torture. This should not surprise us. Not only was torture frequently used in the prosecution of witches, especially in those areas of Europe influenced by Roman law,[13] but as a judicial practice it was particularly open to abuse.

In the seventeenth and early eighteenth centuries the administration of torture in all criminal cases, and particularly in witchcraft proscutions, came increasingly under attack, resulting ultimately in the prohibition of torture in all European jurisdictions. The most influential of these critiques came from Friedrich Spee von Langenfeld, a German Jesuit who held a position as professor of moral theology at the University of Paderborn. Spee had witnessed first-hand a number of witch-hunts that had taken place in his university town and the surrounding region. In *Cautio criminalis*, published anonymously in 1631, he revealed the terrible predicament that innocent persons fell into when tortured, and he condemned the judges and the German princes who had approved the administration of the procedure. In addition to Spee, two Jesuits from Ingolstadt, Adam Tanner and Paul Laymann, wrote large works on moral theology that included sections condemning the use of torture in witchcraft trials.[14] From the Protestant side came treatises by Johann Meyfart, a Lutheran professor from Erfurt whose work betrayed a heavy reliance on Spee, and Johannes Grevius, a Dutch theologian who condemned the use of torture by Christians for any purpose whatsoever.[15]

This body of critical work on torture continued to grow in the late seventeenth century. The appearance of new works at that late date attests to the continued use of the procedure, even after its employment in witchcraft prosecutions had become less frequent. Two of these later works achieved fairly widespread circulation. In 1681 Augustin Nicolas, a judge and royal councillor in Franche-Comté, wrote a closely reasoned assault on the practice, emphasizing the injustice of forcing witches to confess to imaginary crimes.[16] The second work was a dissertation by Christian Thomasius, the jurist at the University of Halle who is known mainly for his earlier treatise, *De crimine magiae* (1701). This condemnation of torture, which was published in 1705, provided the basis for a more comprehensive treatise on criminal procedure in witchcraft cases that was published in 1712.[17] Thomasius drew heavily on the earlier works of Spee, Tanner and Meyfart, but he also gave his treatise a distinctly Protestant flavour. A Pietist known for his anticlericalism, Thomasius argued in the manner of Grevius that torture was an unchristian means of extorting the truth, that it was never mentioned in Scripture, and that the 'tyrannical' papacy had used it to strike down their enemies under the pretext of heresy and witchcraft.[18]

The main criticism of torture in all these works was not so much that the procedure was inhumane,[19] but that the evidence obtained by means of its administration was unreliable, since innocent persons would make false admissions in order to stop the pain. This criticism of torture was therefore just one manifestation of a more general change in attitudes towards legal evidence and proof that will be discussed below. The criticism possessed more than mere academic significance. In those jurisdictions where torture was routinely administered in witchcraft cases, the criticism contributed directly to a reduction in the number of convictions and executions and ultimately to a decline in the number of trials as well.

The seventeenth- and early eighteenth-century critics of torture, writing in the context of witchcraft trials, made three specific points. The first was that torture should not be allowed on the basis of mere ill-fame or insufficient circumstantial evidence. The rationale for torturing witches on the basis of such limited or unsubstantiated grounds was the claim that witchcraft was a *crimen exceptum*, an exceptional crime in which the normal rules of evidence do not apply. Beginning in the 1620s, which was a particularly intense period of witch-hunting in Germany, a number of jurists, most notably Ernst Cothmann, presented the unorthodox but not entirely novel argument that witchcraft was not a *crimen exceptum*.[20] If that were the case, trials for witchcraft would have to conform to the more exacting legal requirements spelled out in the *Carolina*.[21]

The second criticism of torture, which may have done more to reduce the number of prosecutions than any other single factor, was directed at the common practice of torturing those who were named by confessing witches as their accomplices without any supporting evidence. In ordinary crimes such denunciations could not be admitted as evidence, but once again the definition of witchcraft as a *crimen exceptum* allowed the judge to ignore the standard cautionary rules. This practice had become routine in areas where belief in the sabbath was strong, and in some German bishoprics, such as Trier, Bamberg and Würzburg, it had resulted in hundreds of executions. On this issue learned opinion was divided. Bodin and Del Rio had defended the practice in unequivocal terms, but Tanner took a more negative position. Tanner did not deny the propriety of seeking evidence of accomplices from those who had confessed to exceptional crimes, but he objected that mere denunciation, even by more than one confessing witch, did not justify either torture or the conviction of people of good repute.

The final criticism of torture was a rebuttal of the claim that God would intervene in the process in order to protect the innocent. This same argument had served as a defence of the medieval ordeals before their abolition in 1215.[22] Tanner was particularly eloquent in destroying this argument, claiming that if God had permitted martyrdoms, wars and massacres, there was no assurance that he would not permit the execution of innocent persons named as witches by allowing them to incriminate themselves under torture.[23]

The arguments against providential intervention in the torture chamber went hand in hand with criticisms of the swimming of witches, a popular and technically illegal practice which stood as a remnant of the practice of the water ordeal and which had been formally abolished as a method of judicial proof in 1215. Most lawyers, including the German jurist Johann Goedelmann and even Bodin, condemned it, denying that it had any evidentiary value. Goedelmann considered it a superstition invented by the Devil and claimed that judges who used it should be prosecuted.[24] In England the physician John Cotta characterized this 'vulgar trial of witchcraft' as a barbarous exercise of 'uncivil force and lawless violence'.[25] Nevertheless, it did not lack learned or powerful advocates, including King James VI of Scotland, who claimed it could serve as an indication of the divine will.[26] Swimming never became an accepted part of the legal process against witches in England or Scotland, but in some European localities it served as one of the *indicia* that justified the use of torture. In France village judges occasionally authorized its use, although they did so without the permission of the superior courts.[27] In Hungary, where the old ordeals persisted well into the eighteenth century, municipal courts used the swimming test and compurgation on a regular basis.[28] In parts of Westphalia the swimming test apparently served as a final proof of guilt as late as the seventeenth century.[29] German jurists, however, uniformly condemned the procedure, and by the eighteenth century it had become the exclusive property of the popular community.[30]

Restrictions on the use of torture were followed ultimately by its complete abolition. This process occurred in Scotland in 1709, Prussia in 1754, Saxony in 1770, Austria in 1776, Sweden in 1782, France in 1788 and Bavaria in 1806.[31] It is important to note that the actual abolition of torture in most European jurisdictions came after the effective end of witchcraft prosecutions, and sometimes even after formal decriminalization. Most of the prohibitions of torture formed part of a broader reform of criminal procedure that most continental European states undertook in the last quarter of the eighteenth century and first quarter of the nineteenth century. Moreover, the abolition of torture in Europe was in large part inspired by humanitarian concerns that had not been prominent in earlier critiques. The decline in witch prosecutions, therefore, had much more to do with the regulation and limitation of torture than with its formal elimination.

New standards of evidence

As suggested above, the questions raised regarding the administration of torture in witchcraft cases formed part of a more general set of concerns about the admission and evaluation of judicial evidence. During the seventeenth century judges and legal writers throughout Europe showed themselves increasingly reluctant to accept the evidence that was presented to them to justify the conviction and execution of witches. This reluctance led to the realization that the crime of witchcraft was extremely difficult, if not impossible, to prove.[32] This conclusion may have contributed to, or received support from, a more fundamental belief that witchcraft itself was an impossible act, as shall be discussed below. But the legal conclusion, taken by itself, was of incalculable importance in bringing the witch-hunt to an end. It led directly to the increasing number of acquittals that occurred in virtually all jurisdictions, and it also contributed to the ultimate realization that witchcraft as a crime could no longer be effectively prosecuted.

Concerns regarding the sufficiency of evidence in witchcraft cases took a number of different forms. It can be seen, first and foremost, in a growing reluctance among judges and legal writers to accept confessions, traditionally regarded as 'the queen of proofs', as sufficient proof of guilt. This concern was not restricted to those confessions that were adduced under torture, which, as we have seen, had their own special evidentiary problems. Judges and lawyers seemed just as unwilling to accept at face value those confessions that witches had allegedly made 'freely'. The greatest doubt arose when the confessions had a high diabolical content, i.e. when the witches had confessed to either a pact with the Devil or attendance at the sabbath. Reginald Scot had argued that confessions of this sort provided the least reliable evidence, while Johann Weyer attributed them to the mental weakness of the women who had made them. A more sophisticated interpretation of free confessions as the product of dreams or illusions, especially juvenile dreams, emerged during the investigation conducted by Salazar in the great Basque witch-hunt of 1609–11. By the late seventeenth century judges were willing to accept confessions to witchcraft (or any other crime) only if such confessions were in no way extorted, if they contained nothing that was impossible or improbable, and if the person confessing was neither melancholic nor suicidal.[33]

A second and even more frequent expression of judicial caution in the interpretation of evidence was based on the possibility that events attributed to supernatural agency may have had natural causes. This was particularly relevant to charges of *maleficium*, in which it was claimed that witches had inflicted harm by supernatural (i.e. diabolical) means. The sceptical response to such allegations, frequently adopted when lawyers defended witches against such charges, was that the act had natural causes, and that in order to convict a person of the crime, the possibility of natural causation had to be ruled out. Thus in Spain, in the wake of the hunts of 1526 and 1609–11, inquisitors were instructed to ask whether the maleficent deeds that witches confessed to, such as having killed children or destroyed crops, might have had natural causes.[34] Inquiries of this sort became more common in later seventeenth-century trials. In Italy inquisitors insisted that in cases of infanticide by witchcraft, the physicians who had treated the children should be examined to discover whether they could determine 'if the illness was or *could have been* natural'.[35] The burden of proof was on the prosecution; all that was necessary to secure acquittal was evidence that natural causation was *possible*. In a number of trials in Scotland in the late 1620s, advocates for the witches went to great lengths to prove that certain *maleficia* might not have been the product of supernatural intervention.[36] In securing the acquittal of a witch accused of murder by sorcery in 1662, Paul von Fuchs was content to show that the alleged supernatural cause of the disease which killed his victim could not be proved.[37]

Even if the court could be satisfied that harm was done by supernatural means, on the grounds that there was no possible natural explanation of a particular act of 'malefice', cautious lawyers and officials could demand concrete evidence that the witch had actually been responsible for its infliction. Proof of this sort was obviously difficult to obtain, precisely because the very nature of magic was that it could act on substances at a distance, without direct physical contact. The evidence for commission, therefore, could only be circumstantial, such as the pronouncement of a curse on the victim, close physical proximity between the witch and the victim before the misfortune occurred, or even the report of a glance on the victim that could be represented as the evil eye. To sceptical seventeenth-century legal minds such evidence was not terribly persuasive, and it led some lawyers to claim that the only way to establish the guilt of the witch and demonic agency in the infliction of *maleficium* was to prove that she had made a pact with the Devil.[38] Of course, that undertaking had its own evidentiary problems. In the absence of a confession, courts would have to rely on the discovery of the witches' marks, the content of their speech or the testimony of accomplices to prove that they had made a pact.[39] The difficulty of convicting persons on those grounds alone became apparent in colonial Massachusetts, where judges required evidence of the pact for conviction. Because of that requirement, more than 80 per cent of all witchcraft cases brought before the Massachusetts courts prior to the Salem witch-hunt of 1692 resulted in acquittals.[40]

The question of whether afflictions were caused by diabolical or natural means arose in a particularly telling fashion in those cases of witchcraft that involved demonic possession. The revelation that some demoniacs had faked their symptoms contributed to greater caution in the handling of all witchcraft accusations, while the highly publicized exorcisms of possessed nuns in French convents at Loudun, Louviers and Auxonne led theologians, especially Protestants, to entertain and express serious doubts about the extent of demonic interference in the world. The most direct effect, however, was that it made judges uncertain whether the behaviour of possessed persons was sufficient to convict the witches whom they named as the source of their bodily afflictions. In 1697 James Johnstone, the former Scottish secretary of state, shortly after the condemnation of seven witches for causing the possession of the young girl Christian Shaw, observed that 'the parliaments of France and other judicatories who are persuaded of the being of witches never try them now because of the experience they have had that it's impossible to distinguish possession from nature in disorder'.[41] There may have been other compelling reasons why the French did not try witches in 1697, but Johnstone's explanation at the very least forces us to recognize how the evidentiary problems associated with possession could lead to a state of judicial paralysis in witchcraft cases.

A further evidentiary problem related to demonic possession arose in connection with spectral evidence, which was the testimony by possessed persons that they could see the spectres or ghosts of the witches who were responsible for their afflictions. Evidence of this sort had been introduced into witchcraft trials at various times in the seventeenth century. In England it found a place in witchcraft trials as late as 1696, or possibly even 1712.[42] The most effective challenge to its judicial use came from those who claimed that the Devil might have used his powers of illusion to misrepresent innocent persons in spectral form, just as he might have misrepresented innocent

239

persons at the sabbath.[43] It was precisely this line of reasoning that caused the clergy in Massachusetts to abandon the trials that they had originally supported in 1692 and to conclude that some of the victims had been falsely accused. Similar reasoning led German jurists in the late seventeenth century to refuse the admission of spectral evidence unless it was confirmed by other proof.[44]

A final source of judicial caution in matters of evidence concerned the acceptance of the testimony of witnesses. In the trial of ordinary crimes, children, criminals, heretics and the defendant's relatives, servants and alleged accomplices were not allowed to testify against the accused. In many continental jurisdictions, however, these same persons were permitted to testify against witches, on the grounds that witchcraft was a *crimen exceptum* that would otherwise be incapable of legal proof.[45] In the seventeenth century children in particular played an increasingly prominent role as witnesses in witchcraft trials.[46] The policy of allowing them to testify, however, began to encounter opposition as the trials started to take a heavy toll. In 1584 Reginald Scot criticized continental judicial procedure precisely on these grounds.[47] About the same time the Parlement of Paris, denying the entreaties of Jean Bodin, refused to allow testimony from children and other witnesses in witchcraft cases.[48] The exclusion of testimony from unqualified witnesses had the demonstrated ability to bring witch-hunts to a swift end. In 1614 the earl of Dunfermline, the Scottish lord chancellor, successfully derailed a prosecution to which he was opposed by excluding all fourteen of the prosecution's witnesses against the accused, arguing that witchcraft was not a *crimen exceptum* and that therefore there was no reason to admit them.[49]

The disenchantment of the world

The judges, jurists and magistrates who were primarily responsible for reducing the number of witchcraft prosecutions and executions generally believed in the reality of witchcraft. These men often doubted that witches made face-to-face pacts with the Devil or gathered collectively to worship him, but they still thought that witches – defined as practitioners of harmful magic – did exist. Salazar, for example, came to doubt the testimony of the children he interrogated, but never once doubted that witches could perform harmful deeds through the power of the Devil.[50] The lawyers who served as members of the Parlement of Paris during the early seventeenth century may have doubted the guilt of people accused of causing demonic possession, but they nevertheless confirmed the sentences passed against some of the witches brought before them. The German lawyer Paul von Fuchs, defending his client against charges of witchcraft, stated his firm belief that those who actually did perform malevolent magical deeds should be put to death.[51] Friedrich Spee, in his passionate plea for the lives of the witches who were forced to confess in the 1620s, argued that witchcraft was a terrible crime.[52] In Scotland, the famous defender of witches and inveterate critic of those who prosecuted them, Sir George Mackenzie, began his exposition on the subject with an attack on Johann Weyer, 'the great patron of witchcraft', claiming that witches should suffer death not just for poisoning and murder, but also for 'enchanting and deluding the world', and that even charmers were guilty of at least apostasy and heresy.[53]

The jurist who came closest to denying the reality of witchcraft was Christian Thomasius, whose critique of the legal process helped to bring witch-hunting in Germany to an end. Thomasius, who is often identified as a figure of the early Enlightenment, is often celebrated for declaring unequivocally that 'witchcraft is only an imaginary crime'.[54] Indeed, Thomasius launched a devastating attack on the cumulative concept of witchcraft, denying the existence of the pact, the sabbath and the influence of evil spirits on corporeal bodies. He never denied the existence of the Devil, but his concept of demonic power was so limited that it rendered the crime of witchcraft impossible. For Thomasius the power of the Devil was exercised only in the spiritual sphere; it thus had only moral influence.[55] Nevertheless, Thomasius admitted that sorcerers could injure people by occult means and that those individuals should be put to death. When he denied the reality of the 'crime of magic', he was in fact referring exclusively to the pact with the Devil, since according to Prussian and Saxon law this was the essence of witchcraft.

It should be clear, therefore, that the decline of witch-hunting in the late seventeenth and early eighteenth centuries received its direction from men who were unwilling to abandon completely their belief in the reality of witchcraft. Nevertheless, a number of changes occurred in the intellectual world in the late seventeenth century that fostered doubt, if not disbelief, in the power of witches. These changes affected a broad cross-section of the educated elite in Europe, and there is evidence that they contributed to the reluctance of at least some magistrates and judges to prosecute witches.

The first and most basic of these changes – and at the same time the most difficult to trace – was a growing tendency in all fields of thought to reject dogma and inherited authority, to question everything, even the basic principles upon which one's world-view is based. This tendency can be seen most clearly in the work of René Descartes, who in his search for certain knowledge abandoned reliance upon books, rejected the 'authority' of the ancients as well as of the scholastics, and built his philosophical system upon 'clear and distinct ideas'. Descartes denied that he was a sceptic, at least in the traditional Greek sense of doubting even that one could possess knowledge, since he arrived at the certain knowledge of his own existence and also that of God and the material world. But the process by which Descartes arrived at that certainty – the wholesale rejection of dogma and the systematic expression of doubt – became closely identified with his philosophy, known as Cartesianism, which spread throughout Europe in the late seventeenth century.[56] That century, with all its religious intolerance and warfare, may strike us as a time of intense and uncompromising faith. In a certain sense it was. But within the literate elite and among university-educated men it was a period of profound and pervasive doubt. When witch beliefs became the target of such doubt, the prosecution of witches became increasingly difficult to justify.

A second change in the mental outlook of educated Europeans in the late seventeenth century was the growing conviction that the physical world functioned like a machine, in an orderly, regular fashion and in accordance with the immutable laws of nature. Often referred to as the mechanical philosophy, this view of nature had the potential for undermining the belief that the Devil could intervene in the operation of the natural world.[57] That potential was most apparent in the work of the English philosopher Thomas Hobbes, who subscribed to a mechanistic view of nature and denied the existence of all non-corporeal entities, including demons.[58] The extreme materialistic version of mechanical philosophy promoted by Hobbes also represented a serious threat to current religious belief, since it could lead one to deny the existence of God. As Henry More warned in his attack on the mechanical philosophy, 'No spirit, No God.'[59]

SOURCE BOOK

The mechanical philosophy did not necessarily lead to a denial of the reality of witchcraft. Some of the most famous scientists of the seventeenth century, while endorsing a mechanistic view of nature, still found a place for demons in the natural world.[60] The English scientist Robert Boyle, who discovered the laws of nature governing the elasticity of air, firmly believed in a world of demons and witches, and used the story of the witch of Mascon in France to show that the Devil could work through the processes of nature.[61] Another English member of England's Royal Society, Joseph Glanvill, considered stories regarding witchcraft and possession as empirical evidence that had scientific status.[62] Nevertheless, the spread of the belief in a universe governed by immutable laws of nature among the educated, especially towards the end of the seventeenth century, gradually helped to undermine witch beliefs and discourage witchcraft prosecutions during their final days.[63]

Closely related to the belief in a regular, orderly universe was the growing conviction among educated Europeans that there were natural explanations for mysterious or apparently supernatural phenomena. In the fifteenth and sixteenth centuries the natural world was rather narrowly defined. Phenomena that could not be readily explained in fairly simple 'naturalistic' terms were readily attributed to supernatural intervention of some sort, a mode of thought that scholasticism encouraged. The first challenge to this scholastic outlook came not from the mechanical philosophy but from its rival, the magical cosmology of the Neoplatonists. It might seem surprising that Neoplatonism, a philosophy in which magic held such an important place, could be credited with uprooting a scholastic world-view that was in many ways more realistic. But by emphasizing the fact that substances had natural sympathies and antipathies that explain their motion, Neoplatonists discouraged a reliance upon supernatural explanations of extraordinary events and encouraged an exploration of the natural world in a genuinely scientific manner.[64] Even when Renaissance magicians felt compelled to supplement natural with spiritual magic, they helped to undermine the scholastic cosmology, since in the Neo-platonic world the learned magician could compel spirits to respond to his commands and not therefore remain a victim of capricious demonic forces.

In the long run, Neoplatonism, with its belief in a magical world of various occult forces and its acceptance of the existence of demonic as well as angelic spirits within that 'natural' world, proved to be an insufficient foundation upon which to mount an assault on the entire set of learned witch beliefs. A Neoplatonist would have found it difficult to argue that witchcraft and magic were impossible crimes.[65] The other rival to scholasticism, the mechanical philosophy, according to which matter was completely inert and barren and incapable therefore of accommodating any type of magic, natural or spiritual, had much more potential to undermine the cumulative concept of witch-craft. Yet during its period of influence, Neoplatonism helped generations of educated men come to an understanding that extraordinary phenomena had natural causes. It is interesting to note that Reginald Scot, the most radical critic of witch beliefs and witchcraft prosecutions in the late sixteenth century, fully accepted the reality of natural magic.[66] In the late seventeenth century the sceptical physician John Webster, who argued that all diseases had natural causes, subscribed to the magical philosophy of the Neoplatonists.[67] **SOURCE BOOK**

At the same time as educated Europeans were adopting world-views that encouraged them to attribute extraordinary occurrences to natural causes, they were also beginning to discover that many of the unusual diseases and aberrant forms of behaviour that were customarily attributed to witchcraft could be explained without any reference to the supernatural. Beginning in the second half of the sixteenth century, a number of learned men, especially trained physicians, began to argue that many diseases which were allegedly caused by *maleficium* had natural causes; that individuals who made free confessions to witchcraft were either under the influence of drugs or suffering from some form of melancholy, depression or mental disorder; and that persons who were possessed by the Devil had in fact succumbed to some medical malady. The growth of such sentiment was by no means steady, and the medical commu-nity itself was divided on these questions.[68] It has even been suggested that doctors, finding themselves unable to explain a rash of epidemic diseases, actually *caused* the 'witch-craze.'[69] Nevertheless, doctors did eventually succeed in undermining many witch beliefs.[70] The English doctor Edward Jorden, in an attack upon popular witch beliefs and the activities of the cunning men, showed that many of the maladies allegedly inflicted by witches were some **SOURCE BOOK** form of what we would call hysteria, while John Cotta attributed some of the same symptoms to epilepsy.[71] In the late seventeenth century John Webster advanced similar arguments. It took some time before a large proportion of educated Europeans became convinced that all diseases had natural causes; even

Cotta and Jorden were not willing to rule out certain supernatural maladies.[72] And since there remained a number of undiagnosed illnesses, the temptation to attribute them to preternatural forces was strong. Even when doctors were able to identify the natural causes of physical and mental disease, the belief that witchcraft was involved did not evaporate, for it was perfectly plausible to argue that the Devil worked *through* nature, just as the natural theologians made the same claim with respect to God. By and large, however, the educated elite became convinced that the diseases witches were said to cause, the symptoms that demoniacs manifested, and the wild confessions that some witches made all had natural causes and took place without the cooperation of spirits or demons. Even when the actual causes of the disease or exceptional behaviour were not yet known, people were optimistic and confident that those causes would eventually be discovered. By 1756 a Hungarian doctor was able to claim that 'these days physicians leave supernatural matters for the clergy'.[73]

The mental changes we have been describing – the growth of Cartesian doubt, the spread of the mechanical philosophy, and the conviction that there were natural causes of supernatural phenomena – occurred primarily within the upper levels of European society. As far as we can tell, the witch beliefs of common folk changed very little in the late seventeenth and eighteenth centuries. These were simply reclassified by the elite as 'superstition' and treated with contempt, a striking illustration of what Peter Burke has referred to as the withdrawal of the elite from popular culture.[74] Of course, there was some inevitable percolation of learned ideas down to the lower levels of society, just as there had been in the fifteenth and sixteenth centuries when learned ideas of the demonic pact and the sabbath had been transmitted to the uneducated through the media of sermons, catechetical instruction and even witchcraft trials themselves. It is possible that the two groups of educated or semi-educated persons with whom villagers had contact – the clergy and physicians – were able to weaken some popular witch beliefs. The clergy may have been able to convince their congregations that God worked through the processes of nature and that demons were not constantly threatening people with physical harm, while the doctors may have achieved some success in helping their patients to realize that their diseases were not caused super-naturally, as the cunning men had always argued.[75] It would be rash, however, to assume that these two groups of educated professionals achieved a great deal of success in changing popular attitudes. Scepticism regarding the supernatural is much more difficult to instill in people than credulity, and most local clerics and physicians were probably not capable of mounting any sort of effective assault on popular credulity and superstition.[76]

The persistence of superstitious beliefs among the peasantry may have actually contributed, in a somewhat ironic way, to the triumph of scepticism among the elite. One of the tactics that sceptics like Nicolas de Malebranche, Laurent Bordelon and Cyrano de Bergerac used to win support for their views was to ridicule the beliefs of the silly rustic shepherds and other peasants who continued to claim that witches were active in their communities.[77] The same tactics of ridicule and satire, it should be noted, were later used by William Hogarth and Francisco Goya in the paintings and engravings they made on the theme of witchcraft and superstition. The effect of this ridicule was to encourage those who occupied the upper strata of society, even those who were not well-educated, to give at least lip-service to the new scepticism, so as to confirm their superiority over their social inferiors. Scepticism, in other words, became fashionable. During the late seventeenth and early eighteenth centuries the barriers that separated the aristocracy and the wealthy from those who occupied the lower strata of society began to widen throughout Europe. In order to put as much distance as possible between themselves and the common people, the landowners and members of the professions, especially those who were upwardly mobile, did all they could to prove that they shared nothing with their inferiors. Knowledge of the latest scientific discoveries may have been one way to establish one's social and intellectual credentials, but scepticism regarding witchcraft, since it involved the expression of open contempt for the lower orders, was far more effective. The decline of witch beliefs among the wealthy and educated elite may have had as much to do with social snobbery as with the development of new philosophical ideas.

Religious changes

We saw at length in Chapter 4 the ways in which the Protestant and Catholic reformations contributed to the intensification of witch-hunting in the sixteenth and early seventeenth centuries. At the same time, however, we saw how Protestantism could contribute to scepticism regarding witchcraft and a reluctance to prosecute witches. In the late seventeenth century this potential of Protestantism to bring witch-hunting to an end began to be realized.

The decline of religious enthusiasm

The most important religious factor in the decline of witchcraft prosecutions was the reduction in the level of religious zeal or 'enthusiasm'. While it would be misleading to claim that Europe as a whole became more religiously tolerant at this time,[78] there is plenty of evidence to indicate that religious zeal and enthusiasm were waning in Europe after 1650. The clearest illustration of this was the decline of religious warfare after the Peace of Westphalia in 1648. After that time international conflict had much more to do with national self-interest and dynastic aggrandizement than with religious ideology. At the national level the same tendency can be observed in the sources of domestic unrest: after 1650 there were few religious wars in Europe. In theology the reaction to enthusiasm and zeal is evident in the emphasis on the reasonableness of religion,[79] while the most general indication of the new climate was the mistrust of people who claimed to be directly inspired or directed by the Deity.[80] All of this suggests that the age of the Reformation, which had been marked by the intense expression of religious zeal, by religiously inspired warfare, by a preference for the emotional over the rational, and by the presence of ideologically inspired saints or religious fanatics, was gradually coming to an end and that a more secular, more rational age was dawning.

The decline of religious enthusiasm had a number of important effects on the process of witch-hunting. Among theologians, as we have seen, the desire to accommodate religion to philosophy and science led churchmen like the Latitudinarians in England to accept a world-view in which Satan had very little power. The growing distrust of individuals who claimed to have direct contact with the world of spirits made people sceptical of demoniacs, which in turn led them to question the reality of the witchcraft that was so often said to be its source. But the most important effect of the new religious outlook was a decline in the commitment of God-fearing Christians to purify the world by burning witches. It is true of course that not all witchcraft prosecutions required religious zeal or enthusiasm for their sustenance, especially those centring on the alleged practice of *maleficia*. But many witchcraft trials were inspired by the determination of magistrates, clergy and the entire community to purify the world by waging war on Satan's confederates. As this type of militancy and millenarianism declined, so too did the witchcraft prosecutions that they had encouraged.

The decline of religious zeal was also reflected in the new spirit of tolerance that began to characterize some Protestant and even a few Catholic communities in the second half of the seventeenth century.[81] There is a solid foundation for this religious tolerance in the Protestant tradition, most notably in the *Heidelberg Catechism*, even though intolerance was more characteristic of Protestant practice during the first century of the Reformation. This Protestant tolerance was manifested mainly towards members of other religious denominations, but the same sentiment could be extended to those suspected of witchcraft, since they were widely regarded either as heretics or at least as religious transgressors. It is probably no coincidence, therefore, that witch-hunting first began to decline in the Dutch Republic, a country known for its early religious tolerance.[82] When Balthasar Bekker pleaded eloquently in 1691 that Protestants should not pass judgement on other Christians, he was reflecting a Dutch tradition that reached back to Erasmus in the early sixteenth century.[83] It was also no coincidence that Poland, the Roman Catholic 'state without stakes', not only tolerated religious diversity but also did not prosecute many witches in the sixteenth century, although both religious persecution and witch-hunting did develop belatedly in that kingdom in the late seventeenth century.

Not unrelated to this new spirit of tolerance was the abandonment of the determination by both Protestant and Catholic public authorities in many states to use their secular power to create an ideal Christian community. This determination to establish a godly state, which was evident in many small German territories as well as in Scotland, Denmark and colonial Massachusetts, often involved the imposition of a strict moral discipline on the population. In response to clerical pressure, the legislatures of these states had passed laws against blasphemy, drunkenness, adultery and sodomy as well as witchcraft, and on the basis of these laws the courts had prosecuted these crimes with a vengeance. In some cases this effort to impose God's will on the people was inspired by millenarian fervour. In the late seventeenth and eighteenth centuries, however, the various states of Europe abandoned this type of moral crusading, a process indicative of the secularization of both law and politics. At the same time, the theory that the state was a sacred realm, with the king exercising power by divine right, lost much of its persuasive force. The end of witchcraft prosecutions can be linked, at least in general terms, with this change in thinking regarding the nature and purpose of the state.[84]

The sovereignty of God

In similar fashion the Protestant emphasis on the sovereignty of God, which underlay the prosecution of those magicians and witches who were believed to have challenged that sovereignty, could just as easily be invoked to deprive the Devil of much of his alleged worldly power. This line of thought finds its clearest expression in the 'providential' theological tradition that flourished at Tübingen in the sixteenth and seventeenth centuries. Contrary to the position taken in the *Malleus maleficarum*, the theologians at Tübingen attributed all misfortune to the work of a providential God, denying that any intermediate demonic forces played a role in the process. This tradition not only contributed to the moderation and ultimately the decline of witch-hunting in the duchy of Württemberg, but it also made inroads in Denmark, where pastors trained in the Tübingen tradition were largely responsible for the decline of witch-hunting that began there as early as 1625.[85] One finds a similar theme in German Pietism, a religious movement originating in the late seventeenth century which eliminated the belief in a personal Devil and which therefore was able to bring faith and reason into harmony. Pietism has been associated with the decline of learned witch beliefs in Württemberg, Saxony and also in Hungary.[86] In the nineteenth century it apparently contributed to the decline of popular as well as learned witch beliefs in various parts of Germany.[87]

Biblical scholarship

The final religious contribution to the decline of witch-hunting was the effort undertaken by a number of Protestants to use the Bible to discredit the entire process. In the sixteenth century the Protestant sceptics Johann Weyer and Reginald Scot had both used the Bible to show that the 'witches' condemned in the Hebrew Bible were hardly the same type of malefactors as the witches being condemned in their own day.[88] The political theorist Robert Filmer developed the same argument in his comparison of an English and a Hebrew witch in the 1650s.[89] In a similar vein, the Alsatian jurist Andreas Sandherr argued before a court at Colmar in 1650 that witch beliefs had no biblical foundation.[90]

In the late seventeenth century some Protestant biblical scholars went even further by using Scripture to deny the effectiveness of demonic power in the world. The best example of this effort was a massive treatise by the Dutch Calvinist minister Balthasar Bekker, *De betoverde weereld* [The Enchanted World], which was published in four parts in the Netherlands in 1691 and 1693 and translated into English, German and French shortly thereafter. It would be hard to identify a more comprehensive assault upon the cumulative concept of witchcraft before the end of the great witch-hunt. In 1701 the German jurist Felix Brähm hailed the book as the chief assailant of the superstition of witchcraft.[91] Bekker denied the pact with the Devil, the sabbath, metamorphosis, flight, conception by a demon, demonic possession and the very practice of harmful magic itself. At the basis of this denial lay a powerful critique of contemporary demonology. For Bekker the Devil was merely a symbol of evil and was incapable of exercising power over the physical world, even the power of illusion that figured so prominently in the work of Weyer.[92] Once the Devil was reduced to this status, the possibility that a human being could commit the crime of witchcraft vanished. Indeed, Bekker boldly suggested that when accusations of witchcraft are forthcoming, the state should prosecute the accusers, not the accused, a course of action that courts had not yet begun to take.[93]

Bekker's work is usually cited as evidence of the way Cartesian philosophy undermined the cumulative concept of witchcraft. It is certainly true that Bekker was a Cartesian, a rationalist who endorsed the mechanical philosophy and who accepted Descartes's rigid distinction between matter and spirit. But Bekker was first and foremost a biblical scholar in the Erasmian tradition, who argued for a proper historically contextualized interpretation of those scriptural passages that referred to witches and demons. Bekker declared that both Scripture and reason prove that 'the empire of the Devil is but a chimera and that he has neither such a power nor such an administration as is ordinarily ascribed to him', but the book places far more emphasis on Scripture than Cartesian rationalism in challenging contemporary witch beliefs.[94]

However cogent Bekker's treatise was, there are two reasons to question its effectiveness in bringing about the end of witch-hunting. First, it is difficult to measure any real impact the book might have had on the intensity of prosecutions. The Dutch Republic had stopped trying witches nearly a century before Bekker wrote, and even in the neighbouring German territories witch-hunting had almost come to an end.[95] Second, Bekker's attack on witch beliefs did not find much support within clerical and theological circles.

Bekker had directed his work against two of the most respected Calvinist theologians in the Netherlands in the seventeenth century, Johannes Coccejus and Gisbertus Voetius. The leaders of the Reformed Church expelled him from his ministry for his faulty exegesis of the Bible regarding the power of the Devil, and the large number of Dutch polemicists who attacked his book anchored their position in Calvinist theological orthodoxy.[96] If the book had any impact, it simply reinforced a tolerant Erasmian Protestant tradition that had been developing for a number of years.

Social and economic developments

In this discussion of the reasons for the decline of witch-hunting we have focused almost exclusively on the work of those persons who controlled the judicial machinery and the writers who might have influenced them. But what about those who occupied the lower levels of society, who were primarily responsible for bringing the initial accusations of *maleficium* against their neighbours and for testifying against them in court? Without their support witch-hunting would not have been successful, at least not over a long period of time. Could these common folk have been at least partially responsible for the decline of witch-hunting? Did the number of trials decrease because fewer people were attributing their misfortunes to the magical powers of their neighbours? If that were the case, the lower number of accusations might very well be explained by social, economic and demographic change.

There is little doubt that the dramatic changes in the fabric of European social life during the period 1550–1650 contributed to the great European witch-hunt. Over-population, an unprecedented rise in prices, a decline in real wages among the poor, chronic famine and dearth, especially during years of climatic severity, periodic outbreaks of the plague, extraordinarily high levels of infant mortality, migration of the poor from the countryside to the town, pestilence among people and beasts, and the social dislocations that resulted from widespread domestic and international warfare often lay at the root of those personal conflicts that found expression in witchcraft accusations.[97] The question for our purposes is whether there was a sufficient improvement in, or reversal of, these adverse economic and social conditions to bring about a reduction in the number of charges brought before the courts.

It is true that the demographic explosion of the sixteenth and seventeenth centuries came to an end around 1660, and inflation, which had been fuelled primarily by demographic growth, also showed signs of levelling off. Real wages registered some improvement, and the effects of warfare on the civilian population were greatly reduced. But whether these improvements made daily village life more secure and personal tensions in small communities less acute is certainly problematic; one could argue that significant changes in the quality of rural life did not take place in most European countries until the end of the eighteenth century or the beginning of the nineteenth. The same might be said of the quality of medical care in those communities; the country physician did not replace the wise woman in rural areas until long after the witch trials were over. The most that we can say with any degree of certainty is that communal provision for the poor became more systematic and effective in most European countries after 1660, and that may very well have eliminated some of the social tension between the dependent members of the community and their more well-off neighbours.[98]

In the final analysis it remains impossible to determine to what extent the social and economic improvements and the changes in culture that did take place after 1660 helped to reduce the number of formal accusations made by villagers and townspeople. It is difficult enough to identify the social and economic tensions that lay behind the specific quarrels leading to witchcraft accusations, but at least we have some tangible evidence, in the form of depositions taken from witnesses, to work with. But when communities did *not* bring charges of witchcraft against their neighbours, at least not as frequently as they had in the past, they rarely left written evidence regarding the reasons for their inaction. The most that the legal record tells us is the suggestive report from the Scottish Justiciary Court in 1671 that two witches were set free because 'there was no one to insist' (i.e. for lack of a formal accuser).[99] We can only speculate, therefore, whether the decline in formal accusations reflects a real reduction in the number and gravity of personal conflicts at the village level or the more pragmatic calculation that judicial authorities would not be receptive to complaints brought before them.

There are of course other possibilities. One is that popular witch beliefs actually changed, following the same pattern that occurred first among the more highly educated members of society. One possible source of such a transformation would have been the sermons of sceptical and tolerant ministers, such as those delivered by Danish pastors trained in the providential tradition in the middle of the seventeenth century or the more admonitory one given in the next century by Joseph Juxon, the vicar of Twyford, after a local witch-swimming.[100] Sermons served as one of the few vehicles for contact and interaction between popular and learned culture during this period. But there is little evidence that popular beliefs actually changed in response to such religious instruction, either before or after decriminalization, and there is much to suggest that they continued in their earlier form. Indeed, the frequency with which local communities took illegal counteraction against suspected witches suggests strongly that popular witch beliefs persisted for many generations after the trials had stopped. As one scholar has observed, witchcraft 'died hard in the public mind – if it died at all'.[101]

Another possibility is that people stopped bringing charges against witches because the prosecutions themselves became too costly. We know from isolated examples that the confinement and trial of witches could be terribly expensive, even when the assets of the accused were used to defray the cost of incarceration and transportation. These financial burdens arising from the prosecution of witches fell on the entire community. In order to avoid further expenses, a number of accused witches were actually released from gaol, and their release might easily have made villagers more reluctant to support further prosecutions.[102] It is unlikely, however, that the larger patterns of decline can be attributed to such financial considerations. It is more likely that residents of villages and small towns would have abandoned witch-hunting after experiencing the fear that gripped the entire community during the panics. The realization that no one was safe from the cycle of accusations and implications, coupled with the recognition that innocent people were being executed, was just as capable of affecting people in the lower levels of society as the members of the local ruling elite.

In any event, we still do not have any hard evidence showing that people of low social standing became reluctant to accuse and prosecute witches. Faced with a dearth of evidence from popular sources, we can only return to the sources we do have, which are statistics showing a reduction in the number of trials and executions, the records of those trials that ended in acquittals, and the statements of those individuals who criticized the process of witch-hunting. These sources suggest that the main reason for the decline in prosecutions was the increasing reluctance of lay and clerical judicial authorities to convict persons of witchcraft, an attitude that was only occasionally and belatedly reinforced by a growing scepticism regarding the possibility of the crime.

Decriminalization

The long and somewhat erratic decline of witch-hunting led finally to the complete end of prosecutions and the determination that witchcraft was no longer a crime. This process of decriminalization took one of two forms. The first, which is formal or *de jure* decriminalization, involved the explicit repeal of the laws upon which prosecutions were based. *De jure* decriminalization, as we shall see, occurred in very few jurisdictions prior to the end of the eighteenth century, and in those where it did, the repeal of the laws was often incomplete, leaving some activities encompassed within the definition of witchcraft as prohibited. The second form, *de facto* decriminalization, was realized when judicial authorities simply stopped prosecuting and executing witches, either because they had concluded that the crime was incapable of legal proof or because they denied the reality of the crime. Although we can often discover the dates of the last witchcraft trials and executions in various jurisdictions, it is more difficult to identify the time when the members of a ruling and administrative elite came to the conclusion that the crime should no longer be prosecuted, especially since there may have been disagreement among the members of those elites on that very question.

Since the decline and end of witchcraft prosecutions occurred everywhere in Europe, historians often assume that *de jure* decriminalization was a universal phenomenon, with witchcraft laws falling like dominoes throughout Europe. The legislative record, however, does not support this assumption. Before the dawn of the nineteenth century, witchcraft laws were repealed or significantly modified in only seven kingdoms: France in 1682, Prussia in 1714, Great Britain in 1736, the Habsburg Monarchy in 1766, Russia in 1770, Poland in 1776 and Sweden in 1779. Only the last two kingdoms legislated a complete ban on witchcraft trials. The Swedish National Code of 1779 certainly had that effect, since it simply omitted the clause regarding witchcraft in the old Code of 1734, thus rendering prosecutions impossible.[103] The Polish statute, passed by the diet a year after a witch-hunt in the village of Doruchów had claimed the lives of six women, forbade the prosecution of witches by all tribunals, including the court of the small town of Grabów that had conducted the trials. The Polish statute also forbade the use of torture in all criminal cases.[104]

The earlier British statute of 1736 also bears most of the signs of a blanket prohibition of witchcraft prosecutions, since it repealed the English statute of 1604 and its Scottish counterpart of 1563. But by making it an offence to 'pretend to exercise or use any kind of witchcraft, sorcery, enchantment or conjuration or undertake to tell fortunes' on the pain of imprisonment for one year, Parliament failed to decriminalize all those activities that once marched under the broad banner of witchcraft.[105] Prosecutions for conjuration under the statute of 1736 were rare, but they did take place, and the judges who charged grand juries continued to remind them that it was 'very penal' to pretend to be a witch.[106] This provision of the new witchcraft law was not repealed until 1951.[107]

The French royal edict of 1682 achieved even less than the British law of 1736. It is true that the edict, just like the later British statute, referred to magic as 'pretended', possibly to offer protection against imposters. But as far as witchcraft prosecutions were concerned, the law was far more qualified than the British statute. Designed in part to prevent a recurrence of a recent court scandal, it left intact the death penalty for forms of magic that were overtly sacrilegious, and it permitted some of the prosecutions of *maleficium* that continued in France during the following decade. Witchcraft in France was not fully decriminalized until 1791 at the time of the French Revolution. The Habsburg imperial law of 1766 also failed to eliminate all witchcraft prosecutions. While eliminating prosecutions in cases arising from fraud and mental illness, it nonetheless ordered the banishment of those who made pacts with the Devil and even allowed the possibility of the death penalty in cases of *maleficium* performed with the assistance of the Devil.[108]

Russian efforts to decriminalize witchcraft bore a faint resemblance to the Habsburg legislation of 1766. As early as 1731, during the reign of Empress Anna, the Russian Senate had passed a law classifying witchcraft as fraud, but conviction still carried the death penalty. Catherine II's legislation of 1770 reduced the penalty for this special type of fraud to non-capital punishment, but it left open the possibility that the parties involved could be prosecuted for popular superstition. Ten years later the empress encouraged the courts to try cases of alleged witchcraft as fraud, leaving those who made accusations, especially women who claimed to be possessed, to be tried in special courts of conscience for popular superstition. Those same courts of conscience dealt with the criminally insane.[109]

The least comprehensive of these laws was the Prussian edict of 1714, issued by King Frederick William I less than two years after his accession to the throne. This mandate was designed entirely to reform the criminal procedures used in witchcraft trials, so that innocent persons would no longer be tortured, forced to confess, or executed. Its concern with legal procedure reflects the influence of Thomasius, the chancellor at the 'liberal' University of Halle, and indirectly that of Spee, upon whom Thomasius relied heavily in his work. The edict, which was to be proclaimed in the local courts, demanded that all judicial decisions to torture or execute witches be submitted to the king for confirmation before being implemented. This provision, which echoed French policy and anticipated that of the Habsburg Monarchy, provides further evidence of the role played by central authorities in restricting witchcraft prosecutions. The law did not, however, ban witchcraft trials or even executions, although it did require the removal of all the stakes from the public places where witches had been burned. In 1721 a Prussian law abolished the death penalty in all witchcraft trials.[110] Decriminalization came only in 1776.

In all the other countries of Europe *de jure* decriminalization did not take place until after 1800, and in some jurisdictions it never occurred at all. In the duchy of Württemberg, the Provincial Code which had authorized the prosecution of witchcraft was not changed until well into the nineteenth century. The same was true in Saxony, where the code drafted by Benedikt Carpzov in 1635 was not rewritten, with the provisions against witchcraft now omitted, until the period of the Napoleonic wars. Likewise the Bavarian edict of 1611, renewed in 1665 and 1746, remained at least nominally in force until the criminal reforms of 1813.[111] This German pattern of late repeal, long after the *de facto* end of prosecutions, was also followed in Denmark, where the decline of witch-hunting had begun as early as 1625 and where the last legal execution had taken place in 1693. In that kingdom an article authorizing the execution of witches by burning, which had been incorporated into the Danish Code of 1683, was not repealed until 1866.[112]

The formal decriminalization of witchcraft had little bearing on the broader process of decline that we have been discussing. The blanket repeals that took place in Great Britain and Sweden had no effect whatsoever on witchcraft prosecutions in those countries because the last trial had long preceded the legislation effecting the change. The same could be said of the large number of states that repealed their laws only in the nineteenth century. Even in those countries that passed witchcraft statutes before the end of the trials, the new laws had only a limited effect on the volume of prosecutions. The first of these laws, the French edict of 1682, probably prevented prosecutions only in the few outlying regions of the country where trials were still taking place. The same could be said of Frederick William I's edict of 1714, since prosecutions in Prussia had slackened considerably since the 1690s. Only Maria Theresa's imperial law of 1766 seems to have led to a demonstrable curtailment in the number of trials and executions. Even then, however, witch-hunting was taking place only in certain parts of the Habsburg Monarchy, mainly in Hungary. In Austria itself trials had already ended, with the last execution occurring in 1750.[113]

The more common pattern of decriminalization was the *de facto* cessation of trials, without any accompanying edict. This, as we have seen, was achieved at different times in various territories, but in almost all cases the very last trials occurred long after the decline in prosecutions had begun. Table 8.1, which lists both the last execution and the last trial in those territories for which data are available, gives a clear indication of how long witch-hunting continued, at least in some attenuated form.

There have traditionally been two contenders for the dubious distinction of being the last execution for witchcraft in Europe: the burning of Anna Göldi for bewitching her master's child in the Swiss canton of Glarus in 1782 and the execution of two women with inflamed eyes for using magic to harm their neighbours' cattle in the Polish town of Poznan in 1793. As we have seen at length in this chapter, the decline and end of witch-hunting involved a deliberate effort by higher judicial authorities, very often the judges who staffed the central institutions of the state, to supervise and control the trial of witches by local courts. These two incidents illustrate the difficulty of such control. The trial in Glarus, which appears to have resulted in the last legal execution, appropriately occurred in a small canton in which anything even remotely resembling central state power was absent, where witchcraft had not been decriminalized, and where the prohibition of torture lay more than a half-century in the future. Witch-hunting at Glarus and in most of eastern Switzerland remained, even in the late eighteenth century, a strictly local operation.[114]

The execution at Poznan offers us a somewhat different commentary on the relationship between central and local control. Most Polish witchcraft trials in the seventeenth century were conducted by municipal authorities, often in the villages where the charges originated. In 1768 the highest court of the kingdom, the Assessory Court, had prohibited the small towns from conducting this type of trial. The order was not always observed, however, perhaps as much out of ignorance as a spirit of municipal independence. After the executions at Doruchów in 1775, the Polish legislative assembly, the *sejm*, took action and forbade all witchcraft prosecutions. This exercise of central authority seems to have been effective, for after that date witch trials

Table 8.1 Last executions and last trials for witchcraft.

Country or region	Last execution	Last trial
Parlement of Paris	1625	1693
Alsace	1683	1683
Franche-Comté	1661	1667
Cambrésis	1679	1783
Dutch Republic*	1609	1659
Luxembourg	1685	1685
Switzerland	1782	1782
Geneva	1652	1681
England	1685	1717
County of Essex	1645	1675
Scotland	1706	1727
Ireland	1711	1711
New England	1692	1697
Denmark	1693	1762
Sweden	1710	1779
Finland	1691	1699
Württemberg	1749	1805
Würzburg	1749	1749
Westphalia	1728	1732
Kempten	1775	1775
Augsburg	1728	1738
Bavaria	1756	1792
Nuremberg	1660	1725
Prussia	1767	1767
Austria	1750	1775
Hungary	1756	1777
Slovenia	1720	1746
Poland	1775	1776
Spain	1781	1820
Portugal	1626	1802
Palermo	1724	1788

* Does not include executions in the region of Limburg, which did not belong to the Republic. Executions there continued into the 1630s. Source: Gijswijt-Hofstra, 'Witchcraft in the Northern Netherlands', 77–8.

disappeared from the legal record. In 1793, however, Poland was partitioned for the second time, leaving the country temporarily without any central government. A judge in the small town of Poznan, situated in the province of Greater Poland, which was about to pass over to Prussian control, immediately took advantage of this hiatus in government and executed the two women. The legality of the trial remains a subject of controversy: it was undertaken by a member of a properly constituted municipal government but without the sanction of higher state authorities. The royal commission that was overseeing the transfer of power from Poland to Prussia tried to prevent the execution, but it acted too late.[115] We can be fairly certain that if either a Polish or a Prussian royal government had been fully constituted at the time, the trial would not have even taken place. Witch-hunting, even in its last gasp, remained a local affair which central governments tried to control, regulate or eliminate, but not always with complete success.

One of the effects of the decline of witchcraft and its ultimate decriminalization was the breakdown of the cumulative concept of witchcraft into its components. As discussed in Chapter 2, witchcraft as defined in the early modern period was a composite crime. In its most elaborate form it combined maleficent magic with that of diabolism, although judicial authorities in various jurisdictions placed different degree of emphasis on one component or the other. More specifically the crime of witchcraft comprehended a variety of activities that could be prosecuted separately as crimes in the ecclesiastical or secular courts. Witchcraft could denote heresy, apostasy, blasphemy, maiming, murder, poisoning, theft, destruction of crops, killing of livestock, arson, sodomy, fornication, adultery, infanticide, conspiracy or treason. In 1584 the English sceptic Reginald Scot identified fifteen different crimes attributed to witchcraft.[116] In the period of decline, as the concept of witchcraft was breaking down into its components, persons accused of witchcraft were often prosecuted for more specific offences encompassed in the broad definition of the crime. The most common of these was poisoning, which could be interpreted in natural or supernatural terms.[117] Less frequent were prosecutions for making pacts with the Devil, such as those in Sweden between 1680 and 1789; trials for sacrilege in late seventeenth- and eighteenth-century France; and trials for magic in German territories, especially Württemberg and Finland when prosecutions for witchcraft began to wane.[118] Defining the crime of witchcraft in the early modern period has always a matter of controversy. As the trials came to an end, its definition became a matter of little practical concern, leaving the task to modern historians.

Notes

1. Soman, 'Witch Lynching at Juniville', 8–15; idem, 'Parlement of Paris', 31–44.
2. Monter, *Frontiers of Heresy*, 268–9; Knutsen, *Servants of Satan*, 101–3.
3. Henningsen, *Witches' Advocate*, 375.
4. Monter, *Frontiers of Heresy*, 275.
5. Tedeschi, 'Inquisitorial Law and the Witch', 83–118.
6. Scaglia's document was also published by itself in 1657. On the publication and circulation of this work see Ginzburg, *Night Battles*, 200, n. 40; J. Tedeschi, *The Prosecution of Heresy* (Binghamton, 1991): 209. On Carena's treatise, *Tractatus de officio sanctissimae Inquisitionis,* which was first published in 1636, see Martin, *Witchcraft and the Inquisition in Venice*, 71–3.
7. Lea, *Materials*, II: 952–3.
8. In Swabian Austria, the decline of prosecutions can be attributed to the regulation of local witch-hunting by the visitation of commissioners appointed by the central government. See Dillinger, *Evil People*, 166–84.

9. Schormann, *Hexenprozesse in Nordwestdeutschland*, 9–44, 158. On the consultations with the law faculties of the universities of Rostock and Greifswald see Lorenz, *Aktenversendung und Hexenprozess*.

10. Behringer, *Witchcraft Persecutions in Bavaria*, 326–7.

11. Schormann, *Hexenprozesse in Nordwestdeutschland*, 20–1.

12. Ibid., 24, 57.

13. Torture was also used in witchcraft cases in countries like Sweden and Hungary where Roman law had little or no influence. In Sweden its use was forbidden in legal proceedings, but it was allowed in witchcraft cases, sometimes by royal decree. See Ankarloo, 'Sweden', 290.

14. A. Tanner, *Theologia scholastica* (Ingolstadt, 1626/7), III, 'Disputatio VI'; P. Laymann, *Processus iuridicus contra sagas et veneficos* (Cologne, 1629); H. P. Kneubühler, *Überwindung von Hexenwahn und Hexenprozess* (Diessenhofen, 1977); Behringer, *Witchcraft Persecutions in Bavaria*, 322–4.

15. J. Meyfart, *Christliche Erinnerung an gewaltige Regenten und gewissenhaffte Prädicanten wie das abscheuliche Laster der Hexerey mit Ernst auszurotten* (Schleusingen, 1635); J. Grevius, *Doma Tribunal Reformatum* (Hamburg, 1624).

16. A. Nicolas, *Si la torture est un moyen seur à verifier les crimes secret: dissertation moral et juridique* (Amsterdam, 1681), esp. 105. Nicolas attacked Remy, Bodin and Del Rio for defending the procedure.

17. C. Thomasius, *De tortura ex foris Christianorum proscribenda* (1705); idem, *De origine ac progressu processus Inquisitorii contra sagas* (1712); idem, *Über die Hexenprozesse*, ed. R. Lieberwirth (Weimar, 1967).

18. For translated excerpts from *De tortura* see Levack, *Witchcraft Sourcebook*, 184–7.

19. On the importance of the humanitarian argument in the debate over torture in the late eighteenth century see E. Peters, *Torture* (Oxford, 1985): chapter 3.

20. J. G. Goedelmann, *De magis, veneficis et lamiis*, III, chapter 1, n.19, had advanced this idea earlier in his attack on Bodin.

21. *Biblioteca sive acta et scripta magica*, ed. E. D. Hauber (Lemgo, 1738), II: 27–55.

22. Peters, *Torture*; Lea, *Materials*, 649.

23. Tanner, *Theologica scholastica*.

24. Goedelmann, *De magis, veneficis et lamiis*, I, chapter 5, 21–30.

25. J. Cotta, *The Trial of Witch-Craft* (London, 1616): 111. The medical and philosophical faculties of the Leiden also rejected the procedure. Gijswijt-Hofstra, 'Six Centuries of Witchcraft in the Netherlands', 20.

26. James VI, *Daemonologie*, 81. Unsworth, 'Witchcraft Beliefs and Criminal Procedure in Early Modern England', in *Legal Record and Historical Reality*, ed. T. G. Watkin (London, 1989): 96–8.

27. Soman, 'Witch Lynching at Juniville', 11–12; idem, 'Decriminalizing Witchcraft', 6.

28. I. Kristóf, '"Wise Women", Sinners and the Poor: The Social Background of Witch-Hunting in a 16th–18th Century Calvinist City of Eastern Hungary', *Acta Ethnographica* 37 (1991/2): 99–100.

29. Lea, *Materials*, II: 892–3.

30. See, for example, F. Brähm, *Disputatio inaug. de fallacibus indiciis magiae* (Halle, 1709): 47.

31. Peters, *Torture*, 90–1. Other dates of abolition are: Brunswick (1770), Saxony (1770), Denmark (1770), Sweden (1782), Tuscany (1786), France (1788), Lombardy (1789), the Netherlands (1798), Bavaria (1806), Spain (1808), Norway (1819), Portugal (1826), Greece (1827), Gotha (1828) Zurich (1831), Freiburg (1848) and Basel (1850).

32. In 1692 Hugh Hare, a justice of the peace, in his charge to the jury at the Surrey quarter sessions, warned that although witchcraft was a sin and a crime punishable by death, 'it is so hard a matter to have full proof brought of it, that no jury can be too cautious and tender in a prosecution of this nature'. *Surrey Archaeological Collections* 12 (1895): 128–9, cited in Kittredge, *Witchcraft in Old and New England*, 596. For a similar charge to the grand jury in the same year from the Earl of Warrington see M. Gaskill, *Crime and Mentalities in Early Modern England* (Cambridge, 2000): 94.

33. Sir G. Mackenzie, *The Laws and Customes of Scotland in Matters Criminal* (Edinburgh, 1678): 86–7. See also the statement of William Forbes, *The Institutes of the Law of Scotland* (Edinburgh, 1730): 371.

34. Henningsen, *Witches' Advocate*, 371.

35. Ginzburg, *The Night Battles*, 126.

36. Larner, *Enemies of God*, 178.

37. Hauber, *Biblioteca sive acta et scripta magica*, I, 617–21.

38. M. Dalton, *The Country Justice* (London, 1630); Fox, *Science and Justice*, 64–5.

39. See, for example, R. Bernard, *A Guide to Grand Jury Men . . . in Cases of Witchcraft* (London, 1630): 212–21.

40. Godbeer, *The Devil's Dominion*, Chapter 5.

41. *The Manuscripts of the Duke of Roxburghe* (Historical Manuscripts Commission, Fourteenth Report, Appendix III, London, 1894): 132; on Paisley see *History of the Witches of Renfrewshire*, ed. J. Millar (Paisley, 1809).

42. For a list of English cases in which spectral evidence was introduced see Kittredge, *Witchcraft in Old and New England*, 363–4.

43. For the denial of the latter claim by demonologists see Lea, *Materials*, II: 886.

44. Andreas Becker, *Disputatio juridica de jure spectorum* (Halle, 1700).

45. See, for example, Kramer and Sprenger, *Malleus maleficarum*, 209; Bodin, *De la Démonomanie des sorciers*, lib. 4, cap 2; Carpzov, *Practica nova rerum criminalium*, 130.

46. H. Sebald, *Witch-Children* (Amherst, NY, 1995): 104–5.

47. Scot, *Discoverie*, 11.

48. Soman, 'Parlement of Paris', 36–7. The Parlement never accepted the definition of witchcraft as a *crimen exceptum*.

49. Trial of Geillis Johnstone, National Archives of Scotland, JC 1/38.

50. *The Salazar Papers*, ed. G. Henningsen (Leiden, 2004).

51. Hauber, *Biblioteca sive acta et scripta magica*, I, 627–8.

52. F. Spee, *Cautio Criminalis, or a Book on Witch Trials*, tr. M. Hellyer (Charlottesville, 2003): 16–17.

53. Mackenzie, *The Laws and Customes of Scotland*, 81–4. As late as 1730 the Scottish judge William Forbes wrote that, 'Nothing seems plainer to me than that there may be, and have been witches, and that perhaps such are now actually existing'. Forbes, *Institutes*, 32.

54. C. Thomasius, *Dissertatio de crimine magiae* (1701); *Über die Folter*, tr. and ed. R. Lieberwirth (Weimar, 1960).

55. See M. Pott, 'Aufklärung und Hexenglaube: Philosophische Ansätze zur Überwindung der Teufelspakttheorie in der deutsche Frühaufklärung', in *Das Ende der Hexenverfolgung*, ed. S. Lorenz and D. R. Bauer (Stuttgart, 1995): 183–202.

56. See R. H. Popkin, *The History of Scepticism from Erasmus to Descartes* (Assen, 1960): 174–216, esp. 212–13.

57. Easlea, *Witch Hunting*, esp. 196–252.

58. T. Hobbes, *Leviathan* (London, 1651): 209–10, 352–66.

59. H. More, *An Antidote against Atheism* (London, 1655): 278. For More, the existence of witchcraft and other forms of demonic activity provided proof for the

existence of spirits and hence also of God. See A. R. Hall, *Henry More: Magic, Religion and Experiment* (Oxford, 1990): 138–9. See also R. Baxter, *The Certainty of the Worlds of Spirits* (London, 1691).

60. For a statement of the current scholarly consensus that seventeenth-century science, including the mechanical philosophy to which many natural philosophers subscribed, did not contribute in any significant degree to the rejection of witch beliefs, much less the end of the trials, see P. Elmer, 'Science and Witchcraft', in *The Oxford Handbook of Witchcraft in Early Modern Europe and Colonial America*, ed. Brian P. Levack (Oxford, 2013): 548–60.

61. Boyle was responsible for the translation of the French account of this story into English. On Boyle and witchcraft see Clark, *Thinking with Demons*, 308.

62. Glanvill, *Saducismus Triumphatus*.

63. A possible link between Cartesian ideas and a reluctance to prosecute witches comes from Geneva, where Robert Chouet, a magistrate who adopted Cartesiasn ideas and dabbled in scientific experiments, rejected witchcraft beliefs, and discouraged prosecutions. Monter, *Witchcraft in France and Switzerland*, 38–9, 62.

64. Trevor-Roper, 'Witch-Craze', 181.

65. On the difficulty of distinguishing between natural and demonic magic see S. Clark, 'The Scientific Status of Demonology', in *Occult and Scientific Mentalities in the Renaissance*, ed. B. Vickers (Cambridge, 1984): 351–74.

66. Easlea, *Witch Hunting*, 23. Weyer also praised natural magic, although he was hostile to diabolical magic. See L. Thorndike, *A History of Magic and Experimental Science* (New York, 1944), VI: 516.

67. J. Webster, *The Displaying of Supposed Witchcraft* (London, 1677).

68. On early medical opinion see Denis, *Toul*, 13–15.

69. See L. Estes, 'The Medical Origins of the European Witch Craze: A Hypothesis', *Journal of Social History* 17 (1984): 270–84.

70. For a list of physicians critical of witch-beliefs see J. Nemec, *Witchcraft and Medicine, 1484–1793* (Washington, 1974): 4–5.

71. MacDonald, *Mystical Bedlam*, 198–9. See also *Witchcraft and Hysteria in Elizabethan London*, ed. M. MacDonald (London, 1990).

72. For the attempt of Cardinal Barberini to ascertain whether a disease had natural or supernatural causes see Ginzburg, *Night Battles*, 125–6.

73. Quoted in Evans, *Habsburg Monarchy*, 405.

74. P. Burke, *Popular Culture in Early Modern Europe* (London, 1978): 270–81.

75. Delumeau, *Catholicism*, 174, argues that the fear of the Devil diminished as the two Reformations filtered down to the parish level in the late seventeenth century.

76. For the success of one cleric, using the tactics of indifference rather than persuasion, see J. Boswell, *Journal of a Tour to the Hebrides*, ed. R. W. Chapman (Oxford, 1970): 266.

77. Monter, *European Witchcraft*, 113–26; L. Bordelon, *L'Histoire des imaginations extravangantes de Monsieur Oufle* (Paris, 1710).

78. See Drummond and Bulloch, *Scottish Church*, chapter 1.

79. G. Cragg, *From Puritanism to the Age of Reason* (Cambridge, 1960).

80. See M. Heyd, 'The Reaction to Enthusiasm in the Seventeenth Century: Towards an Integrative Approach', *Journal of Modern History* 53 (1981): 258–80.

81. For a full discussion of the relationship between religious pluralism and the end of the witch-hunts see Waite, *Heresy, Magic and Witchcraft*, chapter 6.

82. H. de Waardt, 'Rechtssicherheit nach dem Zusammenbruch der zentralen Gewalt. Rechtspflege, Obrigkeit, Toleranz und witschaftliche Verhältnisse in Holland', in *Das Ende der Hexenverfolgung*, ed. S. Lorenz and D. R. Bauer (Stuttgart, 1995): 129–52.

There is of course no necessary connection between the two, and in the Netherlands there was a brief period of intolerance toward Arminians. Ibid., 140. On Dutch 'tolerance' of witches see M. Gijswijt-Hofstra, 'Witchcraft and Tolerance: The Dutch Case', *Acta Ethnographica* 37 (1991/2): 401–12.

83. G. J. Stronks, 'The Significance of Balthasar Bekker's *The Enchanted World*', in *Witchcraft in the Netherlands from the Fourteenth to the Twentieth Century*, ed. M. Gijswijt-Hofstra and W. Frijhoff (Rotterdam, 1991): 154–5.

84. Larner, *Enemies of God*, 57–9, 193–9; Midelfort, *Witch Hunting in Southwestern Germany*, 127; B. Roeck, 'Christlisher Idealstaat und Hexenwahn zum Ende der Europaischen Verfolgungen', *Historisches Jahrbuch* 108 (1988): 379–405; Ankarloo, 'Sweden', 291–2; I. Bostridge, *Witchcraft and its Transformations, c.1650–c.1750* (Oxford, 1997). For the connection between the end of witch-hunting and the collapse of the confessional state see Clark, *Thinking with Demons*, 545.

85. Jens Christian V. Johansen, 'Witchcraft, Sin and Repentance: The Decline of Danish Witchcraft Trials', *Acta Ethnographica Acad. Sci. Hungarica* 37 (1992): 413–23.

86. M. Gijswijt-Hofstra, 'Witchcraft after the Witch-Trials', in *Witchcraft and Magic in Europe: The Eighteenth and Nineteenth Centuries*, ed. B. Ankarloo and S. Clark (London, 1999): 165–7; A. Várkonyi, 'Connections between the Cessation of Witch Trials and the Transformation of the Social Structure Related to Medicine', *Acta Ethnographica Hungarica* 37 (1991–2): 460–1.

87. A. Gestrich, 'Pietismus und Aberglaube: Zum Zusammenhang von popularem Pietismus und dem Ende der Hexenverfolgung im 18. Jahrhundert', in *Das Ende de Hexenverfolgung*, ed. S. Lorenz and D. R. Bauer (Stuttgart, 1995): 269–88.

88. Weyer, *Witches, Devils, and Doctors*, 93–8; Scot, *Discoverie*, 64–5.

89. R. Filmer, *An Advertisment to the Jury-Men of England Touching Witches together with A Difference betweene an English and Hebrew Witch* (London, 1653). This tract bears comparison with Book VII of Scot, *Discoverie of Witchcraft*.

90. J. Klaits, 'Witchcraft Trials and Absolute Monarchy in France', in *Church, State and Society under the Bourbon Kings of France*, ed. R. Golden (Lawrence, 1982): 163.

91. Brähm, *Disputatio*, 4. On the radicalism of Bekker's book see R. Attfield, 'Balthasar Bekker and the Decline of the Witch-Craze: The Old Demonology and the New Philosophy', *Annals of Science* 42 (1985): 383–95.

92. Trevor-Roper, 'European Witch-Craze', 174; Pott, 'Aufklärung und Hexenglaube', 190–3.

93. See below, 264.

94. Quoted in Easlea, *Witch Hunting*, 218.

95. The one northwestern German territory where witchcraft panics continued to take a heavy toll into the 1690s was the duchy of Westphalia.

96. Stronks, 'Significance of . . . *The Enchanted World*', 152–4. The most bitter attack on Bekker as well as Thomasius came from Peter Goldschmidt, the pastor of Sterup in the duchy of Schleswig, *Verworffener Hexen- und Zauberer-Advocat* (Hamburg, 1705). See J. U. Terpstra, 'Petrus Goldschmidt aus Husum', *Euphorion* 59 (1965): 361–83.

97. Demos, *Entertaining Satan*, 368ff., argues that trials often did not coincide with periods of social conflict but that they could nonetheless originate as delayed responses to such conflict.

98. Thomas, *Religion and the Decline of Magic*, 581, makes this argument for England.

99. *Proceedings of the Justiciary Court from 1661 to 1678*, ed. S. Scott-Moncrieff (Scottish History Society, 1905), II: 56.

100. Johansen, 'Witchcraft, Sin and Repentance', 415–18; Gaskill, *Crime and Mentalities*, 85.

101. W. B. Carnochan, 'Witch-Hunting and Belief in 1751: The Case of Thomas Colley and Ruth Osborne', *Journal of Social History* 4 (1970–1): 389.

102. Monter, *Frontiers of Heresy*, 273, on the costs of the Spanish trials of 1609–11.

103. Ankarloo, 'Sweden', 300.

104. Soldan and Heppe, *Geschichte der Hexenprozesse*, II: 26; Tazbir, 'Hexenprozesse in Polen', 305–6. An anonymous account of this trial, which claimed that the witches had been swum but failed to sink, imprisoned in a lord's grain cellar immured in sauerkraut barrels, and tortured so severely that three of the accused had died, was fictitious. The six witches that were in fact executed were convicted without proof by the small town court of Grabów. Ostling, *Between the Devil and the Host*, 12, 59.

105. 9 Geo. II, c. 5.

106. *Charges to the Grand Jury 1689–1803*, ed. G. Lamoine (Camden Society, 4th ser., vol. 43, 1992): 365.

107. I. Bostridge, 'Witchcraft Repealed', in *Witchcraft in Early Modern Europe: Studies in Culture and Belief*, ed. J. Barry, M. Hester and G. Roberts (Cambridge, 1996): 333. The last conviction on the basis of the British witchcraft statute of 1736 occurred in 1944. M. Gaskill, *Hellish Nell: Last of Britain's Witches* (London, 2001).

108. Paradoxically Maria Theresa's edict both affirmed and denied the reality of witchcraft, undermining any claim that it reflected the spirit of the Enlightenment. E. M. Kern, 'An End to Witch Trials in Austria: Reconsidering the Enlightened State', *Austrian History Yearbook*, 30 (1999): 165–8.

109. Zguta, 'Witchcraft Trials in Seventeenth-Century Russia', 1200–1.

110. Lea, *Materials*, III: 1431.

111. Behringer, *Witchcraft Persecutions in Bavaria*, 287.

112. Henningsen, 'Witch Persecution', 106–7.

113. Byloff, *Hexenglaube und Hexenverfolgung*, 154–6.

114. Bader, *Die Hexenprozesse in der Schweiz*, 207.

115. Scholtz, *Über den Glauben der Zauberei in den letztverflossenen vier Jahrhunderten* (Breslau, 1830): 120, quoted in Soldan and Heppe, *Geschichte der Hexenprozesse*, II: 332.

116. Scot, *Discoverie of Witchcraft*, 18.

117. Giovanna Fiume, 'The Old Vinegar Lady, or the Judicial Modernization of the Crime of Witchcraft', in *History from Crime*, ed. E. Muir and G. Ruggiero (Baltimore, 1994): 65–87.

118. Olli, 'The Devil's Pact', 100–16; Mandrou, *Magitstrats et sorciers*, 496–9; Bever, 'Witchcraft in Wuerttemberg', 378–9; M. Nenonen, *Noituus, taikuus ja noitavainot: Ala-Satakunnan, Pohjois-Pohjanmaan ja Viipurin Karjalan maaseudulla vuosina 1620–1700* [Witchcraft, Magic and Witch Trials in Rural Lower Satakunta, Northern Ostrobothnia and Viipuri Carelia, 1620–1700] (Helsinki, 1992).

WITCH-HUNTING
AFTER THE TRIALS

By the middle of the eighteenth century the judicial prosecution of witches, which had reached its most intense point in the closing years of the sixteenth century and in the early years of the seventeenth century, had finally come to an end. Either witchcraft had been formally decriminalized by the repeal of the laws authorizing the trials or courts had simply stopped initiating prosecutions. Nevertheless, witch-hunts did not disappear but continued in a variety of different forms. First, communities often took justice into their own hands by lynching or otherwise persecuting the people who had been accused of witchcraft. Second, judicial authorities in Europe and America pursued and prosecuted marginal or dissident groups using similar tactics to those that had been employed against witches, thus giving rise to a new, broader definition of the term 'witch-hunt'. Third, in late twentieth-century America and Britain a number of individuals have been prosecuted for satanic ritual abuse, an alleged crime that resembles in many respects the crime of witches in the early modern period. Finally, witch-finding movements have flourished in many African countries since the cessation of colonial rule in the twentieth century.

Witch-lynchings

The lynching of European witches had long pre-dated the decline of prosecutions. At the height of witch-hunting in the period from 1580 to 1630, lynching had served as an alternative to formal prosecution, sometimes to avoid the prohibitive costs of prosecution, at other times to serve the desire of the local populace for summary justice. The latter motive seems to have been operative in the province of Champagne in France in 1587, when villagers in Juniville lynched seven persons suspected of witchcraft, while within a radius of twenty-five miles of Juniville village mobs lynched more than fifty persons in the same year.[1] Other lynchings took place when the courts either refused to prosecute witches or acquitted them. In one Spanish village in the early seventeenth century, a witch was lynched as soon as word of her acquittal by the Inquisition reached her home village. [2] In 1690 the residents of the Polish town of Gnesen took this retaliatory action one step further by trying to lynch *the judge* who had acquitted a witch.[3] Fifteen years later a mob in the fishing village of Pittenweem in Fife, Scotland, dragged an accused witch, Janet Cornfoot, through the streets and then used heavy stones to crush her to death after the Privy Council had refused to allow local magistrates to try her and four other women for their alleged crime.[4]

After the decriminalization of witchcraft, lynchings became the only means by which villagers who believed that witches had caused them harm could bring the alleged malefactors to justice. As long as the popular belief in witchcraft persisted, such illegal attacks on witches could occur.[5] In the Dutch Republic, which had been the first country to stop executing witches, at least three witches were lynched in the years after the trials ended.[6] In the southern provinces of the Netherlands, which later became Belgium, witch-lynchings occurred sporadically from the end of the seventeenth century until 1882. These attacks were almost always directed against women from rural areas, and in many cases they were thrown into fires.[7] A similar case occurred in France in 1818.[8]

The suspicions that provoked these popular attacks on witches resembled those that had led villagers to accuse and testify against their neighbours during the period of the trials. As might be expected, the suspicions involved *maleficia* rather than Devil-worship, since the alleged practice of harmful magic had always been the main concern of villagers. In 1722, for example, a group of villagers from Øster Grønning in Salling, Denmark, burned a woman to death for allegedly killing two children and a number of livestock by witchcraft. The courts tried and executed two of the ringleaders of this lynching for murder, outlawed one of their accomplices, and forced another five to do public penance.[9] At Tring, Hertfordshire, in 1751, a group of villagers suspected Ruth and John Osborne, a poor elderly couple living in a workhouse, of being witches because they had become dependent upon the community for their living. When they were subjected to the swimming test, Ruth Osborne drowned (see Figure 9.1). The ringleader of the mob that attacked her, Thomas Colley, was tried and executed for the murder.[10]

Incidents like these continued to take place from time to time in the nineteenth and twentieth centuries. In Russia there was a rash of witch-burnings by groups of peasants between 1879 and 1889, including one woman who was roasted on a spit with the consent of her son, while a number of men were killed for casting the evil eye on weddings between 1879 and 1895.[11] In 1894 the husband, relatives and friends of Bridget Cleary, a young married woman from Clonmell, Tipperary, in Ireland beat and burned her to death on the suspicion that the real Bridget had been taken away by the fairies and that a witch had been put in her place.[12] In 1911, in the vicinity of Perugia, Italy, farmers seized an old woman reputed to be a witch and burned

Figure 9.1 The swimming of Ruth Osborne by a mob at Tring, Hertfordshire, 1751. As a result of her subjection to this ordeal, Osborne died and the ringleader of the mob was executed for murder.

her to death in a lime kiln.[13] In 1976 residents of a small German village attacked Elizabeth Hahn, a poor, elderly spinster who was widely suspected of being a witch and keeping familiars in the form of dogs. Her neighbours shunned her, threw rocks at her, threatened to beat her to death and eventually set fire to her house, badly burning her and killing all of her animals because they thought she was casting hexes on them.[14] One year later two brothers in a village near Alençon, France, were tried for murdering a village sorcerer who kept a cabin full of magical potions and was known to throw salt on people's gardens.[15] In 1981 a Mexican mob stoned a woman to death after her husband accused her of using witchcraft to incite the attack that took place on the life of Pope John Paul II.[16]

These acts of communal or private justice, all of which are based on a belief in witchcraft, represent one form in which witch-hunting has continued to the present day. The main difference between these lynchings and the witchcraft prosecutions of the past is that established judicial authorities did not participate in the assault upon the suspected witches but instead prosecuted the assailants. Witch-hunting, in other words, became a form of popular, vigilante-style justice that did not have the sanction of the state. The only court cases involving suspicions or accusations of witchcraft have been prosecutions for other crimes, such as assault, fraud and arson, in which witchcraft was alleged as a motive.[17]

Witch-hunts without witches

A very different form of modern witch-hunting, also reminiscent of the past, has been the prosecution of members of dissident groups or individuals without sufficient justification. These modern witch-hunts have involved the use of a variety of judicial tactics to harass, convict or otherwise penalize a group of people who have become the object of widespread fear. The judicial authorities who have conducted these witch-hunts have assumed the guilt of the alleged malefactors, applied pressure (sometimes in the form of torture) to secure confessions, depicted their crime in horrific and often moral terms, and made strenuous efforts to obtain the names of alleged accomplices. The similarity between these witch-hunts and their sixteenth- and seventeenth-century predecessors could not be clearer.

The most common targets of twentieth-century witch-hunts have been political dissidents of one stripe or another. The systematic efforts by totalitarian regimes to repress political dissent, such as those conducted during the Stalinist purges of the 1930s, serve as frightening examples of the effectiveness of such campaigns.[18] The Holocaust conducted by Adolf Hitler's Nazi regime has also evoked comparisons with the witch-hunt of the early modern period.[19] In many countries these tactics include the use of torture, sometimes by means of the *strappado* and other time-tested methods, in order to obtain confessions and the names of accomplices.[20] These tactics may be most common among totalitarian regimes, but the abusive treatment of political dissidents in the Abu Ghraib prison in Iraq during the US-led war in the early years of the twenty-first century reveal that even Western democracies that forbid the use of torture under any circumstances can be persuaded to utilize it when the threat of subversion by terrorists becomes too great to bear.[21]

The episode in the history of the United States in the twentieth century that is most frequently compared to early modern European witch-hunts was the interrogation of hundreds of American citizens by congressional committees in the early 1950s in order to discover the presence of communists in the government, the armed forces and the entertainment industry. The parallels between these hearings and the witch trials of the early modern period were so apparent that Arthur Miller, who testified before the House on Un-American Activities Committee (HUAC), wrote a play, *The Crucible*, to illustrate the similarities between those hearings and the witch-hunt that had taken place at Salem in 1692.[22]

Between these two episodes there were many grounds for comparison. In both cases politically prominent individuals distinguished themselves as witch-hunters and prosecutors. The role of John Hathorne, the main prosecutor in the Salem trials, was assumed by Joseph McCarthy, the demagogic senator from Wisconsin who chaired the Senate committee investigating the matter. The threat to Salem in 1692 and the United States in 1950 was perceived to be both internal and external: the Devil was active both in Salem village and the surrounding areas, including those places where the Indians – who were believed to be Devil-worshippers – lived, just as communists suspected of being in the government were believed to be allied with the forces of Soviet Russia and international communism. What is more, the stereotype of the witch/communist broke down as both hunts progressed. Just as the stereotype of the old, poor female witch broke down at Salem when the wife of Governor Phips of Massachusetts and several wealthy merchants from Boston were named as accomplices, so too the stereotype of the communist as intellectual and playwright broke down when military officers were charged before the Senate Committee. These deviations from the traditional image of both the witch and the communist encouraged the growth of scepticism regarding the validity of the charges that had been brought against both subordinate groups.

The two witch-hunts resembled each other most closely in the area of criminal procedure. Just as a special court of oyer and terminer had been established to hear witchcraft cases in Salem, so special congressional committees (HUAC and the Senate Committee), both of which had special powers of subpoena and interrogation that regular courts did not have, were established to deal with the communist menace. The legal proceedings of the 1950s, just like those of 1692, were based largely on the assumption of guilt, so much so that Senator Hubert Humphrey claimed that the committees were 'turning Anglo-Saxon jurisprudence upside down'. In both cases prosecutors used leading questions in the interrogation of witnesses, and most importantly, enormous pressure was brought to bear on witnesses to reveal the names of accomplices or like-minded associates. It was this pressure to name names (without torture but not without other forms of coercion) that most deeply disturbed Miller and many other victims of the communist-hunt, such as Lillian Hellman. It was also this feature of the hunt that most vividly evoked the horrific memory of the chain-reaction witch-hunt.[23]

Modern witches and Satanists

The widespread practice of witchcraft in late twentieth-century and contemporary Europe and America raises the question as to what extent modern witches have been the target of modern witch-hunts. The question deserves serious consideration, if only because many contemporary witches identify with the witches who were persecuted in the early modern period, while others have been accused of performing similar deeds.

Modern-day witches can be grouped into two broad categories. The first includes all those who practise pagan rituals.[24] Some modern witches, especially the followers of Gerald Gardner, contend that early modern witches, just like themselves, were practitioners of an ancient fertility religion, Wicca, rather than the Devil-worshippers the authorities claimed they were. This contention is based largely on the scholarly work of Margaret Murray, and it has therefore lost credibility as Murray's thesis has been destroyed by her critics. Not only is there no uncontaminated evidence that witches were in fact worshipping pagan gods, but there is not even any solid evidence that witches gathered collectively, like their modern counterparts, for any purpose whatsoever. To the extent that modern witchcraft is organized into covens or even into local and regional organizations, it is qualitatively different from the witchcraft that was actually practised (as opposed to what was believed to be practised) in the past.

Aside from the lack of organization among early modern European witches, there are even more fundamental distinctions between them and modern Wiccans and pagans. Sixteenth- and seventeenth-century witches were always named by other people: one was *called* a witch, even if one did actually practise harmful magic. In the twentieth century, however, witches have defined themselves as such, perhaps reluctantly but nevertheless with a certain amount of pride. Once witchcraft became a self-defined rather than an other-defined activity, it also lost its malevolent character. Early modern European witches were regarded as essentially evil beings, whereas modern Wiccans proclaim themselves to be entirely beneficent and have even established a witch anti-defamation league to counter the negative image that they have inherited from the past. Modern witches insist that the magic they perform is invariably good, whereas the craft of the early modern witch, even if it was performed with good intentions or not performed at all, was represented to society as the quintessence of evil.

The second group of modern witches, who in many ways are seen as the antithesis of Wiccans and other modern pagans, consists of those people who call themselves Satanists.[25] A relatively small number of these 'witches' claim to be members of a religious sect, such as the Church of Satan founded by Anton LaVey in 1966. Members of Satanist churches often promote themselves as being evil, but if LaVey's *Satanic Bible* is any guide, they consider themselves evil only by traditional Christian criteria. LaVey proposed a non-Christian, hedonistic but nevertheless non-aggressive ethic that neither he nor any objective observer could label as evil.[26] A few self-proclaimed 'Satanists' have been accused of destroying animal and occasionally even human life, but these persons do not typify the larger body of ritual Satanists, much less the broader witchcraft movement, and are probably best regarded simply as criminals or sadists rather than witches.[27]

In any event, neither ritual Satanists nor contemporary Wiccans have been the target of witch-hunts, defined in the broad, modern sense of the word discussed above. These groups, especially the Wiccans, have been the victims of widespread popular hostility and occasional discrimination, and they have failed in many instances to win exemption from taxation on the grounds that they belong to a legitimate religion. But they have not been subjected to the legal harassment and prosecution that has become central to the notion of a witch-hunt. They cannot, for example, claim to have been treated in the manner of twentieth-century communists or people falsely accused of terrorism today.

The only so-called Satanists who have been prosecuted in modern times are the alleged practitioners of 'satanic-ritual abuse', all of whom have been falsely accused. In the 1980s and 1990s a small number of people in Britain and the United States were accused of sexually abusing children in ceremonies that bear an eerie resemblance to those described in the demonological literature of the early modern period. The rituals they were accused of performing are the product of sheer fantasy. The charges brought against these people, which reflect the collective anxieties of a troubled society, have no grounding in reality. This is not to assert that the sexual and physical abuse of young children does not take place. The rise in the incidence of this type of violence, at the hands of their parents, friends and strangers, is one of the most troubling developments of contemporary domestic life. But the charges of ritual Satanism that have been grafted on to such charges have no basis in fact.[28] In not one of the legal trials in either Britain or the United States in which charges of satanic-ritual abuse have been brought forward have the charges been proved. In a recent study of a large cluster of such cases in England, the anthropologist Jean La Fontaine has concluded that *none* of the allegations of ritual abuse has been corroborated.[29]

In the United States the allegations of this most perverse, homicidal form of Satanism became known to the public mainly through a series of sensational trials, beginning with the McMartin pre-school trial in Manhattan Beach, California, during the 1980s, which claims the dubious distinction of being the longest and most costly criminal trial in US history. In that trial charges were brought against the owner and six staff members of the school for the sexual abuse of 360 children. The charges included not only sexual molestation but also participation in satanic rites. Another case began in 1983 in Jordan, Minnesota, when James Rud, during a plea bargain to charges that he had sexually abused two children while babysitting, accused eighteen adults of similar behaviour. A total of sixty children eventually testified that their parents, neighbours and even a long-deceased member of the community had molested them. This led to the indictment of twenty-four adults for belonging to two interconnected sex rings engaging in the ritual mutilation and murder of young children. In Reno, Nevada one year later, three employees of a Montessori school were accused of sixty-nine accounts of sexual abuse of twenty-six pupils under their care as part of a series of satanic rituals. In 1988 the children of Paul Ingram, a deputy sheriff from Olympia, Washington, on the basis of recovered memory ten years after the fact, accused their father and his colleagues of involving them in bizarre and violent satanic rituals.[30]

The rituals described in these cases can hardly be compared with those of conventional Satanists like Aleister Crowley or Anton LaVey. Instead of summoning up demons or performing black masses, these Satanists have been accused of physically abusing young children as part of a series of violent and sadistic ceremonies. The alleged rituals do not conform to a single model, but they often involve the presence of sexual predators dressed in robes and wearing masks, the mutilation of human beings and animals, the murder of children, the drinking of human blood, and cannibalism. These modern satanic rites, just like those described in accounts of the witches' sabbath, reverse all the generally accepted norms of moral behaviour. The belief that they actually take place reflects both the secular and religious fears of the late twentieth century – violent harm to the most vulnerable members of society and the subversion of Christianity. Those who articulate these fears tend to exaggerate the extent of the evil at hand. In a series of police workshops conducted in Utah in 1992, those in attendance were informed that satanic cults were sacrificing 50,000 to 60,000 children each year, a figure more than two times higher than the annual total of all homicides in the United States.[31] The failure of authorities to find the bodies of any of these children was attributed to the fact that Satanists had eaten them, just as early modern witches were often alleged to have eaten the bodies of unbaptized infants.

The similarities between modern cases of satanic-ritual abuse and the witchcraft trials of the early modern period are striking. First, the charges against the accused included not only bodily harm – in this case sexual abuse and sometimes murder – but also the practice of Satanism. This is the same frightening mixture of physical harm and religious nonconformity, *maleficium* and apostasy that drove the prosecutions of the early modern period. The way in which the accusations developed also followed the early modern pattern, with the original charges of physical harm being lodged first by the witches' family or neighbours and then being amplified during judicial investigation to include the more fantastic charges of child sacrifice and cannibalism. At this later investigatory stage the number of charges increased dramatically, as either the prosecutors, the victims or the suspects themselves accused others of complicity in the crime. These modern cases, in other words, conform to the classic pattern of the witch-hunt.

Second, the social situations that have given rise to these two different types of prosecutions are strikingly similar. Let us recall that many witchcraft accusations in the past were the product of parental and especially maternal fears regarding the care of newborn children. A majority of witchcraft cases during the early modern period in fact dealt with harm of one sort or another inflicted on young children. In both cases adults projected their own guilt about their inability to care for their children properly on to those with whom they had contracted to assist them. In the process they constructed the image of the child-custodian who harmed rather than nurtured her children. Almost all of the satanic-abuse cases of the 1980s arose in day-care facilities of one sort or another. The staff of the McMartin pre-school at Manhattan Beach and the workers at the Montessori school in Reno therefore became the late twentieth-century counterparts of the lying-in maids in early modern Germany, France and England. All of these persons heightened the insecurities of parents who had been at least temporarily displaced as their children's caregivers.

A third similarity concerns the role of the clergy in encouraging these beliefs and in adducing confessions. During the early modern period the clergy played a crucial role in witch-hunts. Not only did they frequently intervene in the judicial process, sometimes persuading the accused that they were sinners and therefore servants of Satan, but they also contributed to the emotional mood that sustained the prosecutions. In many villages they delivered sermons identifying witchcraft as the source of the community's misfortunes, taking their text from Exodus 22:18, 'Thou shalt not suffer a witch to live'. In the modern cases of satanic-ritual abuse fundamentalist clergymen have been decisive both in arousing fears of Satanism and in eliciting confessions.[32] In the Ingram case the family minister, a member of the Church of Living Water, a Pentecostal congregation, spent hours with Ingram and his children and ended up actually shaping their testimony.

The fourth and most relevant similarity concerns the evidentiary standards that were employed in these cases. Cases of satanic-ritual abuse have relied, almost exclusively, on the testimony of young children. The techniques used to secure children's testimony in these cases, which include the deliberate cueing of the child witnesses to give the answers expected of them, have been subjected to the most severe criticism in the legal literature. The use of recovered memory to gain access to childhood experiences, as in the Ingram case, has likewise come under legal suspicion. Testimony from children was also a prominent feature of many of the witchcraft trials of the sixteenth and seventeenth centuries. As we have seen, the massive witch-hunt in the Basque country in northern Spain in 1609–11 was fuelled by the confessions of almost 2,000 children that adults had taken them to the sabbath. The large Swedish witch-hunt that began in the Mora district of Dalecarlia in 1668 and spread all the way to Stockholm was based on the charges levelled by a fifteen-year-old boy that a number of adults had transported him and other children to Blåkulla, the Swedish mountain where the worship of the Devil allegedly took place. In the witch-hunt at Salem, Massachusetts, in 1692 the main form of evidence came from adolescent girls suffering from some of the symptoms of demonic possession. The girls claimed that they could see the spectres of the witches who were afflicting them.

The testimony of children in any trial is of course always suspect, simply because children are highly suggestible and because they have difficulty distinguishing fantasy from reality. They also are capable of giving false testimony to gain revenge on those who have disciplined them. All this was well known in the judicial literature of the sixteenth and seventeenth centuries, just as it is today. Nevertheless, juvenile testimony was allowed in both periods, since it offered sometimes the only way to prove a crime which contemporaries considered to be of the greatest magnitude. As we have seen, many legal authorities in the early modern period placed the crime of witchcraft in a special category in order to permit such judicial latitude. Witchcraft was labelled a *crimen exceptum*, an excepted crime, one so horrendous that in order to identify and prosecute the malefactors the normal rules of evidence need not be observed. In admitting the testimony of children in modern-day cases of satanic-ritual abuse, judges have come close to endorsing the same exceptional judicial standard.

The only significant differences between these modern cases and the witchcraft trials of yesterday relate to their judicial outcome. Almost all modern cases of satanic-ritual abuse have resulted in mistrials, acquittals or the withdrawal of the charges. These acquittals usually have occurred after the validity of the children's testimony and, in particular, the employment of the techniques of recovered memory have been legally challenged. In the sixteenth and early seventeenth centuries, by contrast, such judicial scepticism did not develop until after some of the worst miscarriages of justice in the history of the West had taken place. This sceptical outlook can be found in the writings of the Spanish inquisitor Alonso de Salazar Frías, who showed that the confessions of the Basque witch children in 1611 were nothing but fantasies and who demanded that all subsequent charges of witchcraft be confirmed by 'external and objective proof'; in the treatises of the German Jesuit Friedrich Spee, who presented a scathing critique of the use of judicial torture in the witchcraft trials at Würzburg and Paderborn during the 1620s; and in the legal works of Sir George Mackenzie, the Scottish Lord Advocate who was almost single-handedly responsible for the end of Scottish witch-hunting. Unfortunately, the judicial caution that these men demanded in witchcraft trials emerged much too late, after thousands of innocent persons had lost their lives.

Witch-hunting in Africa

The attacks against witches that have taken the greatest toll in human life in the nineteenth and twentieth centuries have occurred not in Europe or America but in Africa. The belief in witches in Africa has a long history, and those beliefs resemble European witch beliefs in many respects. Witches in Africa, as in Europe, are believed to be capable of using magical powers to bring harm to their neighbours, their animals and their crops. African witches cause illness and death, especially sudden death, although the deaths of young children are not customarily attributed to them. African witches destroy crops, prevent cows from giving milk, cause women to miscarry and impede fertility. They also are believed to be able to run at great speeds, and among the Cewa, the Tallensi and the Nyakusa witches are believed to be able to fly.[33]

Campaigns to eliminate African witches – known as 'witch-cleansing' movements – pre-dated the beginning of European imperial rule in the nineteenth century. There are records of sustained prosecutions among the Malagasy in Madagascar, the Bechuana in Botswana, the Bakweri and the Ndebele in Cameroon, and the Pondo in South Africa in the late nineteenth century, before the onset of European rule.[34] Tribal chieftains sometimes presided over these movements, but without the state apparatus of European countries, the executions bear a closer resemblance to European lynchings than to the trials held in European courtrooms.

There is little question, however, that these witch-cleansing movements increased in frequency after the establishment of European colonial rule. The reason for this increase is ironically that the 'enlightened' European rulers who had already rejected their witch beliefs tried to put an end to the witch-hunts, a course of action Africans considered to be an assault on their beliefs and traditions. When witches were brought before colonial courts, they were regularly set free on the grounds that the crime could not be proved at law.[35] This refusal to convict witches gave the impression that the law was at the service of the witch rather than the victim. Consequently, African communities often took the law into their own hands, trying witches summarily by means of the ordeal or simply lynching them, thereby undermining the law and order that colonial administrators were trying to maintain.[36]

The emancipation of African colonies from European rule in the second half of the twentieth century has in many ways made the situation worse. Without the restraint imposed by sceptical Western colonial administrators, African communities have experienced a new freedom in pursuing witches. In some countries, most notably the former German, French and British colony of Cameroon, the government has superintended this effort. On the basis of the penal code of 1967, Cameroonian courts have prosecuted people who have disturbed the peace by practising witchcraft, magic or divination. The penalties for this crime – two to ten years' imprisonment and the payment of a hefty fine – are not as harsh as those applied in early modern European courts, but they have resulted in the successful prosecution of individuals for violating the law. The standards for proving the crime in the Cameroonian courts have also been relaxed, allowing conviction on the basis of accusations originating in the village, the confession of the accused or overwhelming circumstantial evidence. With Cameroonian judges who fully believed in the reality of witchcraft now in control, the prosecution of witches in this new African nation has begun to resemble the witchcraft trials that took place in Europe in the early modern period. These trials have not, however, used torture, and therefore no large witch-hunts have taken place.[37]

A second pattern, much closer to the illegal prosecutions that occurred in Europe towards the end of the seventeenth century, became evident in South Africa in the late 1980s and early 1990s. In 1957, shortly after South Africa became a republic controlled by Afrikaners (the descendants of Boers, the original Dutch settlers), the South African parliament passed the Witchcraft Suppression Act No. 3. On the surface the act appears to be similar to the

Cameroonian Act of 1967, for one of its provisions claims that anyone who 'professes a knowledge of witchcraft or the use of charms' shall be guilty of an offence and liable to prosecution. The main thrust of the act, however, was to facilitate the prosecution of someone who has killed a witch or has been serving as a witch-finder or witch doctor. The act, therefore, which was the work of a white, apartheid government, is based solidly in European scepticism regarding the reality of witchcraft. It is intended to suppress a belief in witchcraft. Like the British Act of 1736, moreover, it allows the prosecution of anyone who 'pretends to exercise or use any supernatural power, witchcraft, sorcery, enchantment, or conjuration'.[38] The act, therefore, reflected the spirit of colonial European rule, professing a disbelief in the reality of witchcraft and prescribing the most serious punishments – imprisonment up to twenty years – not for the witches themselves but for those who attacked them.

During the struggle against the Afrikaner government in the 1980s the illegal hunting of South African witches in direct violation of the Witchcraft Suppression Act (which was amended in 1970) became more frequent. The African National Congress (ANC), the main resistance organization, did not endorse these witch-cleansing movements, but many black South Africans involved in the resistance began to take illegal action against those whom they suspected of this activity. In this way the hunting of witches became politicized, and the Witchcraft Suppression Act became a symbol of white insensitivity to native African culture. One of the groups that became involved in a witchcraft eradication campaign during these years was an informal association of male youths known as the Comrades. In 1986 the Comrades attacked more than 150 witches in the Bushbuckridge region of the South African lowveld, killing thirty-six of them.[39] In 1990 a series of unexpected deaths in Green Valley incited groups of the Comrades to conduct another witch-hunt, demolishing the homes of suspected witches, whipping some of them, and conducting witch-finding rituals that pressured others to name their accomplices publicly.[40] In the same year somewhere between 300 and 400 accused witches in Venda sought police protection because their houses had been burned down.

The release of Nelson Mandela from prison in 1991 and the establishment of ANC rule in 1994 did not put an end to the witch-cleansing movements, especially since the Witchcraft Suppression Act remained in force. In 1994, just before the elections that brought the ANC to power, sixty witches were killed in the Northern Province. In Zebediela a spate of such lynchings took place within the space of three months in the late 1990s, including the burning to death of twelve alleged witches. The killings have continued into the twenty-first century, although in reduced numbers. In 2003 five family members were arrested for killing an eighty-year-old woman who was believed to be the cause of a young child's death.[41]

The continuation of witchcraft violence in South Africa after the elections of 1994 prompted a prolonged debate regarding the Witchcraft Suppression

Act of 1957. A commission appointed in 1996 to address the problem of violence against suspected witches concluded that part of the problem was that under the act the state courts continued to suppress the belief in the reality of witchcraft by prosecuting the healers and witch doctors whom people consulted when they thought they had been bewitched. The commission recommended changes in the Witchcraft Suppression Act, but the ANC government has been reluctant to allow even the limited prosecutions of witches that were sanctioned in Cameroon. Consequently, the passage of new legislation against witches (not witch doctors) has become a rallying cry for those who support further Africanization of South African law and politics.

A third pattern of modern African witch-hunting is typified by the murder of witches in various regions of Tanzania. In August 1999 Tanzania's Criminal Investigations Department reported that in the previous eighteen months more than 350 persons had been killed by angry villagers for using witchcraft to kill their loved ones or inflict curses that made them fail in business, or reduced their harvests. Most of the accused witches were old women, some of whose eyes had turned red after years of cooking in the smoke-filled kilns in their huts.[42] This last charge is reminiscent of the final execution for witchcraft in Europe, in the Polish town of Poznan in 1793, when two women with inflamed eyes were executed for bewitching their neighbours' cattle.[43]

The witch murders in Tanzania have continued into the twenty-first century, as villagers in northern regions along the shores of Lake Victoria have been murdering more than a hundred old women each year for allegedly causing illness, death or other misfortunes. One woman who survived such attacks was the eighty-year-old Magdale Ndila, who suffered blows to her head and the severing of her right hand.[44] These attacks have often been incited by traditional healers, who have suggested that if the alleged witches were to be killed, it would help to remedy the harm done. Deteriorating economic conditions have often aggravated these attacks.[45] In size and motivation these Tanzanian witch-hunts bear the closest resemblance to the witch-hunts that occurred in early modern Europe. The main difference, however, is that the Tanzanian hunts lack any legal authority. In that respect they resemble the lynchings of witches that occurred mainly after the great European witch-hunts had ended.

Illegal executions have taken place in other parts of Africa, most notably Kenya, where the lynchings have been conducted, as in Tanzania, without any legal sanction. In September 1998, ten elderly witches in Kenya were killed by a local vigilante group in revenge for the abduction of a villager who was forced to exhume a corpse and then eat the decomposing flesh.[46]

The similarities between modern African and historical European witch-hunting should not be exaggerated. The most striking difference is that the charges brought against African witches deal almost exclusively with harmful magic rather than diabolism. As we have seen, early modern European witchcraft acquired its distinctive character from the imposition of a fairly sophisticated demonology on a body of peasant belief regarding magic and *maleficium*. This demonology has no equivalent in African cultures and can only be found in areas where Christian charismatic movements have helped to demonize the traditional African spiritual world.[47] It is not surprising that the work of anthropologists who have studied African witchcraft has been applied most successfully to the study of English witchcraft, where the crime was defined more in magical and less in diabolical terms than in any other place in Europe.[48]

A second difference between African and historical European witchcraft is that many of the fantastic beliefs and accusations associated with the European sabbath are absent from contemporary African cultures. Since most of these beliefs are rooted in Christian demonology, their absence in pagan cultures is not surprising. Now, it is true that some African peoples believe that witches engage in some of the activities that Europeans claimed took place at the sabbath. Some African people, most notably the Dinka of southern Sudan and the Lugbara of western Uganda, believe not only in the existence of day witches or simple sorcerers but also in night witches. Unlike their more pedestrian diurnal counterparts, night witches are able to turn themselves into animals who can walk upside down, gather at night and feast on corpses, dance naked and go out at night in spirit and attack people, causing indiscriminate damage to crops and barrenness to women.[49] The prevalence of such traditional ideas in non-Christian societies that have only recently been exposed to Western theology suggests that all societies are capable of generating fantasies about people reversing all social and moral norms and engaging in such activities as cannibalistic infanticide. That would suggest that the European image of the sabbath is just one version of a universal nightmare that haunts people whenever the social order appears to be in danger. It is important to note, however, that although the Dinka and the Lugbara can identify and take counteraction against day witches, they cannot specifically identify and prosecute night witches. When day witches are named, moreover, there is never any attempt to attribute to them the activities of night witches. Night witches, in other words, exist only in these people's imagination.[50] When a charge of cannibalism is directed specifically against an African witch, it is only a symbolic way of claiming that the witch has eaten the soul, not the actual flesh of the victim.[51]

The inability of these African societies to identify and prosecute night witches leads us to what is perhaps the single most important difference between early modern European witch-hunting and the witch-cleansing movements in contemporary African cultures. European states during the early modern period, unlike contemporary African societies, developed systems of criminal procedure that were capable of discovering and prosecuting large numbers of individuals for thought crimes or for activities that never took place. As we have seen, most African witch-hunts have taken place without the legal sanction of the state, and when African courts have become involved in the process, as in Cameroon, they have conducted the trials in such a way as to prevent the development of large chain-reaction witch-hunts. They have never allowed the introduction of legal machinery capable of sustaining the type of systematic, deadly and effective prosecution that took place in early modern Europe. One reason for this restraint is that African colonial courts were set up only after the end of the witch-hunting in Europe, and the post-colonial courts that have taken their place, while more sympathetic to native African beliefs, nonetheless remain under the influence of European jurisprudence. Witch-hunting in Africa, therefore, has remained a local, popular and technically (in so far as the state is concerned) illegal operation.

These differences between the legal environment of early modern Europe and that of contemporary African communities, as well as the revival of witch-hunting against Satanists and witch substitutes in the twentieth century, underline the importance of legal procedures in the European witch-hunt. The reasons why that hunt took place are many and varied, as this book has argued. But the hunt was essentially a judicial operation and as such could not have taken place without the growth of the legal powers of Church and state, the introduction of inquisitorial procedure, and the use of torture and other forms of judicial coercion. It is also true that the hunt could not have occurred if the cumulative concept of witchcraft had not yet been formed. This book has shown that the fusion of various witch beliefs by the end of the fifteenth century, coupled with the development of legal procedures at the same time, formed the two essential preconditions of the witch-hunt and explain more than any other factors why the hunt took place when it did. Of course, these two preconditions were intimately connected, since it was only because of the development of new legal procedures that various witch beliefs could be fused. Only when inquisitors were able to coerce individuals into confessing to their fantasies could the cumulative concept of witchcraft acquire the legitimacy that it needed to command credence.

If the adoption of legal procedures proved to be of crucial importance in the origin of the great witch-hunt, their elimination was of no less importance in its decline. As we have seen in the previous chapter, the real turning point in the great hunt occurred when magistrates and judges came to the conclusion that the judicial process had resulted in the execution of innocent human beings, and therefore took steps to prevent such miscarriages of justice from ever happening again. At the same time, a more fundamental philosophical and religious scepticism challenged the very system of belief upon which the great witch-hunt was based, but it is worth noting in conclusion that the decline of the European witch-hunt was much more the work of lawyers, judges and magistrates than of theologians or philosophers. And after the prosecution of witches had dwindled to an occasional prosecution for *maleficium*, it was a series of legislative acts and decrees that brought the European witch-hunt to an end, thus concluding one of the saddest chapters in the legal history of the West.

276

Notes

1. Soman, 'Witch Lynching at Juniville', 8–15.
2. Henningsen, 'Witch Persecution', 110–19.
3. Tazbir, 'Hexenprozesse in Polen', 281n, 299. One historian has speculated that lynchings in Poland may have accounted for as many as half the total number of witchcraft executions, although the figure of 5,000 makes such executions seem unlikely. Baranowski, *Procesy Czarownic*, 180.
4. *An Account of a Horrid and Barbarous Murder in a Letter from a Gentleman in Fife* (Edinburgh, 1705); National Library of Scotland, MS 683, ff. 84–7.
5. In the middle of the nineteenth century the Bishop of Orléans reported that in the countryside the beliefs in witchcraft and the reliance upon cunning men were as widespread as ever. Garrett, 'Witches and Cunning Folk', 57.
6. Waardt, 'Prosecution or Defense', 83.
7. Gijswijt-Hofstra, 'Witchcraft after the Witch-Trials', 115–16; M.-S. Dupont-Bouchat, 'Le Diable apprivoisée: Le sorcellerie revisité; mague et sorcellerie au XIX^c siècle', in *Magie et sorcellerie du moyen âge à nos jours*, ed. R. Muchembled (Paris, 1994): 235–66.
8. Sebald, *Witchcraft*, 52, 42n.
9. Henningsen, 'Witch Persecution', 110–19, 135.
10. Carnochan, 'Witch-Hunting and Belief in 1751', 389–403. Colley's neighbours did not think this was a just sentence for killing 'an old wicked woman that had done so much mischief by her witchcraft'. Gaskill, *Crime and Mentalities*, 86.
11. Ryan, 'Witchcraft Hysteria', 78.
12. P. Byrne, *Witchcraft in Ireland* (Cork, 1975): 56–68; A. Bourke, *The Burning of Bridget Cleary: A True Story* (Harmondsworth, 2001).
13. Soldan and Heppe, *Geschichte der Hexenprozesse*, II: 350.
14. Sebald, *Witchcraft*, 223.
15. Agence France-Press, May 13, 1977. The case is discussed in Henningsen, *Witches' Advocate*, 18.
16. *Newsweek*, 25 May 1981: 33.
17. W. de Blécourt, 'The Witch, her Victim, the Unwitcher and the Researcher: The Continued Existence of Traditional Witchcraft', in *Witchcraft and Magic in Europe: The Twentieth Century*, ed. B. Ankarloo and S. Clark (London, 1999): 176–80.
18. On the comparisons between witch-hunting and the Stalinist purges see R. W. Thurston, 'The Rise and Fall of Judicial Torture: Why it was Used in the Witch Hunts and the Soviet Union', *Human Rights Review* 1 (2000): 26–39.
19. Purkiss, *The Witch in History*, chapter 1, shows that efforts by feminists to establish similarities between witch-hunting and the Holocaust have led to the grossly inflated estimates of the total number of witchcraft executions.
20. *The Observer*, 15 June 1980.
21. A. Lewis, 'Making Torture Legal', *New York Review of Books*, 15 July 2004.
22. A. Miller, *The Crucible* (Boston, 1953).
23. L. Hellman, *Scoundrel Time* (Boston, 1976); A. R. Cardozo, 'A Modern American Witch-Craze', in *Witchcraft and Sorcery*, ed. M. Marwick (London, 1970): 369–77.
24. See R. Hutton, *The Triumph of the Moon: A History of Modern Pagan Witchcraft* (Oxford, 1999).
25. The charges occasionally lodged against neo-pagan witches that they are Satanists have no basis in fact. Pagans do not believe in the existence of any inherently evil forces in the supernatural realm. Charges of this sort resemble those brought against sorcerers in the early modern period. See Hutton, *Triumph of the Moon*, 407–8.
26. A. LaVey, *The Satanic Bible* (New York, 1969): 46–54.

27. See, for example, the claim that two murders in Italy in 2004 were inspired by Satanism. *International Herald Tribune*, 21 June 2004.

28. See J. S. Victor, *Satanic Panic: The Creation of a Contemporary Legend* (Chicago, 1993). The accusations, amplified by uncritical media coverage, led to a moral crusade in which horrified parents, survivors, religious fundamentalists, law enforcement professionals, and prosecutors participated. See M. deYoung, 'One Face of the Devil: The Satanic Ritual Abuse Moral Crusade and the Law', *Behavioral Sciences and the Law* 12 (1994): 389–407.

29. J. S. La Fontaine, *Speak of the Devil: Tales of Satanic Abuse in Contemporary England* (Cambridge, 1998).

30. L. Wright, *Remembering Satan* (New York, 1994).

31. Ibid., 86.

32. See Victor, *Satanic Panic*, on the rhetoric of modern moral crusades, especially against Satanists.

33. Macfarlane, *Witchcraft in Tudor and Stuart England*, 214.

34. Stephen Ellis, 'Witch-Hunting in Central Madagascar, 1828–1861', *Past and Present* 175 (2002): 90–123; Behringer, *Witches and Witch Hunts*, 198–200.

35. See Richard D. Waller, 'Witchcraft and Colonial Law in Kenya', *Past and Present* 180 (2003): 241–75.

36. C. Fisiy, 'Containing Occult Practices: Witchcraft Trials in Cameroon', *African Studies Review* 41 (1998): 148–51. For a description of a witch-finding movement in Nyasaland and Rhodesia in 1934 and another movement in the late 1940s in West Africa see G. Parrinder, *Witchcraft: European and African* (London, 1958): 170–5.

37. Fisiy, 'Containing Occult Practices', 151–61.

38. 'Witchcraft Suppression Act No. 3 of 1957', in *Witchcraft Violence and the Law in South Africa*, ed. J. Hund (Pretoria, 2003): 149–50.

39. I. A. Niehaus, 'The ANC's Dilemma: The Symbolic Politics of Three Witch-Hunts in the South African Lowveld, 1990–1995', *African Studies Review* 41 (1998): 93–9; Parrinder, *Witchcraft: European and African*, 145–7.

40. Parrinder, *Witchcraft*, 99–113.

41. J. Harnischfeger, 'Witchcraft and the State in South Africa', in *Witchcraft Violence and the Law in South Africa*, ed. J. Hund (Pretoria, 2003): 40–72.

42. Reuters, 3 August 1999.

43. Soldan and Heppe, *Geschichte der Hexenprozesse*, II: 332.

44. BBC News World, 29 October 2002. The *Huffington Post* reported in 20012 that 3,000 witches have been lynched in Tanzania between 2005 and 2011 (www.huffingtonpost. com/2012/05/29/tanzania-witchcraft-3000-lynchings-witches_n_1553448.html). Without corroborating evidence, this figure should be viewed with the same caution as the inflated estimate of the number of European executions.

45. See R. Abrahams (ed.), *Witchcraft in Contemporary Tanzania* (Cambridge, 1994).

46. BBC News World, 5 September 1998.

47. A Presidential Commission of inquiry in Kenya, chaired by the Archbishop of Nyeri, reported in 1999 that a cult of Devil-worship existed in the country, but this was not linked to the practice of traditional Kenyan witchcraft, nor were the Devil-worshippers the target of an anti-witchcraft movement. *The Nation*, 4 August 1999.

48. See Macfarlane, *Witchcraft in Tudor and Stuart England*, 211–53.

49. Ibid.

50. See Mair, *Witchcraft*, 36–42.

51. Parrinder, *Witchcraft: European and African*, 147.

SELECT
BIBLIOGRAPHY

Manuscript sources

National Archives of Scotland, Edinburgh
JC 1/38 Trial of Geillis Johnstone
JC 2/10–17 Court of Justiciary Books of Adjournal
JC 10/1–5 Circuit Court Records
JC 26, 27 Court of Justiciary Processes
CH2 Kirk Sessions and Presbytery Records
PA7/23/1 Records of Parliament
National Library of Scotland, Edinburgh
MS 683 Records of the Burgh of Pittenweem

Printed primary sources

An Account of a Horrid and Barbarous Murder in a Letter from a Gentleman in Fife. Edinburgh, 1705.
Baxter, Richard. *The Certainty of the Worlds of Spirits*. London, 1691.
Becker, Andreas. *Disputatio juridica de jure spectorum*. Halle, 1700.
Behringer, Wolfgang (ed.). *Hexen und Hexenprozesse in Deutschland*. Munich, 1988.
Bekker, Balthasar. *De betoverde weereld*. Amsterdam, 1693.
Bernard, Richard. *A Guide to Grand Jury Men ... in Cases of Witchcraft*. London, 1630.
Binsfeld, Peter. *Tractatus de confessionibus maleficarum et sagarum*. Treves, 1596.
Blackstone, William. *Commentaries on the Laws of England*. Oxford, 1796.
Bodin, Jean. *De la Démonomanie des sorciers*. Anvers, 1586.
Bodin, Jean. *On the Demon-Mania of Witches*. Trans. Randy A. Scott. Ed. Jonathan L. Pearl. Toronto, 2001.
Bodó, M. *Jurisprudentia criminalis secundum praxim et constitutiones Hungaricas*. Pozsony, 1751.
Boguet, Henri. *An Examen of Witches*. Trans. E. A. Ashwin. Ed. M. Summers. London, 1929.
Bordelon, Laurent. *L'Histoire des imaginations extravagantes de Monsieur Oufle*. Paris, 1710.
Boswell, James. *Journal of a Tour to the Hebrides*. Ed. R. W. Chapman. Oxford, 1970.
Boyer, Paul and Stephen Nissenbaum (eds). *Salem Village Witchcraft: A Documentory Record of Local Conflict in Colonial New England*. Belmont, 1972.
Brähm, Felix. *Disputatio inaug. de fallacibus indiciis magiae*. Halle, 1709.

Brown, P. H. (ed.). *Register of the Privy Council of Scotland*, 3rd ser., I, 1661–4. Edinburgh, 1908.

Burr, George Lincoln (ed.). *Narratives of the Witchcraft Cases, 1648–1706*. New York, 1914.

Burton, Robert. *Anatomy of Melancholy*. New York, 1932.

Cardano, Jerome. *De rerum varietate*. Basel, 1557.

Carena, Cesare. *Tractatus de officio sanctissimae Inquisitionis*. Cremona, 1641.

Carpzov, Benedikt. *Practica nova rerum criminalium*. Wittenberg, 1635.

Cotta, John. *The Trial of Witch-Craft*. London, 1616.

Dalton, Michael. *The Country Justice*. London, 1630.

Daneau, Lambert. *A Dialogue of Witches*. London, 1575.

Davidson, L. S. and J. O. Ward (eds). *The Sorcery Trial of Alice Kyteler*. Binghamton, 1993.

Del Rio, Martín. *Investigations into Magic*. Ed. and trans. P. G. Maxwell-Stuart. Manchester, 2000.

Erastus, Thomas. *Deux Dialogues. Histoires disputes et discours des illusions et impostures des diables, des magiciens infames, sorcieres et empoisonneurs, des ensorcel*. Paris, 1885.

Filmer, Robert. *An Advertisement to the Jury-Men of England Touching Witches together with A Difference between an English and Hebrew Witch*. London, 1653.

Forbes, William. *The Institutes of the Law of Scotland*. Edinburgh, 1730.

Gibson, Marion (ed.). *Witchcraft and Society in England and America, 1550–1750*. Ithaca, NY, 2003.

Gifford, George. *A Dialogue Concerning Witches and Witchcraftes*. London, 1593.

Gifford, George. *A Discourse of the Subtle Practice of Devils by Witches*. London, 1587.

Glanvill, Joseph. *Saducismus Triumphatus*. London, 1681.

Goedelmann, Johann Georg. *De magis, veneficis et lamiis*. Frankfurt, 1592.

Goldschmidt, Peter. *Verworffener Hexen- und Zauberer-Advocat*. Hamburg, 1705.

Goodcole, Henry. *The Wonderful Discoverie of Elizabeth Sawyer, a Witch, Late of Edmonton*. London, 1621.

Grevius, Johannes. *Doma Tribunal Reformatum*. Hamburg, 1624.

Grien, Hans Baldung. *Prints and Drawings*. Ed. J. H. Marrow and A. Shestack. Chicago, 1981.

Guazzo, Francesco Maria. *Compendium Maleficarum*. Trans. E. A. Ashwin. Ed. M. Summers. London, 1929.

Hall, David (ed.). *Witch-Hunting in Seventeenth-Century New England: A Documentary Collection, 1638–1692*. Boston, 1991.

Hansen, Joseph (ed.). *Quellen und Untersuchungen zur Geschichte des Hexenwahns und der Hexenverfolgung im Mittelalter*. Bonn, 1901.

Hauber, E. D. (ed.). *Biblioteca sive acta et scripta magica*. 3 vols. Lemgo, 1738.

Henningsen, Gustav (ed.). *The Salazar Documents: Inquisitor Alonso de Salazar Frías and Others on the Basque Witch Persecutions*. Leiden, 2004.

Hobbes, Thomas. *Leviathan*. London, 1651.

Hopkins, Matthew. *The Discovery of Witches*. London, 1647.

James VI. *Daemonologie*. Ed. G. B. Harrison. London, 1924 [1597].

Kennett, White. *The Witchcraft of the Present Rebellion*. London, 1715.

Kirkton, James. *The Secret and True History of the Church of Scotland*. Ed. C. K. Sharpe. Edinburgh, 1917.

Kors, Alan C. and Edward Peters (eds). *Witchcraft in Europe, 400–1700: A Documentary History*. 2nd edn. Philadelphia, 2001.

Kramer, Heinrich and James Sprenger. *The Malleus Maleficarum*. Trans. and ed. M. Summers. London, 1928.

Lamoine, G. (ed.). *Charges to the Grand Jury 1689–1803*. Camden Society, 4th ser., 43, 1992.

Lancre, Pierre de. *On the Inconstancy of Witches: Tableau de l'inconstance des mauvais anges et demons* (1612). Ed. and trans. Gerhild Scholz Williams. Tempe and Turnhout, 2006.

Laymann, Paul. *Processus iuridicus contra sagas et veneficos*. Cologne, 1629.

Levack, Brian P. (ed.). *The Witchcraft Sourcebook*. 2nd edn. London, 2015.

Luther, Martin. *A Commentary on St. Paul's Epistle to the Galatians*. London, 1741.

Mackenzie, Sir George. *The Laws and Customs of Scotland in Matters Criminal*. Edinburgh, 1678.

Mammoli, Domenico (ed.). *The Record of the Trial and Condemnation of a Witch, Matteuccia di Francesco, at Todi, 20 March 1428*. Rome, 1972.

The Manuscripts of the Duke of Roxburghe. Historical Manuscripts Commission, Fourteenth Report, Appendix III. London, 1894.

Mather, Cotton. *Memorable Providences Relating to Witchcrafts and Possessions*. Boston, 1689.

Mather, Cotton. *Wonders of the Invisible World*. Boston, 1693.

Mather, Increase. *Cases of Conscience concerning Evil Spirits Impersonating Men*. Boston, 1693.

Meyfarth, Johann. *Christliche Erinnerung an gewaltige Regenten und gewissenhaffte Prädicanten wie das abscheuliche Laster der Hexerey mit Ernst auszurotten*. Schleusingen, 1635.

Millar, J. (ed.). *A History of the Witches of Renfrewshire*. Paisley, 1877.

More, Henry. *An Antidote against Atheism*. London, 1655.

Newes from Scotland. London, 1591.

Nicolas, Augustin. *Si la torture est un moyen seur à verifier les crimes secrets: dissertation moral et juridique*. Amsterdam, 1681.

Normand, Lawrence and Gareth Roberts (eds). *Witchcraft in Early Modern Scotland: James VI's Demonology and the North Berwick Witches*. Exeter, 2000.

Ostorero, Martine, Agostino Paravicini Bagliani and Kathrin Utz Tremp (eds). *L'imaginaire du sabbat: Edition critique des textes les plus anciens (1430 c.–1440 c.)*. Lausanne, 1999.

Perkins, William. *A Discourse of the Damned Art of Witchcraft*. Cambridge, 1608.

Perrault, F. *The Devill of Mascon*. Oxford, 1658.

Remy, Nicolas. *Demonolatry*. Trans. E. A. Ashwin. Ed. Montague Summers. London, 1930.

Scot, Reginald. *The Discoverie of Witchcraft*. Ed. M. Summers. London, 1930.

Scott-Moncrieff, S. (ed.). *Proceedings of the Justiciary Court from 1661 to 1678*. Scottish History Society, Edinburgh, 1905.

Scultetus, Johannes [Antonius Praetorius]. *Gründlich Bericht von Zauberey und Zauberern*. Cologne, 1598.

The Second Part of the Boy of Bilson, or a True and Particular Relation of the Impostor Susanna Fowles. London, 1698.

Sharpe, James (ed.). *English Witchcraft 1560–1736*. 6 vols. London, 2003.

Spee, Friedrich von Langenfeld. *Cautio Criminalis, or a Book on Witch Trials*. Trans. Marcus Hellyer. Charlottesville, 2003.

Stearne, John. *A Confirmation and Discovery of Witchcraft*. London, 1648.

The Surey Demoniack: or, An Account of Satan's Strange and Dreadful Actings in and about the Body of Richard Dugdale of Surey, near Lancashire. London, 1697.

Tanner, Adam. *Theologia scholastica*. Ingolstadt, 1626/7.

Thomasius, Christian. *Über die Folter*. Trans. and ed. R. Lieberwirth. Weimar, 1960.

Thomasius, Christian. *Über die Hexenprozesse*. Trans. R. Lieberwirth. Weimar, 1967.

The Trial of Temple Anneke: Records of a Witchcraft Trial in Brunswick, Germany, 1663. Ed. Peter Morton. Trans. Barbar Dähms. Toronto, 2006.

Webster, John. *The Displaying of Supposed Witchcraft*. London, 1677.

Wesley, John. *The Journal of the Rev. John Wesley, A. M.* New York, 1906.

Weyer, Johann. *Witches, Devils and Doctors in the Renaissance: Johann Weyer's De Praestigiis Daemonum*. Ed. George Mora. Binghamton, 1991.

Whitelocke, Bulstrode. *Memorials of the English Affairs*. London, 1682.

Whitmore, William H. (ed.). *The Colonial Laws of Massachusetts*. Boston, 1889.

Witches Apprehended, Examined and Executed. London, 1613.

Willumsen, Liv Helene. *The Witchcraft Trials in Finnmark Northern Norway*. Trans. Katjana Edwardsen. Bergen, 2010.

Secondary sources

Abrahams, R. (ed.). *Witchcraft in Contemporary Tanzania*. Cambridge, 1994.

Adler, Margot. *Drawing Down the Moon*. Boston, 1979.

Almond, Philip C. *England's First Demonologist: Reginald Scot and 'The Discoverie of Witchcraft'*. London, 2011.

Alver, Bente G. *Heksetro og Trolddom*. Oslo, 1971.

Anderson, Robert D. 'The History of Witchcraft: A Review with Some Psychiatric Comments', *American Journal of Psychiatry* 126 (1970): 69–77.

Andreski, Stanislav. 'The Syphilitic Shock', *Encounter* 58 (1982): 7–26.

Anglo, Sydney. 'Evident Authority and Authoritative Evidence: The *Malleus Maleficarum*', in *The Damned Art: Essays in the Literature of Witchcraft*, ed. S. Anglo. London, 1977: 1–31.

Ankarloo, Bengt. 'Sweden: The Mass Burnings (1668–76)', in *Early Modern European Witchcraft: Centres and Peripheries*, ed. Bengt Ankarloo and Gustav Henningsen. Oxford, 1990: 285–317.

Ankarloo, Bengt. *Trolldomsprocesserna i Sverige*. Stockholm, 1971.

Apps, Lara and Andrew Gow. *Male Witches in Early Modern Europe*. Manchester, 2003.

Ashforth, Adam. *Witchcraft, Violence, and Democracy in South Africa*. Chicago, 2005.

Attfield, Robin. 'Balthasar Bekker and the Decline of the Witch-Craze: The Old Demonology and the New Philosophy', *Annals of Science* 42 (1985): 383–95.

Avis, P. D. L. 'Moses and the Magistrate: A Study in the Rise of Protestant Legalism', *Journal of Ecclesiastical History* 26 (1975): 151–72.

Bader, Guido. *Die Hexenprozesse in der Schweiz*. Affoltern, 1945.

Baeyer-Katte, Wanda von. 'Die Historischen Hexenprozesse: Der Verbürokratisierte Massenwahn', in *Massenwahn in Geschichte und Gegenwart*, ed. W. Bitter. Stuttgart, 1965: 220–31.

Bailey, Michael D. *Battling Demons: Witchcraft, Heresy, and Reform in the Late Middle Ages*. University Park, 2003.

Bainton, Roland. *Women of the Reformation: From Spain to Scandinavia*. Minneapolis, 1977.

Baissac, Jules. *Les Grands jours de la sorcellerie*. Paris, 1890.

Baranowski, Bohdan. *Procesy czarownic w Polsce w XVII i XVIII wieku*. Lodz, 1952.

Barb, A. A. 'The Survival of the Magic Arts', in *The Conflict between Paganism and Christianity*, ed. A. Momigliano. Oxford, 1963: 100–23.

Barry, Jonathan. *Witchcraft and Demonology in South-West England, 1640–1789*. Basingstoke, 2012.

Barry, Jonathan and Owen Davies (eds). *Palgrave Advances in Witchcraft Historiography*. Basingstoke, 2007.

Barstow, Anne L. *Witchcraze: A New History of the European Witch Hunts*. New York, 1994.

Bartlett, Robert. *Trial by Fire and Water: The Medieval Judicial Ordeal*. Oxford, 1986.

Baschwitz, Kurt. *Czarownice. Dzieje procesów o czary*. Warsaw, 1963.

Baschwitz, Kurt. *Hexen und Hexenprozesse*. Munich, 1963.

Baxter, Christopher. 'Jean Bodin's *De la Démonomanie des sorciers*: The Logic of Persecution', in *The Damned Art: Essays in the Literature of Witchcraft*, ed. S. Anglo. London, 1977: 76–105.

Behringer, Wolfgang. '"Erhob sich das ganze Land zu ihrer Ausrottung . . .": Hexen-prozesse und Hexenverfolgungen in Europa', in *Hexenwelten: Magie und Imagination vom 16.–20. Jahrhundert*. Ed. Richard van Dülmen. Frankfurt, 1987: 131–69.

Behringer, Wolfgang. 'Heinrich Kramers *Hexenhammer*: Text und Context', in *Frühe Hexenverfolgung in Ravensburg und am Bodensee*, ed. Andreas Schmauder. Ravensburg, 2001: 83–124.

Behringer, Wolfgang. 'How Waldensians became Witches: Heretics and their Journey to the Other World', in *Communicating with the Spirits*, ed. Gábor Klaniczay and Éva Pócs. Budapest, 2005: 155–92.

Behringer, Wolfgang. 'Kinderhexenprozesse: zur Rolle von Kindern in der Geschichte der Hexenverfolgung', *Zeitschrift für Historische Forschung* 16 (1988): 31–47.

Behringer, Wolfgang. *Shaman of Oberstdorf: Chonrad Stoecklin and the Phantoms of the Night*. Trans. H. C. Erik Midelfort. Charlottesville, 1998.

Behringer, Wolfgang. 'Weather, Hunger and Fear: Origins of the European Witch-Hunts in Climate, Society and Mentality', *German History* 13 (1995): 1–27.

Behringer, Wolfgang. *Witchcraft Persecutions in Bavaria: Popular Magic, Religious Zealotry and Reason of State in Early Modern Europe*. Cambridge, 1997.

Behringer, Wolfgang. *Witches and Witch Hunts: A Global History*. London, 2004.

Ben-Yahuda, Nachman. *Deviance and Moral Boundaries*. Chicago, 1985.

Bethencourt, Francisco. 'Portugal: A Scrupulous Inquisition', in *Early Modern European Witchcraft: Centres and Peripheries*, ed. Bengt Ankarloo and Gustav Henningsen. Oxford, 1990: 403–22.

Bever, Edward. 'Old Age and Witchcraft in Early Modern Europe', in *Old Age in Pre-Industrial Europe*, ed. P. Stearns. Princeton, 1983: 150–90.

Bever, Edward. *The Realities of Witchcraft and Popular Magic in Early Modern Europe: Culture, Cognition and Everyday Life*. Basingstoke, 2008.

Bever, Edward. 'Witchcraft in Early Modern Württemberg', PhD dissertation. Princeton, 1983.

Blauert, Andreas. *Frühe Hexenverfolgungen*. Hamburg, 1989.

Blauert, Andreas (ed.). *Ketzer, Zauberer, Hexen: die Anfänge der Europäischen Hexenverfolgungen*. Frankfurt, 1990.

Blécourt, Willem de. 'The Making of the Female Witch: Reflections on Witchcraft and Gender in the Early Modern Period', *Gender and History* 12 (2000): 287–309.

Blécourt, Willem de. 'The Witch, her Victim, the Unwitcher and the Researcher: The Continued Existence of Traditional Witchcraft', in *Witchcraft and Magic in Europe: The Twentieth Century*, ed. Bengt Ankarloo and Stuart Clark. London, 1999: 141–219.

Bonomo, Giuseppe. *Caccia alle Streghe*. Palermo, 1959.

Borst, Arno. 'The Origins of the Witch-Craze in the Alps', in *Medieval Worlds: Barbarians, Heretics, and Artists in the Middle Ages*. Chicago, 1992: 101–22.

Bossy, John. 'Moral Arithmetic: Seven Sins into Ten Commandments', in *Conscience and Casuistry in Early Modern Europe*, ed. Edmund Leites. Cambridge, 1988: 214–34.

Bostridge, Ian. *Witchcraft and Its Transformations c.1650–c.1750*. Oxford, 1997.

Bostridge, Ian. 'Witchcraft Repealed', in *Witchcraft in Early Modern Europe: Studies in Culture and Belief*, ed. J. Barry, M. Hester and G. Roberts. Cambridge, 1996: 309–34.

Bourke, Angela. *The Burning of Bridget Cleary: A True Story*. Harmondsworth, 2001.

Boyer, Stephen and Paul Nissenbaum. *Salem Possessed: The Social Origins of Witchcraft*. Cambridge, MA, 1974.

Brann, Noel. 'The Conflict between Reason and Magic in Seventeenth-Century England: A Case Study of the Vaughan-More Debate', *Huntington Library Quarterly* 43 (1980): 103–26.

Brauner, Sigrid. *Fearless Wives and Frightened Shrews; The Construction of the Witch in Early Modern Germany*. Amherst, MA, 1995.

Brauner, Sigrid. 'Martin Luther on Witchcraft: A True Reformer?', in *The Politics of Gender in Early Modern Europe*, ed. J. R. Brink, A. Coudert and M. C. Horowitz. Sixteenth Century Essays and Studies 12. Kirksville, MO, 1989: 29–42.

Briffault, Robert. *The Mothers*. New York, 1927.

Briggs, Robin. *Communities of Belief: Cultural and Social Tension in Early Modern France*. Oxford, 1989.

Briggs, Robin. 'Witchcraft and Popular Mentality in Lorraine, 1580–1630', in *Occult and Scientific Mentalities in the Renaissance*, ed. Brian Vickers. Cambridge, 1984: 351–74.

Briggs, Robin. *Witches and Neighbours: The Social and Cultural Context of European Witchcraft*. Harmondsworth, 1996.

Briggs, Robin. *The Witches of Lorraine*. Oxford, 2007.

Briggs, Robin. 'Women as Victims? Witches, Judges and the Community', *French History* 5 (1991): 438–50.

Broedel, Hans Peter. *The* Malleus Maleficarum *and the Construction of Witchcraft: Theology and Popular Belief*. Manchester, 2003.

Brucker, Gene A. 'Sorcery in Early Renaissance Florence', *Studies in the Renaissance* 10 (1963): 7–24.

Burghartz, Susanna. 'The Equation of Women and Witches: A Case Study of Witchcraft Trials in Lucerne and Lausanne in the Fifteenth and Sixteenth Centuries', in *The German Underworld*, ed. Richard J. Evans. London, 1988: 57–74.

Burke, Peter. *Popular Culture in Early Modern Europe*. London, 1978.

Burke, Peter. 'Witchcraft and Magic in Renaissance Italy: Gianfrancesco Pico and his *Strix*', in *The Damned Art: Essays in the Literature of Witchcraft*, ed. S. Anglo. London, 1977: 32–52.

Burr, George Lincoln. 'The Fate of Dietrich Flade', in *George Lincoln Burr: Selections from His Writings*, ed. Lois Oliphant Gibbons. Ithaca, NY, 1943: 190–233.

Burr, George Lincoln. *The Witch Persecutions*. Philadelphia, 1902.

Burstein, Sona R. 'Aspects of the Psychopathology of Old Age Revealed in the Witchcraft Cases of the Sixteenth and Seventeenth Centuries', *British Medical Bulletin* 6 (1949): 63–71.

Byloff, Fritz. *Hexenglaube und Hexenverfolgung in den österreichischen Alpenländern*. Berlin and Leipzig, 1934.

Byrne, Patrick. *Witchcraft in Ireland*. Cork, 1975.

Cardozo, A. Rebecca. 'A Modern American Witch-Craze', in *Witchcraft and Sorcery*, ed. M. Marwick. London, 1970: 369–77.

Carnochan, W. B. 'Witch-Hunting and Belief in 1751: The Case of Thomas Colley and Ruth Osborne', *Journal of Social History* 4 (1970–1): 389–403.

Caro Baroja, Julio. *The World of the Witches*. Trans. O. N. V. Glendinnung. Chicago, 1965.

Carus, Paul. *The History of the Devil and the Idea of Evil*. New York, 1969.

Certeau, Michel de. *The Possession at Loudun*. Trans. Michael B. Smith. Chicago, 1996.

Cervantes, Fernando. *The Devil in the New World: The Impact of Diabolism in New Spain*. New Haven, 1994.

Cervantes, Fernando. *The Idea of the Devil and the Problem of the Indian: The Case of Mexico in the Sixteenth Century*. London, 1991.

Childs, J. *Armies and Warfare in Europe, 1648–1789*. New York, 1982.

Cirac Estopañán, Sebastián. *Los procesos de hechicerías en la Inquisición de Castilla la Nueva*. Madrid, 1942.

Clark, Stuart. 'Inversion, Misrule and the Meaning of Witchcraft', *Past and Present* 87 (1980): 99–127.

Clark, Stuart. 'King James's *Daemonologie*: Witchcraft and Kingship', in *The Damned Art: Essays in the Literature of Witchcraft*, ed. S. Anglo. London, 1977: 156–81.

Clark, Stuart (ed.). *Languages of Witchcraft: Narrative, Ideology and Meaning in Early Modern Culture*. Basingstoke, 1991.

Clark, Stuart. 'Protestant Demonology: Sin, Superstition and Society (c.1520–c.1630)', in *Early Modern European Witchcraft: Centres and Peripheries*, ed. Bengt Ankarloo and Gustav Henningsen. Oxford, 1990: 45–81.

Clark, Stuart. 'The Scientific Status of Demonology', in *Occult and Scientific Mentalities in the Renaissance*, ed. B. Vickers. Cambridge, 1984: 351–74.

Clark, Stuart. *Thinking with Demons: The Idea of Witchcraft in Early Modern Europe*. Oxford, 1997.

Cohn, Norman. *Europe's Inner Demons: The Demonization of Christians in Medieval Christendom*. Rev. edn. Chicago, 1993.

Coudert, Allison P. 'The Myth of the Improved Status of Protestant Women: The Case of the Witchcraze', in *The Politics of Gender in Early Modern Europe*, ed. J. R. Brink, A. Coudert and M. C. Horowitz. Sixteenth-Century Essays and Studies 12. Kirksville, MO, 1989: 61–94.

Cowan, Edward. 'The Darker Vision of the Scottish Renaissance', in *The Renaissance and Reformation in Scotland*, ed. I. B. Cowan and D. Shaw. Edinburgh, 1983: 125–40.

Cragg, Gerald. *From Puritanism to the Age of Reason*. Cambridge, 1960.

Currie, Elliott P. 'Crimes without Criminals: Witchcraft and its Control in Renaissance Europe', *Law and Society Review* 3 (1968): 7–32.

Daly, Mary. *Gyn/Ecology: The Metaethics of Radical Feminism*. Boston, 1978.

Damaska, Mirjan. 'The Death of Legal Torture', *Yale Law Journal* 86 (1978): 860–4.

Darr, Orna Alyagon. *Marks of an Absolute Witch: Evidentiary Dilemmas in Early Modern England*. Farnham, 2011.

Davies, Owen. *Witchcraft, Magic and Culture, 1736–1951*. Manchester, 1991.

Davies, Owen and Willem de Blécourt (eds). *Beyond the Witch Trials: Witchcraft and Magic in Enlightenment Europe*. Manchester, 2004.

Davies, Owen and Willem de Blécourt. *Witchcraft Continued: Popular Magic in Early Modern Europe*. Manchester, 2004.

Davis, Natalie. *The Return of Martin Guerre*. Cambridge, MA, 1983.

Deacon, Richard. *Matthew Hopkins: Witch-Finder General*. London, 1976.

Decker, Rainer. 'Die Haltung der römischen Inquisition gegenüber Hexenglauben und Exorzismus am Beispiel der Teufelsaustreibungen in Paderborn 1657', in *Das Ende der Hexenverfolgung*, ed. S. Lorenz and D. R. Bauer. Stuttgart, 1995: 97–115.

Decker, Rainer. *Witchcraft and the Papacy*. Trans. H. C. Erik Midelfort. Charlottesville, 2008.

Degn, Christian, Hartmut Lehmann and Dagmar Unverhau (eds). *Hexenprozesse: Deutsche und Scandinavische Beiträge*. Neumünster, 1983.

Delcambre, Etienne. 'La psychologie des inculpes Lorrains de sorcellerie', *Revue historique de droit français et étranger*, ser. 4, 32 (1954): 383–403.

Delumeau, Jean. *Catholicism between Luther and Voltaire: A New View of the Counter-Reformation*. London, 1977.

Delumeau, Jean. *La Peur en occident XIVe–XVIIIe siècles*. Paris, 1978.

Demos, John P. *Entertaining Satan: Witchcraft and the Culture of Early New England*. New York, 1982.

Demos, John P. 'Underlying Themes in the Witchcraft of Seventeenth-Century New England', *American Historical Review* 75 (1970): 1311–26.

Denis, A. *La Sorcellerie a Toul aux XVIe et XVIIe siècles*. Toul, 1888.

deYoung, Mary. 'One Face of the Devil: The Satanic Ritual Abuse Moral Crusade and the Law', *Behavioral Sciences and the Law* 12 (1994): 389–407.

Dienst, Heide. 'Magische Vorstellungen und Hexenverfolgungen in den österreichen Alpenländern (15–18 Jahrhundert)', in *Wellen der Verfolgungen in der österreichischen Geschichte*, ed. E. Zöllner. Vienna, 1986: 70–94.

Dillinger, Johannes. *'Evil People': A Comparative Study of Witch Hunts in Swabian Austria and the Electorate of Trier*. Trans. Laura Stokes. Charlottesville, 2009.

Dillinger, Johannes. 'Politics, State-Building and Witch-Hunting', in *The Oxford Handbook of Witchcraft in Early Modern Europe and Colonial America*, ed. Brian P. Levack. Oxford, 2013: 528–47.

Di Simplicio, Oscar. 'Giandomenico Fei, the Only Male Witch: A Tuscan or an Italian Anomaly', in *Witchcraft and Masculinities in Early Modern Europe*, ed. Alison Rowlands. Basingstoke, 2009: 121–48.

Di Simplicio, Oscar. *Inquisizione Stregoneria Medicina: Siena e il Suo Stato (1580–1721)*. Siena, 2000.

Dömötör, Tekla. 'The Cunning Folk in English and Hungarian Witch Trials', in *Folklore Studies in the Twentieth Century*, ed. V. J. Newall. Woodbridge, 1978: 183–7.

Douglas, Mary. *Witchcraft Confessions and Accusations*. London, 1970.

Drummond, A. L. and J. Bulloch. *The Scottish Church 1688–1843*. Edinburgh, 1973.

Duffy, Eamon. *The Stripping of the Altars*. New Haven, 1992.

Dupont-Bouchat, Marie-Sylvie. 'Le Diable apprivoisée: Le sorcellerie revisité; mague et sorcellerie au XIXe siècle', in *Magie et sorcellerie du moyen âge à nos jours*, ed. R. Muchembled. Paris, 1994: 235–66.

Dupont-Bouchat, Marie-Sylvie. 'La Répression de la sorcellerie dans le duché de Luxembourg aux XVIe et XVIIe siècles', in M. Dupont-Bouchat, W. Frijhoff and R. Muchembled. *Prophètes et sorciers dans les Pays-Bas XVie–XVIIIe siècles*. Paris, 1978: 41–154.

Durrant, Jonathan. *Witchcraft, Gender and Society in Early Modern Germany*. Leiden, 2007.

Dworkin, Andrea. *Woman Hating*. New York, 1974.

Easlea, Brian. *Witch Hunting, Magic and the New Philosophy: An Introduction to the Debates of the Scientific Revolution 1450–1750*. Brighton, 1980.

Eiden, Herbert and Rita Voltmer (eds). *Hexenprozesse und Gerichtspraxis*. Trier, 2002.

Eisenstein, Elizabeth L. *The Printing Revolution in Early Modern Europe*. Cambridge, 1983.

Eliade, Mircea. *Occultism, Witchcraft and Cultural Fashions*. Chicago, 1976.

Ellis, Stephen. 'Witch-Hunting in Central Madagascar 1828–1861', *Past and Present* 175 (2002): 90–123.

Elmer, Peter. 'Science and Witchcraft', in *The Oxford Handbook of Witchcraft in Early Modern Europe and Colonial America*, ed. Brian P. Levack. Oxford, 2013: 548–60.

Elmer, Peter. 'Towards a Politics of Witchcraft in Early Modern England', in *Languages of Witchcraft: Narrative, Ideology and Meaning in Early Modern Culture*, ed. Stuart Clark. Basingstoke, 2001: 101–18.

Erikson, Kai. *Wayward Puritans*. New York, 1966.

Estes, Leland. 'The Medical Origins of the European Witch Craze: A Hypothesis', *Journal of Social History* 17 (1984): 271–84.

Evans, R. J. W. *The Making of the Habsburg Monarchy, 1550–1700*. Oxford, 1979.

Favret-Saada, Jeanne. *Deadly Words: Witchcraft in the Bocage*. Trans. Catherine Cullen. Cambridge, 1980.

Ferber, Sarah. *Demonic Possession and Exorcism in Early Modern France*. London, 2004.

Fisiy, Cyprian. 'Containing Occult Practices: Witchcraft Trials in Cameroon', *African Studies Review* 41 (1998): 148–51.

Fiume, Giovanna. 'The Old Vinegar Lady, or the Judicial Modernization of the Crime of Witchcraft', in *History from Crime*, ed. E. Muir and G. Ruggiero. Baltimore, 1994: 65–87.

Flint, Valerie I. J. *The Rise of Magic in Early Medieval Europe*. Princeton, 1991.

Foucault, Maurice. *Les Procès de sorcellerie dans l'ancienne France devant les jurisdictiones séculières*. Paris, 1907.

Fox, Sanford J. *Science and Justice: The Massachusetts Witchcraft Trials*. Baltimore, 1968.

Gareis, Iris. 'Merging Magical Traditions: Sorcery and Witchcraft in Spanish and Portuguese America', in *The Oxford Handbook of Witchcraft in Early Modern Europe and Colonial America*, ed. Brian P. Levack. Oxford, 2013: 412–28.

Gari Lacruz, Angel. 'Variedad de competencias en el delito de brujería 1600–1650 en Aragón', in *La Inquisición española: nueva visión, nueva horizontes*, ed J. Perez Villanueva. Madrid, 1980: 319–27.

Garnier, S. *Barbe Buvée et le pretendue possession des Ursulines d'Auxonne*. Paris, 1895.

Garrett, Clarke. 'Witches and Cunning Folk in the Old Regime', in *The Wolf and the Lamb: Popular Culture in France from the Old Regime to the Twentieth Century*, ed. J. Beauroy, M. Bertrand and E. T. Gargan. Stanford, 1976: 53–64.

Garrett, Clarke. 'Women and Witches: Patterns of Analysis', *Signs* 3 (1977): 461–70.

Gaskill, Malcolm. *Crime and Mentalities in Early Modern England*. Cambridge, 2000.

Gaskill, Malcolm. 'The Devil in the Shape of a Man: Witchcraft, Conflict and Belief in Jacobean England', *Historical Research* 71 (1998): 142–71.

Gaskill, Malcolm. *Hellish Nell: Last of Britain's Witches*. London, 2001.

Gaskill, Malcolm. 'Witchcraft and Power in Early Modern England: The Case of Margaret Moore', in *Women, Crime and the Courts in Early Modern England*, ed. J. Kermonde and G. Walker. Chapel Hill, 1994: 125–45.

Gaskill, Malcolm. 'Witchcraft in Early Modern Kent: Stereotypes and the Background to Accusations', in *Witchcraft in Early Modern Europe: Studies in Culture and Belief*, ed. Jonathan Barry, Marianne Hester and Gareth Roberts. Cambridge, 1996: 257–87.

Gaskill, Malcolm. *Witchfinders: A Seventeenth-Century English Tragedy*. London, 2005.

Gaudemet, J. 'Les ordiales au moyen age: doctrine, législation et pratique canoniques', in *La Preuve*, Receuils de la Société Jean Bodin 17. Brussels, 1965: 99–135.

Gehm, Britta. *Die Hexenverfolgung im Hochstift Bamberg und das Eingrefen des Reichshofrates zu ihrer Beendigung*. Hildsheim, 2000.

Geis, Gilbert and Ivan Bunn. *A Trial of Witches: A Seventeenth-Century Witchcraft Prosecution*. London, 1997.

Gentz, Lauritz. 'Vad förorsakade de stora häxprocesserna?', *ARV* 10 (1954): 33–9.

Gestrich, Andreas. 'Pietismus und Aberglaube: Zum Zusammenhang von popularem Pietismus und dem Ende der Hexenverfolgung im 18. Jahrhundert', in *Das Ende de Hexenverfolgung*, ed. Sönke Lorenz and Dieter R. Bauer. Stuttgart, 1995: 269–88.

Gibson, Marion. *Reading Witchcraft: Stories of Early English Witches*. London, 1999.

Gijswijt-Hofstra, Marijke. 'The European Witchcraft Debate and the Dutch Variant', *Social History* 15 (1990): 181–94.

Gijswijt-Hofstra, Marijke. 'Witchcraft after the Witch-Trials', in *Witchcraft and Magic in Europe: The Eighteenth and Nineteenth Centuries*, ed. Bengt Ankarloo and Stuart Clark. London, 1999: 95–189.

Gijswijt-Hofstra, Marijke. 'Witchcraft and Tolerance: The Dutch Case', *Acta Ethnographica* 37 (1991/2): 401–12.

Gijswijt-Hofstra, Marijke. 'Witchcraft in the Northern Netherlands', in *Current Issues in Women's History*, ed. Arina Angerman *et al*. London, 1989: 75–92.

Gijswijt-Hofstra, Marijke and Willem Frijhoff (eds). *Witchcraft in the Netherlands: From the Fourteenth to the Twentieth Century*. Rotterdam, 1991.

Gillespie, Raymond. 'Ireland', in *Encyclopedia of Witchcraft: The Western Tradition*, ed. Richard M. Golden, vol. II. Santa Barbara, 2006, 567–8.

Ginzburg, Carlo. *Ecstasies: Deciphering the Witches' Sabbath*. New York, 1991.

Ginzburg, Carlo. *The Night Battles: Witchcraft and Agrarian Cults in the Sixteenth and Seventeenth Centuries*. Trans. John and Anne Tedeschi. Baltimore, 1983.

Godbeer, Richard. *The Devil's Dominion: Magic and Religion in Early New England*. Cambridge, 1992.

Godbeer, Richard. *Escaping Salem: The Other Witch Hunt of 1692*. Oxford, 2005.

Golden, Richard M. (ed.). *Encyclopedia of Witchcraft: The Western Tradition*. 4 vols. Santa Barbara, 2006.

Golden, Richard M. 'Notions of Social and Religious Pollution in Nicholas Remy's *Demonolatry*', in *Politics, Ideology and the Law in Early Modern Europe: Essays in Honor of J. H. M. Salmon*, ed. Adrianna E. Bakos. Rochester, NY, 1994: 21–33.

Golden, Richard M. 'Satan in Europe: The Geography of the Witch Hunts', in *Changing Identities in Early Modern France*, ed. Michael Wolfe. Durham, NC, 1997: 216–47.

Goodare, Julian. 'The Scottish Witchcraft Panic of 1597', in *The Scottish Witch-Hunt in Context* Manchester, 2002: 51–72.

Goodare, Julian (ed.). *The Scottish Witch-Hunt in Context*. Manchester, 2002.

Goodare, Julian. 'Women and the Witch-Hunt in Scotland', *Social History* 23 (1998): 288–309.

Goodare, Julian, Lauren Marten and Joyce Miller (eds). *Witchcraft and Belief in Early Modern Scotland*. Basingstoke, 2008.

Goodare, Julian, Joyce Miller and Louise Yeoman. *The Survey of Scottish Witchcraft*. www.shca.ed.ac.uk/Research/witches/.

Goode, William. *Religion among the Primitives*. Glencoe, IL, 1951.

Greenleaf, R. E. *Zumarraga and the Mexican Inquisition 1536–1543*. Washington, 1962.

Greenleaf, R. E. *The Mexican Inquisition of the Sixteenth Century*. Albuquerque, 1969.

Gregory, Anabel. *Rye Spirits: Faith, Faction and Fairies in a Seventeenth Century English Town*. London, 2013.

Gregory, Anabel. 'Witchcraft, Politics and "Good Neighbourhood" in Early Seventeenth-Century Rye', *Past and Present* 133 (1991): 31–66.

Hall, A. R. *Henry More: Magic, Religion and Experiment*. Oxford, 1990.

Hansen, Chadwick. *Witchcraft at Salem*. New York, 1969.

Hansen, Joseph. *Zauberwahn, Inquisition and Hexenprozess im Mittelalter*. Munich, 1900.

Harley, David. 'Historians as Demonologists: The Myth of the Midwife-Witch', *Social History of Medicine* 3 (1990): 1–26.

Harner, Michael J. 'The Role of Hallucinogenic Plants in European Witchcraft', in *Hallucinogens and Shamanism*, ed. Michael J. Harner. New York, 1973: 125–50.

Harnischfeger, Johannes. 'Witchcraft and the State in South Africa', in *Witchcraft Violence and the Law in South Africa*, ed. J. Hund. Pretoria, 2003: 40–72.

Harrington, Joel. *The Faithful Executioner: Life and Death, Honor and Shame in the Turbulent Sixteenth Century*. New York, 2013.

Harris, H. A. *Sport in Greece and Rome*. Ithaca, NY, 1972.

Harris, Marvin. *Cows, Pigs, Wars and Witches*. New York, 1974.

Heikkinen, Antero. *Paholaisen Liittolaiset*. Helsinki, 1969.

Heikkinen, Antero and Timo Kervinen. 'Finland: The Male Domination', in *Early Modern European Witchcraft: Centres and Peripheries*, ed. Bengt Ankarloo and Gustav Henningsen. Oxford, 1990: 319–38.

Heinemann, Evelyn. *Hexen und Hexenglauben*. Frankfurt, 1986.

Heinsohn, Gunnar and Otto Steiger. 'The Elimination of Medieval Birth Control and the Witch Trials of Modern Times', *International Journal of Women's Studies* 5 (1982): 193–214.

Hellman, Lillian. *Scoundrel Time*. Boston, 1976.

Henderson, Ebenezer. *Annals of Dunfermline*. Glasgow, 1879.

Henningsen, Gustav. 'The Papers of Alonso de Salazar Frías', *Temenos* 5 (1969): 85–106.

Henningsen, Gustav. 'Witchcraft in Denmark', *Folklore* 93 (1982): 131–7.

Henningsen, Gustav. *The Witches' Advocate: Basque Witchcraft and the Spanish Inquisition, 1609–1614*. Reno, 1980.

Henningsen, Gustav. 'Witch Persecution after the Era of the Witch Trials', *ARV. Scandinavium Yearbook of Folklore* 144 (1988): 103–53.

Herzig, Tamar. *Christ Transformed into a Virgin Woman: Lucia Brocadelli, Heinrich Institoris and the Defense of the Faith*. Rome, 2013.

Herzig, Tamar. 'The Demons' Reaction to Sodomy: Witchcraft and Homosexuality in Gianfrancesco Pico della Mirandola's *Strix*', *Sixteenth Century Journal* 34 (2003): 53–72.

Herzig, Tamar. 'Witchcraft Prosecutions in Italy', in *The Oxford Handbook of Witchcraft in Early Modern Europe and Colonial America*, ed. Brian P. Levack. Oxford, 2013: 249–67.

Hester, Marianne. *Lewd Women and Wicked Witches: A Study of the Dynamics of Male Domination*. London, 1992.

Heyd, Michael. 'The Reaction to Enthusiasm in the Seventeenth Century: Towards an Integrative Approach', *Journal of Modern History* 53 (1981): 258–80.

Hitchcock, James. 'George Gifford and Puritan Witch Beliefs', *Archiv für Reformationsgeschichte* 58 (1967): 90–9.

Hoffer, Peter Charles. *The Devil's Disciples: Makers of the Salem Witchcraft Trials*. Baltimore, 1996.

Holmes, Clive. 'Popular Culture? Witches, Magistrates and Divines in Early Modern England', in *Understanding Popular Culture: Europe from the Middle Ages to the Nineteenth Century*, ed. S. Kaplan. Berlin, New York and Amsterdam, 1984: 85–111.

Holmes, Clive. 'Women: Witnesses and Witches', *Past and Present* 140 (1993): 43–78.

Horsley, Richard A. 'Who Were the Witches? The Social Roles of the Accused in the European Witch Trials', *Journal of Interdisciplinary History* 9 (1979): 689–715.

Houlbrooke, Ralph R. 'The Decline of Ecclesiastical Jurisdiction under the Tudors', in *Continuity and Change*, ed. R. O'Day and F. Heal. Leicester, 1976: 239–86.

Hund, John (ed.). *Witchcraft Violence and the Law in South Africa*. Pretoria, 2003.

Hutton, R., *The Triumph of the Moon: A History of Modern Pagan Witchcraft*. Oxford, 1999.

Huxley, Aldous. *The Devils of Loudon*. New York, 1952.

Jobe, T. H. 'The Devil in Restoration Science: The Glanvill–Webster Witchcraft Debate', *Isis* 72 (1981): 343–56.

Johansen, Jens Christian V. 'Denmark: The Sociology of Accusations', in *Early Modern European Witchcraft: Centres and Peripheries*, ed. Bengt Ankarloo and Gustav Henningsen. Oxford, 1990: 339–65.

Johansen, Jens Christian V. 'Witchcraft, Sin and Repentance: The Decline of Danish Witchcraft Trials', *Acta Ethnographica Acad. Sci. Hungarica* 37 (1992): 413–23.

Kahk, Juhan. 'Estonia II: The Crusade against Idolatry', in *Early Modern European Witchcraft: Centres and Peripheries*, ed. Bengt Ankarloo and Gustav Henningsen. Oxford, 1990: 273–84.

Kamber, Peter. 'La Chasse aux sorciers et aux sorcières dans le Pays de Vaud: Aspects quantitatifs (1581–1620)', *Revue historique vaudoise* 90 (1982): 21–33.

Kamensky, Jane. 'Words, Witches and Woman Trouble: Witchcraft, Disorderly Speech and Gender Boundaries in Puritan New England', *Essex Institute Historical Collections* 128 (1992): 286–307.

Karlsen, Carol. *The Devil in the Shape of a Woman: Witchcraft in Colonial New England*. New York, 1987.

Kern, Edmund M. 'An End to Witch Trials in Austria: Reconsidering the Enlightened State', *Austrian History Yearbook* 30 (1999): 159–235.

Kieckhefer, Richard. *European Witch Trials: Their Foundations in Popular and Learned Culture, 1300–1500.* London, 1976.

Kieckhefer, Richard. 'The First Wave of Trials for Diabolical Witchcraft', in *The Oxford Handbook of Witchcraft in Early Modern Europe and Colonial America*, ed. Brian P. Levack. Oxford, 2013: 159–78.

Kieckhefer, Richard. *Magic in the Middle Ages.* 2nd edn. Cambridge, 2000.

Kieckhefer, Richard. *The Repression of Heresy in Medieval Germany.* Philadelphia, 1980.

Kittredge, George L. *Witchcraft in Old and New England.* Cambridge, MA, 1929.

Kivelson, Valerie A. *Desperate Magic: The Moral Economy of Witchcraft in Seventeenth-Century Russia.* Ithaca, NY, 2013.

Kivelson, Valerie A. 'Through the Prism of Witchcraft: Gender and Social Change in Seventeenth-Century Muscovy', in *Russia's Women: Accommodation, Resistance, Transformation*, ed. B. E. Evans, B. A. Engel and C. D. Worobec. Berkeley, 1991: 74–94.

Klaits, Joseph. *Servants of Satan: The Age of the Witch Hunts.* Bloomington, 1985.

Klaits, Joseph. 'Witchcraft Trials and Absolute Monarchy in France', in *Church, State and Society under the Bourbon Kings of France*, ed. Richard Golden. Lawrence, 1982: 148–72.

Klaniczay, Gábor. 'Benandante-kresnik-zduhac-táltos', *Ethnographia* 94 (1983): 116–34.

Klaniczay, Gábor. 'Decline of Witches and Rise of Vampires under the Eighteenth-Century Habsburg Monarchy', *Ethnologia Europaea* 17 (1987): 168–88.

Klaniczay, Gábor. 'Hungary: The Accusations and the Universe of Popular Magic', in *Early Modern European Witchcraft*, ed. Bengt Ankarloo and Gustav Henningsen. Oxford, 1990: 219–55.

Klaniczay, Gábor. 'Shamanistic Elements in Central European Witchcraft', in *Shamanism in Eurasia*, ed. Mihaly Hoppal. Göttingen, 1984: 130–50.

Klaniczay, Gábor. 'Witch Hunting in Hungary: Social or Cultural Tensions?', *Acta Ethnographica* 37 (1991–2): 67–91.

Klaniczay, Gábor. *The Uses of Supernatural Power.* Princeton, 1990.

Klaniczay, Gábor and Éva Pócs (eds). *Communicating with the Spirits.* Budapest, 2009.

Kneubühler, Hans Peter. *Die Überwindung von Hexenwahn und Hexenprozess.* Diessenhofen, 1977.

Knutsen, Gunnar W. *Servants of Satan and Masters of Demons: The Spanish Inquisition's Trials for Superstition: Valencia and Barcelona, 1478–1700.* Turnhout, 2009.

Konig, David. *Law and Society in Colonial Massachusetts.* Chapel Hill, 1980.

Kristóf, Ildikó. '"Wise Women", Sinners and the Poor: The Social Background of Witch-Hunting in a 16th–18th Century Calvinist City of Eastern Hungary', *Acta Ethnographica* 37 (1991/2): 99–100.

Kunstmann, Harmut H. *Zauberwahn und Hexenprozesz in der Reichsstadt Nürnberg.* Nuremberg, 1970.

Kunze, Michael. *Highroad to the Stake: A Tale of Witchcraft.* Trans. William E. Yuill. Chicago, 1987.

Kunze, Michael. *Der Process Pappenheimer.* Ebelsbach, 1981.

Labouvie, Eva. 'Männer im Hexenprozess: Zur Sozialanthropologie eines "männlichen" Verstandnisses von Magie und Hexerei', in *Hexenverfolgung in der dörflichen Gesellschaft*, ed. W. Schieder. Göttingen, 1990: 56–78.

Labouvie, Eva. *Zauberei und Hexenwerk: Ländlicher Hexenglaube in der frühen Neuzeit.* Frankfurt, 1987.

La Fontaine, J. S. *Speak of the Devil: Tales of Satanic Abuse in Contemporary England.* Cambridge, 1998.

Lamont, William M. *Godly Rule: Politics and Religion, 1603–1660.* London, 1969.

Langbein, John. 'The Criminal Trial before the Lawyers', *University of Chicago Law Review* 45 (1978): 263–316.

Langbein, John. *Prosecuting Crime in the Renaissance*. Cambridge, MA, 1974.

Langbein, John. *Torture and the Law of Proof*. Chicago, 1977.

Lange, Ursula. *Untersuchungen zu Bodins Démonomanie*. Frankfurt, 1970.

Lapoint, Elwyn C. 'Irish Immunity to Witch-Hunting 1534–1711', *Eire-Ireland* 27 (1992): 76–92.

Larner, Christina. '*Crimen Exceptum*? The Crime of Witchcraft in Europe', in *Crime and the Law*, ed. V. A. C. Gatrell, Bruce Lenman and Geoffrey Parker. London, 1980: 49–75.

Larner, Christina. *Enemies of God: The Witch-Hunt in Scotland*. Baltimore and London, 1981.

Larner, Christina. 'James VI and I and Witchcraft', in *The Reign of James VI and I*, ed. A. G. R. Smith. London, 1973: 74–90.

Larner, Christina. *Witchcraft and Religion: The Politics of Popular Belief*. Oxford, 1984.

Larner, Christina, C. H. Lee and H. V. McLachlan. *Source-Book of Scottish Witchcraft*. Glasgow, 1977.

LaVey, Anton S. *The Satanic Bible*. New York, 1969.

Le Roy Ladurie, Emmanuel. *Les Paysans de Languedoc*. Paris, 1966.

Lea, Henry C. *A History of the Inquisition in Spain*. 4 vols. New York, 1906–7.

Lea, Henry C. *A History of the Inquisition of the Middle Ages*. 3 vols. New York, 1955.

Lea, Henry C. *Materials toward a History of Witchcraft*. Arr. and ed. Arthur C. Howland. 3 vols. New York, 1957.

Lea, Henry C. *The Ordeal*. Ed. Edward Peters. Philadelphia, 1973.

Lea, Henry C. *Torture*. Ed. Edward Peters. Philadelphia, 1973.

Lenman, Bruce and Geoffrey Parker. 'The State, the Community and the Criminal Law in Early Modern Europe', in *Crime and the Law*, ed. V. Gatrell, Bruce Lenman and Geoffrey Parker. London, 1980: 11–48.

Leutenbauer, Siegfried. *Hexerei- und Zaubereidelikt in der Literatur von 1450 bis 1550*. Berlin, 1972.

Levack, Brian P. 'The Decline and End of Witchcraft Prosecutions', in *Witchcraft and Magic in Europe: The Eighteenth and Nineteenth Centuries*, ed. Bengt Ankarloo and Stuart Clark. London, 1999: 1–93.

Levack, Brian P. *The Devil Within: Possession and Exorcism in the Christian West*. New Haven and London, 2013.

Levack, Brian P. 'The Horrors of Witchcraft and Demonic Possession', *Social Research* 81 (2014): 921–39.

Levack, Brian P. 'Judicial Torture in Scotland during the Age of Mackenzie', in *The Stair Society Miscellany IV*, ed. H. L. MacQueen. Edinburgh, 2002: 185–98.

Levack, Brian P. (ed.). *The Oxford Handbook of Witchcraft in Early Modern Europe and Colonial America*. Oxford, 2013.

Levack, Brian P. 'State-Building and Witch Hunting in Early Modern Europe', in *Witchcraft in Early Modern Europe: Studies in Culture and Belief*, ed. Jonathan Barry, Marianne Hester and Gareth Roberts. Cambridge, 1996: 96–115.

Levack, Brian P. *Witch-Hunting in Scotland: Law, Politics and Religion*. London, 2008.

Levack, Brian P. 'Witch-Lynching: Past and Present', in *Swift to Wrath: Lynching in Global Historical Perspective*, ed. William D. Carrigan and Christopher Waldrep. Charlottesville, 2013: 49–67.

Levy, Leonard W. 'Accusatorial and Inquisitorial Systems of Criminal Procedure: The Beginnings', in *Freedom and Reform*, ed. H. Hyam and L. Levy. New York, 1967: 16–54.

Lewis, Anthony. 'Making Torture Legal', *New York Review of Books*, 15 July 2004.

Lorenz, Sönke. *Aktenversendung und Hexenprozess: Dargestellt am Beispiel der Juristen fakultäten Rostock und Greifswald (1570/82–1630)*. 2 vols. Frankfurt, 1982–3.

Lorenz, Sönke. 'Johann Georg Goedelmann – Ein Gegner des Hexenwahns?', in *Beiträge zur Pommerschen und mecklenberischen Geschichte*, ed. R. Schmidt. Marburg, 1981: 61–105.

Lorint, F. E. and J. Bernabe. *La Sorcellerie paysanne*. Brussels, 1977.

Luhrmann, T. M. *Persuasions of the Witch's Craft: Ritual Magic in Contemporary England*. Cambridge, MA, 1989.

McAuliffe, Mary. 'Gender, History and Witchcraft in Early Modern Ireland: A Re-reading of the Florence Newton Trial', in *Gender and Power in Irish History*, ed. Mary Ann Gialenella Valiulis. Dublin, 2009: 39–58.

McCaghy, C. *Deviant Behavior*. New York, 1976.

MacDonald, Michael. *Mystical Bedlam: Madness, Anxiety and Healing in Seventeenth-Century England*. Cambridge, 1981.

MacDonald, Michael (ed.). *Witchcraft and Hysteria in Elizabethan London: Edward Jorden and the Mary Glover Case*. London, 1990.

Macdonald, Stuart. *The Witches of Fife: Witch-Hunting in a Scottish Shire, 1560–1710*. East Linton, 2002.

Macfarlane, Alan. *Witchcraft in Tudor and Stuart England*. New York and London, 1970.

Madar, Maia. 'Estonia I: Werewolves and Poisoners', in *Early Modern European Witch-Craft: Centres and Peripheries*, ed. Bengt Ankarloo and Gustav Henningsen. Oxford, 1990: 257–72.

Mair, Lucy. *Witchcraft*. New York, 1969.

Mandrou, Robert. *Magistrats et sorciers en France au XVII siècle*. Paris, 1968.

Martin, Ruth. *Witchcraft and the Inquisition in Venice, 1550–1650*. Oxford, 1989.

Marwick, Max (ed.). *Witchcraft and Sorcery*. London, 1970.

Marx, J. Jean. *L'Inquisition en Dauphiné*. Paris, 1914.

Masters, R. *Eros and Evil*. New York, 1966.

Maxwell-Stuart, P. G. *Satanic Conspiracy: Magic and Witchcraft in Sixteenth-Century Scotland*. East Linton, 2001.

Maxwell-Stuart, P. G. *Witch Hunters: Professional Prickers, Unwitchers and Witch Finders of the Renaissance*. Stroud, 2003.

Merchant, Carolyn. *The Death of Nature: Women, Ecology and the Scientific Revolution*. New York, 1980.

Merzbacher, Friedrich. *Die Hexenprozesse in Franken*. Munich, 1957.

Michelet, Jules. *Satanism and Witchcraft*. Trans. A. R. Allison. New York, 1939.

Midelfort, H. C. Erik. 'Catholic and Lutheran Reactions to Demon Possession in the Late Seventeenth Century: Two Case Histories', *Daphnis* 15 (1986): 622–48.

Midelfort, H. C. Erik. 'Heartland of the Witchcraze: Central and Northern Europe', *History Today* 31 (1981): 27–31.

Midelfort, H. C. Erik. 'Johann Weyer and the Transformation of the Insanity Defense', in *The German People and the Reformation*, ed. R. Po-Chia Hsia. Ithaca, NY, 1988: 234–61.

Midelfort, H. C. Erik. 'Witchcraft, Magic and the Occult', in *Reformation Europe: A Guide to Research*, ed. S. Ozment. St Louis, 1982: 183–209.

Midelfort, H. C. Erik. 'Witch-Hunting and the Domino Theory', in *Religion and the People, 800–1700*, ed. James Obelkevich. Chapel Hill, 1979: 277–88.

Midelfort, H. C. Erik. *Witch Hunting in Southwestern Germany, 1562–1684: The Social and Intellectual Foundations*. Stanford, 1972.

Miller, Arthur. *The Crucible*. Boston, 1953.

Miller, Perry. *The New England Mind: From Colony to Province*. Cambridge, MA, 1953.

Mitchell, Stephen A. *Witchcraft and Magic in the Nordic Middle Ages*. Philadelphia, 2011.

Monter, E. William. *European Witchcraft*. New York, 1969.

Monter, E. William. 'French and Italian Witchcraft', *Witchcraft Today* 30 (1980): 31–5.

Monter, E. William. *Frontiers of Heresy: The Spanish Inquisition from the Basque Lands to Sicily*. Cambridge, 1990.

Monter, E. William. 'The Pedestal and the Stake: Courtly Love and Witchcraft', in *Becoming Visible: Women in European History*, ed. Renata Bridenthal and Claudia Koonz. Boston, 1977: 119–36.

Monter, E. William. *Ritual, Myth and Magic in Early Modern Europe*. Athens, OH, 1983.

Monter, E. William. 'La sodomie à l'époque moderne en Suisse romande', *Annales* 29 (1974): 1023–33.

Monter, E. William. 'Toads and Eucharists: The Male Witches of Normandy, 1564–1660', *French Historical Studies* 20 (1997): 563–95.

Monter, E. William. 'Witch Trials in Continental Europe, 1560–1660', in *Witchcraft and Magic in Europe: The Period of the Witch Trials*, ed. Bengt Ankarloo and Stuart Clark. London, 2002: 1–52.

Monter, E. William. *Witchcraft in France and Switzerland: The Borderlands during the Reformation*. Ithaca, NY, 1976.

Morgado García, Arturo. *Demnios, magos y brujas en la España moderna*. Cadiz, 1999.

Mormando, Franco. 'Bernardino of Siena, Popular Preacher and Witch-Hunter: A 1426 Witch Trial in Rome', *Fifteenth-Century Studies* 24 (1998): 84–118.

Mormando, Franco. *The Preacher's Demons: Bernardino of Siena and the Social Underworld of Early Renaissance Italy*. Chicago, 1999.

Muchembled, Robert. *Les derniers bûchers: Un village de Flandres et ses sorcières sous Louis XIV*. Paris, 1981.

Muchembled, Robert. *Popular Culture and Elite Culture in France, 1400–1750*. Trans. L. Cochrane. Baton Rouge, 1985.

Muchembled, Robert. 'Satanic Myths and Cultural Reality', in *Early Modern European Witchcraft: Centres and Peripheries*, ed. Bengt Ankarloo and Gustav Henningsen. Oxford, 1990: 139–60.

Muchembled, Robert. 'Satan ou les hommes? La chasse aux sorcières et ses causes', in M. Dupont-Bouchat, W. Frijhoff and R. Muchembled. *Prophètes et sorciers dans les Pays-Bas XVIe–XVIIIe siècle*. Paris, 1978: 13–39.

Muchembled, Robert. 'The Witches of the Cambrésis: The Acculturation of the Rural World in the Sixteenth and Seventeenth Centuries', in *Religion and the People, 800–1700*, ed. James Obelkevich. Chapel Hill, 1979: 221–76.

Murray, Alexander. 'Medieval Origins of the Witch Hunt', *The Cambridge Quarterly* 7 (1976): 63–74.

Murray, Margaret A. *The Divine King of England*. London, 1954.

Murray, Margaret A. *The God of the Witches*. London, 1933.

Murray, Margaret A. *The Witch-Cult in Western Europe*. Oxford, 1921.

Naess, Hans E. 'Norway: The Criminological Context', in *Early Modern European Witchcraft: Centres and Peripheries*, ed. B. Ankarloo and G. Henningsen. Oxford, 1990: 367–82.

Naphy, William G. *Plagues, Poisons and Potions: Plague Spreading Conspiracies in the Western Alps c. 1530–1640*. Manchester, 2002.

Nauert, C. G. *Agrippa and the Crisis of Renaissance Thought*. Urbana, 1965.

Nemec, J. *Witchcraft and Medicine, 1484–1793*. Washington, 1974.

Nenonen, Marko. *Noituus, taikuus ja noitavainot: Ala-Satakunnan, Pohjois-Pohjanmaan ja Viipurin Karjalan maaseudulla vuosina 1620–1700* [Witchcraft, Magic and Witch Trials in Rural Lower Satakunta, Northern Ostrobothnia and Viipuri Carelia, 1620–1700]. Helsinki, 1992.

Newton, John and Jo Bath (eds). *Witchcraft and the Act of 1604*. Leiden, 2008.

Niehaus, Isak A. 'The ANC's Dilemma: The Symbolic Politics of Three Witch-Hunts in the South African Lowveld, 1990–1995', *African Studies Review* 41 (1998): 93–118.

Niehaus, Isak A. *Witchcraft, Power and Politics: Exploring the Occult in the South African Lowveld*. London, 2001.

Norton, Mary Beth. *In the Devil's Snare: The Salem Witchcraft Crisis of 1692*. New York, 2002.

Notestein, Wallace. *A History of Witchcraft in England*. Washington, DC, 1911.

Nottingham, Elizabeth. *Religion: A Sociological View*. New York, 1971.

Oates, Caroline. 'The Trial of a Teenage Werewolf, Bordeaux, 1613', *Criminal Justice History* 9 (1988): 1–29.

Oberman, Heiko A. *Luther: Man between God and the Devil*. Trans. E. Walliser-Schwarzbart. New Haven and London, 1989.

Oberman, Heiko A. *Masters of the Reformation*. Cambridge, 1981.

Oesterreich, Traugott K. *Possession, Demoniacal and Other*. Trans. D. Ibberson. New York, 1966.

O'Keefe, Daniel L. *Stolen Lightning: The Social Theory of Magic*. New York, 1982.

Olli, Soili-Maria. 'The Devil's Pact: A Male Strategy', in *Beyond the Witch Trials: Witchcraft and Magic in Enlightenment Europe*, ed. Owen Davies and Willem de Blécourt. Manchester, 2004: 100–16.

O'Neil, Mary. 'Magical Healing, Love Magic and the Inquisition in Late Sixteenth Century Modena', in *Inquisition and Society in Early Modern Europe*, ed. Stephen Haliczar. Totowa, 1987: 88–114.

Ostling, Michael. *Between the Devil and the Host: Imagining Witchcraft in Early Modern Poland*. Oxford, 2011.

Ostling, Michael. 'Witchcraft in Poland', in *The Oxford Handbook of Witchcraft in Early Modern Europe and Colonial America*, ed. Brian P. Levack. Oxford, 2013: 318–33.

Ostorero, Martine. *Le Diable au sabbat: Littérature démonologique et sorcellerie (1440–1460)*. Florence, 2011.

Pagels, Elaine. *The Origin of Satan*. New York, 1995.

Paiva, José Pedro. *Bruxaria e superstição num País sem 'Caça às Bruxas', 1600–1774*. Lisbon, 1997.

Parke, Frances Neal. 'Witchcraft in Maryland', *Maryland Historical Magazine* 31 (1936): 271–98.

Parker, Geoffrey. 'Some Recent Work on the Inquisition in Spain and Italy', *Journal of Modern History* 54 (1982): 519–32.

Parrinder, Geoffrey. *Witchcraft: European and African*. London, 1958.

Paulus, Nikolaus. *Hexenwahn und Hexenprozesse, vornehmlich im 16 Jahrhundert*. Freiburg, 1910.

Pearl, Jonathan L. 'Bodin's Advice to Judges in Witchcraft Cases', *Proceedings of the Annual Meeting of the Western Society for French History* 16 (1989): 95–102.

Pearl, Jonathan L. *The Crime of Crimes: Demonology and Politics in France, 1560–1620*. Waterloo, Ontario, 1999.

Pearl, Jonathan L. 'Humanism and Satanism: Jean Bodin's Contribution to the Witchcraft Crisis', *Canadian Review of Sociology and Anthropology* 19 (1984): 541–8.

Pearl, Jonathan L. 'Witchcraft in New France in the Seventeenth Century: The Social Aspect', *Historical Reflections* 4 (1977): 191–205.

Peters, Edward. *Inquisition*. Berkeley, 1989.

Peters, Edward. *The Magician, the Witch and the Law*. Philadelphia, 1978.

Peters, Edward. *Torture*. Oxford, 1985.

Pfister, C. 'Nicolas Remy et la sorcellerie en Lorraine la fin du XVI siècle', *Revue Historique* 93 and 94 (1907): 225–39, 28–44.

Pitt-Rivers, Julian. 'Honour and Social Status', in *Honour and Shame: The Values of Mediterranean Society*, ed. J. G. Peristiany. Chicago, 1966: 19–78.

Pitts, John L. *Witchcraft and Devil Lore in the Channel Islands*. Guernsey, 1886.

Pohl, Herbert. *Hexenglaube und Hexenverfolgung im Kurfürstentum Main.z* Geschichtliche Landeskunde 32. Stuttgart, 1988.

Pollock, Adrian. 'Social and Economic Characteristics of Witchcraft Accusations in Sixteenth- and Seventeenth-Century Kent', *Archaeologia Cantiana* 95 (1979): 37–48.

Poole, Robert (ed.). *The Lancashire Witches: Histories and Stories.* Manchester, 2002.

Popkin, Richard H. *The History of Scepticism from Erasmus to Descartes.* Assen, 1960.

Pott, M. 'Aufklärung und Hexenglaube: Philosophische Ansätze zur Überwindung der Teufelspakttheorie in der deutsche Frühaufklärung', in *Das Ende der Hexenverfolgung*, ed. Sönke Lorenz and Dieter R. Bauer. Stuttgart, 1995: 183–202.

Purkiss, Diane. *The Witch in History: Early Modern and Twentieth-Century Representations.* London, 1996.

Rabb, Theodore. *The Struggle for Stability in Early Modern Europe.* New York, 1975.

Radford, G. H. 'Thomas Larkham', *Reports and Transactions of the Devonshire Association* 24 (1892): 96–146.

Rafnsson, Magnùs. *Angurgapi: The Witch-Hunt in Iceland.* Hólmavik, 2003.

Rapley, Robert. *A Case of Witchcraft: The Trial of Urbain Grandier.* Montreal, 1998.

Riezler, S. *Geschichte der Hexenprozesse in Bayern.* Stuttgart, 1896; repr. Aalen, 1968.

Robbins, Rossell Hope. *The Encyclopedia of Witchcraft and Demonology.* New York, 1959.

Robisheaux, Thomas. *The Last Witch of Langenburg: Murder in a German Village.* New York, 2009.

Roeck, B. 'Christlisher Idealstaat und Hexenwahn zum Ende der Europaischen Verfolgungen', *Historisches Jahrbuch* 108 (1988): 379–405.

Roper, Lyndal. 'Evil, Imaginings and Fantasies: Child Witches and the End of the Witch Craze', *Past and Present* 167 (2000): 107–39.

Roper, Lyndal. *Oedipus and the Devil: Witchcraft, Sexuality and Religion in Early Modern Europe.* London, 1994.

Roper, Lyndal. *Witch-Craze: Terror and Fantasy in Baroque Germany.* New Haven, 2004.

Roper, Lyndal. *The Witch in the Western Imagination.* Charlottesville, 2012.

Rose, Elliot. *A Razor for a Goat.* Toronto, 1962.

Rosen, George. 'Psychopathology of the Social Process: (I) A Study of the Persecution of Witches in Europe as a Contribution to the Understanding of Mass Delusion and Psychic Epidemics', *Journal of Health and Human Behavior* 1 (1960): 13–44.

Rothkrug, Lionel. 'Icon and Ideology in Religion and Rebellion, 1300–1600: *Bauerfreiheit* and *religion royale*', in J. M. Bak and G. Benecke (eds) *Religion and Rural Revolt.* Manchester, 1984: 31–61.

Rothkrug, Lionel. 'Religious Practices and Collective Perceptions: Hidden Homologies in the Renaissance and Reformation', *Historical Reflections* 7 (1980): 103–50.

Rowlands, Alison. 'Eine Stadt ohne Hexenwahn. Hexenprozesse, Gerichtspraxis und Herrschaft im frühneuzeitlichen Rothenburg ob der Tauber', in *Hexenprozesse und Gerichtspraxis*, ed. Herbert Eiden and Rita Voltmer. Trier, 2002: 331–47.

Rowlands, Alison. 'Stereotypes and Statistics: Old Women and Accusations of Witchcraft in Early Modern Europe', in *Power and Poverty: Old Age in the Pre-Industrial Past*, ed. Susannah R. Ottaway, L. A. Botelho, and K. Kittredge. Westport, 2002: 167–86.

Rowlands, Alison (ed.). *Witchcraft and Masculinities in Early Modern Europe.* Basingstoke, 2009.

Rowlands, Alison. 'Witchcraft and Old Women in Early Modern Germany', *Past and Present* 173 (2001): 50–89.

Rowlands, Alison. *Witchcraft Narratives in Germany: Rothenburg, 1561–1652.* Manchester, 2003.

Rummel, Walter. *Bauern, Herren und Hexen: Studien zur Sozialgeschichte sponheimischer und kurtrierischer Hexenprozesse, 1574–1664.* Göttingen, 1991.

Rummel, Walter and Rita Voltmer. *Hexen und Hexenverfolgung in der Frühen Neuzeit*. Darmstadt, 2008.

Russell, Jeffrey B. *Witchcraft in the Middle Ages*. Ithaca, NY, 1972.

Ryan, W. F. *The Bathhouse at Midnight: Magic in Russia*. University Park, 1999.

Ryan, W. F. 'The Witchcraft Hysteria in Early Modern Europe: Was Russia an Exception?', *Slavonic and East European Review* 76 (1998): 49–84.

Sabean, David W. *Power in the Blood: Popular Culture and Village Discourse in Early Modern Germany*. Cambridge,1984.

Sawyer, Ronald C. '"Strangely Handled in all her Lyms": Witchcraft and Healing in Jacobean England', *Journal of Social History* 22 (1989): 461–85.

Schmauder, Andreas (ed.). *Frühe Hexenverfolgung in Ravensburg und am Bodensee*. Konstanz, 2001.

Schmidt, Jürgen M. *Glaube und Skepsis. Die Kurpfalz und die abendländlische Hexenverfolgung 1446–1685*. Bielefeld, 2000.

Schormann, Gerhard. *Hexenprozesse in Deutschland*. Göttingen, 1981.

Schormann, Gerhard. *Hexenprozesse in Nordwestdeutschland*. Hildesheim, 1977.

Schulte, Rolf. *Hexenmeister: Die Verfolgung von Männern im Rahmen der Hexenverfolgung von 1530–1730 im Alten Reich*. Frankfurt, 1999.

Scribner, Robert. 'Ritual and Popular Religion in Catholic Germany at the Time of the Reformation', *Journal of Ecclesiastical History* 35 (1984): 44–77.

Scribner, Robert. 'Witchcraft and Judgement in Reformation Germany', *History Today* 40 (1990): 12–19.

Sebald, Hans. *Witch-Children*. Amherst, NY, 1995.

Sebald, Hans. *Witchcraft: The Heritage of a Heresy*. New York, 1978.

Seitz, Jonathan. *Witchcraft and Inquisition in Early Modern Venice*. Cambridge, 2011.

Segl, Peter (ed.). *Der Hexenhammer: Enstehung und Umfeld des Malleus Maleficarum von 1487*. Cologne, 1988.

Seth, Ronald. *Children against Witches*. New York, 1969.

Seymour, St John. *Irish Witchcraft and Demonology*. Dublin, 1913.

Shapiro, Barbara. *Probability and Certainty in Seventeenth Century England*. Princeton, 1983.

Sharpe, J. A. *Instruments of Darkness: Witchcraft in England, 1550–1570*. London, 1996.

Sharpe, J. A. *Witchcraft in Seventeenth-Century Yorkshire: Accusations and Counter Measures*. [Borthwick Paper No. 81]. York, 1992.

Sharpe, J. A. 'Witchcraft and Women in Seventeenth-Century England: Some Northern Evidence', *Continuity and Change* 6 (1991): 179–99.

Shumaker, Wayne. *The Occult Sciences in the Renaissance*. Berkeley, 1972.

Silverblatt, Irene. *Moon, Sun and Witches: Gender Ideologies and Class in Inca and Colonial Peru*. Princeton, 1987.

Simon, Maryse. *Les affaires de sorcellerie dans le Val de Lièpvre (XVe et XVIIe siècles)*. Société Savante d'Alsace, 2006.

Sluhovsky, Moshe. *Believe Not Every Spirit: Possession, Mysticism, and Discernment in Early Modern Catholicism*. Chicago, 2007.

Sluhovsky, Moshe. 'The Devil in the Convent', *American Historical Review* 107 (2002): 1379–411.

Sneddon, Andrew. 'Witchcraft Belief and Trials in Early Modern Ireland', *Irish Economic and Social History* 39 (2012): 1–25.

Soldan, Wilhelm G. and Heinrich Heppe. *Geschichte der Hexenprozesse*. Ed. M. Bauer. Munich, 1912.

Soman, A. F. 'Decriminalizing Witchcraft: Does the French Experience Furnish a European Model?', *Criminal Justice History* 10 (1989): 1–22.

Soman, A. F. 'The Parlement of Paris and the Great Witch Hunt (1565–1640)', *Sixteenth Century Journal* 9 (1978): 31–44.

Soman, A. F. 'Le Rôle des Ardennes dans la décriminalisation de la sorcellerie en France', *Revue historique Ardennaise* 23 (1988): 23–45.

Soman, A. F. 'Trente procès de sorcellerie dans le Perche (1566–1624)', *L'Orne littéraire* 8 (1986): 42–57.

Soman, A. F. 'Witch Lynching at Juniville', *Natural History* 95 (1986): 8–15.

Sörlin, Per. *'Wicked Arts': Witchcraft and Magic Trials in Southern Sweden, 1635–1754.* Leiden, 1999.

Souza, Laura de Mello e. *The Devil and the Land of the Holy Cross: Witchcraft, Slavery and Popular Religion in Colonial Brazil.* Trans. Diane G. Whitty. Austin, 2003.

Stafford, Helen. 'Notes on Scottish Witchcraft Cases 1590–91', in *Essays in Honour of Conyers Read*, ed. N. Downs. Chicago, 1953: 96–118.

Stephens, Walter. *Demon Lovers: Witchcraft, Sex, and the Crisis of Belief.* Chicago, 2002.

Stokes, Laura. *Demons of Urban Reform: Early European Witch Trials and Criminal Justice, 1430–1530.* Basingstoke, 2011.

Stronks, G. J. 'The Significance of Balthasar Bekker's *The Enchanted World*', in *Witchcraft in the Netherlands from the Fourteenth to the Twentieth Century*, ed. M. Gijswijt-Hofstra and W. Frijhoff. Rotterdam, 1991: 149–56.

Szasz, Thomas. *The Myth of Mental Illness.* New York, 1961.

Tausiet, María. *Urban Magic in Early Modern Spain: Abracadabra Omnipotens.* Basingstoke, 2014.

Tazbir, Janusz. 'Hexenprozesse in Polen', *Archiv für Reformationsgeschichte* 71 (1980): 280–307.

Tazbir, Janusz. *A State without Stakes.* Trans. A. T. Jordan. Wydawniczy, 1973.

Teall, John L. 'Witchcraft and Calvinism in Elizabethan England: Divine Power and Human Agency', *Journal of the History of Ideas* 23 (1962): 21–36.

Tedeschi, John. 'Inquisitorial Law and the Witch', in *Early Modern European Witchcraft: Centres and Peripheries*, ed. B. Ankarloo and G. Henningsen. Oxford, 1990: 86–118.

Tedeschi, John. 'Preliminary Observations on Writing a History of the Roman Inquisition', in *Continuity and Discontinuity in Church History*, ed. F. F. Church and T. George. Leiden, 1979.

Tedeschi, John. *The Prosecution of Heresy.* Binghamton, 1991.

Terpstra, J. U. 'Petrus Goldschmidt aus Husum', *Euphorion* 59 (1965): 361–83.

Thomas, Keith. *Religion and the Decline of Magic.* London, 1971.

Thorndike, Lynn. *A History of Magic and Experimental Science.* 8 vols. New York, 1941.

Thurston, Robert W. *Witch, Wicce, Mother Goose: The Rise and Fall of the Witch Hunts in Europe and North America.* London, 2001.

Toivo, Raisa Maria. *Witchcraft and Gender in Early Modern Society: Finland and the Wider European Experience.* Aldershot, 2008.

Tourney, Garfield. 'The Physician and Witchcraft in Restoration England', *Medical History* 16 (1972): 143–55.

Trevor-Roper, H. R. 'The European Witch-Craze of the Sixteenth and Seventeenth Centuries', in H. R. Trevor-Roper, *The European Witch-Craze of the Sixteenth and Seventeenth Centuries and Other Essays.* New York, 1969: 90–192; and in *Religion, the Reformation and Social Change.* London, 1967.

University of Oslo. *Trolldomsprosesser* Witchcraft Trials. www.edd.uio.no/ikos/heksearkiv/prosesser.html.

Unsworth, C. R. 'Witchcraft Beliefs and Criminal Procedure in Early Modern England', in *Legal Record and Historical Reality*, ed. T. G. Watkin. London, 1989: 71–98.

Unverhau, Dagmar. 'Akkusationsprozess-Inquisitionsprozess: Indikatoren für die Intensität der Hexenverfolgung in Schleswig-Holstein?' In *Hexenprozesse: Deutsche und skandinavische Beitrage*, ed. C. Degn, H. Lehmann and D. Unverhau. Neumünster, 1983: 59–143.

Unverhau, Dagmar. 'Kieler Hexen und Zauberer zur Zeit der grossen Verfolgung (1530–1676)', *Mitteilungen der Gesellschaft für Kieler Stadtgeschichte* 68 (1981): 41–96.

Valentinitsch, Helfried (ed.). *Hexen und Zauberer: Die grosze Verfolgung – ein europäisches Phänomen in der Steiermark*. Graz, 1987.

Valletta, Frederick. *Witchcraft, Magic and Superstition in England, 1640–70*. Aldershot, 2000.

Várkonyi, A. 'Connections between the Cessation of Witch Trials and the Transformation of the Social Structure Related to Medicine', *Acta Ethnographica Hungarica* 37 (1991–2): 426–77.

Victor, Jeffrey S. *Satanic Panic: The Creation of a Contemporary Legend*. Chicago, 1993.

Volk, Franz. *Hexen in der Landvogtei Ortenau und der Reichsstadt Offenburg*. Lahr, 1882.

Voltmer, Rita. 'Hexenprozesse und Hochgerichte: zur herrschaftlich-politischen Nutzung und Instrumentalisierung von Hexenverfolgungen', in *Hexenprozesse und Gerichtspraxis*, ed. Herbert Eiden and Rita Voltmer. Trier, 2002: 475–525.

Voltmer, Rita. 'Witch-Finders, Witch-Hunters or Kings of the Sabbath? The Prominent Role of Men in the Mass Persecutions of the Rhine-Meuse Area (Sixteenth-Seventeenth Centuries)', in *Witchcraft and Masculinities in Early Modern Europe*, ed. Alison Rowlands. Basingstoke, 2009: 74–99.

Waardt, Hans de. 'Prosecution or Defense: Procedural Possibilities following a Witchcraft Accusation in the Province of Holland before 1800', in *Witchcraft in the Netherlands from the Fourteenth to the Twentieth Centuries*, ed. Marijke Gijswijt-Hofstra and W. Frijhoff. Rotterdam, 1991: 79–90.

Waardt, Hans de. 'Rechtssicherheit nach dem Zusammenbruch der zentralen Gewalt. Rechtspflege, Obrigkeit, Toleranz und wirtschaftliche Verhältnisse in Holland', in *Das Ende der Hexenverfolgung*, ed. Sönke Lorenz and Dieter R. Bauer. Stuttgart, 1995: 129–52.

Waardt, Hans de. *Toverij en samenleving. Holland 1500–1800*. The Hague, 1991.

Waite, Gary K. *Eradicating the Devil's Minions: Anabaptists and Witches in Reformation Europe, 1525–1600*. Toronto, 2007.

Waite, Gary K. *Heresy, Magic, and Witchcraft in Early Modern Europe*. Basingstoke, 2003.

Wakefield, W. L. and A. P. Evans (eds). *Heresies of the High Middle Ages*. New York, 1969.

Walinski-Kiehl, Robert S. 'The Devil's Children: Child Witch-Trials in Early Modern Germany', *Continuity and Change* 11 (1996): 171–89.

Walinski-Kiehl, Robert S. 'Godly States: Confessional Conflict and Witch-Hunting in Early Modern Germany', *Mentalité-Mentalities* 5 (1988): 13–24.

Walinski-Kiehl, Robert S. 'Males, "Masculine Honor" and Witch Hunting in Seventeenth-Century Germany', *Men and Masculinities* 6 (2004): 254–71.

Walinski-Kiehl, Robert S. 'Pamphlets, Propaganda and Witch-Hunting in Germany c.1560–c.1630', *Reformation* 6 (2002): 49–74.

Walker, D. P. *Spiritual and Demonic Magic: From Ficino to Campanella*. London, 1958.

Walker, D. P. *Unclean Spirits: Possession and Exorcism in France and England in the Late Sixteenth and Early Seventeenth Centuries*. London and Philadelphia, 1981.

Waller, Richard D. 'Witchcraft and Colonial Law in Kenya', *Past and Present* 180 (2003): 241–75.

Watkins, S. C. 'Spinsters', *Journal of Family History* 9 (1984): 310–25.

Watt, Jeffrey R. *The Scourge of Demons: Possession, Lust and Witchcraft in a Seventeenth-Century Convent*. Rochester, 2009.

Weisman, Richard. *Witchcraft, Magic and Religion in Seventeenth-Century Massachusetts*. Amherst, 1984.

West, Robert H. *Reginald Scot and Renaissance Writings on Witchcraft*. Boston, 1984.

White, Lynn, Jr. 'Death and the Devil', in *The Darker Vision of the Renaissance*, ed. R. S. Kinsman. Berkeley, 1974: 25–46.

Wiers-Jenssen, Hans. *Anne Pedersdotter: A Drama in Four Acts*. Trans. John Masefield. Boston, 1917.

Wilby, Emma. *The Visions of Isobel Gowdie: Magic, Witchcraft and Dark Shamanism in Seventeenth-Century Scotland*. Brighton, 2011.

Williams, Gerhild Scholz. *Defining Dominion: The Discourses of Magic and Witchcraft in Early Modern France and Germany*. Ann Arbor, 1995.

Williamson, Arthur. *Scottish National Consciousness in the Age of James VI*. Edinburgh, 1979.

Willis, Deborah. *Malevolent Nurture: Witch-Hunting and Maternal Power in Early Modern England*. Ithaca, NY, 1995.

Willock, I. D. *The Origins and Development of the Jury in Scotland*. Edinburgh, 1966.

Willumsen, Liv Helene. *Witches of the North: Scotland and Finnmark*. Leiden, 2013.

Wilson, Eric. 'Institoris at Innsbruck: Heinrich Institoris, the *Summis Desiderantes* and the Brixen Witch-Trial of 1485', in *Popular Religion in Germany and Central Europe*, ed. Bob Scribner and Trevor Johnson. New York, 1996: 87–100.

Wolf, Hans-Jürgen. *Geschichte der Hexenprozesse*. Erlensee, 1995.

Wootton, David. 'Reginald Scot/Abraham Fleming/The Family of Love', in *Languages of Witchcraft: Narrative, Ideology and Meaning in Early Modern Culture*, ed. Stuart Clark. Basingstoke, 2001: 119–38.

Wright, A. D. *The Counter-Reformation*. New York, 1982.

Wright, Lawrence. *Remembering Satan*. New York, 1994.

Wüst, Wolfgang. 'Inquisitionsprozess und Hexenverfolgung im Hochstift Augsburg im 17. und 18. Jahrhundert', *Zeitschrift für Bayerische Landesgeschichte* 50 (1987): 109–26.

Wyporska, Wanda. 'Poland', in *Encyclopedia of Witchcraft: The Western Tradition*, vol. III, ed. Richard M. Golden. Santa Barbara, 2006: 907–10.

Wyporska, Wanda. *Witchcraft in Early Modern Poland, 1500–1800*. Basingstoke, 2013.

Yates, Frances. *The Occult Philosophy in the Elizabethan Age*. London, 1979.

Zagorin, Perez. *Rebels and Rulers: 1500–1660*. 2 vols. Cambridge, 1981.

Zguta, Russell. 'Was There a Witch Craze in Muscovite Russia?', *Southern Folklore Quarterly* 40 (1977): 119–27.

Zguta, Russell. 'Witchcraft Trials in Seventeenth-Century Russia', *American Historical Review* 82 (1977): 1187–207.

Zika, Charles. *The Appearance of Witchcraft: Print and Visual Culture in Sixteenth-Century Europe*. London, 2007.

Zika, Charles. *Exorcising Our Demons: Magic, Witchcraft and Visual Culture in Early Modern Europe*. Leiden, 2003.

Zilboorg, G. *The Medical Man and the Witch during the Renaissance*. New York, 1941.

INDEX